ECONOMIC FOREIGN POLICY OF THE UNITED STATES

ECONOMIC FOREIGN POLICY
of the
UNITED STATES

BY

BENJAMIN H. WILLIAMS

NEW YORK

Howard Fertig

1967

First published in 1929

Howard Fertig, Inc. edition 1967
Published by arrangement with the McGraw-Hill Book Company

Library of Congress Catalog Card Number: 67-24600

PRINTED IN THE UNITED STATES OF AMERICA
BY NOBLE OFFSET PRINTERS, INC.

TO
Helene Ogsbury Williams

PREFACE

Wholesale participation in the economic affairs of the world has come to the United States with comparative suddenness. Vast forces, hitherto felt but faintly, now assert their place in American life and press for expression through the channels of diplomacy. There are urgent reasons why these new phenomena should be carefully studied. Their significance in the affairs of our country and, indeed, their importance in the future of western civilization are too obvious for comment. The difficult task is here attempted of assembling from a literature, that is often filled with partisan criticism and official defense, an objective account of the economic foreign policies of the United States.

Much assistance has been received, and a general acknowledgment must suffice to express my gratitude for the many aids and suggestions which have come from a multitude of sources. The courtesy and spirit of helpfulness on all sides have been encouraging and are deeply appreciated. More particularly, thanks are due to the editors of the *Political Science Quarterly* for their permission to use an article by myself on "Capital Embargoes," which was published in the issue of the *Quarterly* for June, 1928. This article appears as Chapter V. Several members of the faculty of the University of Pittsburgh have been patient enough to read portions of the manuscript and they have all given valuable suggestions. Howard C. Kidd, Marion K. McKay, Robert L. Jones, and my colleagues in the Political Science Department, Elmer D. Graper, Ralph S. Boots, Martin L. Faust, Gustav L. Schramm, and James C. Charlesworth, have assisted in this way. They have been particularly kind in giving suggestions with regard to imperfections in the various chapters. The defects of fact and judgment which remain are, of course, to be charged against myself alone. Dr. Raymond Leslie Buell generously permitted me to see the proofs of his valuable chapters on Liberia in "The Native Problem in Africa," before that work had come from the press. My wife has done more than anyone to help carry the burden of detail in connection with the preparation of material. Her assistance has been indispensable.

Benjamin H. Williams.

Pittsburgh, Pennsylvania,
December, 1928.

CONTENTS

ix

PART II

THE DIPLOMACY OF COMMERCE

ECONOMIC FOREIGN POLICY
OF THE UNITED STATES

ECONOMIC FOREIGN POLICY

OF THE

UNITED STATES

CHAPTER I

INTRODUCTION: THE PLACE OF THE ECONOMIC MOTIVE

In international relations, as in any other branch of learning, a knowledge of causation is important. Accurate thinking with regard to present or future situations is not possible if, in the study of existing data, attention is paid only to legal acts, agreements, troop movements, and pronouncements, which are the symbols of governmental policies. The real investigator must go farther. He must acquire a factual background as to the conditions precedent. He must raise eternally the question: Why, in any emergency, do governmental officials act as they do? This is not a simple inquiry. National policies are seldom entered upon for single reasons. More frequently do they arise from a complex of motives. Emotions of national pride in the expansion of power, the fear of aggression, the love of peace, the desire for national economic betterment, the influence of high-powered spokesmen for commercial or financial groups, departmental loyalty, or the weight of tradition—these are some of the reasons for action. Any two or more of them may combine to create a state of mind in governmental circles. The hundreds of citizens and officials who have appreciable weight in policy formation may all want substantially the same thing but for different reasons. Hence, with regard to any announced policy, it is often difficult to say just what are the influencing motives and what importance must be attached to each.[1]

[1] For an excellent discussion of motives, see MOON, PARKER THOMAS, "Imperialism and World Politics," Chap. IV, The Macmillan Company, New York, 1926.

1

The acquisitive instincts of merchants, bankers, investors, ship owners, and larger groups have set up strong influences in shaping the policies of nations. We all recognize that the desire for gain is a powerful force in the life of the individual. From the necessity of daily bread in the case of the humblest citizen to the desire for a few extra millions on the part of the great captain of finance, practically all of society gives attention to the economic problem. In domestic politics, likewise, it is apparent that tariff adjustment, business regulation, labor legislation, taxation, and other issues which affect the pocketbook, are of the utmost concern. In international relations, however, the economic motive is frequently given less importance than is its due. Trained historians have long recognized its significance. Economists have stressed its importance. Economic determinists have overemphasized it. And yet, to the general public, the dollar and cents realities of world politics are oftentimes seen but dimly if, indeed, they are recognized at all. Before 1914, the international public thought but little of the far-flung economic struggle that was to result in a world cataclysm. Signs of conflict were seen, but they were generally interpreted in political terminology and such is still the tendency despite the lessons of the war.

A reason for the partial submergence of the economic motive in the effective publicity on international relations is probably to be found in the less perfect receptivity of the public to the drab details of wide commercial movements as contrasted with its eagerness and capacity to absorb accounts of the seemingly simple and heroic acts of great men. Biography is admittedly fascinating. Certain types of publicists have for this reason come to describe history as something of a drama in which the fate of nations is determined by the decisions of outstanding statesmen who, for all that is said to the contrary, may have derived their light from their inner consciousnesses. But, except in the new biography, heroes are philanthropic, idealistic, humanitarian. They are not influenced by thoughts of mere gain. Hence, when we describe the acts of nations in terms of the deeds of famous individuals, the economic motive is often thrust unconsciously into the background.

To the general public the doctrine of the open door in China was put forth by John Hay as a dramatic move to save the weak and helpless Chinese nation from the onslaughts of European powers. But in the Hay Open Door Notes there is a great deal that is popularly overlooked. The commercial ambitions that formed the background of the notes have been forgotten. The trade bodies, the manufacturers, and the exporters who were interested in the possibilities of commerce with 400,000,000 Chinese have faded from the picture. The fact that chambers of commerce and American business men, both in this country and in the Orient, as well as many merchants of Great Britain and Japan, had declared for the open door before the Hay notes were thought of is a matter of knowledge among special students of the subject. The fact that Hay did not originate the idea or the wording of the notes but adapted them from a draft written by W. W. Rockhill, who was familiar with the needs of American commerce in China, is likewise known to those who are particularly interested. The general public, however, has regarded the sending of the notes as an act of intervention arising from generosity. Such a conception is simpler. It is more self-satisfying. But the principal motive of commercial profit does not fit into the story.

In lieu of a hero, writers on international relations frequently resort to the convenient device of hypostasizing, or personifying the state and making it appear to act with the unity of the individual. This device is useful on account of the simplicity which it frequently gives to the presentation of international situations. It is by no means to be condemned. But it should be used with care, for it sometimes leads to erroneous thinking. In personification we are apt to create the illusion of an exalted individual, a tribal deity, and endow it with a different set of motives than actuate the complex political mechanism. And this leads us into errors similar to those which are associated with the great man theory of history.

It should be taken as an axiom of diplomatic psychology that no nation can act consistently from motives of spiritual satisfaction such as give pleasure to superior individuals. Such emotions as the love of a father for a son or the mutual attachment of friends for each other cannot, by the nature of things, have more than a temporary influence in the international world. Policies are not based on pure sympathy for the oppressed. There can be no mandate over Armenia, no American intervention in Korea or Syria. When Russia objected to the Austrian ultimatum out of supposed brotherly love for little Serbia, when Great Britain entered the war allegedly because of the despoliation of Belgium, or when the marines of the United States were sent into Haiti out of a declared desire to assist the negro inhabitants of the Black Republic, the nations avowing these comparatively lofty reasons were throwing themselves open to the shafts of cynics. If the officials of any government pursue policies which sacrifice the national interest or involve the nation in commitments and entanglements without the hope of material gains, they are so fiercely set upon by adversely affected groups within the country that they are soon forced to change their policies or give way to another set of officers.

Perhaps there are instances of high mindedness divorced from self-interest. "Missionary diplomacy" is sometimes entered into at the instance of faithful advocates of religious ideas. It has, however, proved to be practically impossible to separate entirely the political support of evangelism from mercenary considerations. The missionary has too frequently been "used" to further the aims of the trader and the territorial expansionist. Occasional acts of international generosity may be cited. There is the $20,000,000 contribution made by the United States to relieve starvation in Russia. That act was constitutionally defended, however, only on the ground that it in some way promoted the "general welfare" of the United States. Peace policies represent a splendid ideal, but they could gain little support were it not for the realization that in war "there is no victor." A conflict between the United States and a united Europe would cost each party perhaps $100,000,000,000 and possibly much more. Arbitration and the outlawry of war are moves in the direction of the most practical and intelligent material self-interest. One of the errors in hypostasizing, then, is the assumption that purely philanthropic motives can have much importance in governmental psychology.

There is a special reason why the causes for international policies are not always expounded with scientific accuracy and perspective. The facts in current diplomacy are not well known. This is true in the United States as in other countries. The efforts which the Department of State has put forth in the protection of American interests have partially absorbed the energy which it might otherwise have put into publications. *Foreign Relations*, a series which contains the most complete available account of American diplomacy, and which was once published with meticulous promptness, has now fallen in arrears until it is eleven years late, the last issue being for 1917. But these eleven years have witnessed such an emigration of capital from this country as has not been duplicated in world history. Sources of knowledge of the events and negotiations which have reshaped diplomacy to fit the demands of investors and concessionaires are incomplete. The department always responds with courtesy and with all possible promptness to requests for such publications as it issues. But these are not adequate. Scientific writing in the field of American foreign relations is accordingly rendered exceedingly difficult and the general public is forced to place heavy reliance upon official interpretative statements issued to the press.

The official, however, is always on the defensive. Memories of the 1900 Democratic campaign against American imperialism, of the criticisms of the "dollar diplomacy" of Secretary Knox, of the Harding charges against the Wilson policies in Haiti—all of these and many more bear heavily upon the official spokesman. The continuous criticisms of the liberal press are always in his mind. In his interpretations, he is careful to give no more ammunition to the enemy than is necessary, and anything which smacks of a coalition between Washington and Wall Street is studiously avoided. The profits of capitalists are, accordingly, not mentioned.

American business men have come into a position of unprecedented influence, socially and politically. No one doubts that they present their claims to Washington with force and skill, nor that they frequently persuade the government to take action in their behalf. When moved to act, however, the departmental official is apt to rationalize his policy in terms that will satisfy the public and refute anticipated criticisms. "Rationalizing," says James Harvey Robinson, "is the self-exculpation which occurs when we feel ourselves, or our group, accused of misapprehension or errors." And thus national defense, humanitarianism, the will for peace, the maintenance of order, and the rendering of economic assistance to small states are apt to be given greater emphasis than are the acquisitive desires of special groups of citizens.

No finer example of rationalizing exists in the whole literature of official statement than the remarks of Secretary Lansing at the time of the military occupation of Haiti.   Laying aside the mask of the spokesman, he said:

> We have only one purpose to serve,—that is, to help the Haitian people and prevent them from being exploited by irresponsible revolutionists . . . The United States has no purpose of agression and *is entirely disinterested*[1] in promoting this protectorate.

These words entirely ignored the economic interests that were seeking to bring about American intervention.   Indeed, relying on the statement of reasons, which purported to be all inclusive, one would not have known that there were any American economic interests in Haiti at all.   Nothing was said of the fact that the State Department had been engaged in hot dispute with the Haitian government concerning a bank and a railroad, and that both the bank and the railroad, as well as other interests, were to be greatly assisted by intervention.[2]

There are many illustrations of the covering over of the idea of business profits with the mystifying generalizations of great doctrines and principles.   The Monroe Doctrine is sometimes used to defend economic policies in Latin America which have no logical relation to the ideas of Monroe.   The notion of Manifest Destiny has been used as a colossal smoke screen to obscure or conceal the multitude of economic gains that have been part and parcel of expansion.   Reciprocity, sometimes forced from others by means of penalty tariffs, was said by James G. Blaine, in 1890, to be in accordance with international justice.   The doctrine of equality, which is today practiced by the United States and which is sometimes stressed diplomatically for the purpose of preventing reciprocity among other nations which will endanger American commerce, is explained by Secretary Kellogg as embodying the only fair notion of trade.   The two doctrines are based on contrary principles.   The purpose of urging each through diplomatic means has been the expansion of markets for American goods, and the original method used in the time of Blaine has lately been reversed to fit a new situation created by economic evolution.   To describe either as arising out of a respect for the eternal right, rather than from motives of commercial advantage, is certain to contribute to confused thinking.

[1] My italics.

[2] The desire to keep European nations out of Haiti, which was probably the leading motive, was given emphasis in other official statements.   But the economic motive was consistently ignored.

The euphemist who overlooks economic realities is a poor pedagogue for he explains events in terms of a fictitious causation. On the other hand, one should not become doctrinaire on the subject of the economic determination of national policies. There are many different kinds of reasons for action. There are often powerful psychological forces, springing from other than economic causes, which bear down upon foreign offices and state departments and persuade or coerce them into their decisions. The function of the scholar is to sift what evidence he has and to determine the motives as best he can with an unswerving loyalty to the ideal of truth. He cannot, of course, attain perfection in this endeavor. The social sciences offer no such opportunities for mechanical and mathematical accuracy as do the physical sciences. But he may at least set for himself a scientific goal.

PART I
THE DIPLOMACY OF INVESTMENT

CHAPTER II

BACKGROUND AND GENERAL PRINCIPLES OF INVESTMENT DIPLOMACY

I. THE TRANSITION FROM A DEBTOR TO A CREDITOR NATION

From the time of the Declaration of Independence to the World War the United States viewed the world from the standpoint of the borrowing nation and American policies gave evidence of that coincidence which is so commonly observed between international idealism and the lack of surplus wealth. The reaction of indebtedness upon American policies was not due, as in the case of many weaker countries, to an attitude of shrinking from the political demands of powerful money-lending nations. In the case of the United States the fear of the intervention of strong creditors was removed at an early stage by the establishment of sound government, by the distance of Europe, and by the ability to take care of most purely governmental needs with domestic capital. The negative influence of the debtor position upon this country was nevertheless of great importance. Having almost no loans or investments to protect, the Department of State was free from those pressures which were contributing to drive creditor nations into careers of imperialism. The United States, also, because of the desire to keep European governments out of Latin America, was disposed generally to sympathize with the case of the debtor nation. Patriotic moralists during this period took pleasure in drawing contrasts between the American love of human rights and international democracy, handed down from the Revolution, and the aggressive policies adopted for the protection and promotion of foreign investments by certain strong nations of Europe.

Early Financial Distress.—The first financial requirements of the thirteen states were the demands made for the military purposes of the Revolution. Loans were sought in France, Spain, and Holland, and the distress at home which prompted these requests abroad was indeed profound. The following note

11

from Franklin to Vergennes, of Feb. 13, 1781, indicates the desperate need for funds:

> The Marquis de Lafayette writes to me, that it is impossible to conceive, without seeing it, the distress which the troops have suffered for want of clothing, and the following is a paragraph from General Washington, which I ought not to keep back from your Excellency, viz. "I doubt not that you are so fully informed by Congress of our political and military State, that it would be superfluous to trouble you with anything relative to either. If I were to speak on topics of the kind, it would be to show that our present situation makes one of two things essential to us; a peace or the most vigorous aid of our allies, particularly in the article of *money.*" . . .
>
> . . . .
>
> I am grown old. I feel myself much enfeebled by my late long illness, and it is probable I shall not long have any more concern in these affairs. I therefore take this occasion to express my opinion to your Excellency, that the present conjuncture is critical, that there is some danger lest the Congress should lose its influence over the people, if it is unable to procure the aids that are wanted; and that the whole system of the new government in America may thereby be shaken.[1]

France, although rendering valuable aid, looked with a critical eye on some of these requests and was disposed to consider the Americans as unduly supplicant as may be seen from the following instruction from Vergennes to the French minister in America:

> . . . do not conceal from Mr. Morris that we are astonished at the demands which they continue to make on us, while the Americans obstinately refuse to pay taxes, and that it seems to us much more natural to levy on them than on the subjects of the King the taxes necessary for the defense of their cause. As to the payment of interest [on the American loans] you may declare peremptorily that the King will not undertake it, and that any dissatisfaction which may result from this determination will serve only to measure at their just value the gratitude and attachment of the Americans for France.[2]

The sums secured by borrowing during the Revolution are tabulated by Dewey as follows:

---

[1] Sparks, Jared, "Diplomatic Correspondence of the Revolution," Vol. III, p. 187, Nathan Hale and Gray and Bowen, Boston, 1829.

[2] Sumner, William Graham, "The Financier and Finances of the American Revolution," Vol. II, p. 59, Dodd, Mead & Company, New York, 1892.

	France	Spain	Holland*
1777	$ 181,500		
1778	544,500		
1779	181,500		
1780	726,000		
1781	1,737,763	$128,804	
1782	1,892,237	45,213	$ 720,000
1783	1,089,000		584,000
Total...........	$6,352,500	$174,017	$1,304,000

* In addition to these loans gifts were received, mostly from France, amounting to $1,996,500. DEWEY, DAVIS RICH, "Financial History of the United States," p. 47, Longmans, Green & Co., New York, 1922.

Following the Revolution, there ensued under the Articles of Confederation a critical period in American public finance. Payments on the principal and interest of the foreign debt were neglected and the United States was temporarily exposed to the threat of intervention by creditors. Acquisition of Rhode Island by France was the subject of current rumor.[1] The anxiety created by the foreign debt furnished a good argument for the adoption of the Constitution and eventually brought about the establishment of the public credit upon a sound basis. Foreign borrowing by the national government continued for a time under the Constitution, but successive secretaries of the treasury applied themselves to the difficult task of repayment. During the first half of the nineteenth century these various debts were gradually extinguished and the federal government ceased to be under obligation to foreign creditors.

The Repudiated State Debts.—The efforts to develop their internal resources by borrowing and by guaranteeing the debts of private companies involved some of the states in extreme financial embarassment. By 1836, over $90,000,000 was placed in canals and railways in the northern states. One-half of that sum was a charge upon public credit. The larger part of it was British. In the South the capital for the planting and marketing of cotton was obtained through banks, many of which were either owned or guaranteed by the state governments. Much of the funds for the organization of the banks came from London. Aid for the development of cotton raising was considered good

[1] FISH, CARL RUSSELL, "American Diplomacy," 3rd ed., p. 78, Henry Holt & Company, New York, 1922.

policy by textile and banking interests in Great Britain. The return of 5 or 6 per cent upon state bonds and of 9 or 10 per cent upon the bonds of southern banks was attractive to the British investor who knew little of American state finance. Most of the state governments failed to assign definite funds to meet their debt charges. The crisis of 1837 plunged the states into difficulties and their situation grew progressively worse for several years. In 1841–1842, nine of them failed for the time to meet their interest payments. Two of these definitely repudiated their debts and a third disclaimed a portion of its obligations. The sentiment in England against the defaulting debtors became exceedingly bitter. Yankees were temporarily unpopular in London and American credit reached a low point. When, in 1842, the federal government sought to obtain a loan abroad, the bankers of London and Paris disdainfully refused to consider the matter.[1]

Another distressing period of state finance in the South came during the Reconstruction Period when seven states repudiated all or a part of their indebtedness, which had been incurred mostly for internal improvements.[2] Altogether, according to an estimate as of July 1, 1928, eight states are still in default in capital sums totalling $75,200,000 with defaulted interest amounting to $252,821,000. These sums are exclusive of the Confederate loans.[3]

There seems to be merit in the contention of some of the states that the circumstances surrounding a number of the issues were such as to have placed creditors on their guard, because of the low price of the bonds and the fact that the money was to be used or misused by the non-representative carpetbag governments which were held in place by northern troops. Regardless of these circumstances and of the allocation of blame as between the federal government and the states, the repudiated debts are a blot upon the record of the United States and have been a minor perturbing element in its foreign relations.

The fear that the creation of a system of arbitration might bring the matter of the state debts before an international tribu-

[1] JENKS, LELAND HAMILTON, "The Migration of British Capital to 1875," Chaps. III and IV, Alfred A. Knopf, Inc., New York, 1927.

[2] SCOTT, WILLIAM A., "The Repudiation of State Debts," Crowell, New York, 1893; RAYMOND TURNER, "Repudiation of Debts by States of the Union," *Current History*, January, 1926, p. 475.

[3] WINKLER, MAX, "Defaults and Repudiation of Foreign Loans," *Foreign Policy Association Information Service*, Vol. IV, No. 11, p. 244.

nal for examination has promoted, to some extent, senatorial opposition to arbitration treaties. Such opposition was manifest at the time the ill-fated arbitration treaties of 1897, 1904, and 1911 with Great Britain were before the Senate. In the debate on the 1911 treaty, Senator Bacon of Georgia said:

The fundamental proposition upon which the Southern States base their refusal to pay these bonds is that they are not their bonds; that they did not make the bonds; that there were others in high places who had usurped authority for which they were in no manner responsible; and that they were not liable for their acts except in so far as they had received the benefit of those bonds.

As I have had occasion to say before, Mr. President, there are not simple safes and vaults full of these bonds; there are absolutely cords of them, which could be piled up like corded wood, to pay which would bankrupt the Southern States . . .

. . . It is regarded as a closed incident, and it matters not whether the result of such an arbitration should ever exact one dollar of payment from either one of those states; it is a matter we do not wish that any outside party should ever have the right to say to the Senate of the United States, you must arbitrate that.[1]

Accordingly, Senator Bacon introduced an amendment to the resolution of concurrence which, among other things, exempted from the operation of the treaty "the question of the alleged indebtedness or monied obligations of any state of the United States."

Similar objections arose at the time of the debates upon American adherence to the Permanent Court of International Justice. The question of the state debts was, however, considered sufficiently safeguarded from arbitration by the reservations attached to the Senate resolution of adherence providing against advisory opinions without the consent of the United States and providing that disputes could not be submitted to the Court until a general or special treaty should be concluded.

The debts have given cause for some criticism of the position of the United States in demanding that other nations perform their obligations. The Corporation of Foreign Bondholders, in its 1925 Annual Report, said:

The Council regret to report that while the government of the United States has, during the past year, devoted much attention to the payment of obligations incurred by its allies during the great war, no steps have

[1] *Cong. Rec.*, Vol. 48, p. 2869.

been taken by the defaulting states of the Union to recognize and pay their debts.

The repudiated obligations are an embarassment to a great creditor nation which is forced by its new position to place every possible emphasis upon the sanctity of contracts; and their payment by the federal government, although a remote possibility, would doubtless be a good stroke of business. The debts remain as a reminder of the debtor period in American history. A study of them and of the circumstances under which they were contracted should be productive to some degree of sympathy for the financial difficulties of other governments—a sympathy which is too often conspicuous by its absence.

Private Investments in Railways and Other Industries.—Notwithstanding the early disasters in railways finance, the rapid development of the United States opened up splendid industrial and railway opportunities which soon reawakened the interest of British and continental capitalists. In time many of the railway systems in this country were to a large extent owned by foreigners and were also mortgaged for the payment of bonds held abroad. The period around 1898 appears to have marked a decrease in foreign ownership. The United States had so prospered that prophecies of approaching financial independence were heard. A number of railway consolidations necessitated domestic control and large blocks of railroad shares were repurchased by Americans. The following table will show the shifting in ownership in nine important railroads during this period:

	Percentage of foreign-owned stock*	
	1890–1896	1905
Illinois Central...................	65	21
Pennsylvania....................	52	19
Louisville & Nashville............	75	7
New York, Ontario & Western......	58	12
New York Central & Hudson River.	37	9
Reading........................	52	3
Great Northern..................	33	2
Baltimore & Ohio................	21	17
Chicago, Milwaukee & St. Paul....	21	6

* Ripley, William Z., "Railroads: Finance and Organization," p. 5, Longmans, Green & Company, New York, 1915.

European ownership of other industrial and financial projects was, in general, less than in the case of railways, but the total European investment was considerable. Before the World War there were evidences that the period of financial dependency was drawing to a close. In 1900, the prosperous condition of American business prompted the prediction that New York was soon to become the world's money center. This was a temporary illusion. Borrowing from Europe was shortly thereafter resumed as an offset to the balance of international payments which otherwise continued to run against the United States.[1] In 1914 the United States was debtor to Europe in a sum estimated in the neighborhood of from $4,500,000,000 to $5,000,000,000. As against this there were American investments in such neighboring countries as Canada, Mexico, and Cuba which amounted to possibly $2,500,000,000.[2] Thus at the outbreak of the World War the United States was a debtor to the extent of from $2,000,000,000 to $2,500,000,000.[3]

The Effect of the War Period.—And then came the events of July, 1914. As the atmosphere was charged with the war spirit following the Austrian ultimatum of July 23, sales of stocks and bonds by holders in European countries became epidemic. Quotations were forced down and thus the security for bank loans began to melt away. One by one, the stock exchanges closed their doors. The London exchange, the last important European exchange to remain open, suspended business on July 31, the day of the German ultimatum to Russia. New York had likewise been deluged with orders to sell. European holders seemed determined to unload American securities at any cost. Fearing the demoralization of prices and a consequent

---

[1] NOYES, ALEXANDER D., "The War Period of American Finance, 1908–1925," p. 104, G. P. Putnam's Sons, New York, 1926.

[2] It was difficult to arouse the interest of American bankers in foreign investments. A memorandum of the Department of State in 1909 stated that the department had for some years sought to interest American capital in the refunding of the Honduran debt, "but with the rich opportunities of domestic investment there had never seemed to be much hope that American capital would flow into this channel." *Foreign Relations of the United States* (hereafter cited as *For. Rel.*) 1912, p. 551.

[3] See WINKLER, MAX, "America the World's Banker," Foreign Policy Association *Information Service*, Vol. III, Special Supplement No. 3; YOUNG, ARTHUR N., "The Department of State and Foreign Loans," an address at the Institute of Politics, Williamstown, Aug. 26, 1924, *State Department Press Release*, Aug. 26, 1924.

financial panic, the governors of the New York Stock Exchange within thirty minutes of the opening hour of July 31 reached a sudden decision to close. The sale of securities was, however, begun after a few weeks in the "outlaw market" on the sidewalk of Wall Street. By Dec. 12, restricted trading in stocks was permitted and by Apr. 1, 1915 unrestricted trading was allowed. From that time on, capitalists in this country continued without restraint to buy back from Europe the stocks and bonds of American industry.[1]

Repurchases of American securities were made possible in the United States chiefly because of the sale of enormous quantities of food, materials, and munitions to Europe. A large excess of exports over imports was established, and this favorable balance has continued after the war. The strong position of New York as an international money market, due partly to the necessary British embargo on external loans, brought to Wall Street large sums of foreign capital, and thus further strengthened the purchasing power of the United States. It was inevitable that under such circumstances the investors of this country should buy from Europe a large part of the stocks and bonds of American industry which were held abroad. Two billion dollars' worth of securities and possibly more were repurchased in the years between 1914 and 1919,[2] and the movement did not cease with the peace. An illustration of the way in which foreign ownership of American industry dwindled during the period of American neutrality is shown in the following table:

FOREIGN HOLDINGS IN THE UNITED STATES STEEL CORPORATION*

Date	Common shares	Per cent	Preferred shares	Per cent
March 31, 1914	1,285,636	25.29	312,311	8.67
Dec. 31, 1914	1,193,064	23.47	309,457	8.59
Dec. 31, 1915	696,631	13.70	274,588	7.62
Dec. 31, 1916	502,632	9.89	156,412	4.34

* *Commercial and Financial Chronicle*, p. 1740, Oct. 20, 1923. During the period of American participation in the war the sales of foreign holdings in this corporation dropped off, but after the armistice the process continued.

[1] The above account is taken largely from NOYES, *op. cit.*, Chap. II.

[2] DUNN, ROBERT W., "American Foreign Investments," p. 4, Huebsch and the Viking Press, New York, 1926.

Loans and investments in foreign countries soon began on a large scale. Ministers of finance acquired the habit of looking to New York as a market for their securities, and the organization of banking for purposes of loans to governments and industries in every quarter of the earth was a striking phenomenon in the development of Wall Street.

From the position of a debtor owing a net sum between $2,000,000,000 and $2,500,000,000 at the beginning of 1914 the United States became in fourteen years, exclusive of political loans, a net creditor to the extent of from $8,000,000,000 to $11,000,000,000. The estimates of the Department of Commerce of foreign investments in the United States at the end of 1927 place the figure at $3,700,000,000.[1] The private American investments abroad were computed to be between $11,500,000,-000 and $13,500,000,000 distributed as follows:

Latin America	$ 4,322,000,000 to	$ 5,222,000,000
Europe	3,171,000,000 to	3,671,000,000
Canada and Newfoundland	3,037,000,000 to	3,537,000,000
Asia, Australia, and rest of the world	970,000,000 to	1,070,000,000
Total	$11,500,000,000 to	$13,500,000,000[2]

II. THE VALUE OF LOANS AND INVESTMENTS FROM THE PUBLIC STANDPOINT

Before proceeding to examine the specific governmental policies that have been followed in connection with the encouragement and discouragement of investments and with their protection, it is advisable to consider the general reasons why capital exports may be desirable or undesirable and also to mention the special influences which are sometimes at work to

[1] "The Balance of International Payments of the United States in 1927," compiled by Ray Hall, Assistant Chief Finance and Investment Division, *Trade Information Bull.* 552, p. 25.

[2] *Ibid.*, p. 20. The figures of Dr. Max Winkler are somewhat higher. They are for the end of 1927 as follows:

Europe	$ 4,327,000,000
Canada	3,922,000,000
Latin America	5,161,100,000
China, Japan, and Philippines	726,500,000
Miscellaneous	363,400,000
Total	$14,500,000,000

Source: "The Ascendancy of the Dollar," Foreign Policy Association *Information Service*, Vol. IV, Supplement No. 1.

stimulate political action concerning them. These are the considerations which lie behind the diplomacy of a great creditor nation.

Markets.—In an expanding foreign market, when other items in the international exchange tend to show a heavy favorable balance, loans and investments become a necessity to trade. The large quantities of foodstuffs, materials, and munitions which were sent by the United States to Europe during the World War could have been financed only by loans. The proceeds of the loans were used up in the establishment of accounts in this country which were drawn against for the purchase of the needed materials.[1]

The maintenance of a favorable balance of trade since the war has likewise depended upon foreign loans and investments. Other countries have been unable to ship to America the gold necessary to balance accounts, and an extension of credits in one form or another has been essential to the maintenance of the so-called favorable trade balance. Loans have also helped to reestablish the productive capacity of Europe and have thus made possible an increase in the ability of Europe to purchase from the United States.

Frequently investments abroad are placed in construction projects that require materials which the creditor country is able to supply. Clauses are sometimes incorporated in loan contracts requiring that the materials purchased shall be bought in the country in which the loan is placed. Railway loans in China have contained such contract provisions and the advantage to be derived from the sale of American steel products was stressed by President Taft in support of the aggressive negotiations for the inclusion of American capital in the Hukuang Railway loan. Secretary of State Knox, who conducted the negotiations in an insistent manner, was, from his previous service as counsel for the Carnegie Steel Company, able to see clearly the advantages which would accrue to the American iron and steel industry by the placing of the loan.[2]

[1] An excellent description of these transactions is found in RATHBONE, ALBERT, "Making War Loans to the Allies," *Foreign Affairs*, April, 1925, p. 371.

[2] A contract which was devised for the purpose of assisting American exports was announced in *The New York Times* of Nov. 22, 1925. The Universal Pictures Corporation of the United States agreed to loan 15,000,-000 marks to the German Universal Film Company on the condition that

Even without the inclusion of a purchase clause in a loan contract, the operation of the laws of international exchange frequently makes it advisable to expend the proceeds of the loan directly in the lending country. Thus, if an Italian company borrows dollars in New York for the purchase of electrical equipment it will ordinarily be more economic to make purchases in the United States than to transfer the credits from New York to a third country. In a debate in the British Parliament on the East India Loan Bill, in 1923, an amendment was proposed requiring that at least 75 per cent of any sum raised must be spent in Great Britain. The government replied that without such a clause 95 per cent of the India loans raised in Great Britain for the year ending Mar. 1, 1923 was spent directly in Great Britain.[1]

The export of capital has sometimes been complained against as an injury to American trade in that it stimulates industries abroad that compete with producers in this country. Congressman Ralph F. Lozier of Missouri, speaking in the House of Representatives in 1925, after citing an author on the effects of American loans in stimulating industry abroad, said:

Here we have a statement from one well qualified to speak on the subject, that by our lavish and excessive foreign loans we are putting European factories on their feet, and as an obvious result of our short-sighted foreign loan policy, these factories that have been restored by American money are fighting to take our South American and other world trade away from us . . . We are lending money to Europe with which to fight us.[2]

American capital exported to Germany has thus been used by Germans in their contest with American manufacturers for the market in France and other European countries.[3]

Economists are inclined to refute such criticisms with the argument that although certain industries in the lending country may suffer by competition yet a readjustment of investments at home by shifting into those undertakings in which the lending country

---

the American corporation was to have two of the five votes on the executive committee of the German company, which was bound to throw open its 134 theaters to Universal productions.

[1] *Parliamentary Debates*, House of Commons, Vol. 166, p. 2080.

[2] *Cong. Rec.*, Vol. 66, p. 5425.

[3] See also HOWE, FREDERICK C., "Some Overlooked Dangers in Foreign Investments," *Annals of the American Academy of Political and Social Science*, Vol. CXXXVIII, p. 21.

can compete successfully will in the long run be to the national advantage. Furthermore the gains to the world at large which arise from the export of capital into productive industry will doubtless spread to every country.[1]

Raw Materials.—The development of needed supplies of raw materials is a service which is frequently rendered by the placing of capital abroad. British investments have resulted in the creation of supplies of food and materials without which the industrial progress at home could not have taken place. An illustration cited by Hobson is that of the development of rubber plantations by British capital. The world's rubber shortage was relieved by British investments and many industries that depended upon rubber were able to expand.

During the rubber "boom" of 1910 the price of Para rubber rose to 12s. 10d. per pound, but two years later the price was little more than one-third of that amount. Both the output and the consumption increased prodigiously, with much benefit to the national income of the United Kingdom and other countries. Great advantage accrued to the producers of rubber goods, rubber tires, and motor cars, as well as to consumers and investors in rubber concerns.[2]

When American manufacturers became alarmed over the safety of the rubber supply, following the imposition of the restrictions under the Stevenson Plan, a government investigation was set under way to determine what were the suitable areas for the development of plantations by American capital. The Firestone project in Liberia is an energetic attempt to insure a supply of rubber. Mr. Firestone has announced plans for planting 1,000,000 acres and for investing $100,000,000.[3] The Ford plans for growing rubber in Brazil are likewise worthy of note. There are numerous other illustrations of foods and materials that have been supplied to the consumers and manufacturers of the United States through the export of capital. Investments in the sugar plantations, refineries, and railroads of Cuba have greatly augmented the sugar supply available from that country. The work of American capitalists in carving plantations out of

[1] Hobson, C. K., "Export of Capital," p. 63, Constable and Company Ltd., London, 1914.

[2] *Ibid.*, p. 62.

[3] See Mr. Firestone's statement in *The New York Times*, Oct. 15, 1925. Also Buell, Raymond Leslie, "The Native Problem in Africa," Vol. II, p. 820, The Macmillan Company, New York, 1928.

the jungles of Central America has made possible a large importation of bananas. After the exportation of tin ore to the United States from the Federated Malay States was prohibited by a heavy tax, American capital found a source of supply in the tin mines of Bolivia.[1]

The Interest Rate.—The rates on foreign loans have since the war been 1 or 2 per cent higher than on domestic loans.[2] The taking of capital out of the country by foreign loans removes some of the surplus funds from the American market and tends to maintain domestic interest rates in times of accumulating wealth. The proportionate share of the social product which goes to the investing part of the community is accordingly kept higher than it would otherwise be and this influential class may be expected to favor such policies as will encourage capital exports. The detriment to the more numerous borrowing classes is correspondingly great; and objections to foreign loans are sometimes voiced by those who are interested in finding funds for the promotion of domestic enterprises. Complaint has been made by advocates of farming interests that the financing of Europe has deprived American agriculture of the capital necessary for its rehabilitation.[3]

The answer commonly given to such criticisms is that the most economical employment of capital demands that it shall be placed in those industries which are best able to bid for it throughout the world. Furthermore the stimulation of trade and the increase in the world's wealth will help to improve the conditions of domestic enterprise. Thus, if loaning money to Italy will aid in the recovery of that country and increase its power to purchase American products, the net gain to domestic enterprise will be considerable in the long run.

Currency Stabilization.—Loans and investments abroad are sometimes useful in order to prevent the influx of an oversupply of gold. There was need for such a preventive in the United States, when the importation of $294,072,395 of gold during

---

[1] For further discussion of the influence of foreign investments on the supply of raw materials see EARLE, EDWARD MEAD, "International Financial Control of Raw Materials," *Proceedings of the Academy of Political Science,* July, 1926, p. 188.

[2] The difference is sometimes greater than this. In 1925, a $60,000,000 bond issue of New York City was sold to the public at a price that yielded a return of 3.25 to 4.05 per cent. Later in the same year the $100,000,000 Italian government loan was priced so as to yield 7.48 to 7.56 per cent.

[3] See, for example, *Cong. Rec.,* Vol. 66, pp. 4470, 5425.

1923 and the continuation of heavy imports into the middle of 1924 brought the amount in this country well above the $4,000,-000,000 mark. The United States possessed about one-half of the world's supply. Low interest rates and an abundance of funds for lending resulted. Certain financial writers predicted that should this movement continue gold inflation would send values soaring and upset the stability of the currency. The gold import was checked to a large extent, however, by foreign loans, some of which resulted in a shipment of gold during the latter part of the year. Thus, in December, 1924 there was a shipment of gold to Germany as part of the proceeds of the $110,000,000 loan floated in the United States under the Dawes Plan. Since that time loans have contributed to the stability of the currency.[1]

Profits Accruing to Special Groups.—The commissions of investment bankers earned through the flotation of foreign loans, while not important from the public standpoint on account of the relatively small number of persons engaged in such work, are still of significance because the political influence of the banking class is vastly out of proportion to its numerical strength. The amount of compensation received for placing securities in the hands of the investing public is ordinarily not a matter of record, although it is said to be larger in the case of foreign bonds than in that of domestic issues. Thomas W. Lamont, of the firm of J. P. Morgan & Co., stated that in the case of the $100,000,000 Italian loan of 1925, the bonds were purchased by the syndicate at 90 and offered to the investing public at 94½, leaving a margin of $4,500,000 to be distributed among the members of the syndicate for expenses and commissions. J. P. Morgan & Co., the firm which negotiated the loan and organized the syndicate, received for its services slightly less than one-fourth of 1 per cent or something under $250,000.[2] The spread between the price paid to the borrower and that fixed for sale to the public is frequently much greater than 4½ per cent, but the risk that the bonds will not be sold is then, as a rule, correspondingly

[1] During reverse conditions at an earlier period in American history large borrowings from Europe prevented the draining away of gold by heavy payments which were necessary on account of an unfavorable international balance. BOLLES, ALBERT S., "The Financial History of the United States from 1789 to 1860," p. 456, D. Appleton & Company, New York, 1894.

[2] Letter to Congressman LaGuardia, dated Jan. 14, 1926, *Cong. Rec.*, Vol. 67, p. 2135. The press reported that the bonds sold at a figure slightly above 94½.

larger. In other ways the compensation of the international banker is sometimes quite high. An answer to a question in the British House of Commons on May 14, 1927, indicated that for its services in granting the British government a credit of $100,000,000 in 1925, which credit was never used, the Morgan firm, together with allied banking houses, received a commission of $2,500,000.[1]

Concessionaires and speculators are other special groups interested in promoting the export of capital. The concessionaire obtains a contract with a foreign government which gives him special rights in return for services to be rendered, usually in the development of economic resources. He is then faced with the task of procuring the necessary capital to carry out the project, and has a decided interest in securing diplomatic protection which will create conditions favorable to investment. He frequently calls upon the Department of State for aid in controversies which arise out of the performance of the contract. The speculator who goes into another country and makes a purchase of low-priced land expecting to dispose of it later at an advanced figure to his fellow countrymen is likewise intent upon obtaining the exportation of capital into his project and may seek political assistance to insure favorable conditions. The former activities of land companies in the Isle of Pines are a case in point. Large tracts of land were purchased by the companies, following the Spanish American War. An unauthorized statement of an Assistant Secretary of War that the island had been ceded by Spain to the United States and was therefore American territory was seized upon by the promoters and published in their advertisements. A great deal of effort was expended in attempting to influence the United States government to lay claim to the island. Largely due to this effort, the treaty with Cuba settling the title to the island was kept before the Senate for twenty-two years before favorable action could be obtained upon it.[2]

The more conservative industrial, shipping, and banking groups, which seek to extend their business abroad by the erection

---

[1] *Parliamentary Debates*, House of Commons, Vol. 205, p. 1627; *The New York Times*, May 5 and 6, 1927.

[2] See *Sen. Doc.* 166, Sixty-eighth Congress, Second Session; JENKS, LELAND HAMILTON, "Our Cuban Colony," p. 144, The Vangard Press, N. Y., 1928; and also an article by the author in *Foreign Affairs*, July, 1925, p. 689.

of warehouses, factories, and power plants and the organization of banks and other creative agencies represent a force which is now becoming predominant in the exportation of American capital. The interest of these groups in foreign policy is frequently that of obtaining security and stability in weaker countries.

Loans for Non-productive Purposes.—The building up of armaments, the financing of revolutions and war, the subsidizing of venal governments, and the promotion of unsound schemes for development are examples of enterprises which result in the diversion of capital to non-productive purposes. With some exceptions, such expenditures may be set down as inimical to the interests of mankind in general and, therefore, undesirable from the world viewpoint. According to Secretary Hoover, if foreign loans for such purposes could be prevented a great number of benefits would follow.

There could be no question as to the ability to repay; with this increasing security, capital would become steadily cheaper, the dangers to national and individual independence in attempts of the lender to collect his defaulted debts would be avoided; there would be a definite increase in the standard of living and the comfort and prosperity of the borrower. There would be no greater step taken in the prevention of war itself.[1]

While there can be but little disagreement as to the evils of loans of the destructive type, there is, on the other hand, but little agreement as to methods of preventing such loans. Secretary Hoover proposed that this be done by the development of sentiment in the commercial and financial groups of each country. As this would make it necessary for banking houses to forego voluntarily large commissions, there is but little possibility that such a sentiment will develop. The more effective method of prevention by a government embargo of non-productive loans has thus far received little support in the United States and is assured of the positive opposition of financial groups, which shrink from government interference with the functions of the banker.

Purely Political Considerations.—The political considerations surrounding loans will be dealt with in greater detail in subsequent chapters. It may be sufficient here to outline the main points under this heading and to suggest that the government of

[1] Remarks at the opening of the Pan-American Commercial Conference, May 2, 1927.

the United States has not been unmindful of these matters. In the Caribbean and Central America the State Department, since the time of Secretary Knox, has favored the refunding of British investments by the flotation of American loans. This has been deemed important in removing a powerful motive for British intervention in an area of vital interest to the United States. American participation in Chinese loans was supported by Secretary Knox partly in order that he might be able to exert an influence in Chinese affairs in opposition to the policies of European creditor nations. In some cases, the United States has favored the making of loans by American bankers in order to support favored or "puppet" governments in weaker countries, such as the Estrada and Diaz governments in Nicaragua, the Dartiguenave and Borno governments in Haiti, and the Jimenez government in the Dominican Republic.

The Effect of Loans upon War and Peace.—Loans and investments carry with them influences which make for war as well as counter influences which make for peace. The pressures exerted by investors to secure political action favorable to their interests are among the most powerful of the secret influences which tend to cause governments to embark upon aggressive and inconsiderate policies. Such policies not only create feelings of hostility among the people of the offended country but intensify suspicions and criticism on the part of rival creditor nations. Latin-American distrust of the United States because of interventions in Central America and the Caribbean is probably a menace to future harmony in the Western Hemisphere and has given Europeans a pretext for roundly criticizing the motives and methods of this country.

Loans to Europe, on the other hand, constituting as they do the weakest spot in the defense armor of the United States, tend to predispose this country towards a peaceful settlement of disputes with European governments. In case European states should wage war with the United States they would probably confiscate American property within their borders. Large and powerful capitalistic interests in the United States are accordingly anxious that there be no war with European countries. On the other hand, the easy method of cancellation of indebtedness by a declaration of war may, from the European viewpoint, be conceived of as an influence which in some future dispute may add to the reasons for hostility.

CHAPTER III

POLITICAL ENCOURAGEMENT TO CAPITAL EXPORTS

American capitalists and diplomats have on many occasions joined in their efforts to create better opportunities for the making of investments abroad. The motives behind this partnership are economic and political, and it is sometimes difficult to determine which of the two is the primary moving force. At times the Department of State has been stirred into activity at the behest of banking groups. The desire to overthrow barriers erected against foreign capital by nationalists in backward countries, the prospect of rich concession contracts, or the fear of the consequences of destructive insurrections are reasons which have caused the sending of telegrams to Washington or the hurried visit to the national capital of attorneys for financial interests. At other times, the first request for action has come to the bankers from the Department of State, which has sought to bring about the investment of American money as a counteractant against foreign influence. Loans in the strategically important area of the Caribbean and Central America have been requested in order to preempt the territory as against the citizens of other strong creditor nations. Key investments, such as those in the building of railroads or the organization of treasury service banks in backward countries, have been considered desirable for political purposes. Loans which involve the collection of the revenues of weaker governments have been urged for the purpose of advancing policies. Whether the profit to be obtained by the American capitalist or the additional control to be secured by the government is the dominating motive, the international financier and the diplomat have been joined together. While the two parties may have their controversies, there seems to be in this field no likelihood of that divorce of business from government which is so urgently recommended by conservative groups in domestic politics.

PROTECTION AS AN ENCOURAGEMENT TO CAPITAL EXPORTS

The protection of capital after it has gone abroad will be taken up more fully in later chapters, but the effect of such action in promoting the investment of additional capital is sufficiently important to deserve mention in the present chapter. When a government engages actively in the protection of the property of its citizens abroad, investors became reassured and are more willing to make additional ventures. The effect of the intervention and debt control clauses of the Platt Amendment has been important in stimulating American enterprise in Cuba. The anti-revolution and fiscal supervision policies pursued in other countries of the Caribbean and Central America have given such confidence to capital that the bonds of several of those countries have been raised from the status of greatly depreciated paper to the position of first-rate investments. The following comparison of certain government bond prices on June 14, 1928, will serve to indicate the standing of some of the countries under American protection:

Government	Interest rate	Price
United Kingdom	5	99⅝
Panama	5½	103
Cuba	5½	102
Belgium	6	100
Haiti	6	100
Argentina	6	99
Uruguay	6	97½
Chile	6	95
France	7½	115¾
Germany	7	106¼
Salvador	8	112

The comparatively high values of the bonds of Cuba, Panama, and Haiti show the power of the securities of financially supervised governments to attract capital, and likewise suggest a close relationship between strong protection policies and credit rating.[1]

One or two illustrations will show the effect of protection upon the return to the investor and make clear why the capitalist

[1] The question may be raised as to whether it is for the best interests of the weaker country to maintain sound credit at the cost of its independence. To the materially minded individual who grades persons and nations according to their financial standing there will be one answer. To the idealist who considers that the affairs of the spirit are much more important than those of the flesh there will be another. But there can be little doubt as to the influence of protection policies upon the export of capital.

frequently waits upon the express or implied assurance of diplomatic support before embarking upon new ventures abroad.[1] The American China Development Company obtained in 1900 a concession to construct a railway in China from Canton to Hankow. In order to forestall the sale of the concession to the nationals of a more imperialistic government than the United States, the Chinese insisted upon a clause providing that "the Americans cannot transfer the rights of these agreements to other nations or people of other nationality." The stock, nevertheless, was placed in the open market, and a majority control was purchased by Belgians who took charge of the company. The Chinese government thereupon annulled the concession.[2] The stock was repurchased by American financiers and China was informed that the United States could not "tolerate such an act of spoliation as the forfeiture of the concession would be."[3] The Chinese government finally settled with the company for $6,750,000, which, according to W. W. Willoughby, was $3,750,000 in excess of the amount that the Americans had spent.[4]

The work of the Department of State in supporting the claims of the National Railroad Company of Haiti as against the Haitian government also illustrates clearly why a strong policy of protection is likely to encourage investments. The concession was obtained from the Haitian government by an American adventurer under suspicious circumstances. A dispute later arose during the building of the road as to whether the interest payments on construction bonds guaranteed by the Haitian government were to be made on each section as it was completed, as the railroad claimed, or upon the whole road after completion, as was claimed by the Haitian government. In 1914, Haiti suspended payments on the ground that although five completed sections were to be delivered every twelve months only six sections had been delivered in four years. Forfeiture of the

[1] The department seldom, if ever, makes a public promise of support to any enterprise. Investors are, nevertheless, frequently given every reason to believe that protection will be extended.

[2] The British pressed China to cancel the contract, DENNETT, TYLER, "Roosevelt and the Russo-Japanese War," p. 155, Doubleday, Page and Company, Garden City, 1925.

[3] *For. Rel.*, 1905, p. 131.

[4] WILLOUGHBY, WESTEL W., "Foreign Rights and Interests in China," (Rev. Ed.), Vol. II, p. 1071, The Johns Hopkins Press, Baltimore, 1927.

concession was contested by the United States. After American military occupation the Haitian government was compelled to resume interest payments on the uncompleted road. The bonds, which had been largely French owned, found their way into the hands of the National City Bank of New York. Payments of back interest and the increase in price of the bonds made a profit for the bank or its clients, which has been estimated to be more than $2,000,000.[1]

Knowledge of the above-described transactions and other similar ones tends to strengthen the belief of investors and concessionaires that the Department of State will give them support in times of trouble. Accordingly, they are more willing to venture their money abroad. If, however, the Department of State should disapprove of a particular loan or investment, few capitalists would be willing to proceed with the project, for in such instances the department would be able to withhold diplomatic support. The power to refuse protection constitutes the sanction behind the department's policy of capital embargoes.

PRESENTING THE CASE OF THE AMERICAN CONTRACTOR AND CONCESSIONAIRE

While the Department of State does not ordinarily advocate the claims of one set of American interests at the expense of another, it seeks to employ all proper methods for the assistance of American business men abroad by seeing that their applications are duly presented to the authorities and that they receive a fair hearing on a basis of equality with proposals from other countries. According to the advice of Hugh Gibson, testifying as a representative of the United States diplomatic service, an American desiring to secure a contract in a foreign country should go first to the American legation or embassy. The staff members stand ready to assist him in meeting the officials who have the authority to grant the concession, and to give him aid in drawing up his contract. Diplomatic advice as to the terms which he should offer and as to the form of contract which will avoid future difficulties will be given and will be of especial value in the initial stages of the negotiations.

[1] DOUGLAS, PAUL H., "The American Occupation of Haiti," *Political Science Quarterly*, Vol. XLII, pp. 230, 383. See also, *For. Rel.*, 1915, p. 538; 1916, p. 368; 1917, p. 815.

Protection will later be offered against the attempts of rivals to upset the contract by putting over competing arrangements.[1]

Sometimes the efforts of the diplomat are intensified into an argument for the superiority of American enterprise, and an admonition against rejecting American proposals. The following rather fanciful statements to the Tsung-li-Yamen, or Chinese board of foreign affairs, made in 1897 for the purpose of securing an important contract for the American China Development Company, may be taken as an extreme instance of this sort. Mr. Denby in his statement before the Yamen had urged:

. . . that it was conceded by all the officials who had been consulted on railroad questions that Americans could better than any other people build great railroads; that the government had been distinctly advised on all sides to treat with Americans for building its great lines of railroads; that it had gone out all over the world that contracts would be made with Americans; that from a political point of view it was conceded on all hands that the work of developing China should be conceded to Americans, because the United States had and could have no ulterior designs on Asiatic territory; that to refuse now to grant contracts to Americans might develop a bad feeling among our people at home and make them less friendly than they always had been to China; that a few weeks ago it was understood that the contract for building the Hankow-Pekin line was actually let to Americans—a preliminary contract had been made with the American China Development Company; that this company was composed of men who were worth several hundred millions of taels; that it was beyond all peradventure able to execute any contract it might make; that at the instance of Sheng Taotai and other distinguished persons (meaning Li Hung Chang) well-known experts and financiers had come to Shanghai; that they were there in consultation with Sheng, and they had represented to me that Sheng was not disposed to treat them fairly; that it would be a breach of good faith to fail to make a contract with these representatives of American interests, and I had to demand that they wire to Sheng to contract with the American company for the building of the Hankow-Pekin line; that I did not desire to go into details of the contracts to be made, but would leave them to the parties concerned.[2]

---

[1] "Foreign Service of the United States," Hearings before the Committee on Foreign Affairs of the House of Representatives, pp. 42–43, Government Printing Office, Washington, 1924.

[2] *For. Rel.*, 1897, p. 57. The State Department commended the efforts of Minister Denby but urged upon him greater caution in making representations that might be understood as giving government endorsement to the financial standing of persons seeking the contract. The statement

SECURING THE REMOVAL OF RESTRICTIONS SET UP BY BACKWARD NATIONS

Undeveloped nations, reading in the lessons of history the inevitable domination of weak borrowing countries by stronger creditor nations, have sometimes sought to guard their independence by setting up restrictions against foreign capital. Barriers of this sort are apt to become irksome to foreign investors, who naturally pine for the high returns which are sometimes found in virgin investment fields. The benevolent interest of the stronger nation in the development of the weaker one may also be mentioned among other reasons as a cause for anxiety in demanding the removal of the restrictions.

Protests against Chinese Mining Regulations.—The Treaty of 1903 between the United States and China contained a clause safeguarding the free investment of foreign capital in Chinese mines by pledging China to

. . . recast its present mining rules in such a way as, while promoting the interests of Chinese subjects and not injuring in any way the sovereign rights of China, will offer no impediment to the attraction of foreign capital nor place foreign capitalists at a greater disadvantage than they would be under generally accepted foreign regulations.[1]

In 1908, the Chinese Government adopted regulations which provided that the Chinese authorities might order work stopped at the mines in their discretion and that any consequent loss must be sustained by the operators. Secretary of State Root protested that:

Besides being unreasonably restrictive and prejudicial to the industrial development of China itself, some of these regulations violate the spirit, if not the letter, of our treaty stipulations with China.[2]

A regulation promulgated in 1914, providing that foreigners were not to be allowed to hold more than one-half of the total

---

that the American-China Development Company "was composed of men who were worth several hundred millions of taels" was irrelevant as the company itself was a limited liability company with a very small capital. *Ibid.*, pp. 59–60.

[1] *Treaties, Conventions, International Acts, Protocols, and Agreements between the United States of America and Other Powers*, Vol. I, pp. 265–266. (Source hereafter cited as *Treaties, etc. between the United States and Other Powers*.)

[2] *For. Rel.*, 1908, p. 175.

number of shares in mining concerns, brought out a further protest based on the above-quoted stipulation that China would "offer no impediment to the attraction of foreign capital."[1]

Removing Land-owning Restrictions from the Haitian Constitution.—One of the most notable and probably the most aggressive of the attempts by the United States to remove barriers from the path of American capital occurred with reference to the landholding restrictions in Haiti. The Treaty of 1915, which was obtained from Haiti during American military occupation, provided in Art. I:

> The government of the United States will, by its good offices, aid the Haitian government in the proper and efficient development of its agricultural, mineral, and commercial resources and in the establishment of the finances of Haiti on a firm and solid basis.[2]

The article, which was apparently an expression of a purely philanthropic attitude, was soon subjected to an unusual interpretation which well illustrates the elasticity of treaty provisions when construed against a weak country by a strong power. A clause had existed in the Haitian Constitution since 1805 prohibiting foreigners from owning land. To the Haitians this was a cherished defense against foreign domination and had been retained in the constitution during more than a half dozen revisions. The State Department took the view that the prohibition prevented the development of Haiti and made it impossible to give the proper effect to Art. I of the treaty. To what extent the opposition to the constitutional clause came originally from the State Department and to what extent it was developed in the minds of American capitalists who were desirous of buying up land in Haiti it is impossible to state accurately. Both parties probably had a part in the conception of the plan.[3] The particu-

---

[1] *For. Rel.*, 1914, p. 134.

[2] *Treaties, etc. between the United States and Other Powers*, Vol. III, p. 2674.

[3] H. P. Davis, who was interested in an American corporation which was seeking to secure land in Haiti for the raising of castor seed, wrote in the *Pan American Magazine* as follows:

. . . I believe that never in the history of the Americas has there existed an equally favorable opportunity for profitable investment by properly equipped American organizations, as that afforded by the present situation in Haiti and Santo Domingo. (March, 1917, p. 241.) . . .

The development of the agricultural lands of Haiti to their full extent will not be accomplished, however, until after the repeal of Article Six of the Haitian Constitution. All intelligent Haitians who really desire the

lar methods by which the clause was eliminated constitute an instructive chapter in the history of American Caribbean diplomacy.

The Haitian President, who was almost entirely under the control of the United States, called the legislative chambers together in 1917 as the National Assembly to consider the revision of the constitution in order to strike out the clause prohibiting foreign landholding. The sentiment of the Assembly, however, was strongly opposed to the elimination of the clause. Brigadier General Cole of the United States Marine Corps, who was in command of the forces of occupation, suggested in his reports that the American minister warn the Haitians that the United States would not accept a constitution unless the clause should be stricken out. He further stated:

> If national assembly refuses to heed such warning, it will be necessary to dissolve assembly to prevent passage. The number marines in Haiti should be increased by at least eight full companies to prevent disorders that may follow dissolution assembly.[1]

A few days later he reported:

> Unless contrary instructions received, if necessary to prevent passage proposed constitution, [which still contained the objectionable prohibition of foreign landholding] I intend dissolve national assembly, through President, if possible; otherwise direct.[2]

When it appeared certain that the assembly would pass the constitution retaining the clause, General Cole decided to act. He had been promised a decree of dissolution by the evidently reluctant President Dartiguenave; but when General Butler was sent to obtain it, the decree had not yet been signed. General Butler had been instructed to tell the President that if he did not sign the decree the national assembly would be suppressed and that a military government would be recommended for the country. When confronted with the possibility of losing his

---

regeneration of their country agriculturally must see that this provision of their constitution, which prohibits the ownership of land by foreigners, must be eliminated before they can expect the realization of the full potential value of their lands. (October, 1917, p. 327.)

[1] "Inquiry into the Occupation of Haiti and Santo Domingo," a record of the hearings before a select committee of the United States Senate, Vol. I, p. 698, Govt. Printing Office, Washington, 1922.

[2] *Ibid.*, p. 701.

position, the President signed the decree.[1] General Butler then took the decree to the assembly, promulgated it, cleared the hall of deputies and senators, and placed guards at the doors to prevent further meetings.

The next step in the program of eliminating the restriction was to pass a new constitution, containing the desired amendment, by popular vote. A constitutional plebiscite of this sort was not provided for in the existing constitution, but it was decided to hold one on an extra-legal basis. The new document was drafted and submitted to the voters in an election conducted by the Haitian gendarmerie, which was officered by American marines. The officers waged a campaign for the adoption of the proposed constitution.[2] On the election day an officer of the gendarmerie was placed in every voting place. There was evidence that the election was in no sense free. An American missionary testified before the senatorial committee that the Haitians were terrified by the exhibition of armed force, and that, in the polling place which he observed, the negative votes were not untied, and only the affirmative votes lay loose.[3] A light vote was cast and the constitution was carried almost unanimously. Since the restriction against foreign ownership of land has passed out of the Haitian constitution, the purchase of real estate by American firms has begun, and a number of American corporations have now acquired large holdings in Haiti.[4]

Mexican Barriers against Foreigners.—In 1879, the United States objected to a law of Mexico which provided that citizens of adjoining nations could not acquire public lands in the Mexican states bordering such nations. The law was doubtless designed to prevent American land ownership and consequent political encroachment in the northern tier of Mexican states. The Department of State in complaining to Mexico against the law described it as an invidious and unnecessary discrimination

[1] *Ibid.*, p. 702.

[2] *Ibid.*, p. 566.

[3] *Ibid.*, p. 191–192.

[4] Dunn, "American Foreign Investments," p. 135. Concerning this episode and the rumor that Franklin D. Roosevelt, Assistant Secretary of the Navy, drafted the remodelled constitution, Senator Harding declared during the presidential campaign of 1920 that if elected he would not "empower an Assistant Secretary of the Navy to draft a constitution for helpless neighbors in the West Indies and jam it down their throats at the point of bayonets borne by United States Marines." *The New York Times,* Aug. 29, 1920.

"quite incompatible with those friendly relations which the obvious interests of both countries requires should be maintained between them." The Mexican government refused to alter its laws under American protest. Thirty-four years later the Department of State cited the stand of Mexico with approval while defending the California Alien Land Law against the protests of Japan.[1]

Acquiescence in the Mexican position became complete following the adoption of the Constitution of 1917 and subsequent legislation imposing severe restrictions upon the acquisition of property by foreigners.[2] Concerning the disabilities of aliens, Secretary Kellogg said:

> Every sovereign state has the absolute right within its own jurisdiction to make laws governing the acquisition of property acquired in the future. This right cannot be questioned by any other state. If Mexico desires to prevent the future acquisition by aliens of property rights of any nature within its jurisdiction, this government has no suggestion whatever to make.[3]

Perhaps this concession was due to the experience of the United States with Japan, or perhaps it was made for the purpose of emphasizing the American protest against disabilities as to property which had already been acquired. At any rate, the statement was an admission that prohibitions on investments in the future are not properly a subject of protest.

PROMOTING THE PRINCIPLE OF THE OPEN DOOR

Rivalry between creditor nations for the privilege of investing in backward areas has become a common form of international competition since the exportation of capital began on a large scale in the second half of the nineteenth century. One of the most dangerous types of controversy growing out of capitalistic rivalry results from the attempts of governments to set up investment monopolies for their nationals within designated zones. With the development of the United States as a lending nation, this country has become a party to such disputes in several sections of the world.

[1] *For. Rel.*, 1913, p. 647.
[2] See below, p. 113.
[3] "Rights of American Citizens in Certain Oil Lands in Mexico," Sen. Doc. 96, Sixty-ninth Congress, First Session, p. 22.

Spheres of Interest in China.—Beginning about 1897, the great European powers began to claim monopolies for economic exploitation within certain areas in China which were called "spheres of interest."[1] The claims of the powers were based upon three kinds of agreements: (1) those made with China, in which China bound herself not to cede any part of the territory to any other power,[2] (2) agreements with the Chinese central government or with local officials in which a preference was promised to the bankers of the power claiming the sphere in case foreign capital was to be used in certain specific developments, and (3) agreements with third powers in which such third powers promised not to seek economic privileges within the sphere. Upon these types of agreements the powers claimed exclusive rights of investment in railway construction, mining enterprises, and public works.   During the epidemic of aggressions upon China from 1897 to 1899, the British claimed a sphere in the Yangtse Valley; the French one in South China along the Indo-China border and in the Island of Hainan; the Germans one in Shantung; and the Russians one in Manchuria.   Japan laid claim to a sphere in the Province of Fukien in 1898, and in 1904 secured whatever title the Russians had to a sphere in Southern Manchuria.   In 1914, Japanese troops wrested the Shantung sphere from Germany.

The United States, which claimed no special areas, brought into opposition to the spheres of interest the doctrine of the "open door."   While the policy as set forth by Hay in 1899 and agreed to by the powers was confined to rights of commerce, this original meaning was soon afterwards expanded to include the freedom to invest in any part of China.   In 1901 and 1902, it became known that under coercion of Russia, which occupied Manchuria with military force, the Chinese government had been forced to grant to the Russo-Chinese Bank certain railway concessions.   In addition, Russia obtained a promise that, should outside financial support be needed by China for the development of Manchuria, application should always be made to the bank.   Strong opposition to the concession was promptly expressed on the part of the United States and Japan.   On

---

[1] The term "sphere of influence" is also applied, although this term seems to be more properly attached to areas in backward countries that are marked out for annexation.

[2] See below, p. 309.

Feb. 3, 1902, Charlemagne Tower, the American ambassador in St. Petersburg, presented the following note to the Russian Foreign Office:

I am instructed to say that the government of the United States could look only with concern upon any arrangement by which China should extend to a corporate company the exclusive right within its territory to open mines, construct railways, or to exert other industrial privileges.

It is the belief of the government of the United States that by permitting or creating a monopoly of this character, China would contravene the treaties which it has already entered into with foreign powers and would injure the rights of American citizens by restricting legitimate trade; also that such action would lead to the impairment of Chinese sovereignty and tend to diminish the ability of China to meet its obligations. Other powers as well might be expected to seek similar exclusive advantages in different parts of the Chinese Empire, which would destroy the policy of equal treatment of all nations in regard to navigation and commerce throughout China.

I am further instructed to convey to your excellency the sentiment of the United States government that the acquiring by any one power of exclusive privileges in China for its own subjects or its own commerce would be contradictory to the assurances repeatedly given by the Imperial Russian ministery for foreign affairs to the United States of the intention of the Russian government to maintain the policy of the open door in China as that policy has been advocated by the United States and accepted by all the powers who have commercial interests within the Chinese Empire.[1]

In reply Count Lamsdorff, Minister for Foreign Affairs of Russia, reflected the closed door sentiment of his government in refusing the American request. He said that there was no thought of attacking the principle of the open door, but affirmed that negotiations carried on by two entirely independent powers, such as China and Russia, could not be made the subject of approval or disapproval by other states. He further expressed a belief that the demands of the Russo-Chinese Bank did not exceed those so often formulated by other foreign companies and that accordingly it would not be easy for the government of the Czar to refuse support to the bank.[2]

[1] *For. Rel.*, 1902, p. 928. A similar note was presented at Peking and copies were handed to the governments of Austria-Hungary, Belgium, France, Germany, Great Britain, Italy, Japan, The Netherlands, and Spain.

[2] *Ibid.*, p. 929.

In 1915, when the Japanese government presented its famous twenty-one demands to China, Art. VI of the original demands provided:

> In case the Province of Fukien requires foreign capital for railway construction, mining, harbor improvements and shipbuilding Japan shall be first consulted.[1]

In a note to the Japanese ambassador of Mar. 13, 1915, Secretary Bryan outlined the American case against the exclusive spheres for economic exploitation. He mentioned the American position during the Russian agressions in Manchuria in 1901 and 1902 and the fact that at that time the Japanese government was making a similar protest against a Russian economic sphere. He then made reference to the Root-Takahira Agreement between the United States and Japan of 1908, in which the two countries agreed to support the principle of equal opportunity for commerce and industry of all nations in the Chinese Empire. With particular reference to the proposed Fukien monopoly for Japanese capital Mr. Bryan said:

> American citizens may claim a right to share in the commercial development not only in Fukien but in other provinces as well. The United States is not unmindful that many serious disadvantages would result to its commercial and industrial enterprises if special preference is given to one nation in the matter of concessions . . . The United States, as well as every other nation, has the right to have its citizens free to make contracts with the Central and Provincial governments without having the exercise of their rights interrupted or regarded as unfriendly by a third power; for each American enterprise in China is treated on its own merits as to its usefulness and prospective benefit, and without any regard to the possible effect it might have on China's future political status in the Orient.[2]

The Japanese demands with regard to Fukien were modified and were finally satisfied by an exchange of notes in which China assured Japan:

> . . . that the Chinese government hereby declares that it has given no permission to foreign nations to construct, on the coast of Fukien Province, dock-yards, coaling stations for military use, naval bases, or to set up other military establishment; nor does it entertain an intention of

[1] *For. Rel.*, 1915, p. 95.
[2] *Ibid.*, pp. 108–109.

borrowing foreign capital for the purpose of setting up the above-mentioned establishments.[1]

This promise was given to reassure the Japanese who were disturbed because of a rumor that the Bethlehem Steel Corporation had contracted to construct for the Chinese government a naval station at Mamoi on the Fukien coast.[2]

The Siems-Carey Contracts.—The difficulties encountered by American financiers in seeking investments in a land of spheres and monopolies are well illustrated by the experience of the Siems-Carey Company, an American railway contracting firm, which was backed by the American International Corporation. The company secured contracts from the Chinese government in 1916 for the building of 1,500 miles of railways in various parts of China. To their disappointment, however, the contractors encountered everywhere the official opposition of great powers, which claimed the right to prevent American trespassers from entering their respective spheres.

One of the roads was to be constructed from Fengcheng in Shansi to Ninghsia in Kansuh through territory lying in a westerly direction from Peking and somewhat to the north. The Russian government objected to the concession on the ground that it conflicted with a prior promise of China to Russia that Russian capital would have the preference in this region. The promise, which was made in 1899, concerned railways *north or northeast* of Peking. In acknowledging the promise the Russian Minister had used the words "north and northeast of Peking or in any other direction." The addition of the words "or in any other direction" was without the authority of China, although China did not call attention to the error.[3] As the railroad route which was promised to the Siems-Carey Company lay to the north and west of Peking it would seem that it did not come within the prior promise of China to Russia. The Secretary of State instructed the American minister in Peking that the United States would not recognize the enlarged claim of Russia to railway construction preferences in the area in dispute.

[1] *For. Rel.*, 1915, p. 204.

[2] WILLIAMS, EDWARD THOMAS, "China Yesterday and Today," p. 506, Thomas Y. Crowell Company, New York, 1923.

[3] *For. Rel.*, 1916, p. 198. Text of notes are printed in MACMURRAY, JOHN V. A., "Treaties and Agreements with and Concerning China 1894–1919," Vol. I, pp. 207–208, Oxford Univ. Press, New York, 1921.

This position was made clear to China and likewise to the Russian minister in Peking.[1]   Construction of the line, however, was deferred, evidently due to the unwillingness of the company to proceed in face of the Russian opposition.

Another line considered for construction was to run from Chuchow in Hunan to Yamchow in Kwangtung through the Province of Kwangsi.   The French government objected to the building of this road by American capital on the ground that by a former agreement, which had been kept secret, the Chinese had promised preferential rights on railway and mining enterprises in the Province of Kwangsi to the French.   The United States questioned the validity of the agreement because of its secret nature and because it violated the principle of the open door, a principle which France had repeatedly affirmed.   The plans for building the line, however, were abandoned.[2]

A proposed route through the Province of Hupeh, which is in the Yangtse Valley, was objected to by the British because of a secret agreement between a Chinese Viceroy and a British Consul General providing that British capitalists should have the first opportunity of railway construction in Hupeh.   Secretary Lansing defended the right of the American company and informed the British ambassador:

> The reservation of whole provinces and larger areas in China for railway construction, for mining or for other industrial enterprises by any one Power, appears to the American government to be decidedly at variance with the policy of the "open door" and equality of commercial opportunity to which the British government has subscribed.
>
> It is the opinion of the American government that none but agreements or contracts for specific enterprises can be held to be of force under the policy of the "open door," and that such contracts if not executed within a reasonable period, ought not to operate to prevent the necessary development of the region concerned.[3]

The British reply, while acknowledging the desirability of the "open door," pointed out that unfortunately the régime of special spheres had been established, and that as British railway contractors were excluded from many regions in China, Great Britain could not throw open to competition the only sphere in which her investors had a privilege position.   It was inti-

[1] *For. Rel.*, 1916, pp. 205–206.
[2] For the diplomatic exchanges see *For. Rel.*, 1917, p. 183*ff*.
[3] *Ibid.*, p. 191.

mated, however, that cooperation between British and American capital in railway construction might be welcomed, inasmuch as British capitalists were at that time unable to proceed with their projects owing to the financial demands of the European War.[1]

A project for the improvement of the Grand Canal, which crosses Shantung, was then considered. The Japanese, however, claimed as successors to Germany an option on public works requiring foreign capital in Shantung. Against the evident wishes of Chinese officials and against the better judgment of Paul S. Reinsch, American Minister to China, a compromise was arranged by which Japanese capitalists were to have a participation amounting to five-twelfths of the proposed loan. The fear that Japan would otherwise defeat the American project and the evident willingness of the American International Corporation for Japanese participation were the considerations which influenced the Department of State to acquiesce in the compromise arrangement.[2]

While the validity of none of the foregoing objections was admitted by the United States, their combined effect was to play havoc with the plans of the American company.[3]

The Work of the Washington Conference.—One of the most important accomplishments of the Washington Conference was the passage of a resolution which was intended to abolish spheres of interest in China and make impossible the monopolistic claims of various powers to the rights of economic development in special areas. In Art. III of the Nine-power Treaty Relating to Principles and Policies Concerning China, the powers agreed:

With a view to applying more effectually the principles of the Open Door or equality of opportunity in China for the trade and industry of all nations, the Contracting Powers, other than China, agree that they will not seek, nor support their respective nationals in seeking.

(a) any arrangement which might purport to establish in favor of their interests any general superiority of rights with respect to commercial or economic development in any designated region of China;

[1] *For. Rel.*, 1917, pp. 195, 196.

[2] For an account of the affair see WILLIAMS, *op. cit.*, p. 427; WILLOUGHBY, *op. cit.*, Vol. II, p. 1087; *For. Rel.*, 1917, p. 207*ff*.

[3] Another American railway project which was defeated because of foreign objections was that for building the Chinchow-Aigun line. It was opposed by both Japan and Russia. See below, p. 47.

(b) any such monopoly or preference as would deprive the nationals of any other Power of the right of undertaking any legitimate trade or industry in China, or of participating with the Chinese government, or with any local authority, in any category of public enterprise, or which by reason of its scope, duration, or geographical extent is calculated to frustrate the practical application of the principle of equal opportunity.[1]

A resolution of the conference provided that there should be established at the subsequent Special Tariff Conference a Board of Reference to which any questions arising in connection with the above quoted provision as well as concerning Art. V of the same treaty should be referred.[2] The Board of Reference provided for has not been created, and probably will not come into existence, owing to the opposition to such a board in China. The Tariff Conference which met in Peking in 1926 did not even consider the question of creating the board.[3]

JOINT INVESTMENTS SOMETIMES PROPOSED

As a derivative of the open door policy in finance, the United States has on several occasions advocated cooperation between the banking groups of rival creditor nations in their investments in weak countries. Such companionship has by no means been proposed by the State Department as a universal policy. In the Caribbean and Central American countries, the United States has not desired joint action, preferring rather to work toward single control. In the Far East and Middle East, however, where other strong countries have political aims and influence, and where American capital is threatened with exclusion, the cooperation policy has been advocated. The purpose has been to secure participation for American financiers in investments and to neutralize the imperialistic influences which are certain to be exerted where a single creditor country gains a monopoly of the right to supply capital in a backward region. The desire to prevent imperialism is, in turn, probably due to the fear of further economic exclusion which would result therefrom.

[1] *Treaties, etc. between the United States and Other Powers*, Vol. III, p. 3122.
[2] *Ibid.*, p. 3138.
[3] WILLOUGHBY, *op. cit.*, Vol. I, p. 122. For other efforts of the Department of State in behalf of the open door principle see below, Chap. IV, where the equality principle concerning oil in the Middle East is discussed.

The Hukuang Railways Loan.—When Philander C. Knox became Secretary of State in 1909, he found a situation in China which engaged his best efforts in behalf of what was to become his favorite policy, the extension of American finance or, as it is generally termed, "dollar diplomacy." At that time British, French, and German banking groups were completing a complicated negotiation to arrange terms and shares in the construction of a magnificently conceived railway system in China. The project involved the building of lines from the southern city of Canton to Hankow, the great industrial center on the Yangtse, and thence west to the populous Szechwan Province, which was not accessible by river traffic because of the dangerous Yangtse gorges. The possibilities for such a railway system, both in the supply of materials for construction and in financial opportunity, seemed to American bankers and to Secretary Knox as too attractive to permit of the exclusion of American capital.

A promise given by China to the United States in 1904, to the effect that if it should become necessary to draw upon outside capital for the construction of the Hankow-Szechwan line American and British capitalists would be notified simultaneously, furnished Secretary Knox with a basis for intervention. A little more than two months from the time the Taft administration had come into office, the press reported that after a long negotiation an agreement had been reached between the French, German, and British bankers for the construction of the railways. The contract had been initialed and was ready for the Chinese Imperial edict which would complete the transaction. At this juncture Secretary Knox with some boldness asked that the matter be stopped and that the United States, under the agreement of 1904, should be given a share in the furnishing of capital and materials. The claim was pressed simultaneously in London, Paris, Berlin, and Peking. The European powers, as well as China, took the position that while they agreed to American participation in principle, it was then a little too late to rearrange the pending transaction, as the matter was virtually concluded. They intimated, however, that there would doubtless be other loans in which the United States would be allowed to participate. Secretary Knox would not for a moment accept this answer but began a vigorous campaign against odds to force American capital into the enterprise. For two months there was a continuous interchange of communications with the governments concerned, during which time the European bankers were secretly pressing their diplomats to conclude the loan immediately on the agreed basis. China, caught between two fires, was in a difficult and unhappy situation. On June 13, 1909, the American chargé in Peking wired the Department of State that the Chinese government was under pressure and desired to petition the throne for the edict which would close the deal as an affair between European bankers. Two days later, the United States resorted to an unusual method in diplomatic procedure. President Taft sent a persuasive telegram over his own signature to Prince Chun, the Regent of the Chinese Empire, which read in part as follows:

> I am disturbed at the reports that there is certain prejudiced opposition to your government's arranging for equal participation by American capital in the present railway loan, . . . I have an intense personal interest in making the use of American capital in the development of China an instrument for the promotion of the welfare of China, and an increase in her material prosperity without entanglements or creating embarassments affecting the growth of her independent political power and the preservation of her territorial integrity.[1]

At the same time Secretary Knox instructed the American chargé in more vigorous language, stating that if the United States should be blocked, the responsibility would solely rest upon China which "would have acted with singular unfriendliness to the United States."[2]   The Prince Regent ordered the Chinese foreign office to admit the American bankers, and the State Department took up the task of arranging the detailed terms of participation.   Dollar diplomacy had triumphed.[3]

The American Proposal to Internationalize the Manchurian Railways.—One of the outstanding attempts to apply the formula of internationalization was staged in the land of the Manchus, where a great American railway financier, ambitiously seeking to encircle the globe, found himself hopelessly enmeshed in the entanglements of Japanese and Russian policies. After the Russo-Japanese War, Manchuria was partitioned into two spheres of interest, and the railways in each sector were under the control of the government claiming the sphere. In the northern area, the Chinese Eastern Railway, which is a part of

---

[1] *For. Rel.*, 1909, p. 178.

[2] *Ibid.*, p. 179.

[3] For the diplomatic correspondence, see *ibid.*, p. 144*ff.*

the Trans-Siberian Railway connecting Russia with the Pacific, remained under Russian ownership guarded by Russian troops. In the southern sphere, the South Manchurian Railway system was in the hands of the Japanese. The South Manchurian Railway connects Peking and Tientsin with the Trans-Siberian railroad and derives much importance from the fact that it is thus a link in the chain of railway transportation between China and Europe. E. H. Harriman, rising to fame as a power in the American railway world, had dreamed of controlling the Trans-Siberian road and of linking it up with a warm-water port on the Pacific by a similar control in the South Manchurian Railway. He then expected to install a line of steamships between a Baltic port and New York. These, with his American transcontinental line and his trans-Pacific steamers, would complete his around-the-world system.

Approaching the government of Japan concerning the South Manchurian Railway, Mr. Harriman at first met with some success.[1] Eventually, however, the Japanese opposed his participation in the control of their road and secured such financial assistance as Harriman had offered by a bond issue in London. When Harriman found himself defeated in this project he became interested in building another road further west to link up with the Trans-Siberian Railroad. Willard Straight, the energetic and able young American Consul General in Mukden, who had obtained his position partially through Harriman's influence, was fully cognizant of the railway wizard's desires and was himself deeply interested in introducing American capital into Manchuria. From his position in Mukden, he conducted negotiations with the Chinese officials to this end. Later, when he left the consular service and returned to China as the agent for an enlarged banking group, which was working in harmony with Harriman, he entered into an agreement for the construction of a railroad from Chinchow to Aigun by British interests backed by American capital. This line would have furnished the desired link. The purpose in obtaining the concession was that the holding of a definite agreement with China for constructing a road which would compete with the South Manchuria Railway for through traffic to Europe would given an undoubted advan-

[1] For an excellent and intimate account of this subject see CROLY, HERBERT, " Willard Straight," p. 238*ff*, The Macmillan Company, New York, 1925.

tage in further bargaining with Japan for the control of the South Manchuria Railway. In case such bargaining should turn out to be futile, the new concession would furnish in the last resort an independent connecting line.[1] Before the preliminary agreement was signed on Oct. 2, 1909, however, Harriman had died and the dynamic force behind the American plans was gone. Eventually the Chinchow-Aigun project was abandoned, due to the opposition from Russia and Japan.[2]

The immediate importance of the conclusion of the Chinchow-Aigun agreement was the part which it played as a point of departure for the internationalization schemes of the Department of State. With Harriman's death the department became the directing agency for the extension of American interests in Manchuria. Secretary Knox devised a plan for the participation of the capitalists of a number of countries in the financing and control of all of the railways in Manchuria. Manchuria was to become a buffer state under the single control of neither Russia or Japan. The open door to capital was to be assured through the principle of internationalization.

The British government was the first to which the subject was mentioned. In an instruction to the American Ambassador in London, dated Nov. 9, 1909, Secretary Knox brought attention to the Chinchow-Aigun agreement and suggested that it might be opened to the participation of other powers. From this point Mr. Knox went on to suggest:

> Perhaps the most effective way to preserve the undisturbed enjoyment by China of all political rights in Manchuria and to promote the development of those Provinces under a practical application of the policy of the open door and equal commercial opportunity would be to bring the Manchurian highways and the railroad under an economic and scientific and impartial administration by some plan vesting in China the ownership of the railroads through funds furnished for that purpose by the interested Powers willing to participate.[3]

China, Russia, Japan, France, and Germany were also approached.

While the Knox plan was seemingly equitable from the international point of view, it failed to take into consideration the immense practical difficulties due to the nationalistic aims of

[1] CROLY, *op. cit.*, p. 297.

[2] WILLOUGHBY, *op. cit.*, Vol. I, p. 88; *For. Rel.*, 1910, p. 261.

[3] *For. Rel.*, 1909, p. 211.

both Russia and Japan in an area which seemed to them to have vital importance from the standpoint of their national existence. China agreed to the plan, but Great Britain was lukewarm and evasive, while Russia and Japan were flatly opposed. Russia stated that the Chinese Eastern Railway was an integral part of the great Trans-Siberian route and was extremely important in the line of communication between the Russian possessions in the Far East and the rest of the Empire. The Russian government refused to agree to placing the railway under international administration. The Japanese government was equally positive in its opposition. Among other reasons, the necessity for protecting Japanese enterprise in Manchuria was stressed as follows:

In the regions affected by the Japanese railways in Manchuria there have grown numerous Japanese industrial and commercial undertakings which owed their inception, as they owe their continual existence, to the fact that the Imperial government, possessing the railways in question, are able to extend to those enterprises and to the persons engaged in them due protection and defense against attack and pillage by lawless bands that still infest the country. In the development of these enterprises, which are contributing in such a marked degree to the prosperity and progress of Manchuria, a large number of Japanese subjects and large sums of Japanese money are enlisted, and the Imperial government could not in good faith or with a due sense of their responsibility consent to surrender the means by which such protection and defense are made possible.[1]

Thus the necessity of protection as an excuse for imperialism was set forth in one of its manifold forms. In its final outcome, the Knox proposal for internationalization in Manchuria was a failure.

The Consortium.—A more comprehensive attempt to secure the adoption of the principle of internationalization was seen in the development of the consortium for Chinese loans which was perfected at the close of the World War. A brief historical sketch of the antecedent attempts at combination may serve to explain the evolution of the cooperative idea with regard to investments in China. For some years the bitterness of the competition of financial groups seemed to make it advisable to compromise national rivalries in an international merger. Bankers in Great Britain, Germany, France, and the United

[1] *For. Rel.*, 1910, p. 251.

States had combined in 1909 to finance the Hukuang Railways loan. In 1913, the American group withdrew owing to the unwillingness of the Wilson administration to request their participation in the Chinese reorganization loan. In a burst of idealism, President Wilson disapproved of the pledging of particular taxes and the administration of those taxes by foreign agents as compromising the administrative independence of China.[1]

A complete reversal of the Wilsonian policy was accomplished within four or five years as the United States was rapidly transformed from an idealistic debtor to a practically minded world creditor. With this transformation there developed a tendency to emphasize security in loans and correlatively to minimize the importance of the administrative independence of borrowers. The fear that during the preoccupation of Europe in the World War Japan would secure a financial stranglehold on China provided the direct incentive to revive the consortium, while the cooperation with Great Britain, France, and Japan as allies in the war, made joint action in this regard comparatively easy.[2]

In 1918, the United States brought to the attention of the governments of Great Britain, France, and Japan a proposal for the formation of a new consortium which should make all loans to China in the future. The proposal was accepted. In due time banking groups were formed in the four countries. Representatives of these groups met in New York and signed the consortium agreement on Oct. 15, 1920.[3] The agreement was made with the knowledge and acquiescence of the governments concerned and has official sanction. The banking groups are given a monopoly of the diplomatic support of their governments with regard to those loans in China which come within the scope of the consortium. The loans included under the terms of the agreement are described as follows:

This agreement relates to existing and future loan agreements which involve the issue for subscription by the public of loans to the Chinese government or to Chinese government departments or to provinces of China or to companies or corporations owned or controlled by or on

[1] See below, p. 85.

[2] *For. Rel.*, 1917, p. 114*ff* sets forth some of the correspondence during the transition in the American attitude.

[3] Since the organization a Belgium group has been added.

behalf of the Chinese government or any Chinese provincial government or to any party if the transaction in question is guaranteed by the Chinese government or Chinese provincial government but does not relate to agreements for loans to be floated in China. Existing agreements relating to industrial undertakings upon which it can be shown that substantial progress has been made may be omitted from the scope of this agreement.[1]

The agreement, as may be seen, includes not only loans to the Chinese central and provincial governments but also all loans in which the transaction is guaranteed by such governments.

One of the chief purposes of the consortium was to open the door to capital in China by breaking down spheres of interest. The new plan was well devised to accomplish this purpose, but at the outset its proponents were met with the claim of Japan to a sphere of interest in southern Manchuria and eastern Inner Mongolia. The Japanese urged that these regions were vital to the safety of Japan and that it would jeopardize her security if the key investments were opened to international control. In 1920, Thomas W. Lamont, representing not only the American bankers but speaking also for those of Great Britain and France, journeyed to Tokyo in the role of the banker-diplomat and sought to persuade the Japanese to abandon their special claim. The Department of State and the British Foreign Office also took up the contest against the withholding of reserved territories by any member of the consortium. The two governments pointed out to the Japanese that the intention of the consortium was to abolish special spheres, and that the Japanese claim would only serve to revive similar claims of other nations. They declared that there was no intention to interfere with the vested interests of the Japanese or to demand participation in works already built or under construction and upon which substantial progress had been made. Furthermore, the assurance was given that in the operation of the consortium the United States and Great Britain would refuse to countenance any projects inimical to the interests of Japan. After some further discussion and an agreement that a number of specified railway enterprises were to be left solely to Japan, the Japanese government announced that it was willing to withdraw its reservations.

The consortium has thus far been inactive, due to the fact that conditions in war-stricken China have been unfavorable

---

[1] *Treaties etc. between the United States and Other Powers*, Vol. III, p. 3823.

to the lending of money. The principle of the consortium seems, however, to be well adapted to the needs of American policy in China. Russia and Japan both consider that the problem of their national security is vitally connected with Chinese affairs and each is willing to take steps, if necessary, to insure its position by force. Great Britain, with her immense Asiatic possessions and commerce, is also certain to take a great political interest in China. The United States, on the other hand, has no such vital concern in the Far East, and political entanglements in that region would seem to be extremely unwise. Consequently the open door policy supported by some such practical device as the consortium seems best calculated to safeguard without aggression the interest of the United States. On the other hand, as the Chinese demand for capital increases, American bankers may come to consider the consortium as too restrictive, since it confines the United States to an equal share with the other member nations. Economically, the United States is equipped to supply a much greater proportion.[1]

The American Sphere.—While the United States has stressed equal opportunities and joint investments in China and the Middle East, a different policy has been followed in the region of the Caribbean and Central America. This area, because of its proximity to the United States, its opportunities for trade and investment, and its situation with regard to the Panama Canal, has become transcendingly important in American foreign relations. During the first decade of the twentieth century the United States government gradually formed the opinion that European loans and investments in the public debt and key industries of the countries of this section constituted a threat to the Monroe Doctrine. By the time the conviction was firmly established, many of the governments were under obligation to Europe in sums, which, considering the paucity of public revenues, amounted to a comparatively heavy indebtedness. The United States accordingly developed a policy of counteracting European financial influence and replacing European capital with American.

Philander C. Knox, victor of the Hukuang Railway loans controversy, ranks as the most energetic of all American diplo-

[1] For a general treatment of the consortium, see WILLOUGHBY, *op. cit.*, Vol. II, p. 1025*ff*, and Carnegie Endowment for International Peace (Division of International Law), *Pamphlet* 40.

mats in the attempts to use investments in other countries for the extension of political influence; and the financial policy of the United States in the Caribbean and Central America bears the stamp of his personality. Efforts to refund the British-owned debts of Nicaragua, Honduras, and Guatemala, although not successful, together with the introduction of American capital in Haiti and the assistance to American concessionaires against foreigners in Cuba and Panama, constitute the record of Knox in the creation of an American-controlled sphere. Secretary Knox was not supported, as were his successors, with great reserves of surplus capital; but, nevertheless, his efforts fixed the outlines of American policy in the region under consideration, a policy which was strengthened in the hands of later Secretaries of State as the United States was transformed into a creditor nation.

Following the overthrow of the arbitrary Zelaya in Nicaragua in 1910, Secretary Knox set his heart upon refunding the Ethelburga loan to the Nicaraguan government, which had been obtained in London the previous year, the interest on which was in default because of the anti-Zelayist revolution. A treaty was negotiated to give sufficient guarantees to the bankers and a $15,000,000 loan was tentatively agreed upon. The treaty was defeated, however, in the United States Senate and the loan failed. The insistence upon the loan in the instructions issued from the department reveals the fact that the Secretary regarded it as a major objective, even though it was opposed by what seems to have been the predominant sentiment in Nicaragua.[1] Upon defeat of the treaty a loan of $1,500,000, providing for the appointment of an American to supervise the customs collections, was made by the bankers, Brown Brothers and J. and W. Seligman of New York. The outcome in Nicaragua was therefore partially successful.

Opposition by Secretary Knox to British attempts to refund their nominally enormous paper claims against the government

[1] See *For. Rel.*, 1911, for documents concerning the loan. The text of the Dawson agreements containing a promise of Nicaraguan leaders to seek a loan in the United States is on pages 652–653. An instruction stressing the primary importance of the loan is on page 667. A dispatch showing the sentiment against the loan in Nicaragua is on page 639 and another asking that a war vessel be stationed at Corinto until the loan could be put through is on pages 661–662. The text of the defeated loan convention is in *For. Rel.*, 1912, p. 1074.

of Honduras[1] made it necessary for him to interest bankers in an American refunding plan. A New York syndicate became interested in the situation and a proposal was made. A customs-control convention to guarantee the loan was negotiated but met defeat in the Honduran Congress. The plan was then dropped.[2]

The conflict between the Department of State and the British Foreign Office over a similar attempt to refund the British-owned debt in Guatemala showed again the determination of Secretary Knox to rid Central American governments of their indebtedness to British capitalists. In 1912, Secretary Knox attempted to dissuade the British government from making demands upon Guatemala for back payments of interest and for a restoration of the coffee revenues to the service of the loan, the revenues having been originally pledged and later diverted to other purposes. In lieu of the proposed action, the Secretary offered a plan for refunding by American bankers and for taking over the British bonds at a figure to be agreed upon. When the British government showed a disinclination to suspend its demands and await the proposed refunding, Secretary Knox spoke sharply of the predominant interests of the United States in this section. The following instruction of Jan. 7, 1913 indicates the ruffled temper of the American diplomat:

As has been pointed out orally to Mr. Mitchell Innes of the British Embassy, the attitude of Great Britain in demanding one and only one solution of the difficulty, especially when the solution is one likely to block the development of a well-recognized policy of the United States in a sphere in which this government is preeminently interested, would not appear consistent with even an ordinary regard for the broad interests and policies of the United States.[3]

The above-quoted instruction rings with the language of the special sphere and is in sharp contrast with the notion of equality of investment supported by the United States in the Far East. However, after the affair had dragged for a few months longer the British summarily applied the pressure of gunboat diplomacy. The Guatemalan government being threatened by a warship

[1] In 1911 the amount was estimated at $124,000,000.
[2] *For. Rel.*, 1912, p. 549*ff.*
[3] *For. Rel.*, 1913, pp. 558–559.

agreed to restore the coffee revenues to the service of the debt and the matter was terminated.[1]

The work of Secretary Knox in introducing American capital into Haiti was attended by far-reaching political results. The National Bank of the Republic of Haiti, a French corporation owned by French and German capitalists, occupied a position of importance with regard to the Haitian government, being entrusted with the service of the treasury. All governmental revenues were deposited with the bank and disbursements were made by order upon it. To Secretary Knox, the foreign ownership of an institution so likely to provide the cause for diplomatic intervention was not desirable in a region which was vital to the United States. When the bank was reorganized in 1910, Secretary Knox demanded that American financiers should participate in its ownership, and 8,000 of the 40,000 shares were allotted to four New York banks, 2,000 shares going to each. From that time on, intervention in Haitian affairs on behalf of the bank by the Department of State became frequent, and the bank was an influence in bringing about American military occupation in 1915. After the outbreak of the World War the department became interested in obtaining complete ownership for Americans, and, in 1917, the bank became the property of the National City Bank of New York. According to the testimony of the bankers, the department, desirous of replacing French financial control in Haiti with American control, had urged the purchase.[2] Secretaries Bryan and Lansing merely carried out under more favorable conditions the policy started by Knox.

In other ways, American policy in Haiti brought about the replacement of foreign by American capital. The American Financial Adviser in seeking to refund the Haitian foreign debt spent a large part of his time in the United States. Finally, when a loan was arranged in 1922, it was floated in New York, and the ownership of the Haitian debt passed from France to the United States. This change was probably due, however, more to economics than politics as the center of world finance had now shifted to the American metropolis.

---

[1] The correspondence is found in *For. Rel.*, 1912, p. 500*ff*; 1913, p. 557*ff*.

[2] "Inquiry into the Occupation of Haiti and Santo Dimingo," Vol. I, pp. 105–106, 119. For the numerous controversies waged by the Department of State on behalf of the bank see *For. Rel.*, 1914 and 1915.

In Cuba, the United States placed a strict limitation upon foreign borrowing under the Platt Amendment which became a part of the Treaty of 1903 between the two countries. The amendment was interpreted to give to the United States a sort of advisership with regard to Cuban loans. Later Secretary Knox expanded the amendment to give the right of supervision over concessions granted by Cuba to foreigners. In this way, American capital was favored and British capital discouraged.[1]

For strategic reasons, the United States has exercised the right of supervising railway concessions in Panama, and has deemed the acquiring of exclusive railway rights by foreigners in that country as detrimental to American interests. The Dziuk concession, backed by British and German capital, was opposed by the United States in 1912. Panama cancelled the concession nominally for non-fulfilment of contract but actually to please the United States.[2] At another time, when the government of Panama was contemplating the construction of a railway, Colonel Goethals and Minister Price were requested by the Department of State to make recommendations upon the plan. The two agreed that the Department of State should require the bonds for the project to be floated in the United States.[3]

The difference in the American investment policy in the Far East and that in the region of the Panama Canal is due primarily to the remoteness of the one area and the vital importance of the other in the scheme of national defense.

[1] See below, pp. 200–203.
[2] *For. Rel.*, 1912, p. 1198.
[3] *For. Rel.*, 1914, p. 1030.

CHAPTER IV

AIDING THE EXPORT OF CAPITAL INTO FOREIGN OIL FIELDS

THE SUDDEN IMPORTANCE OF OIL

Among the most remarkable examples of the work of the State Department in aiding the investment of American capital in enterprises abroad are its efforts to secure concessions for the exploitation of the oil resources of foreign countries. During the years from 1920 to 1923, the extremely nervous state of the international public and official opinion regarding oil led to unprecedented diplomatic activity to obtain the priceless "black gold." To understand this situation, a brief review of the development of the uses of petroleum and the consequent rivalry for supplies is necessary.

The Military Uses of Oil.—The World War gave unquestioned proof of the value of oil as a military material. The motorization of transportation revolutionized the fuel problem.[1] On Dec. 15, 1917, Premier Clemenceau, facing the desperate prospect of the exhaustion of oil stocks and pleading for a transfer of American oil tankers from the Pacific to the Atlantic, telegraphed President Wilson:

If the Allies do not wish to lose the war then, at the moment of the great German offensive, they must not let the French lack the petrol which is as necessary as blood in the battles of tomorrow.

Because of their control of the sea the Allies were able to draw upon the American oil fields, and, accordingly, after the necessary ships had been made available, the allied supplies were ample. The Germans had depended upon American petroleum prior to 1914; but during the war they were cut off from this source. Gallicia, Rumania, and the Russian Caucasus were accordingly invaded. When reverses came upon the eastern front, however, and oil supplies from that direction were diminished, there ensued for the German army a veritable

[1] See below, p. 361.

57

petroleum famine.   Oil was lacking for motor lorries and air-planes.   As the conflict drew towards its ultimate climax the allies had great advantages in the speed of troop movements. According to Henry Berenger, the French authority:

> If hostilities had lasted only a few days more, our victorious troops would have taken, in the Ardennes, whole armies whose line of retreat was becoming so congested that they must have fallen into our hands without resistance.   Hence the Germans hastily accepted the conditions which were imposed upon them without either hesitation or discussion.[1]

Oil had played an important part in the victory of the allies.

The Economic Uses of Oil.—The war and postwar periods have been characterized by rapidity of movement.   The auto-mobile, the motor truck, the oil-burning locomotive, the Diesel engine, and the ocean-leaping airplane are the outstanding moderisms in transportation.   The advantages of oil as a fuel in ship propulsion have moved some writers to make radical predictions as to its significance in the economic order of the future.   Oil is far more easily loaded aboard ship than coal, and an oil-burning ship can be fueled from a tanker at sea.   Stoking is eliminated.   The space required for engine and fuel is reduced to less than one-half; and the cruising radius is increased.   The merchant marine of the future will be dependent on oil.   De la Tramerye writes:

> The nation which controls this precious fuel will see the wealth of the rest of the world flowing towards it.   The ships of other nations will soon be unable to sail without recourse to its stores of oil.   Should it create a powerful merchant fleet, it becomes the mistress of ocean trade. Now, the nation which obtains the world's carrying trade takes toll from all those whose goods it carries, and so has abundant capital.   New industries rise around its ports, its banks become clearing houses for international payments.   At one stroke the controlling centre of the world's credit is displaced.[2]

Without examining into the soundness of these statements the above quotation stands as an illustration of the values attributed to the control of petroleum and explains to some extent the feverish anxiety of foreign offices in their rivalries to obtain possession of the world's oil.

[1] DE LA TRAMERYE, PIERRE L'ESPAGNOL, "The World Struggle for Oil," p. 109, Alfred A. Knopf, Inc., New York, 1924.

[2] *Ibid.*, pp. 10–11.

The United States Faces the End of Its Oil Resources.—While the desirability of oil as a means of achieving national military and economic greatness became apparent towards the end of the World War, the feeling also arose in the United States that this country, which had ranked first for many years in its oil production, was approaching the end of its supplies. A joint committee of the American Association of Petroleum Geologists and the United States Geological Survey published in 1922 an estimate that of the original 15,000,000,000 barrels, recoverable by present methods, about 9,000,000,000 barrels remained in the ground. The American fields have for several years yielded more than 700,000,000 barrels per year and in 1927 the production was 905,800,000 barrels. In 1926, the Federal Oil Conservation Board reported:

The total present reserves in pumping and flowing wells in the proven sands has been estimated at about 4½ billion barrels.[1]

If the estimates above cited are approximately correct and production is maintained at the present rate and according to present methods of recovery, the end of American oil will be reached in four or five years. This period is, of course, too short for, as the supply diminishes, the output will decrease while improved methods of recovery and new wells will extend production further into the future. Whatever allowances may be made, however, it is apparent that the wealth of American petroleum, so generously granted by Nature, is being rapidly used up. It is doomed to short duration in terms of the life of a nation.[2]

The distress arising from the lack of petroleum in the future may be alleviated by the extraction of oil from shale or by the manufacture of synthetic gasoline from coal. A process invented by Dr. Friedrich Bergius, in Germany, has attracted much

[1] *Report of the Federal Oil Conservation Board*, Part I, p. 6, Govt. Printing Office, Washington, 1926.

[2] Business men who have been interested in securing new capital in the oil industry have decried these predictions as prophecies of gloom and as "exhaustion bogies." The traditionally short-sighted view of the practical man who is interested in the next year's dividends is here contrasted with the estimates of the theorists. The discussion exemplifies the interesting contrast between the exploitation point of view and the social viewpoint. For an account of this controversy see ISE, JOHN, "The United States Oil Policy," Chap. XXVII, Yale University Press, New Haven, 1926.

attention.   From this and similar processes the German chemical trust expects to meet the national demands for gasoline by 1937.[1]   The Federal Oil Conservation Board places much faith in the American supply of shale.   The board assuringly states:

> The oil-shale and oil-sand deposits of this country are of more promise in the future outlook.   Very large areas of such shales exist, many of them yielding as much as a barrel of oil per ton of shale.   Their utilization is solely a question of price.   There can be no doubt that these shales will some day be brought into production.   They form an almost unlimited reserve and may, therefore, be taken as the final protection of our people in the matter of essential supply.[2]

FOREIGN RESTRICTIONS

The need of convenient sources of oil from which to serve their foreign markets has caused United States oil companies to search for wells in distant countries.   As the prospectors of the great American trusts have gone abroad, however, they have met with a cold reception.   Restrictions either in laws or administrative regulations have barred them from many coveted fields.   Reports of these discriminations were dispatched to Washington in the years immediately following the World War and created official indignation.   Investigations of the system of foreign exclusions were ordered and reports were rendered by both the Department of State and the Federal Trade Commission.   Some of the principal findings are presented in the following pages.[3]

British Restrictions.—In British India, the government has held to the practice of granting prospecting or mining leases only to British subjects or to companies controlled by British subjects.   The sale of concessions to foreigners is also apparently forbidden.   A number of applications were made to the Indian government by Standard Oil companies and their subsidiaries

[1] DENNY, LUDWELL, "We Fight for Oil," p. 239, Alfred A. Knopf, Inc., New York, 1928.

[2] *Report*, p. 12.

[3] The reports referred to are: "Restrictions on American Petroleum Prospectors in Certain Foreign Countries," Sen. Doc. 11, Sixty-seventh Congress, First Session; "Oil Prospecting in Foreign Countries," Sen. Doc. 39, Sixty-seventh Congress, First Session; "Oil Concessions in Foreign Countries," Sen. Doc. 97, Sixty-eighth Congress, First Session; Federal Trade Commission, *Report on Foreign Ownership in the Petroleum Industry*, Govt. Printing Office, Washington, 1923.

for prospecting licenses in Burma, but they were refused. An application for permission to erect tanks for the storage of oil in Burma was likewise refused by the government of Burma, no reason being assigned. An appeal to the Indian government was fruitless. In Trinidad, British Guiana, British Honduras, Nigeria, Kenya Colony, and Brunei, the lessees of Crown lands must be British subjects or British-controlled companies. In Canada exploitation is limited to companies of British registry, a regulation which does not preclude the development by American capital. On the other hand, there are no restrictions as to nationality in the United Kingdom, and the same situation prevails in many of the other British possessions. Due to the fact that 60 per cent of the production of the British Empire comes from India and 20 per cent from Trinidad, the British authors, Davenport and Cooke, raise the question: "Is it not fair and accurate to say that the bulk of British oil production is closed to foreign companies?"[1]

Other Countries.—With regard to French territory, the Department of State reported that the regulations were not clear but that it seemed probable that concessions would not be granted to alien groups in France, Algeria, West French Africa, and Madagascar unless they should form a part of a French stock company of which two-thirds of the directors should be French citizens. It is not certain whether these restrictions apply to Morocco and Tunis. The Sinclair Consolidated Oil Corporation reported:

In practice it has been found that France and the French colonies are more completely closed to development by American companies than in any other part of the world.[2]

In the Dutch East Indies, the production rights belong either to the government or to companies under contract with the government. Contracts may be granted only to Dutch subjects, inhabitants of the Dutch East Indies, inhabitants of The Netherlands or Dutch East Indies, and to Dutch companies, on the boards of directors of which there must be a majority of Dutch subjects. This regulation does not exclude

[1] "Oil Trusts and Anglo-American Relations," p. 176, The Macmillan Company, New York, 1924. The treatment of American companies in Mesopotamia, a country under British influence, is discussed later (see p. 64).

[2] Federal Trade Commission, *op. cit.*, p. 52.

Americans residing in The Netherlands or the Dutch East Indies, or Dutch companies backed by American capital.[1] The practice has been, however, to award the production contracts in the important petroleum fields to the Royal Dutch-Shell interests.

In certain backward countries, such as Mexico, the petroleum deposits cannot be acquired by foreigners. This restriction, which is a defense against foreign capitalistic control, has occasioned notable diplomatic controversy where the provisions have been retroactive.

TUGGING AT THE BRITISH DOOR

The sense of the enormous importance of oil, combined with a dread of the coming scarcity and a belief that the door abroad was closed against the United States, produced a frame of mind among public officials, certain congressmen, officers of oil companies, some journalists, and a part of the general public which was almost akin to hysteria. The United States was, they believed, in the position of a strong man deprived of his rights and shut in by his potential enemies. To quote again the French writer, de la Tramerye:

> If the United States does not succeed in acquiring new oil fields in the rest of the world, the position will become so serious that they will only be able to avoid war at the price of economic vassalage.[2]

The opinion was important because it was representative.

The chief petroleum controversy in which the United States engaged was a rather heated series of exchanges with the British government. The British had sought, during and immediately after the World War, to challenge the American oil supremacy. Lord Curzon stated on Nov. 21, 1918, that "the allies floated to victory on a wave of oil," and this was evidently one of the waves which Britannia intended to rule. By the time of the armistice the British plans for the control of oil sources in many parts of the world were well laid. They had extended their control over Mesopotamia and Palestine.[3] Ambitions in North Persia were set forward by the purchase of the Khostaria con-

[1] *Federal Trace Commission, op. cit.,* pp. 53–54.

[2] *Op. cit.,* p. 40.

[3] Their troops had also gone into the Russian Caucasus, but from that area they had been forced to retire.

cession by the Royal Dutch-Shell, and British capital had been active in Latin America. The result was that while the United States still maintained the greater part of the current production of petroleum, the major part of the oil resources were either in territory controlled by Great Britain or were owned by British capitalists. Sir Mackay Edgar, a British oil man, in an article published in *Sperling's Journal* of September, 1919, under the title of "Britain's Hold on the World's Oil," wrote somewhat boastfully as follows:

They [the Americans] are diligently scouring the world for new oil fields—only to find, almost wherever they turn, that British enterprise has been before them and that the control of all the most promising properties is in British hands . . . The British position is impregnable. All the known oil fields, all the likely or probable oil fields, outside the United States itself, are in British hands or under British management or control, or financed by British capital. We shall have to wait a few years yet before the full advantages of the situation begin to be reaped. But that the harvest will eventually be a great one can be no matter of doubt. To the tune of many million pounds a year America before very long will have to purchase from British companies, and to pay for in dollar currency, a progressively increasing proportion of the oil she cannot do without and is no longer able to furnish from her own stores.[1]

The Department of State was not slow to respond to the British challenge and diplomatic negotiations began over the exclusion of Americans from Mesopotamia and Palestine and over rival rights in North Persia. Throughout the correspondence the British took the position that they were not trying to preempt the world's oil supply and that there were no restrictions against Americans excepting in certain British territories where the production was not great. The United States was also reminded that the great bulk of petroleum production was still American. Lord Curzon stated:

I would like here to make a passing reference to the very mistaken impressions which appear to be current in the United States in regard to the oil policy of His Majesty's government. The output of oil within the British Empire is only about 2½ per cent of the world's production, and if the production of Persia be included, in virtue of certain oilfields in that country being owned by a British company, the total amounts to about 4½ per cent. Against this small percentage, the United States produces some 70 per cent of the world's output,

[1] Quoted in ISE, *op. cit.*, p. 461.

besides which United States companies, who own at least three-fourths of the Mexican output, are estimated to produce a further 12 per cent of the world's output. This overwhelming proportion, over 80 per cent of the petroleum production of the world is under American control, and the predominance of the United States in regard to oil production is assured for many years to come. There is, in any case, no justification for supposing that Great Britain, whose present oil resources are altogether insignificant in comparison, can seriously threaten American supremacy, and any prophecies as to the oil-bearing resources of countries at present unexplored and quite undeveloped must be accepted with reserve.[1]

In reply to this, Secretary of State Colby pointed out that according to estimates only one-twelfth of the petroleum resources of the world were possessed by the United States, whose supplies had already been drawn upon for foreign needs to a greater extent than those of any other country.[2] Here was a plain difference in point of view, the British stressing current production, in which the United States was supreme, and the Americans emphasizing potential resources, of which the greatest share was apparently in the hands of the British.

Mesopotamia.—The existence of oil in Mesopotamia had been well known for several years and there had been some rivalry for the right to develop the oil fields when, in 1914, the Turkish Petroleum Company secured a tentative concession. This company was an international group and its shares were owned by the Anglo-Persian Oil Company, 50 per cent; the Deutsche Bank, 25 per cent; and the Royal Dutch-Shell, 25 per cent. An incomplete promise of the Turkish government to lease the fields was given to the company following diplomatic representations by both the British and German governments, and was in the nature of a communication from Said Halim Pasha, Grand Vizier, addressed in identic form to the British and German ambassadors at Constantinople.[3] The date of the note was June 28, 1914, and the matter stood thus as the World War began. During the war the British invaded Mesopotamia, reaching Bagdad in 1917 and advancing to Mosul shortly after the armistice. Great Britain was awarded a mandate over the territory at the San Remo Conference. Although the

---

[1] *International Conciliation*, No. 166, pp. 313–314.
[2] *Ibid.*, pp. 323–324.
[3] A portion of the letter is quoted below, p. 67.

mandate did not go into effect, the treaty of alliance between Great Britain and Iraq, signed Oct. 10, 1922,[1] gave a large amount of political control to Great Britain.

The San Remo Conference, at which the Class *A* Mandates were awarded, also saw the conclusion of a secret agreement between Great Britain and France with regard to oil. This agreement, in brief, provided that in case a private company should be used to develop the Mesopotamian oil fields the British government should place at the disposal of the French government a share of 25 per cent in such company at a price no greater than that paid by the other participants. The company was to be under permanent British control. The French in their turn agreed to permit the construction of pipe lines across territory within their sphere to a port or ports on the Eastern Mediterranean. In other words, the French received an opportunity to purchase the 25 per cent share of the Deutsche Bank in the Turkish Petroleum Company, which share had been expropriated by the British government during the war, and Great Britain received the promise of a right of way for a pipe line across Syria. The date of this agreement was Apr. 24, 1920.

On May 12, in ignorance of the oil agreement at San Remo but aware of the mandate allotment, the American government presented through Ambassador Davis at London a note expressing the hope that no exclusive concessions would be granted in the mandated territory and that the principle of treatment in law and fact equal to that accorded to the nationals or subjects of the Mandatory power should be guaranteed to the nationals or subjects of all nations.[2] This note was prompted by the belief that the British authorities were quietly preparing for a monopolistic development of the oil resources in Mesopotamia.

When in July, 1920, the news of the San Remo Agreement was published, the United States was prompt to file a protest with the British foreign office and the discussion continued for several years. The main arguments as presented in the published notes may be summarized without regard to their chronological sequence as follows:

The Principles Underlying Mandates.—Lord Curzon was averse to a discussion of the terms of the mandates with the

---

[1] Replaced by the Treaty of Dec. 14, 1927.

[2] *International Conciliation* No. 166, p. 304.

United States and suggested that the only proper place for such an exchange of views was before the Council of the League of Nations. Secretary Colby replied that rights over the mandates were an evolution from the war against the Central Powers, and that the United States, having contributed to the successful issue of the war, could not consider itself debarred from the discussion of the subject. Certain principles were proposed by the Department of State as appropriate to be applied in the class *A* mandates. In brief, the suggestions were that the spirit of trusteeship behind the mandate conception at the peace negotiations at Paris should continue to prevail, that there should be accorded equality of economic treatment to the nationals of all countries, that no monopolistic concessions should be granted, and that reasonable publicity should be given in the matter of concessions. It was also requested that the draft mandate forms should be communicated to the American government for consideration prior to submission to the Council of the League. The rejoinder of Lord Curzon was to the effect that he could see nothing in the mandate principle which compels the mandatory power to discriminate against its own nationals by setting aside their just rights. He gave no pledge of compliance with the American request.

The Preferential Treatment of France as a Discrimination against the United States.—The United States claimed that the preferential treatment shown to France in the provision for the transfer of shares was not in consonance with the principle of equality of treatment which should have been maintained in the mandates. The British government in reply cited the historic contention of the United States in support of the conditional interpretation of the most-favored-nation clause:

> . . . that special privileges conceded to particular countries in return for specific concessions cannot in virtue of such a clause be claimed by other countries not offering such concessions.

France had given a definite *quid pro quo* in the form of a right of way for a pipe line across Syria and, according to the British contention, there was no inequality in granting a particular concession in oil in return.

The Validity of the Turkish Petroleum Company's Claims.— The identic note which was addressed by the Turkish Grand Vizier to the British and German ambassadors on June 28, 1914, and which formed the basis of the claims of the Turkish Petroleum Company, read as follows:

The Ministry of Finance being substituted for the Civil List with respect to petroleum resources discovered, and to be discovered in the vilayets of Mossoul and Bagdad, consents to lease these to the Turkish Petroleum Company, and reserves to itself the right to determine hereafter its participation as well as the general conditions of the contract.[1]

The British government took the view that this was a valid contract which could not be questioned. It further alleged that to challenge the rights thus acquired would not be consistent with the attitude of the United States toward the oil properties of American citizens in Mexico as affected by Art. 27 of the Mexican Constitution. The American State Department, however, saw in the Grand Vizier's letter no definite and binding agreement, as the extent of the participation of the Ministry and the general conditions of the lease were to be left to later negotiations. The British Foreign Office had submitted no evidence of progress toward securing the approval of the Turkish Parliament. The whole affair seemed to be a matter in contemplation rather than a concluded bargain. The Department of State suggested arbitration as a suitable means for determining the validity of the contract.

The Settlement.—Just how the conflicting claims of American and British interests over oil in Mesopotamia were adjusted is not a matter of definite record. While the governments were addressing notes to each other over the principles of the open door and mandatory trusteeship, representatives of the oil companies came together and effected an agreement. To what extent the Mesopotamian accord was part of a larger oil bargain between the Standard Oil on one hand and the Royal Dutch-Shell and Anglo-Persian on the other is not clear, although during the same general period the difficulties over Northern Persia and Palestine were smoothed out. After several years of negotiation it was definitely announced that a group of American companies was to have the privilege of purchasing 25 per cent of the shares of the Turkish Petroleum Company. The allotment was to come from the shares held by the Anglo-Persian Company. Five American companies were to participate in

[1] Text given in "Oil Concessions in Foreign Countries" p. 49.

the American portion, including the Standard Oil Company of New Jersey, the Standard Oil Company of New York, the Gulf Refining Company, the Atlantic Refining Company, and the Pan-American Petroleum and Transport Company. All of the companies, excepting Gulf Refining, are of the Standard Oil family. This arrangement was hailed by the Standard Oil officials as the first instance in history of the development of oil fields according to a "practical open-door policy."[1] The process of putting into effect the above-mentioned agreement was, however, not easy. For a time the claims of C. S. Gulbenkian, a wealthy Armenian, who had been prominent in the affairs of the Turkish Petroleum Company during the period before the war when it had obtained the promise from the Turkish government, proved to be an obstacle. Likewise the overgenerous act of the Anglo-Persian Company in parting with half of its Turkish Petroleum holdings in order to appease the Americans was evidently regretted by the management of that company. After many months of negotiations, the shares in the Turkish Petroleum Company were finally rearranged as follows: Anglo-Persian, 31.25 per cent; Royal Dutch-Shell, 21.25 per cent; French interests, 21.25 per cent; American interests, 21.25 per cent; C. S. Gulbenkian, 5 per cent.[2]

Palestine.—The Standard Oil Company of New York had secured concessions in Palestine and had begun prospecting prior to the World War. After the interruptions due to that conflict the company sought to recommence operations in 1919, but its representative was arrested in Jerusalem by the orders of the British Governor of Palestine. The British government explained that all such work was to be discontinued for the time being. The American embassy in London requested that the company be allowed to resume its work. Great Britain agreed to permit this with the understanding that such consent did not commit the government in favor of the legal claims of Standard Oil. A further condition that the company should furnish to the government of Palestine a full and complete report of its investigations was demurred to by the Department of State which could see no good reason for such a report. The British government insisted that such returns were necessary as the government of Palestine had no facilities for making

[1] DENNY, *op. cit.*, p. 151; *The New York Times*, Apr. 24 and May 16, 1926.
[2] DENNY, *op. cit.*, pp. 156–157.

geological surveys and must, therefore, take advantage of the findings of private companies holding mineral concessions. The United States finally assented to this demand and in time the company proceeded with its investigations.[1]

NON-BRITISH TERRITORY IN THE EAST

Djambi.—The Djambi oil fields are considered by American oil experts to be the richest in the Dutch East Indies, and rights to exploit them have been coveted particularly by Standard Oil because of the proximity to its distribution systems in the Far East. Sinclair was also eager to secure an interest in oil production in this region; and when the matter of a contract for exploitation was under consideration the United States made diplomatic representations urging that Americans should be permitted a share in the development. This plea was disregarded and the Dutch government proceeded to award the contract to the *Bataafsche Petroleum Maatschappij*, which is a subsidiary of the Royal Dutch. Thus, the richest field of the Dutch East Indies was turned over for exploitation to a company representing Dutch and British capital. In the worldwide struggle between Standard Oil and Royal Dutch-Shell, the latter had scored an undoubted victory.

The United States government took the view that the award to the Royal Dutch subsidiary amounted to closing the door in the face of American capital and that the act was particularly unfair because the United States had made no discrimination against Dutch or British capital in the development of the oil resources of this country. The Roxana Petroleum Company and the Shell Company of California are among some of the important Royal Dutch-Shell companies established in American territory, and through its various subsidiaries the combination holds large leases in the public domain and in Indian lands. The United States informed the Dutch government that it was very greatly concerned over the granting of a monopoly to a company in which foreign capital other than American is so largely interested. In this case the capital other than American referred to was the British interest in the Royal Dutch-Shell combination. Threats were made to retaliate under the United

---

[1] See "Oil Concessions in Foreign Countries," pp. 59–67 for the correspondence concerning this matter.

States Mineral Leasing Act of 1920 which forbids leases on the public domain to nationals of countries which do not extend similar privileges to American citizens.

The Dutch reply was to the effect that the contract had already been promised to the Bataafsche Petroleum Company even before the American companies had approached the government on the subject, that the accord reached with the company was such as to give the government an influence in the management of the enterprise to such an extent that it tended to take the form of an exploitation by the state itself, that there were other fields in the Dutch East Indies which were open to Americans, and that, after all, the exploitation of the field by a Dutch company would not deprive the United States of oil or exert any influence on the international distribution of oil. The Dutch government further objected to the statement that its policy was any less in line with the principle of the open door than that of the United States.

Retaliation by the United States was actually begun. On Sept. 12, 1922, Albert Fall, Secretary of the Interior, refused the request of the Shell Company of California for a lease on public lands in Utah and gave them sixty days in which to file evidence that the government of The Netherlands would permit similar concessions to citizens of the United States. The company withdrew its application. In March, 1923, the Secretary refused to permit the assignment of Indian leases to the Roxana Petroleum Corporation. This decision was later reversed by the successor of Mr. Fall, Hubert Work, on the ground that Secretary Fall had exceeded his authority under the Leasing Act, as Indian lands belong to the Indians in fee and are not a part of the public domain.[1] After several years of negotiations the State Department announced that the two governments had settled their differences over oil exploitation by a friendly understanding. The Netherland government assured the United States that its laws and policies were such as would permit participation by Americans in the development of oil lands in the Dutch East Indies. The United States in turn agreed to consider The Netherlands as a reciprocating country under the terms of the 1920 mineral leasing act, which construction restores to Dutch nationals the privilege of leasing public mineral lands.[2]

[1] Ise, *op. cit.*, pp. 471–472.
[2] *State Department Press Release*, Sept. 17, 1928.

Persia.—Prior to the war Persia had been torn into two spheres of influence, the Russian on the north and the British on the south. The mineral oil resources in the south had been conceded to the Anglo-Persian Oil Company while those in the north were claimed by Akaky Khostaria, a national of Russia. Following the war, Persia was in financial difficulties and sought to secure assistance from the United States, partially because Persian leaders believed that capital thus obtained would not subject the country to foreign intervention. On Sept. 15, 1921, the Persian minister at Washington sent to the Secretary of State a memorandum explaining the fiscal needs of Persia. Prominent among the reasons set forth to interest the capitalists of the United States was the assertion that "Plenty of oil of the best quality, which is one of the great requirements of America, is to be found throughout the north, as well as the south, of Persia."[1]

The Standard Oil Company of New Jersey approached the Persian government and an agreement was arranged for a $5,000,000 loan and an oil concession.[2] This concession was voted by the Persian Madjless or Parliament on Nov. 24, 1921. The Khostaria concession, which was in conflict with the Standard Oil grant, was disregarded by Persia for the reason that the concession to Khostaria was granted in 1916 during a time when Russian troops were in the country and the Persian Madjless was not in session. According to Art. 22 of the Constitution of Persia such a grant requires the approval of the Madjless. Not having received the required parliamentary sanction, the Persian government looked upon the concession as null and void. However, in May, 1920, the Anglo-Persian Oil Company, in which the British government owns the controlling interest, purchased Khostaria's rights.[3] Thus the Standard Oil came into conflict with the Anglo-Persian.

To counteract British opposition to the American company the Department of State made representations at Teheran. The following instruction was sent to the American Legation on Jan. 21, 1922:

You may inform the Persian government that the government of the United States is deeply interested in the Open Door and that it would

[1] "Oil Concessions in Foreign Countries," p. 91.

[2] *Ibid.*, p. 120 for text of the concession.

[3] FISCHER, LOUIS, "Oil Imperialism," p. 213, International Publishers, New York, 1926.

insist upon this principle in its exchanges with the British or any other government. The American government attaches the greatest importance to the preservation in Persia of such opportunity for American interests as is enjoyed by the interests of any other nation. The Persian Minister and the British Ambassador have been informed.[1]

The concession which had been voted to the Standard Oil Company contained a provision that the rights under it could not be transferred nor could the grantee enter into partnership with any other company without the consent of the Madjless.   Nevertheless, as a part of the great Anglo-American oil bargain, the Standard finally agreed to include the Anglo-Persian Company with it on a basis of equal participation.   This arrangement not only violated the explicit stipulation of the Standard Oil concession against transfer but aroused the opposition of Moscow. The Soviet government was not anxious to see the Anglo-Persian interests entrenched in a territory so near to the Caspian.[2] Supported by Russia, the Persian government refused to accede to the new arrangement.

In December, 1923, the Sinclair Consolidated Oil Company was given a concession for the North Persian fields,[3] and the Standard Oil objected, basing its claim now upon the Khostaria concession in which it had acquired an interest through its association with the Anglo-Persian Company. This was the claim which the Standard Oil Company had considered null and void when it had applied for its own concession two years before. So far as is known, the Department of State took no further part in forcing upon Persia the claims of either of the American companies. In January, 1924, less than a month after the granting of the Sinclair concession, the news of the Teapot Dome scandal attracted worldwide attention. About the same time a rumor was started in Russia to the effect that Sinclair had merged with the Standard Oil, which report also arrayed against him the opposition of the Soviet government.[4] The Sinclair project fell through due to the inability of the Sinclair Company to provide the $10,000,000 loan which was a part of the bargain.[5]

[1] "Oil Concessions in Foreign Countries," p. 99.

[2] FISCHER, *op. cit.*, p. 228.

[3] The terms are set forth in FATEH, MOUSTAFA KHAN, "The Economic Position of Persia," p. 43, King, London, 1926.

[4] FISCHER, *op. cit.*, p. 234.

[5] FATEH, *op. cit.*, p. 43.

Up until the present time no foreign concessionaire has received the grant to the North Persian field.

Russia, a Matter for Future Consideration.—The Russian situation, while it does not come logically within the subject of this chapter, is too important to be passed by without comment. The 1917 Revolution, the breakdown of production, and the antagonisms between the Soviet government and the capitalistic world have temporarily obscured the importance of Russia as a factor in the world's petroleum problem. It seems clear, however, that the United States will be commercially and diplomatically interested in Russian oil in the future. The drain upon American resources will make it inevitable that American companies which distribute in Europe and the East will desire to secure large amounts of oil from the rich Russian fields. Already two American companies, the Standard Oil Company of New York and the Vacuum Oil Company, have been buying from Russia, and their influence is on the side of an understanding with the Soviet government. Non-economic influences, however, have thus far prevailed in the policies of the American government and assistance to American business and investment by the resumption of diplomatic relations with Russia has been deemed subordinate to other considerations.[1]

THE CARIBBEAN AREA

While the "open door" has been the chief reliance of American diplomacy in the East, this principle has scarcely been mentioned with regard to the oil fields in and near the Caribbean. Rather has this country at times sought to exclude foreign companies.

Colombia: the Cowdray Concession.—In 1913, the Lord Cowdray interests of London had under negotiation a large oil concession in Colombia which was to include the right to build docks and to make harbor improvements. The United States opposed this concession and forced the concessionaires to abandon their negotiations. Ambassador Page estimated that Lord

---

[1] For a more thorough discussion of the international importance of Russian oil and the rivalry of the great oil trusts over it see FISCHER, *op. cit.*; DENNY, *op. cit.*, Chap. X. See also the issues of *The New York Times* for July 20, 21, 22, 26, 29, and 30, 1927, for the dispute between the Standard Oil Company of New York and the Vacuum Oil Company on one side and the Standard Oil Company of New Jersey and the Royal Dutch-Shell group on the other over the question of dealing with the Soviet government.

Cowdray lost, that is, failed to make, $100,000,000 by the intervention of the American government.[1] President Wilson explained the general principles which lay behind the action of his government in the celebrated speech before the Southern Commercial Congress at Mobile, Ala. on Oct. 27, 1913, as follows:

. . . states that are obliged, because their territory does not lie within the main field of modern enterprise and action, to grant concessions are in this condition, that foreign interests are apt to dominate their domestic affairs, a condition of affairs always dangerous and apt to become intolerable. What these states are going to see, therefore, is an emancipation from the subordination, which has been inevitable, to foreign enterprise and an assertion of the splendid character which, in spite of these difficulties, they have again and again been able to demonstrate. . . . I rejoice in nothing so much as in the prospect that they will now be emancipated from these conditions, and we ought to be the first to take part in assisting in that emancipation. I think that some of these gentlemen have already had occasion to bear witness that the Department of State in recent months has tried to serve them in that wise.[2]

The "Wilson Doctrine," as Ambassador Page termed it, was designed to prevent foreign financial control of the Latin-American republics. The idealistic epigrams of the scholar-statesman seemed to have a universal application and were doubtless intended for all alike. Whatever may have been in the mind of the President, the practical effect of the doctrine was, however, to keep out British capital and to permit development by Americans. Some of the most "dominating" of concessions in Latin America have been granted to citizens of the United States in the years following 1913.

Helping the Oil Men in Colombia.—The efforts of Wilson and Bryan to discourage British capital from developing Colombian oil have been supplemented by official assistance given to Americans in their attempts to secure concessions. The principal instances of such aid were in connection with the ratification of the treaty which was negotiated to make amends for the Panama incident of 1903. The people of Colombia, following 1903, were bitter toward the United States and various administrations

[1] HENDRICK, BURTON J., "The Life and Letters of Walter Hines Page," Vol. I, p. 227, Doubleday, Page and Company, Garden City, 1923.

[2] *President Wilson's State Papers and Addresses*, pp. 34–35, George H. Doran Company, New York, 1917.

sought to mollify unfriendly sentiment. Attempts were made to conclude a treaty which would grant to Colombia an indemnity and certain commercial rights in the Canal Zone. Until 1921, these attempts had failed, largely at first through the disinclination of Colombia to accept a small indemnity and later through the opposition in the United States Senate of the friends of President Roosevelt. The objections of the latter were directly mainly at a so-called "regrets" clause, which was placed in the negotiated treaty during the Wilson administration. They also objected to the principle of an indemnity.

By 1919, petroleum had thrown a new light upon the discussions. In a note of Jan. 20, 1920, the American Minister at Bogota alluded to the possibility of a deal which would include the ratification of the treaty by the United States in exchange for oil concessions to American capitalists.

It has been entirely in a spirit of friendly interest for the prosperity of Colombia that Mr. Philip has taken the liberty of expressing his personal opinion to President Suarez to the effect that the celebration by Colombia of important contracts with citizens of the United States at this time would, in all probability, have a most favorable bearing upon the treaty situation.[1]

Colombia was not willing to make petroleum rights a subject for consideration in the treaty and maintained that that instrument should deal with nothing more than the Panama dispute. It was intimated, however, that if the matter of the treaty should be satisfactorily disposed of, Colombia would feel more kindly inclined toward American concessionaires. As the President of Colombia stated:

Under the present conditions it would be possible for Colombia to say to the United States: "Give my right (literal in the imperative—make effective my right) and fulfill your obligations, which act will open the door to many friendly acts." But the United States would have no right to say to Colombia: "If you do not grant favors to my citizens I will not fulfill my previous obligations."[2]

In other words Colombia was not willing to make a promise of favorable treatment a condition expressed in the treaty but

[1] "Diplomatic Correspondence with Columbia in Connection with the Treaty of 1914, and Certain Oil Concessions," Sen. Doc. 64, Sixty-eighth Congress, First Session, pp. 59–60.

[2] *Ibid.*, p. 58.

was willing to leave it to implication that if the treaty should be ratified favorable treatment would follow.

A strong faction in the United States Senate which had previously been in opposition was willing to accept this as a gentlemen's agreement and was thereby influenced to support the treaty as is shown by the reversal in attitude of the group leader, Senator Lodge of Massachusetts. Senator Lodge had previously been much opposed to the treaty. In 1917, he had signed a minority report of the Senate Committee on Foreign Relations, roundly criticising it. He had given to the press a statement of his opposition, which read as follows:

It [the treaty] begins with an apology and ends with paying Colombia $25,000,000 for nothing in particular except her doubtful good will after payment . . The objections to the treaty on its merits seem to me conclusive . . . Even if I favored the treaty I would not support it now because I am not willing to have my country blackmailed.[1]

Coincident with the entrance of the oil question into the treaty controversy, Senator Lodge changed his mind. In speaking for the treaty on Apr. 12, 1921, he elaborated the argument that oil is essential to the great maritime nations and dwelt on the danger of a British monopoly. He introduced a map furnished by Secretary of Interior, Albert Fall, to show the principal sources of supply and marketing affiliations of the Royal Dutch-Shell combination together with an imposing list of the producing, distributing, and marketing companies belonging to those interests. He also brought forth two letters from Secretary Fall, who was seemingly the liason agent between the oil interests and the senatorial group. A letter from the Secretary, of Mar. 21, 1921 read in part as follows:

Thus far it is undoubtedly true that American oil interests are much interested in the friendly settlement of all outstanding difficulties with Colombia and in drawing more closely the commercial relations of the two countries through political friendship.

Activities of the oil companies are directed, generally, by intelligent, broad-minded American business men, who, of course, realize as do other thinking American citizens, that upon governmental action largely depends the success of individual investment and consequent trade wealth.

Believing, as Theodore Roosevelt and others believed, that friendly and very close relations with Colombia are absolutely necessary for the

[1] *The New York Times*, Mar. 14, 1917.

safety of the Panama Canal, and of American interests, and realizing, as they do, that friendly relations between the two governments must exist as a preliminary and as a prerequisite to the development of Colombia's natural resources by American capital, it is doubtless true that American oil companies are urging ratification of the present treaty.[1]

Due to the support of Republicans who had previously opposed the settlement, the treaty was approved by the Senate on Apr. 20, 1921 by a vote of sixty-nine to nineteen. Following the ratification of the treaty, American investments have increased in Colombia by leaps and bounds, oil companies and other concessionaires being treated with hospitality by the Colombian government.[2]

The Question of Recognizing Huerta.—When the Madero régime was overthrown by Huerta, a long period followed in which the United States refused to recognize the new government while Great Britain extended recognition. The American refusal was based on the moral grounds that Huerta had come into power by lawless means. This was an unorthodox notion in the practice of recognition, but there is no reason to believe that there was an ulterior dominating motive. However, it was suspected by both President Wilson and Secretary Bryan that the Huerta administration was favorable to British oil producers. Colonel House wrote to Ambassador Page on Nov. 14, 1913:

I talked the Mexican situation out thoroughly with him [Bryan] and one of your dispatches came while I was there. I found that he was becoming prejudiced against the British government, believing that their Mexican policy was based purely upon commercialism, that they were backing Huerta quietly at the instance of Lord Cowdray, and that Cowdray had not only already obtained concessions from the Huerta government, but expected to obtain others. Sir Lionel was also all to the bad.

I saw the President and his views were not very different from those of Mr. Bryan.[3]

In the course of time, due partly to the yielding of the United States in regard to the Panama Canal tolls, the British Government withdrew recognition of Huerta, and American policy triumphed. To what extent the desire to exclude British oil interests affected the American policy it is impossible to determine,

[1] *Cong. Rec.*, Vol. 61, p. 167.
[2] Dunn, "American Foreign Investments," p. 74.
[3] Hendrick, *op. cit.*, Vol. I, p. 206.

but it seems reasonable to say that opposition to the suspected grants by Huerta to Cowdray did something at least to stiffen the opposition to Huerta.[1]

CRITICISMS OF THE REASONS ADVANCED FOR OIL DIPLOMACY

As has been stated, whenever several considerations enter into the national policies of any nation the public statements made by those who are responsible for the policies and by the members of the public who support them are not always accurate in stressing the various reasons according to their actual importance. Motives which appeal to the instinct of national self-preservation are often emphasized far beyond their due, while others which are less popular, such as seeking advantages for certain special groups, may be minimized or omitted altogether. The public statements with regard to oil diplomacy have placed too much emphasis upon national defense and the need of raw materials, and have failed to give sufficient attention to the fact that a very important effect of such policies will be to admit American oil companies to a share in the natural wealth of other countries. What is primarily a matter of financial advantage has been explained to the public as a question of defense policy and raw material diplomacy.

Will American Investments Abroad Bring Oil into the United States in Time of War?—The belief that the investment of American capital in the oil fields of other countries will be an aid to this country in case of war is largely an illusion. In war time the supply of oil, as of any other material imported from abroad, will depend upon the control of transportation routes. This is

---

[1] The British claimed at the time that the United States was playing the game of the Standard Oil in Mexico. The British government has likewise charged American interference against British concessions in Haiti and Costa Rica. In his note to Ambassador Davis of Aug. 9, 1920, Earl Curzon alleged as follows: "On the occupation of Hayti by United States forces in 1913 [sic], the United States Administration refused to confirm an oil concession which had been approved by the Haytian government and Legislature and for which the caution money had been deposited in the republic; and more recently the United States representatives at San Jose urged the present Costa Rican government to cancel all concessions granted by the previous government, the only concession in question being an oil concession granted to a British subject." *Int. Conciliation*, No. 166, p. 34. Denny states: "American dominance was easy to achieve in countries over which the United States government or its so-called 'treaty officials' exercise wide authority." *Op. cit.*, p. 104.

a naval problem. If a nation at war has control of the seas, it will be able to purchase materials from other countries, whether such materials are financially controlled by its nationals or not. If the seas are in the hands of the enemy, however, overseas commodities cannot be directly secured, and the modern extension of the doctrine of ultimate destination has made it next to impossible to import such commodities indirectly. After the outbreak of the World War the Allies, because of their naval supremacy, were able to draw upon the United States for oil and other supplies during the years of American neutrality, independent of any investment which they may have had in this country. Germany was prevented from securing access to materials, even to those which had been developed by German capital. In case of war between the United States and a formidable European combination the investments of American companies in oil in the Near East would be wholly lost to the United States and would accrue only to the advantage of the European belligerents. Such investments are actually preparing the sinews of war for a possible enemy.

Will American Investments Abroad Bring Oil into the United States in Time of Peace?—The large needs of the United States for oil in the future for economic purposes have been greatly emphasized in the discussion of the question of American investments in foreign lands. It has been assumed that if American companies are permitted to obtain properties in other countries the oil which they produce will be available to the United States just as if it were produced in this country. The assumption is much too sweeping. In times of peace, the import of raw materials depends upon an adequate production abroad, financial ability to purchase, and the absence of restrictions against exportation from the producing country. American capital may, it is true, assist in promoting greater production abroad, but in those areas in which it must be forced by diplomatic action, such as in Mesopotamia, the need is evidently not for more capital, as the rivalry between capitalists is already very great.

When oil is once produced abroad it becomes an article in the international market and will go to those countries which are best able to bid for it regardless of the nationality of the producer. The ability of the United States with its present wealth and income to purchase oil sufficient for its needs can hardly be questioned. A possible advantage in American ownership arises from the fact that an American company producing abroad is ordinarily but a subsidiary of a larger distributing corporation and that it will be inclined to sell to the parent concern, the distributing machinery of which is set up in the United States. This would be a factor making for importation but would be subject to strict limitations as to the price of oil here and abroad. On the other hand, an important reason why large American interests seek foreign petroleum wells is that they may have more convenient supplies for their distributing systems in Europe and Asia. In such case, the oil produced will not come to the United States. The great companies that have so stressed the need for oil in the United States as a justification for a strong oil policy have been for many years vigorously shipping oil out of the country on a large scale. It is possible that such companies in obtaining oil for their foreign markets from their subsidiary producers abroad, which oil might otherwise be shipped from the United States, will to that extent conserve the American supply.

Will Export Restrictions on Oil Be Less Likely if Production Is Controlled by Americans?—The legal power of a foreign country to impose export restrictions remains intact regardless of the nationality of the capital within its borders. The United States would retain its right to object to such restrictions whether American capital were involved in the restricted product or not. It must be admitted, however, that with the growing tendency for the political influence of the United States to follow American capital into backward countries this country would, because of investments, probably be in a better position to prevent unfavorable legislation. A very significant statement in this connection was made in the *Report of the Federal Oil Conservation Board:*[1]

That American companies should vigorously acquire and explore such fields is of first importance, not only as a source of future supply, but supply under control of our citizens. Our experience with the exploitation of our consumers by foreign-controlled sources of rubber, nitrate, potash, and other raw materials should be sufficient warning as to what we may expect if we should become dependent upon foreign nations for our oil supplies.

The board which made this recommendation consisted of four cabinet officials, Secretaries Work (chairman), Davis, Wilbur, and Hoover. Two of them were to be shortly elevated to the

[1] Page 12.

highest places in the Republican party. Their recommendation could only be based on the doctrine that the political influence of the United States will extend to lands in which petroleum supplies are under the control of American oil companies, and that it will there be used to prevent legislative policies which are opposed to the interests of consuming nations. But, if the anticipated oil controls in foreign countries shall be for the purpose of enhancing the price and should they have the support of the producers, as was the case at the time of forming the monopolies in rubber, nitrate, potash, and several other raw materials, the influence of American oil companies producing in those countries may be thrown energetically on the side of the controlling nation. In such a situation their persuasive powers exerted upon the Department of State will offset, to some extent, the pressure of the American consumers.[1] At any event it is doubtful if the power of the United States can be effectively exerted in a sphere as remote as the Near East, where some of the most important of American companies have objectives.

The main reason to which must be ascribed the interest of American capital in foreign oil production is not that of securing oil in the United States but of participating in the generous returns which frequently follow the opening of virgin fields. The high profits of the Royal Dutch-Shell, the princely returns from the operations of the Anglo-Persian, and the large number of fabulous American oil fortunes, all attest the possibilities of dividends in the production and distribution of petroleum. The attraction of rich foreign fields for American oil companies has been great and this has been reflected in diplomatic activity. Naturally, however, considering the dubious state of public opinion regarding oil "trusts" in the United States, the probabilities of high returns to such interests have not been emphasized in the public discussion of the question. To state openly that the principal effect of the government's effort is to make possible large dividends for the stockholders of oil companies would hardly arouse public enthusiasm.

---

[1] See p. 395 for the situation regarding the sugar control.

CHAPTER V

CAPITAL EMBARGOES

GENERAL CHARACTER

The influence of diplomacy in international finance is not always encouraging and stimulating to investments. It takes on a negative aspect when the power of statecraft is used to prevent the flotation of foreign loans. The capital embargo is an effective weapon in the hands of government officials. The nation which would keep abreast of the rapidly moving tide of material development must have capital, and hence free access to the money markets of the world is highly desirable to those countries that are unable to supply their needs from internal sources. Industrial development, currency stabilization, military and naval requirements, and the refunding of maturing loans are among the chief reasons which impel finance ministers and entrepreneurs to approach the bankers of creditor nations for financial assistance. Inability to obtain the desired funds may sometimes result in a serious crisis or a substantial retardation of national development. The officials of creditor nations are therefore able to use the much desired privilege of admission to their money markets as a valuable *quid pro quo* in the diplomatic game.

There are two methods by which the ban on foreign loans may be accomplished: (1) by formal legal action such as is authorized by the laws of France, Belgium, and Italy, and (2) by extralegal influence, which is the means used in Great Britain, Japan, and the United States.

In France, the Minister of Finance must give his permission before a foreign loan is admitted to quotation on the Paris Bourse. The finance minister always consults with the foreign office[1] and thus the Minister for Foreign Affairs has the opportunity to inject into the matter considerations of French foreign policy, which may be entirely divorced from the question of the

[1] VIALLATE, ACHILLE, "Economic Imperialism," p. 58, The Macmillan Company, New York, 1923.

soundness of the loan. Prior to the war, when the savings of the French people were placed in large amounts in foreign public bonds, the French government frequently took the occasion to barter for diplomatic advantages in exchange for the permission to list securities. Threats of withdrawing the listing privilege were made in 1909 when the Danish government contemplated raising the import duty on French wines.[1] The awarding of an artillery contract by the Argentine government to the German Krupps in 1908 brought about a complaint by the Schneider firm in France that an unfair preference had been given to their German rivals. Accordingly, in 1909, the French government forbade the listing on the Paris Bourse of the Argentine internal loan of 1895 and also of the then pending 5 per cent loan which was to be placed in Paris.[2] Likewise in 1909 a Bulgarian loan was refused by the French government for the reason that none of the proceeds was to be spent in orders for materials in France.[3] In 1914 the French government proposed to withdraw the listing privilege from Turkish state bonds unless certain contracts should be placed in France.[4]

The second or extralegal method, which consists in merely advising the bankers against making certain foreign loans, differs from the first in form more than in effect. The recommendation of the government against a loan appears to be as certain to put a stop to the public flotation of the issue as would a legal disqualification. Few bankers would care to purchase the bonds of a foreign country and attempt to sell them to domestic investors in the face of the disapproval of their own government. The investing public, learning of the official opposition, would become apprehensive and the bankers would run a heavy risk of being left with a large block of unsold securities on their hands. In 1912, the London firm of C. Birch Crisp & Co., which was outside of the British banking group in the consortium for loans to China, attempted to handle an issue of £10,000,000 for the Chinese Republic. The British Foreign Office was opposed to the loan.[5] The result was that only

[1] LASSWELL, HAROLD, "Political Policies and the International Investment Market," *Jour. of Political Economy*, Vol. 31, p. 389.

[2] *Ibid.;* also U. S. Federal Trade Commission, "Cooperation in American Export Trade," Vol. I, p. 76, Govt. Printing Office, Washington, 1916.

[3] U. S. Federal Trade Commission, above cited.

[4] *Ibid.*, p. 77.

[5] *For. Rel.*, 1912, p. 152.

40 per cent of the first installment of £5,000,000 offered in London could be disposed of and the second installment was never issued.[1] So far as is known no American banker has shown any inclination to proceed with a loan which has been disapproved by the Department of State.

DEVELOPMENT OF THE AMERICAN POLICY

In the United States, the practice of exercising a veto over undesirable foreign loans and of using the threat of a veto in bargaining for an advantage made its appearance soon after American capital began to seek investment abroad. Up to 1922, there had been a number of instances in which the Department of State had been instrumental in preventing loans, and there were other cases where a loan veto had been threatened. During the Chinese Revolution of 1911, Yuan Shih-kai, premier under the Manchu régime, requested a foreign loan to tide over the desperate financial crisis which confronted his government. The revolutionary faction, on the other hand, urgently asked the Department of State to restrain American financiers from assisting the Manchus.[2]   During this uncertain struggle, Secretary Knox took a neutral position between the two factions and disapproved of any loan to Yuan Shih-kai as inconsistent with the spirit of neutrality.   He also opposed loans which would conflict with the broad plans of the governments which were backing up the consortium.   In response to a request for a statement of the policy of the United States the department informed the British Ambassador:

> In view of the possible effect upon the lives, property, and trade of its nationals in the disaffected districts of any departure from the policy hitherto consistently pursued by common consent among the powers, the American government believes that any loans to China at the present juncture would be inopportune, except upon the conditions already laid down, namely strict neutrality as between Chinese factions and broad participation by the interested foreign powers.
>
> While the American government would be inclined to favor financial assistance to China on the above conditions, it is felt to be a corollary of this policy to discourage loans by its nationals unless assured that such loans are in harmony with the above views.[3]

[1] WILLOUGHBY, "Foreign Rights and Interests in China," Vol. II, pp. 991–992.

[2] *For. Rel.*, 1912, p. 106.

[3] *Ibid.*, p. 107.

Early in 1913, the American group in the six-power consortium was contemplating with the other consortium members a $125,-000,000 reorganization loan to the Chinese government. On Mar. 4, 1913, the Taft administration gave way to that of Woodrow Wilson and the next day Willard Straight, acting for the American bankers, wrote a letter of inquiry to Secretary Bryan to ascertain his wishes as to the reorganization loan.[1] On Mar. 18, President Wilson gave the answer for his administration in a statement to the press declining to request the continuation of the group in the loan because of the conditions to be imposed upon China. The President used the following language:

The conditions of the loan seem to us to touch very nearly the administrative independence of China itself, and this administration does not feel that it ought, even by implication, to be a party to those conditions. The responsibility on its part which would be implied in requesting the bankers to undertake the loan might conceivably go the length in some unhappy contingency of forcible interference in the financial, and even the political, affairs of that great oriental state, just now awakening to a consciousness of its power and of its obligations to its people. The conditions include not only the pledging of particular taxes, some of them antiquated and burdensome, to secure the loan, but also the administration of those taxes by foreign agents. The responsibility on the part of our government implied in the encouragement of a loan thus secured and administered is plain enough and is obnoxious to the principles upon which the government of our people rests.[2]

Immediately following this disapproving statement, the American group announced to the other national groups and to the Chinese government that it had withdrawn from the negotiations for the loan. From this incident, the power of the government in discouraging foreign loans was made clear. The Chinese loan was so dependent upon governmental support that the refusal of the Department of State to approve the loan, implying a disinclination to accept the responsibility of protecting it, was an insurmountable obstacle.

When the World War broke out, American bankers asked the attitude of the Department of State concerning loans to belligerent countries. Secretary Bryan, expressing the first reaction of the government upon the matter, advised against such financial assistance. In a telegram to J. P. Morgan and Company, he

[1] Text in *For. Rel.*, 1913, p. 167.
[2] *Ibid.*, pp. 170–171.

said: "In the judgment of this government, loans by American bankers to any foreign nation which is at war are inconsistent with the true spirit of neutrality."[1] Powerful economic forces gradually developed against this policy and after Mr. Bryan left the Department of State the decision was reversed. The unprecedented surpluses of exports over imports, rising to more than a billion in 1915 and to over two billions in 1916, could be balanced only by lending to the buyers. The grim might of overpowering economic interest made it almost impossible that the moral doctrine of Secretary Bryan should prevail.[2] During 1915 and 1916, something over a billion dollars was loaned to Great Britain and France.

In 1917, during a controversy with the government of Ecuador concerning the payment of claims of the American-owned Guayaquil and Quito Railroad Company, the State Department specifically mentioned its power of withholding approval from loans. In an instruction to the American Minister at Quito the department said:

You may intimate orally to the Minister for Foreign Affairs that in no case will the Department give its approval to any loan by American bankers to Ecuador until interest is paid and daily deposits resumed.[3]

In the controversy with The Netherlands over the admission of American oil interests to participation in the development of the Djambi oil fields in the Dutch East Indies, the State Department in its instructions of Apr. 19, 1921, to the American Minister at The Hague included a declaration that retaliation in kind against Dutch interests might ensue in case of exclusion of American oil companies, and there was a further ambiguous threat of additional action should this not be sufficient. The nature of the additional action was disclosed to some extent a few days later in an instruction that the exclusion of American interests "would create an unfavorable impression and a situation of general discouragement to prospective American participants

---

[1] *For. Rel. Supplement*, 1914, p. 580.

[2] It is not contended that Mr. Bryan's position was in accord with the precedents in international law, but nevertheless, the enormous assistance which American trade and loans gave to the Entente lends much support to his statement as to the inconsistency of such aid with the true spirit of neutrality.

[3] *For. Rel.*, 1917, p. 738.

in other branches of Dutch industry."[1] While very indefinite in meaning, the unlikelihood that the Djambi dispute would deter American capital from entering into legitimate and profitable Dutch enterprises without some official pressure makes it impossible to interpret this passage as other than a veiled threat of a capital embargo to be instigated through department advices.

Formulation of a Definite Policy by the Department of State.— Toward the latter part of the World War and for a few years after the armistice, the United States held an incomparable position in world finance, due to its growing capital surplus and to the embarrassment of other creditor countries by the demands of the war. Great Britain, which prior to 1914 had furnished the largest share of capital for international financing, was forced to cease loaning abroad, and about the only available funds procurable by borrowing nations were in the United States. Aware of its power, due to this temporary monopoly, the Department of State began to consider definite methods and procedures in controlling loans.

On May 25, 1921, President Harding conferred with certain members of his cabinet and a number of leading investment bankers at the White House and it was agreed that the bankers would keep the Department of State informed of foreign loans so that it might have an opportunity to object should it care to do so. Secretary Mellon is authority for the statement that it was the prospect of default upon American war debts which made this policy seem advisable.[2] Either some of the bankers did not quite get the meaning of this agreement or they did not understand why they must forego their lucrative commissions, for on Mar. 3, 1922, the Department of State issued an announcement for the purpose of clearing up the matter. After referring to the preceding conference and to the fact that the desirability of cooperation did not seem to be sufficiently well understood in banking and investment circles, the announcement read as follows:

The flotation of foreign bond issues in the American market is assuming an increasing importance and on account of the bearing of such operations upon the proper conduct of affairs, it is hoped that American concerns that contemplate making foreign loans will inform the Depart-

[1] "Oil Concessions in Foreign Countries," p. 72.

[2] *Annual Report of the Secretary of the Treasury*, 1925, p. 54.

ment of State in due time of the essential facts and subsequent developments of importance. Responsible American bankers will be competent to determine what information they should furnish and when it should be supplied.

American concerns that wish to ascertain the attitude of the department regarding any projected loan should request the Secretary of State, in writing, for an expression of the department's views. The department will then give the matter consideration and, in the light of the information in its possession, endeavor to say whether objection to the loan in question does or does not exist, but it should be carefully noted that the absence of a statement from the department, even though the department may have been fully informed, does not indicate either acquiescence or objection. The department will reply as promptly as possible to such inquiries.

The Department of State cannot, of course, require American bankers to consult it. It will not pass upon the merits of foreign loans as business propositions, nor assume any responsibility whatever in connection with loan transactions. Offers for foreign loans should not, therefore, state or imply that they are contingent upon an expression from the Department of State regarding them, nor should any prospectus or contract refer to the attitude of this government. The department believes that in view of the possible national interests involved it should have the opportunity of saying to the underwriters concerned, should it appear advisable to do so, that there is or is not objection to any particular issue.[1]

Vetoing of Loans to Governments Which Have Failed to Fund Their Indebtedness to the United States.—As has been intimated, the policy of consultation outlined above was formulated for the purpose of controlling loans to the allied governments which had borrowed money from the United States, and it is in this connection that the policy has had its most important applications.

The Rumanian Case.—In the fall of 1922, the Rumanian government was engaged in negotiations to refund its indebtedness through a $175,000,000 loan to be obtained in New York, London, and Paris. At the same time that government had made no attempt to fund its obligations to the United States, which amounted to $37,992,675.42, and which constituted a first lien

---

[1] *State Department Press Release*, Mar. 3, 1922.

A discussion of this policy is contained in the address by Dr. Arthur N. Young on "The Department of State and Foreign Loans," delivered at Williamstown, Mass., Aug. 26, 1924. See also DULLES, JOHN FOSTER, "Our Foreign Loan Policy," *Foreign Affairs*, October, 1926, p. 33.

on Rumanian assets. During the loan negotiations, the Department of State protested against the incurring of further obligations by Rumania until action had been taken to arrive at a satisfactory funding agreement with the United States. The result of this protest was that a commission shortly left Rumania for Washington to negotiate a settlement of the debt, which settlement was eventually signed on Dec. 4, 1925. While from the meager accounts of the affair which reached the public it did not appear that American bankers had been advised against the Rumanian loan, yet the protest to Bucharest undoubtedly derived its effect from the willingness of the Department of State to prevent any flotation in New York. In the face of this attitude, the prospect for the Rumanian government of completing the loan without first appeasing the United States would have been negligible.

France.—It is a strange turn in the wheel of fortune that France, the nation which had used the capital embargo so energetically and for such diverse purposes, should herself be made to suffer from this device at the hands of her former ally. Seldom has a first-rate power been subjected to such financial pressure as has been applied to France in the last few years with regard to the war-debt settlement with the United States. At the close of 1924, France was the largest postwar borrower in the American market. Three times the French government had come to New York for $100,000,000 loans for the stabilization of the franc. Provincial, municipal, railway, and other loans had been floated, the whole totaling almost a half-billion dollars. At the beginning of 1925, there were a number of new French loans, private and municipal, under consideration in New York; but already suspicions that France intended to ignore her war debt to the United States had begun to militate against their success. Late in December, 1924, there had been indications of sentiment in Congress against further loans by American bankers to France unless a debt settlement should be reached within a reasonable time.[1] And then events occurred which effectually killed French credit in the United States.

In January of 1925, Deputy Louis Marin, a former minister in the Poincaré administration, delivered in the Chamber of Deputies an address denying the moral obligation of France to repay the American debt. His speech was dramatic:

[1] *The New York Times*, Dec. 31, 1924.

While war still raged, statesmen in every country appealed in the common cause. Some gave their ships, some munitions, some the lives of their sons, some money, and today only those who gave money come saying to us: "Give back what we loaned."

Yet during the war money was munitions. It was not more valuable than the lives given by 1,450,000 Frenchmen who died on the field and 300,000 who died of their wounds.

Cheers from all parts of the Chamber indicated that the speaker had expressed the inmost thought of the French people. The application of financial pressure in Washington followed immediately. The next day's dispatches from New York brought tidings that plans for the sale of new issues of French industrial and municipal bonds had been hurriedly dropped by American bankers at the instance of Washington.[1] From that time on French financing ceased to progress in the United States, although the bonds of other nations were sold in large quantities.

In an effort to arrange a settlement the French Debt Commission visited the United States and conducted negotiations with the American World War Foreign Debt Commission during September, 1925. No permanent funding plan could be agreed upon, and the French commission carried back to Paris the American proposal for a temporary arrangement for five years, during which time France was to pay the sum of $40,000,000 annually. Hostile sentiment concerning this temporary settlement was manifested by denunciations from the French press. Undoubtedly it was an unpopular arrangement in France and would have stood but little chance of ratification unless further pressure should be brought to bear. From Washington came the intimation for a second time that further French loans were dependent upon ratification of the plan.[2] This announcement had its effect on the French government. M. Caillaux, in a speech at a Socialist Congress at Nice shortly afterward, took occasion to warn his hearers against imprudent words "which might endanger the system of loans to which this country is certain to have to resort again."[3]

The Berenger-Mellon Agreement.—Spurred to renewed efforts, the French government took up the matter of reaching an understanding with the United States, and on Apr. 29, 1926, an

[1] *The New York Times*, Jan. 23, 1925.
[2] *Ibid.*, Oct. 12 and 22, 1925.
[3] *Chicago Tribune*, Oct. 17, 1925.

agreement was signed in Washington between the French Ambassador, M. Berenger, and the American World War Foreign Debt Commission. This accord was subject to severe criticism in France, and a parade of French World War veterans was held in Paris to show disapproval of its allegedly severe terms. It has not been ratified by the French Parliament.

The Fall of the Franc and the Deprivation of Loans Arouse French Feeling.—The matter of the indebtedness became a subject of primary concern following the tragic drop in the value of the franc in the summer of 1926. During this national economic crisis it was evidently expected by French officials that loans could be secured from the United States for purposes of stabilization even before the ratification of the signed agreement, as was the case in the dealings with Italy. The French government was informed, however, that no money could be expected until the final concurrence of their Parliament. The falling franc was at the time wiping out the accumulated savings of hundreds of thousands of French men and women. In the bitterness of feeling over the loss of property, the United States was roundly denounced for its embargo on loans.

Loans to France for the purpose of refunding outstanding issues have been dealt with differently from new issues. By the latter part of 1927, the improved condition of French finances, which made it possible to borrow at lower rates of interest, brought about an attempt to refund a $78,000,000 debt, which was the outstanding portion of the $100,000,000 loan obtained through J. P. Morgan & Co. in 1920 at 8 per cent. The Department of State announced that it would not disapprove of the refunding loan,[1] and the funds were accordingly obtained, for the most part, in New York.[2]

The embargo against France was partially lifted in January, 1928, when the Department of State sent letters to American bankers withdrawing its opposition to the flotation of French industrial securities. The reasons for the change were not made public. Coming as it did shortly after the Franco-American tariff dispute, there is good reason to infer that the raising of the ban on industrial loans was intended to bring about a more

[1] *State Department Press Release*, Oct. 10, 1927.

[2] In refunding, the French government sold $75,000,000 of 5 per cent bonds to the Swedish Match Company, of which a $50,000,000 portion was repurchased by an American company, the International Match Corporation, which obtained its money by a bond issue in New York.

favorable attitude in France with regard to the proposed commercial treaty as well as to create sentiment for the ratification of the debt-funding agreement. A regard for the interests of American investors was probably a contributing cause.[1]

During 1925, the capital embargo was extended to apply as a general policy to all other countries that had not funded their obligations to the United States. Secretary Mellon has explained this action as follows:

> Early in 1925, after much consideration, it was decided that it was contrary to the best interests of the United States to permit foreign governments which refused to adjust or make a reasonable effort to adjust their debts to the United States, to finance any portion of their requirements in this country. States, municipalities, and private enterprises within the country were included in the prohibition. Bankers consulting the State Department were notified that the government objected to such financing. While the United States was loath to exert pressure by this means on any foreign government to settle its indebtedness, and while this country has every desire to see its surplus resources at work in the economic reconstruction and development of countries abroad, national interest demands that our resources be not permitted to flow into countries which do not honor their obligations to the United States and through the United States to its citizens.[2]

Aside from France, the principal debtor nations affected by the embargo were Belgium and Italy. In the case of each of these countries the American policy produced renewed efforts to reach an accord. Debt-funding commissions were speedily sent from both countries to the United States. The Belgian agreement was signed on Aug. 18, 1925, and less than two months later negotiations were commenced for a loan, the larger part of which was to be floated in New York. The agreement with Italy was signed on Nov. 15, 1925, and negotiations for a $100,000,000 loan were immediately begun in New York. The loan was consummated before the funding arrangements were approved by the legislative bodies in either country, the embargo being lifted upon the signing of the agreement. A number of senators in subsequently opposing the funding arrangement made claims that the influence of powerful New York banking houses had been brought to bear upon the administration to hasten the

[1] *The New York Times*, Jan. 15, 1928.
[2] *Annual Report of the Secretary of the Treasury*, 1925, pp. 54–55.

agreement so that the way might be cleared for the rich commissions which they were to reap in the floating of the loan.[1]

Russia.—The Soviet government which repudiated the debts incurred by previous Russian governments has likewise come within the scope of the embargo. In 1926, W. A. Harriman was requested to drop plans which he had under way in Berlin to advance $35,000,000 to finance German exports into Russia. German capital for this purpose was evidently scarce, as the German banks were asking 11 per cent for discounting Moscow's acceptances of drafts based on Soviet orders for German goods. In explanation of its disapproval, the Department of State let it be known that because of the Russian policy concerning debts it would not look with favor upon loans made directly to Russia or to other countries for promoting their trade with Russia.[2]

Another instance of opposition to financial aid to Russia was the extension of the embargo policy, which ordinarily applies only to publicly floated loans, to include an arrangement for the private sale of bonds in this country. In January, 1928, the Department of State, urged on by the New York Life Insurance Company, the First International Securities Corporation, and other holders of repudiated Russian securities, intervened to stop an attempt to sell Russian railway bonds directly to American investors through the mail. The Chase National Bank of New York and banks in Chicago and San Francisco had been selected to act as agents for the payment of interest and retirement charges. The bankers were notified, however, by the Department of State, that there were serious objections to the plan. In a public announcement of its opposition the department stated:

The department objects to financial arrangements involving the flotation of a loan in the United States or the employment of credit for the purpose of making an advance to the Soviet régime. In accordance with this policy the department does not view with favor financial arrangements designed to facilitate in any way the sale of Soviet bonds in the United States. The department is confident that the banks and

[1] The loan took up a $50,000,000 bank credit extended by J. P. Morgan & Co., while the Morgan house received a large commission for its part in forming the American syndicate. See above, p. 24.

[2] *The New York Times*, Apr. 10 and 11, 1926. Another reason advanced was that the department failed to perceive any advantage that would come to the United States through promoting the trade of some other country with Russia.

financial institutions will cooperate with the government in carrying out this policy.[1]

EMBARGOES AGAINST LOANS TO SUPPORT RAW MATERIAL MONOPOLIES

On several occasions in the past, American capital has been used to support foreign raw-material monopolies in their price-raising efforts. The result has been that American money has been used to increase the cost of commodities purchased by the American consumer. When, in 1906, the State of São Paulo in Brazil decided to go into the various markets of the world to purchase coffee and thereby raise the price, it could at first receive no financial assistance in Europe and consequently obtained the needed funds in New York. As a result of its valorization efforts, the price of coffee was for the time being materially raised. Congressman Norris claimed that the artificial advance in price amounted to a charge of about $35,000,000 per year to the American people.[2] A government commission in Yucatan which was backed by New York bankers helped to raise the price of sisal in 1916 from 6⅝ to 14 cents per pound, and created a great deal of dissatisfaction among agriculturists in the United States on account of the effect upon the price of binding twine.[3]

As a result of such use of American money, Secretary Hoover, in his campaign against foreign raw material monopolies, recommended that American capital should not be used to finance such combinations,[4] and on several occasions the embargo policy has been followed with regard to them.

Embargo on Coffee Loans.—In 1925, plans for a bond issue to be sold in New York for the state of São Paulo for coffee valorization were under way when the bankers were informed that the Department of State would not approve of the loan. The following statement of Secretary Hoover was issued:

The Administration does not believe the New York banking houses will wish to provide loans which might be diverted to support the coffee speculation which has been in progress for the last year at the hands of the coffee combination in São Paulo, Brazil. Such support would simply bolster up the extravagant prices to the American consumers.[5]

[1] *State Department Press Release*, Feb. 1, 1928.
[2] See below, p. 400.
[2] See below, p. 392.
[4] *Report of Secretary of Commerce*, 1926, p. 38.
[5] *The New York Times*, Nov. 13, 1925.

In December, 1925, a similar ban was placed upon a proposed loan to the German Potash Syndicate. An issue of $50,000,000 was planned, of which $25,000,000 was to be disposed of in New York through an American syndicate. The American end of the loan was abandoned because of the disapproval of the government.

THE EMBARGO ON GERMAN LOANS THAT ARE APT TO INTERFERE WITH REPARATION PAYMENTS

The possibility that extensive loans to the states and communes of Germany might create a condition in that country which would make the payment of reparations under the Dawes Plan impossible led the Department of State in 1927 to adopt an attitude of careful scrutiny of such loans. This policy was in accordance with the tenor of the note of S. Parker Gilbert, Agent General for Reparation Payments, of Oct. 20, 1927, in which he criticized the extravagant tendencies in Germany's fiscal policies. Mr. Gilbert pointed out that German states and communes had borrowed heavily abroad, and that such large-scale indebtedness would have the tendency of impairing public credit and of giving an artificial stimulus to German economic life. A condition of high costs of production, high prices, and increased imports, resulting from large public expenditures, would, according to the Agent General, interfere with the payments of the sums called for in the Dawes Plan, in that it would make more difficult the raising of funds in Germany and would increase the foreign exchange obstacles to payments.[1] Shortly before it had been announced from Washington that the Department of State was considering an embargo upon American loans to German states and communes where they were of such character as to hamper payments under the Dawes Plan.[2]

CONCLUDING OBSERVATIONS ON THE AMERICAN LOAN EMBARGO POLICY

Legality.—The unconstitutionality of the embargo policy has been alleged on several occasions. Typical of such allegations were the remarks of Senator Glass, a former Secretary of the Treasury, who recently contended:

[1] The text of the note was in *The New York Times*, Nov. 6, 1927.

[2] *Ibid.*, Sept. 27, 1927. See also Nov. 8, 1927.

. . . The State Department has no more right to establish a practice or adopt a policy of approving or disapproving the foreign loans of private individuals, concerns, or corporations in the United States than it has to embargo the export commodity trade of this country.[1]

While there is no positive constitutional authority for the specific practice, it appears that the right to announce in advance the attitude of the department upon loans concerning which its assistance may later be sought is a natural derivative from the right to protect American investments abroad. Granting the power of protection, it must be admitted that the selection of the types of investments which are to be protected is a matter of discretion for the Department of State. It cannot be maintained that the department must protect investments which it considers contrary to the national interest. Conceding that there are certain types of investments which need not be supported, it becomes a matter of clear right for the department to announce such disapproval in advance to the investing public for the same reason that it may make a public annoucement of any of its policies. The embargo is then a part of the larger unwritten constitution, deriving its validity from the nature of the powers which every government must entrust to its foreign office.

Effectiveness.—The effectiveness of the capital embargo depends upon the urgency of the need on the part of the prospective borrower and the completeness of the capital monopoly on the part of the prospective lender. As the need of France for financial assistance in 1925 may be said to have been urgent, so the embargo placed upon loans had a real effect upon the fiscal and industrial condition of that country. The fall of the franc in the latter part of the year could no doubt have been arrested to some extent by a loan for currency purposes. Accordingly, the disaster to the savings of the French people which was dealt by the falling of the franc created some bitterness against the United States. At the same time, renewed endeavors to reach an agreement on the war debt were stimulated.

Experience with the embargo has shown, however, that it is not altogether effective as an obstruction to the financing of an enterprise, inasmuch as it neither prevents the borrower from going elsewhere for capital nor shuts off the flow of capital from the country imposing the embargo to the country under the

[1] *Proceedings of the Academy of Political Science*, January, 1928, p. 47.

ban. When on Nov. 3, 1925, the general proscription of foreign loans in London was lifted, the United States lost its position as the world's sole bond market of importance. Both the São Paulo coffee loan and the German Potash Syndicate loan of that year, which were refused in New York, were floated in Great Britain. The success of these loans in London caused criticism of the State Department's attitude by some American financiers who claimed that the only effect of the embargo was that London bankers received the commissions which otherwise would have gone to New York houses.

Under the present policy of the Department of State, American capital cannot be entirely restrained from entering the country against which the embargo is invoked. Except in the case of Russia, the department's policy has pertained to public flotations only. No attempt has been made to give advice concerning bank credits or sales of securities which are floated abroad. But the extension of credits is an effective method of exporting capital for short periods. Large American exports to Russia have been financed in this way despite the embargo on loans. Furthermore, bonds which are publicly floated in Europe may be purchased by bankers and sold in the United States without the formality of a public flotation. In the case of the São Paula coffee loan, which was sold in London, an American banking house purchased a considerable block of the bonds and resold them in the United States at a figure in advance of the price at which they had been offered in London. Thus, one effect of the embargo was to compel American investors to pay a higher price for the bonds than would have been necessary had they been originally offered in New York. Likewise as financial conditions in France improved during 1927, American capital was attracted to the securities of that country despite the attitude of Washington. City of Paris bonds, issued in Holland, were purchased in large amounts by American bankers, who resold them privately to friends in the United States. In this instance the bankers were able to secure them at the original sales price on the same basis as the Dutch bankers.[1] The general rise of French bonds in the New York markets has reflected the demand for other issues in the United States.

In addition to these forms of capital leakage, an embargo against a particular issue may suffer from the fact that loans for

[1] *The New York Times*, Feb. 8, 1927; May 29, 1927.

other purposes may so ease the financial situation in the country in need of capital as to make possible the diversion of funds to the enterprise condemned by the State Department. Although American loans to Germany for the purpose of assisting in exports to Russia are forbidden, yet the loaning of money to Germany for other purposes has helped to make possible the use of German funds for the extension of credits to Russia. Thus, the United States has indirectly loaned to Germany money with which to conduct her trade with Russia.

Business Aspects of Loans.—In some countries the power of embargo is maintained for the purpose of protecting the public against unsound issues. This practice is similar to the function performed under the Blue Sky laws of various states. In the United States, however, the capital embargo has not thus far been applied to prevent unsound investments. Only matters of national policy have entered into the consideration of department officials. It has been suggested, however, that should the standards of American bankers prove to be not sufficiently high, and should issues be sold to the public which later go into default, the extension of the policy to cover the soundness of the loan would possibly follow.[1]

Duty of Consultation with Department Delays Bankers.—From the standpoint of the bankers, it is urged that the duty to consult with the Department of State on all contemplated foreign bond issues is a real handicap, in that the delay entailed may mean the loss of the loan in cases where negotiations move rapidly. The time which is required for the State Department to look into the matter and to consult the Commerce and Treasury departments, which is always done, may vary from twenty-four hours to several weeks. The State Department has requested that the bankers shall not submit bids contingent upon receiving the approval of the department. If requests for competitive bids are cabled to the bankers of several nations at once the delay necessary on the part of the American bankers for purposes of obtaining the approval may cause them to lose the contract.[2]

Resentment against Capital Embargoes.—The advisability of the embargo has been properly called into question on account

---

[1] Address of Dr. Arthur N. Young, *loc. cit.* See WINKLER, "Defaults and Repudiation of Foreign Loans," p. 236, for examples of misleading prospectuses describing questionable issues.

[2] DULLES, *loc. cit.*, pp. 34–35.

of the ill feeling which is certain to follow its use. A proud nation resents the application of pressure to compel it to revise its policies contrary to its own judgment. The implication of the partial loss of political independence through financial dependence is an undoubted humiliation. The assurance of sovereignty is one of the most highly prized values in world politics, and its importance in the minds of other peoples is apt to be underestimated by a nation rising to the heights of economic power. A large part of the world criticism directed against the so-called financial imperialism of the United States has been caused by the embargo policy, and in all probability the injury to American prestige has exceeded any resultant gains.

CHAPTER VI

PROTECTION OF AMERICAN INVESTMENTS ABROAD: GENERAL PRINCIPLES

THE GROWTH OF FORCES MAKING FOR STRONGER PROTECTION POLICIES

The export of capital in recent years has elevated the policy of protection of investments abroad to a position of supreme importance in American foreign policy. Not only has the mantle of the State Department been spread to shelter interests that are vastly greater than formerly, but with a correspondingly larger and more important part of the community interested in foreign investments, a dynamic force for the strengthening of the doctrines of protection has appeared in American life. Minorities of a most aggressive character have been active in calling upon the government to protect their interests abroad. While it cannot be expected that the Department of State has been or will be persuaded to accept fully the suggestions of these minorities, their vigorous and frequent requests for action have had an unmistakable effect. Financial houses, corporations, chambers of commerce, and associations of investors interested in enterprises abroad must be counted among the dynamic forces responsible for the changing American diplomacy.

The desire of those who hold property abroad for strong policies of protection is well illustrated by the attitude of the American business community in China as contrasted with that of the missionary interests. The success of the efforts of the latter depends upon the good will of the Chinese and, hence, missionaries have generally in recent years desired moderate and equal treatment of China. On the other hand, American business men resident in that country have shown a somewhat different inclination. In June of 1923, following some disorders, the American Chamber of Commerce in Shanghai telegraphed to the Department of State a request for a vigorous and crushing policy which would include the disarmament and disbandment of Chinese troops, the placing of Chinese finances under foreign supervision, the imposition of foreign control over all means of communication, the suspension of the return of the Boxer indemnity, the suspension of benefits to China resulting from the Washington Conference, and cooperation with Great Britain to remedy existing conditions.[1]

During the events of 1926–1927, when the Kuomintang was establishing its control in the Yangtse Valley, the Department of State advised American citizens to leave the interior ports of the Yangtse and to seek protection for the time being in the International Settlement in Shanghai. The advice to abandon properties in the interior created a profound dissatisfaction with the department's policy among American business men in China, many of whom were favorable to a policy of force. The American Chamber of Commerce in Shanghai adopted a declaration in favor of military intervention which read in part as follows:

It is obvious that the protective policy applying to Shanghai alone will not enable China to put her house in order, nor prevent enormous losses resulting from the evacuation of the interior districts.

We are convinced that the future welfare of the Chinese people and the ultimate safety of American and other foreign residents throughout China can be attained only through unified action by the Powers to suppress disorder and restore conditions favorable to the formation of a responsible government.

We believe that immediate concerted action by the Powers to restore a condition of security for foreign lives and property in all treaty ports and to recover all foreign properties which have been destroyed or confiscated will have a far-reaching influence throughout China to the ultimate benefit of the Chinese people. This result should not be difficult to attain with the naval forces now in Chinese waters.[2]

One American steamship man, whose business between I-chang and Chunking upon the Yangtse River had been interfered with by the disorders was disposed to advise the Department of State to institute a policy of reprisals through the bombardment of Chinese towns. In a published statement he said:

The Chinese see in our kindness only weakness. If we would reply to continual firing on American vessels by cleaning up a town or two and taking it over, the air would clear immediately.[3]

---

[1] *London Times*, June 25, 1923.

[2] *The New York Times*, Apr. 4, 1927.

[3] *Ibid.*, May 14, 1927.

Thus is seen a tendency among some business men who suffer from political conditions abroad to turn to their own government for a remedy.

A similar influence for inducing strong action on the part of the United States government has been set up by American investments in the Philippines. The foremost Philippine leaders have been convinced that the growth of our investments in the islands will create strong influences against the achievement of native independence and, accordingly, they have at times opposed long-term concessions to American capitalists. That this fear is not without foundation is indicated by the words of Captain H. L. Heath, President of the American Chamber of Commerce in Manila, and one of the wealthiest property holders in the islands. In a statement published in December, 1926,[1] Captain Heath criticised the administration of General Wood as weak and called for a stronger type of Governor General to be chosen from among American business men. He asserted that the American community in the Philippines was "up in arms" against the too-liberal policy of the United States and described the innocent notion that Congress has constitutional power to alienate the Philippine Islands as "the veriest poppy-cock, the effluvia of fearful, altruistic, and eleemosynary minds."

The attitudes of American investors cannot be said to be universally of this character, many of them undoubtedly being in accord with the accepted principles of international fair dealing. Furthermore, the United States government has by no means been willing in all cases to act upon the requests made. The refusal to adopt the recommendations of the American Chamber of Commerce in Shanghai is a case in point. Yet on the whole it cannot be gainsaid that as investments in weaker countries expand the vocal elements urging stronger policies increase.

On the other hand, investments in European countries are a real force for peace and moderation. The liability of such investments to be confiscated in case of war has given the investors an interest in the maintenance of pacific relations. The action of allied countries in seizing the property of alien enemies and the clause in the Treaty of Versailles[2] which reserved to the allied countries the right to retain and liquidate property belonging to Germans furnish precedents for the taking of enemy property

[1] *The New York Times*, Dec. 5, 1926
[2] Article 297.

which would be exceedingly dangerous to the interests of a creditor nation in case of war with other strong powers. Accordingly, influences for peaceful settlement of differences have been created which should have an important effect upon American policies. These considerations do not apply, however, in the backward countries where the inequality in military strength makes it improbable that the debtor country would be able to confiscate American property in the face of forcible action on the part of the United States.

THE CHANGING CHARACTER OF AMERICAN POLICIES

During the last decade of economic expansion a shifting of emphasis on certain international values has been noticeable. The right of American property holders abroad to receive energetic protection has been proclaimed in business and official circles so often and with such force that the opposition that was formerly raised against such interventions has been largely subdued. At the same time, the sovereign right of other nations to the control of their own affairs, once so exalted in American official rhetoric, appears to have lost much of its reality in the new diplomacy. The extreme statement made by President Coolidge that *"the person and property of a citizen are a part of the general domain of the nation, even when abroad,"*[1] is illustrative, on the one hand, of the sweeping character of the more recent claims to the power of protection and, on the other, of the diminishing importance placed upon the concept of the sovereignty of debtor countries.

The nature of the protective function itself has been changed. Until recent years, the protection policies of the Department of State were concerned mainly in obtaining security for the persons of American citizens. But in the last few years the chief application of protection has been in the support of economic rights. Thus, despite the personal danger to American citizens in Mexico, Mr. Hughes, in the early months of his term as Secretary of State, correctly announced: "The fundamental question which confronts the government of the United States in considering its relations with Mexico is the safeguarding of property rights against confiscation."[2]

The scope of the policy of protecting American interests abroad, as it is at present taking form, is wide and includes the

[1] *The New York Times*, Apr. 26, 1927, my italics.
[2] *State Department Press Release*, May 8, 1926.

claim of right to scrutinize a variety of governmental acts in other countries. Policies of undeveloped nations which affect property, including attempts to safeguard their natural resources against foreign exploitation, efforts to make capital more amenable to the power of the state, taxation measures, the regulation of currency which diminishes the value of outstanding accounts, the application of juristic systems which differ from the common law in both the substantive and adjective aspect, have now a concern for American holders of shares in foreign enterprises. The whole conflict of capital and labor in the backward countries, including the regulations of the state to improve the condition of the workmen and the efforts of labor organizations in industries in which American capital is invested, may conceivably be included in the future field of American interest.[1] In the age-old struggle between the defenders of property and those who, either wisely or foolishly, seek to protect and foster human and political values by means of legislation, the influence of the United States in backward countries is certain to be thrown more and more upon the side of property. On the other hand, the assistance of the United States will likewise be extended to promote the welfare of the individual in such countries through economic development and insistence upon stability in government. Doctrinaire writers upon the question, who write wholeheartedly either in praise or condemnation of protection policies, have confused the subject by attempting to explain into it an artificial simplicity which does not exist in the facts. The results of activities in support of investments are certain to be mixed with good and evil and they will be overwhelmingly important in the future of the United States as well as in that of the smaller nations within the American sphere.

THE CONTENTION THAT A GOVERNMENT MAY PROTEST AGAINST FOREIGN REGULATIONS WHICH ADVERSELY AFFECT THE INVESTMENTS OF ITS CITIZENS

There is little in the settled principles of international law which will throw light upon the question of the right of one government to protest against the internal economic policy of

---

[1] For the complaint of the United States against the labor laws of the State of Sonora see *For. Rel.*, 1917, p. 1056. For protests against strikes involving American oil companies in Mexico see *ibid.*, pp. 1028–1030. The difficulties of foreign business men in China are, to some extent at least, due to conflict with native labor organizations.

another. Debtor nations, struggling to maintain as much as possible of their independence of action, frequently deny the right of diplomatic intervention. Strong creditor nations, on the other hand, insist staunchly that they have an interest in the regulative acts of the debtor country and its treatment of private companies so far as such acts affect the investments of their citizens.

The United States has frequently maintained the right of diplomatic intervention in cases of this kind. When the Department of State protested against the Carranza decree of May 1, 1916, concerning mining taxes the Mexican Secretary of Foreign Relations was directed by General Carranza to reply:

. . . that the subject matter of the above-mentioned representations lies exclusively within the province of the Mexican authorities and that, under the principles of international law there is no ground whatever for its being discussed through the diplomatic channel.[1]

Secretary Lansing in reply instructed the American special agent to inform the Mexican authorities that the government of the United States emphatically dissented from such a doctrine and held that it was amply justified in intervening diplomatically because of the confiscatory character of such taxes and the resulting detriment to American citizens.[2] The American view was again expressed in a dispute with Ecaudor over the right of intervention in the case of the Guayaquil and Quito Railway.[3] In that instance Mr. Lansing found "ample warrant" for intervention "in the needed protection for large American interests threatened with destruction through failure of government of Ecuador to respect its contractual obligations, and in the whole record of the dealings by that government with these American interests." The right of intervention in such cases is thus a matter of dispute between creditor and debtor nations. In the last analysis the question of effective intervention depends upon the power of the intervening government and the weakness of its adversary and not upon any definite principles of law.

THE EFFECT OF A WAIVER OF PROTECTION

The diametrically opposite points of view of creditor and debtor nations are likewise clearly shown by the sharp manner

[1] *For. Rel.*, 1917, p. 1039.
[2] *Ibid.*, p. 1040.
[3] *Ibid.*, pp. 734–737.

in which they have disagreed upon the right of an investor to waive the diplomatic support of his government and upon the effect of such a waiver. The borrowing nations of Latin America have felt that investments by foreigners within their territories have had a powerful effect in limiting their sovereignty and in interfering with domestic policies by drawing after them the diplomatic influence of foreign governments. In seeking to prevent this restriction upon their independence of action, many of the Latin-American nations have resorted to express provisions in their constitutions that no concession shall be granted to a foreigner unless he agrees that he will not seek the diplomatic backing of his government in support of his claim.[1] In Art. 27 of the Mexican Constitution of 1917, it is stated that the right of land ownership outside of the prohibited zones may be granted to foreigners provided they agree to be considered as Mexicans in respect to such property and not to invoke the protection of their governments with regard to the same. In case of the breach of the agreement, the penalty provided is the forfeiture of the land. Some governments seek to protect themselves against diplomatic intervention by inserting in concession contracts a clause to the effect that the support of the foreign concessionaire's government will not be sought by the concessionaire. These provisions are called Calvo clauses after the great Argentine jurist and champion of non-intervention. As to the validity of the clause in a contract there has been a wide difference of opinion among international tribunals.[2]

The United States, in common with some other creditor nations, such as Great Britain and Germany (before the war), has been an implacable foe of the so-called Calvo clauses and has contended in a multitude of cases that such stipulations are of no effect.[3] Where the charter of the National Bank of the Republic of Haiti included such a clause and Americans bought stock in the bank the department intervened in their behalf on numerous occasions, ignoring the protests of the Haitian government. In the recent controversies with Mexico over the rights

[1] See BORCHARD, EDWIN M., "The Diplomatic Protection of Citizens Abroad," p. 856, Banks, New York, 1915, for citations to constitutions and laws containing this clause.

[2] *Ibid.*, p. 800*ff*; RALSTON, JACKSON H., "The Law and Procedure of International Arbitration," pp. 58–72, Stanford University Press, Stanford University, California.

[3] BORCHARD, *op. cit.*, p. 797*ff*.

of American investors the department has stated the same principle in the following words:

Under the rules applicable to intercourse between states, an injury done by one state to a citizen of another state through a denial of justice is an injury done to the state whose national is injured. The right of his state to extend what is known as diplomatic protection can not be waived by the individual. If states by their unilateral acts or citizens by their individual acts were permitted to modify or withhold the application of the principles of international law, the body of rules established by the custom of nations as legally binding upon states would manifestly be broken down.

The right of diplomatic protection is not a personal right, but exists in favor of one state against another. It is a privilege which one state under the rules of international law can extend or withhold in behalf of one of its nationals. Whether or not one of its citizens has agreed not to invoke the protection of his government, nevertheless his government has, because the injury has been inflicted by one state against the other, the right to extend what is termed diplomatic protection.[1]

The Mexican Minister for Foreign Affairs put forth the view of the liberty of the individual to bar himself from the protection of his government as follows:

It appears that the foregoing statement is due to some confusion. It is evident that an individual may not compel the state of which he is a citizen to refrain from asserting a right that belongs to it, and in this sense the American doctrine is entirely correct; but the article under consideration makes no such assertion, since that which is required is that the alien shall consider himself a national with respect to the property which may belong to him in the Mexican corporations which he enters, and shall not invoke in regard thereto the protection of his government.

It is therefore an obligation assumed individually and producing effects only between the contracting party and the Mexican government, in no wise infringing upon any of the rights of the foreign state. But if the individual who assumed the obligation violates it, the infraction must be sanctioned [punished], because a law without sanction is not a law. And if the infraction only affects the individual privately, without

[1] Secretary of State Kellogg to the Mexican Minister for Foreign Affairs, Jan. 28, 1926, "Rights of American Citizens in Certain Oil Lands in Mexico," Sen. Doc. 210, Sixty-ninth Congress, Second Session, pp. 22–23. For a Mexican decree issued in 1916 requiring foreigners to renounce their national protection when acquiring rights to certain real property see "Investigation of Mexican Affairs," Sen. Doc. 285, Sixty-sixth Congress, Second Session, Vol. II, p. 3173, and for Secretary Lansing's answers, p. 3174.

in any way infringing the rights of the state to which he belongs, it is not understood how it can be contrary either to international law or to the thesis sustained by your excellency's government.[1]

The United States has also lent its influence against the making of contracts of this character. On one occasion the Department of State advised the Republic of Panama to eliminate a clause in a contract with Americans which renounced future claims through diplomatic channels. The particular significance of this rejection lay in the fact that the contract as drawn set forth the principle of arbitration as a substitute for diplomatic intervention. The tribunal set up provided that two of the three arbiters should be appointed by the Panaman government, one by the President and the other by the Supreme Court of Justice. The third was to be appointed by the contractors. While the composition of the proposed tribunal was open to objection, yet Secretary Knox directed his efforts, not to reforming the tribunal, but to casting out the Calvo clause.[2]

The doctrine of protection as applied by the United States with increasing vigor has taken the following forms:

1. The attempt to apply a "due process of law" doctrine in certain Latin American countries:
    (a) to substantive law,
    (b) to procedure.
2. The attempt to prevent revolutions:
    (a) through diplomatic and legal action,
    (b) by the use of armed forces.

The following chapters will have but little to do with the international law of protection. Within the sphere where principles are well worked out and agreed upon by members of the community of nations, protection must be extended in the future as it has in the past. The practice within this sphere has been fairly well defined and admirably described.[3] Outside of the scope of the accepted law there is, however, a large field where the practice is unsettled and where no common principles are agreed to. In this field, the political implications are vast and it is with this aspect of American policy that the following chapters will deal.

[1] "Rights of American Citizens in Certain Oil Lands in Mexico," p. 29. For the American rebuttal see p. 37; also Dept. of State, "American Property Rights in Mexico," pp. 14, 15, Govt. Printing Office, Washington, 1926.

[2] *For. Rel.*, 1912, p. 1203.

[3] BORCHARD, *op. cit.*

CHAPTER VII

THE DUE PROCESS DOCTRINE

Within recent years the protests of the Department of State against laws which have an allegedly confiscatory effect upon American holdings have given promise of the development of a doctrine of great importance in the relations between the United States and the countries of Latin America. The statement that American property should not be confiscated is so simple in itself and so apparently just that it would present little opportunity for comment were it not for the fact that the doctrine is capable of much interpretation and expansion under precedents which are amply furnished in American jurisprudence. The clearest parallel to the anti-confiscation doctrine is to be found in the clauses of the Fifth and Fourteenth Amendments to the Constitution of the United States which, respectively, prohibit the federal and state governments from depriving persons of life, liberty, or property without due process of law. The significance of the "due process" clauses lies in their enormous expansibility which has enabled the courts to apply them to legislation which affects property adversely and, in the eyes of the court, unreasonably, even if such applications were infinitely remote from the conception in the minds of those who placed the clauses in the Constitution. The Department of State, in determining the question of what is confiscation of American property, will find many analogies in American judicial decisions and will, accordingly, discover in such decisions a bountiful array of precedents for interpretative expansion. The doctrine is now in the earliest stages of what may ultimately become a grand Fourteenth Amendment for Latin America.[1]

[1] For articles discussing the difficulty of imposing the above-described doctrine upon other nations see BORCHARD, E. M. "How Far Must We Protect Our Citizens Abroad?" *New Republic*, Apr. 13, 1927, p. 214; LIPPMANN, WALTER "Vested Rights and Nationalism in Latin America," *Foreign Affairs*, April, 1927, p. 353; WARREN, CHARLES "What is Confiscation?" *Atlantic Monthly*, August, 1927, p. 246; BULLINGTON, JOHN P., "Problems of International Law in the Mexican Constitution of 1917," *Am. Jour. International Law*, October, 1927, p. 685.

In his speech of Apr. 25, 1927, before the United Press Association at New York City, dealing with the protection policies of the United States, President Coolidge unmistakably presaged the development of such a doctrine as that above outlined in the following passage:

We have set up our institutions, established our ideals, and adopted our social standards. We believe that they are consistent with right and truth and justice. We live under a system that guarantees the sanctity of life and liberty through public order and protects the rights of private property under the principle of due process of law. We have thrown every possible safeguard around the individual in order to protect him from any invasion of his rights even by the government itself. It is peculiarly an American doctrine, now usually accepted in principle if not adopted in practice by all civilized countries, that these are inalienable rights, that they ought to belong to all persons everywhere, and that it is the chief function of government to provide instrumentalities by which these rights can be secured and protected. We have adopted these ideals because we believe that they are of universal application and square with the eternal principles of right. But we may as well realize that they will not continue to prevail unless we are prepared constantly to put forth great efforts and make large sacrifices for their support.

While we have not been willing to assume any general attitude of crusading toward other nations, and, realizing that institutions cannot be bestowed but must be adopted, have left them for the most part secure in their right to work out their own destiny, yet we have always been willing to encourage and assist, in so far as we could in harmony with international law and custom, other people in securing for themselves the benefit of these principles and ideals.

. . . .

It would seem to be perfectly obvious that if it is wrong to murder and pillage within the confines of the United States, it is equally wrong outside our borders. The fundamental laws of justice are universal in their application. These rights go with the citizen. Wherever he goes, these duties of our government must follow him.[1]

THE SUBSOIL AND LAND QUESTION

It is particularly with regard to Mexico that the anti-confiscation doctrine has thus far been applied. The principal motivating force in the Mexican Revolution has been the desire to wrest the natural resources of the country, especially agri-

[1] *The New York Times*, Apr. 26, 1927.

cultural land, from the hands of the few and to distribute it more evenly or to control it for the good of the many. The real commencement of economic reforms began under the Constitutionalists whose aims included the dissolution of large landholdings, the destruction of monopolies in natural resources, and labor legislation.[1] The complete program was written into the Mexican Constitution of 1917. Such a policy could not but affect property holdings in general, and those of American capitalists along with the others. There is no doubt that the reforms were partly actuated by the fear that Mexico would come under the control of foreign capitalists, especially in the mining and petroleum industries. The program in that respect may be said to have been directed against foreigners, particularly Americans. The events in Mexico may be said to foreshadow what may be expected in other countries whose desire for the development of their natural resources is not unmixed with apprehension as to the foreign domination that may thereby be established.

Decrees and Laws Concerning Mines in Mexico.—During the unsettled revolutionary period in Mexico after 1910 it became increasingly difficult for American mine owners to keep their mines in operation. At times the Department of State advised Americans to leave Mexico. Lawlessness was so rampant in certain parts of the country as to make it impossible to continue work. The cessation of such an important industry as mining occasioned distress in the communities dependent upon it and deprived the government of revenue. The Mexican revolutionary leaders were desirous of preventing the holding of large tracts in idleness for purpose of speculation, and, in line with their general intention to break up large estates, they wished to divide the mining areas into as many small properties as possible. A decree issued at Monterey, Mar. 19, 1915, by Francisco Villa, who at that time maintained control over a large area, stipulated that whenever the operation of a mine should be abandoned for a period of sixty days, except in cases of accident or *force majeur*, the Secretary of Fomento should have the right to declare the forfeiture of the property involved. In order to facilitate the breaking up of the large holdings of mineral lands the decree further stipulated that exploitation work must

[1] See the Declaration and Decree of Venustiano Carranza issued at Vera Cruz, Dec. 12, 1914, *For. Rel.*, 1914, p. 632.

be conducted on each five contiguous *pertenencias*.[1] Mining men in the areas controlled by Villa sent strenuous objections to the Department of State which in turn protested to Villa. The department contended that the decree was confiscatory of American property and pointed out the impossibility of continuous operation of the mines because of revolutionary conditions. The department further asserted that it was practically impossible on large mining properties to operate every five *pertenencias* at the same time and also argued the injustice of the provision which left the matter of the amount of work to be performed to the discretion of officials without the right of appeal to any court. After a number of protests through the American special agent and a visit by General Scott, American Chief of Staff, who seemed to exercise great influence with the Mexican leaders, Villa agreed that the decree would not be enforced.[2]

A somewhat similar decree issued by the Carranza government from Mexico City on Sept. 14, 1916, similarly declared that a suspension of operations for more than two months in succession or of three months interruptedly in any one year would subject the mining property to forfeiture. Permits to suspend operations for not more than three months in any year could be obtained from the Secretary of Fomento upon the showing of just cause.[3] The purposes of the decree were amply set forth in the preamble which stated that the mining laws of the previous régimes, making no requirements as to the operation of the mines, favored big speculations and the concentration of all important concerns in the hands of foreigners. It was stated that the idleness of the mines left the majority of the mining populations without the means of subsistence and deprived the treasury of the revenues which were ordinarily produced by the industry. The decree also alleged that the foreign nationality of the owners was a real obstacle to the work of establishing sound government on account of the practice of invoking the intervention of other countries in Mexican affairs.

The American government emphatically requested the annulment of the decree on the grounds that it was confiscatory of the

[1] A *pertenencia* is a unit equal to one hectare or a little less than two and one-half acres.

[2] Text of the decree and correspondence relative to it are found in *For. Rel.*, 1915, pp. 893–940.

[3] Text of the decree in *For. Rel.*, 1916, p. 731.

property of American mine owners who found it necessary to close their mines. They were unable to operate because of the drastic tax and wage decrees, uncertain railway service, excessive freight charges, the confiscation of supplies, the high cost of materials, the withdrawal from Mexico of American managers and technical staffs, and the lack of adequate protection. Reopening of the mines was declared to be inadvisable because of the fear of a repetition of the tragic Santa Ysabel massacre, the prevalence of typhus in central and northern parts of Mexico, and the lack of smelting facilities.[1]

In response to this objection, the Mexican Department of Fomento issued circulars making provision for the granting of a suspension of the order to those companies who would make a proper showing before the department setting forth their reasons for failure to resume operations.[2]

The Controversy over the Confiscation of Oil Rights in Mexico. The subsoil provisions of Art. 27 of the Mexican Constitution of 1917 and the laws and decrees issued under them have furnished grounds for a number of serious disputes. One of the avowed purposes of the Constitutionalist party before its accession to power was "the revision of laws relative to the operation of mines, oil fields, water rights, forests, and other natural resources of the country, in order to destroy the monopolies created under the past régime and to avoid the creation of others in the future."[3] On Feb. 5, 1917, Carranza proclaimed the new Mexican Constitution.[4] Article 27 contained the principal economic reforms with regard to ownership of land and the subsoil products. The provisions concerning land raised distinct diplomatic questions which will be dealt with later, leaving those evoked by the clauses concerning subsoil products to be treated under the present heading.

Article 27 provided that "In the Nation is vested direct ownership of all minerals or substances which in veins, layers,

[1] *Ibid.*, p. 734.

[2] *For. Rel.*, 1917, pp. 1044, 1048.

[3] From the Declaration and Decree Issued by General Carranza at Vera Cruz on Dec. 12, 1914, *For. Rel.*, 1914, p. 632.

[4] The text of the Constitution is found in *For. Rel.*, 1917, p. 950. A similar translation arranged in parallel columns with that of the Constitution of 1857 is in the *Supplement to The Annals of the American Academy of Political and Social Science*, May, 1917. Reprints are issued from the Government Printing Office, Washington, 1926.

masses or beds constitute deposits whose nature is different from the components of the land." In this category are included minerals and petroleum. The article goes on to provide that while the ownership is vested in the nation, concessions may be granted on condition that the resources be regularly developed and that certain legal provisions be observed. Concessions may be granted to foreigners provided they agree in advance to be considered as Mexicans in regard to the concession and not to invoke the protection of their government in connection with the same.[1]

The importance of Art. 27 to Americans holding mining and petroleum properties in Mexico has hinged upon the question whether it is retroactive in character and therefore applicable to properties acquired before May 1, 1917, the date on which the constitution took effect. Under laws which had come into existence during the Diaz administrations the purchaser of the land obtained title not only to the surface but also to the subsoil. Prior to May 1, 1917, Americans had bought many thousands of acres of land relying on the Mexican law as it then stood to give them the title to the mineral and petroleum deposits under the surface. A retroactive interpretation of Art. 27 would wipe out these titles representing several hundred millions of dollars.

For several years after the promulgation of the constitution, the attitude of the Mexican officials concerning the retroactivity of the article was not made entirely clear to the Department of State.[2] The United States, however, insisted from the beginning that the clause should not be given a retroactive effect as regards the property of American citizens. When Obregon became President of Mexico on Dec. 1, 1920, the American government sought to make a non-retroactive interpretation of the article a condition precedent to his recognition and negotiations to that effect continued for more than two years.[3] A treaty containing the desired interpretation was suggested by the United States

[1] For a discussion of the American attitude toward such clauses see above, p. 106.

[2] For the dispute over the tax decree of Feb. 19, 1918, which was involved in this question see below, p. 127.

[3] For an account of these negotiations as well as for an excellent summary of the whole question see HACKETT, CHARLES WILSON, "The Mexican Revolution and the United States," 1910–1926 (World Peace Foundation *Pamphlets*, Vol. IX, No. 5).

but rejected by Mexico. After numerous proposals and counter proposals a United States-Mexican Commission met in Mexico City in May, 1923, and reached an agreement upon the question that was not entirely definite. The Mexican commissioners in outlining their position divided the holders of land titles or petroleum rights into two classes, those who had performed some positive acts looking toward making use of or obtaining the oil under the surface and those who had not performed such acts. To those of the first class, Art. 27 should not have a retroactive application. Those of the second class were to be retroactively affected but they were to be granted preferential rights to the oil in the subsoil and the Mexican government would grant them permission to exploit the oil to the exclusion of any third party who had no title to the land or subsoil. This was not intended, however, to constitute an obligation for an unlimited time. The American commissioners reserved diplomatically all the rights of American citizens in the subsoil.[1] This mutual statement was part of the basis of the recognition of Obregon by the United States on Aug. 31, 1923.[2]

The matter rested quietly until the passage by the Mexican Congress of the Petroleum Law of Dec. 26, 1925.[3] The law provided that oil rights might be exchanged for a concession of not more than fifty years, providing positive acts looking toward oil exploitation had been performed prior to May 1, 1917. "Positive acts" meant, in the case of the owner of the land, that he should have begun actual exploitation work before the date mentioned. In the case of a lease or other contract right in the land, the contract must have been for the express purpose of oil exploitation. The confirmation of these rights was to be applied for within one year or they would be forfeited.

To this law the Department of State made continued objection on the grounds that it violated international law and equity by confiscating American property and that it was a breach of the agreement made between the American and Mexican commissioners in the meetings in Mexico City during the summer

[1] Department of State, *Proceedings of the United States-Mexican Commission Convened in Mexico City,* May 14, 1923, pp. 47–49, Govt. Printing Office, Washington, 1925.

[2] This was however disclaimed in a subsequent stage of the controversy by the Mexican Minister for Foreign Affairs, "American Property Right in Mexico," pp. 13–14.

[3] For the text of the law see HACKETT, *op. cit.,* p. 425.

of 1923. More specifically, the American objections to the law were of the following kinds:

1. It was alleged that the law failed to give recognition to the rights of surface owners who had performed no positive acts looking toward petroleum exploitation. The controversy over this point brings out an interesting contrast between Anglo-Saxon and Spanish concepts of property. The United States has based its contentions upon the Mexican laws of 1884, 1892, and 1909 which declared the subsoil deposits to be the exclusive property of the owner of the soil and that the same might be developed and enjoyed by him without the formality of entry or special adjudication. As the property to the subsoil was vested in the surface owner by these laws there was, according to the American contention, no need of positive acts to perfect the title and any attempt to wrest the subsoil from such owner was sheer confiscation. The Mexican officials, however, contended that according to the traditional rule of Spanish law the subsoil belonged to the state. The laws above mentioned which reversed the rule were donations to the surface owner. These donations could be revoked unless meanwhile the surface owner had taken some action to possess himself of the petroleum. Numerous civil law authorities were cited to the effect that a right is not acquired until it is exercised.

Secretary Kellogg recalled that the Mexican commissioners at the Mexico City conference in 1923 had agreed to give preferential rights to the surface owners who had not performed positive acts. The Mexican Minister for Foreign Affairs answered that it was specifically stated at the conference that the obligation to give such preferential rights was not to exist for an unlimited time.[1]

2. The United States government further contended that, conceding the necessity of a positive act to complete the title to the subsoil, the new law and the regulations thereunder were such as to narrow the evidence as to positive acts so that many owners who had really performed such acts, according to the interpretations given by the Mexican commissioners in 1923, would still be barred under the new law. One of the recognized

---

[1] For the opposing views as to the above points see *Proceedings of the United States-Mexican Commission*, pp. 16–23; "Rights of American Citizens in Certain Oil Lands in Mexico," pp. 14, 16, 32; "American Property Rights in Mexico," pp. 2, 4, 17, 18.

positive acts was the making of a contract of purchase or lease for the purpose of exploiting the petroleum. The regulations under the new law required that the evidence of such purpose must be found in the terms of the contract itself. Secretary Kellogg contended that there had been no such restriction of evidence indicated in the decisions of the Mexican Supreme Court of Justice or in the statements of the Mexican commissioners. He argued that the formal listing of petroleum properties prior to May 1, 1917, as required by law, should be considered as sufficient evidence of the object for which the property had been acquired. The Mexican Minister for Foreign Affairs replied that the laws of Vera Cruz, the state where most of the petroleum lands were located, required that all contracts implying a division of property, where the value exceeds 200 pesos, must be of record in a public instrument and that therefore all the contracts would doubtless be available as evidence. If any contract had not been recorded or had not expressed the purpose on its face, and the owner of the petroleum rights had nevertheless listed the property as required by law, the matter could be passed upon by the Department of Industry on terms of equity or could be referred to the courts.[1]

3. Probably the central problem of the oil dispute arose over the requirement that owners who had performed positive acts must exchange their titles for fifty-year concessions on pain of forfeiture. The United States contended that this was confiscation. The Mexican commissioners had agreed in 1923 that their government would be bound by the decisions of the Mexican Supreme Court of Justice which had declared that Art. 27 of the constitution of 1917 was not retroactive as to those persons who had performed positive acts and that such persons would be given drilling permits upon the land. Secretary Kellogg pointed out that the fifty-year period was to run from the date of the positive act, and that if such act had been performed in 1885 there would be left (in 1926) only a nine-year period for the use of the petroleum property. Secretary Kellogg said:

The operation would be nothing but a forced exchange of a greater for a lesser estate. That a statute so construed and enforced is retroactive

[1] *Proceedings of the United States-Mexican Commission*, p. 47; "Rights of American Citizens in Certain Oil Lands in Mexico," pp. 14, 17; "American Property Rights in Mexico," pp. 6, 7, 19, 20.

and confiscatory, because it converts exclusive ownership under positive Mexican law into a mere authorization to exercise rights for a limited period of time, is in the opinion of my government not open to any doubt whatever.

The Mexican Minister for Foreign Affairs answered that the concession conferred upon the owner the right to engage in the same activities which he could engage in under the original title, that the time set was ample to permit him to exhaust a petroleum deposit, and that the period of the concession might be extended. This right of extension, he contended, removed any justifiable objection to the limitation of the term.[1]

At midnight on Dec. 31, 1926 the law became effective and the companies which had not yet applied for a confirmation of their titles were declared to have forfeited them by the terms of the law. Some of the more important American companies representing a large proportion of Mexican production failed to make application.[2]

The matter had come to a seeming *impasse* when on Nov. 17, 1927, the Mexican Supreme Court in the case of the Mexican Petroleum Company of California rendered a decision which revived hopes of an amicable settlement. Certain of the drilling permits of the company in question had been cancelled by the Department of Industry, Commerce, and Labor on account of the failure of the corporation to apply for the confirmation of title. The company then appealed to the courts for an *amparo* restraining the department from the act of cancellation. In an unamious opinion, the Mexican Supreme Court granted the restraining order, and, in so doing, declared unconstitutional Sec. 14 of the petroleum law. The section thus voided was that which provided for substituting a fifty-year concession for titles held by those who had performed positive acts.[3]

---

[1] For this dispute see *Proceedings of the United States-Mexican Commission*, pp. 47–49; "Rights of American Citizens in Certain Oil Lands in Mexico," pp. 13, 27, 34, 39, 44; "American Property Rights in Mexico," pp. 4, 21, 22.

[2] For the conflicting statements of Secretary Kellogg and Minister Morones as to the number of companies failing to make application see *Current History*, April, 1927, p. 136. "Oil Concessions in Mexico," Sen. Doc. 210, Sixty-ninth Congress, Second Session, gives the list furnished by Secretary Kellogg.

[3] A translation of the decision is given in the *Am. Jour. International Law* Vol. 22, p. 421.

Closely following the decision, President Calles submitted to the Mexican Congress an amendment to the oil laws which was promptly enacted. The bill was signed by President Calles on Jan. 3, 1928. The new law provided for the confirmation by concession without limitation as to time, of (1) rights derived from lands on which petroleum exploitation had commenced prior to May 1, 1917; (2) rights derived from contracts closed before May 1, 1917 with surface owners for the purpose of oil exploitation; and (3) rights of those operating pipe lines and refineries under concessions or authorizations issued by the Department of Industry, Commerce, and Labor. The effect of the law was to remove from discussion the most serious cause of trouble between the two countries, that is the limitation of time as to the petroleum rights upon which positive acts had been performed.[1]

The Subsoil Question in Colombia.—In 1919, the United States was engaged with Colombia in the negotiation of a treaty to compose the outstanding differences between the two countries arising from the Panama Revolution of 1903. On June 20, 1919, the President of Colombia issued a decree concerning subsoil deposits which, among other things, nationalized petroleum deposits, prevented the surface owner from executing leases for oil, and declared that permits for petroleum exploration must be obtained from the government.[2] American holders of petroleum rights in Colombia were filled with apprehension as to the possible retroactive effect of this decree. In response to their demands Senator Lodge, Chairman of the Senate Committee on Foreign Relations, asked that the treaty be returned to his committee, and in so asking made the following remarks:

I ask that the treaty with Colombia, which was reported to the Senate as in open executive session a few days ago, be recommitted to the Committee on Foreign Relations. Information has reached the committee from the State Department in regard to a recent decree by Colombia very similar to the Mexican decree which would amount, probably, if enforced, to a confiscation of private property in oil, and the committee feel that the matter should be examined with care before taking up the treaty.

The treaty having been referred to a subcommittee, an amendment was drafted binding each of the two governments to respect

[1] For the text of the amendment see *State Department Press Release*, Jan. 12, 1928; *Current History*, March, 1928, p. 882.

[2] For a summary of the decree see *The New York Times*, Aug. 9, 1919.

titles acquired by citizens of the other to real estate, mines, petroleum, or any other like property situated within its territories. The amendment was rejected by the Colombian government on the ground that the introduction of any clause foreign to the subject matter of the treaty—that is, the secession of Panama —would result in such objections as would make it impossible to secure the approval of the legislature. Colombia was then informed that the treaty would probably not be reported out of the committee until the Colombian government would define in a binding agreement its purpose respecting property rights. A separate treaty, drafted by the United States to make the proposed guarantees, was rejected by Colombia. A favorable decision of the Colombian courts and a law of the Colombian Congress, passed on Jan. 2, 1920, seemed to give the desired guarantees against retroactivity and the objections of the United States were removed.[1]

Mexican Land Regulations.—The land problem has been the central one in the Mexican program of economic reform since the beginning of the Mexican Revolution. Due chiefly to the unwise decrees of Porfirio Diaz the communal lands of the Mexican villages, which once furnished the livelihood for the greater part of the Indian population of Mexico, were prior to 1910, largely broken up and incorporated in the vast estates of the proprietors. The Mexican villagers, mostly Indians, were left to drift eventually into peonage as agricultural workers held for debt. In 1910, 3,103,402 men were counted as peons. These with their families aggregated nine or ten million people or from three-fifths to two-thirds of the population of Mexico.[2] The attempt of the newer Mexican leaders, Carranza, Obregon, and Calles, to reverse this tendency toward monopoly and redistribute the land among the people is one of the most praiseworthy efforts of statesmanship which the western hemisphere has witnessed in the present century.

Madero pledged himself to a redistribution of lands in 1910, but it remained for Carranza to make the first constructive effort to accomplish this purpose by his agrarian decree of January 6, 1915. The decree set aside the past alienations of village

[1] For an account of this matter see "Diplomatic Correspondence with Colombia in Connection with the Treaty of 1914, and Certain Oil Concessions," Sen. Doc. 64, Sixty-eighth Congress, First Session, pp. 48–57.

[2] See HACKETT, *op. cit.*, p. 339*ff*.

communal lands and provided for the expropriation of lands for villages which were in need of them. Article 27 of the Constitution of 1917 carried the program one step farther by writing into the fundamental law the plan of the division of large estates, the development of small land holdings, and the provision of lands for villages by expropriation. The article further forbade the ownership of land by foreigners within a zone extending 100 kilometers from the frontiers or 50 kilometers from the sea coasts.

At the meeting of the United States-Mexican Commission in Mexico City in May, 1923, there was some controversy between the commissioners of the two countries over the method of indemnification of the property holders whose lands were being taken for the villages. The American commissioners claimed that the holders should be indemnified in cash for the just value of their lands at the time of the taking. The Mexican commissioners held that a payment in bonds at the value fixed by the landholders for taxation purposes was sufficient. The matter was arranged, so far as the purpose of the commission was concerned, by a statement of the Mexican commissioners that the acceptance for expropriations for village lands of federal bonds, which were to be 5 per cent, twenty-year bonds, should not be considered as taken by the United States as a precedent for the payment by bonds for expropriations for any other purpose. It was understood by the Mexican commissioners that the United States would bind its citizens to accept bonds in payment for such expropriated lands up to 1,755 hectares. The American commissioners made it plain that they would expect payment in cash for any lands expropriated in excess of 1,755 hectares, and also that they reserved the right to make claims for damages against American citizens for any loss or damage suffered at the hands of the Mexican government.[1]

The next occasion for controversy was the Alien Land Law of Dec. 31, 1925, which was a thoroughgoing attempt by the

[1] *Proceedings of the United States-Mexican Commission*, p. 37*ff.* Another instance of objection to the method of payment for lands was the protest regarding the Agrarian Law of the State of Sonora of 1918 which adopted a policy of the division of lands but made no provision for the payment of compensation other than that persons to whom the land should be transferred by the state should make annual payments to the owners. No penalty was provided for failure to make the payments. The United States protested against this as confiscatory. "Investigation of Mexican Affairs," Vol. II, p. 3174*ff.*

Mexican Congress to oust foreigners from the ownership of real property in Mexico.[1] The provisions of the law may be summarized as follows:

1. No alien shall acquire nor be a shareholder in a Mexican company which shall acquire the title to real estate within the prohibited zones mentioned in Art. 27.

2. In order that an alien may form part of a Mexican company which shall acquire land or concessions for the exploitation of mines, waters, or combustible minerals he must agree not to invoke the protection of his government with reference thereto, under penalty of forfeiture of his property.

3. Aliens shall not be permitted to acquire an interest in Mexican companies owning rural properties when by such acquisition there remains in foreign hands 50 per cent or more of the total interests of the company.

4. Aliens holding 50 per cent or more of the interests of companies owning rural property for agricultural purposes may retain it until their death, if physical persons, or for ten years in the case of moral persons (corporations).

5. Other rights which aliens may not hold, which are the object of the present law, may be preserved by the owners until their death.

6. Aliens receiving prohibited property by inheritance or adjudication must transfer the same within a period of five years to a person having capacity to hold it.

Assurances were given by the Mexican Minister for Foreign Affairs that Arts. 1, 2, and 3 were not to be retroactive in effect. This cleared away most of the grounds for dispute. Article 4 has, however, been the subject of controversy.

That part of Art. 4 which limits foreign corporations holding 50 per cent or more of the interest in any company owning rural property for agricultural purposes to a period of ten years during which they must dispose of their holdings has brought forth much opposition from the United States. The Department of State has complained that

. . . a plainly vested interest through ownership of stock is divested by compelling the holder, without his desire or consent, to dispose of the same within a limited time under conditions which may or may not be favorable to the transfer.[2]

The Mexican government pointed out that a natural person holding such stock could retain the same until his death and that the ten-year provision applied only with regard to artificial persons (corporations). These have immortality, and in order to divest them of their holdings a fixed term must be set. The

[1] For the text of the law see HACKETT, *op. cit.*, p. 414.
[2] "American Property Rights in Mexico," p. 4.

law, according to the Mexican view, is free to amplify, modify, or restrict the capacity of artificial persons. Furthermore, it is claimed, the law does not confiscate the property but gives to the corporations a period of ten years in which to sell their holdings.

The limitation in many instances of the right of alien natural persons to inherit a full title to real estate by the requirement that they must dispose of the same within five years after they have succeeded to it seems to have brought forth but little complaint from the Department of State further than the comment that this "only mitigates and postpones but does not eliminate the confiscatory feature."[1]

The Mexican Foreign Office, on the other hand, has devoted much attention to this phase of the question and has claimed that the right to prevent inheritance of real property by aliens is in strict conformity with municipal and international law, "since in such cases there are no acquired rights, but merely an expectation of acquiring them."[2] It was further pointed out that the statutes of Kansas, Kentucky, Minnesota, Oklahoma, Missouri, and Washington provide that an alien not domiciled in the country is incapacitated from acquiring real property, except if he be an heir of an alien who has previously acquired property. In such case, he must divest himself of the inherited property within a period varying from three to six years under penalty of forfeiture to the state.[3] The principle of cutting off inheritances of real property has seemingly been established by Mexico without serious opposition from the United States.

PROTESTS AGAINST TAXATION MEASURES

As American capital has flowed into backward countries for the purpose of developing their natural resources the tendency of fiscal programs in such countries has been in some instances to shift the burden of taxation onto those industries which are stimulated to greater productivity by the introduction of the new capital. Such a policy is in line with the fiscal developments in the more advanced countries which have come to raise larger percentages of their revenues from industries which are best

[1] "Rights of American Citizens in Certain Oil Lands in Mexico," p. 6.
[2] *Ibid.*, p. 11.
[3] *Ibid.*, p. 31. See also "American Property Rights in Mexico," p. 23.

able to bear a substantial load. The tendency conforms to Adam Smith's first rule of taxation.

In Mexico since the beginning of the Revolution there has been a disposition on the part of the various administrations to obtain a large share of income from the mineral and petroleum industries in which American capital has been heavily invested and from such commercial ventures as are conducted largely by foreigners. Factional chiefs and heads of *de facto* governments have found themselves desperately in need of funds to finance their military operations and to meet other unusual expenses made necessary by the disturbed conditions. They have, accordingly, been forced to resort to a large number of unusual taxes.

The Department of State has taken the position that it would make no objection to taxes properly levied by a government in control of the territory[1] if such taxes were not confiscatory or discriminatory. In instructing an American vice-consul in 1914, the department stated:

> You are instructed that there appear to be no treaty provisions bearing upon the payment by American citizens of contributions or taxes in Mexico. Furthermore, in case of a contribution or tax levied according to the laws of Mexico, general and uniform in its character and operation and not confiscatory, it would appear that American citizens owning property in the sections covered by the contribution or tax would be legally bound to make payment thereof.[2]

In 1915, General Obregon issued a decree which affected Mexico City, exacting a payment of three-fourths of 1 per cent of the capital of corporations and individuals. The Department of State took the position that since the decree was not discriminatory against Americans and the amount of the tax seemed to be insufficient to be confiscatory, it did not consider that it would be justified in protesting if the decree were issued according to law and with reasonable conditions as to compliance.[3] The

[1] In certain sections there have been duplicate demands made upon property owners by different factions which have alternated in control. The United States has stood by the principle of international law that the property holder has a right to pay taxes to any *de facto* government which is in control and that taxes for that period need not be paid to other governments which may later gain control. *For. Rel.*, 1914, pp. 732, 756, 757; *For. Rel.*, 1915, pp. 982, 983, etc.,

[2] *For. Rel.*, 1914, p. 780.

[3] *For. Rel.*, 1915, p. 987.

time allowed for payment in this case was, however, only a few days and penalties of confiscation, appointment of receivers, and imprisonment for thirty days were provided for non-payment. As these conditions seemed unreasonable, a protest was entered and the decree was annulled in so far as it affected Americans and other foreigners.

Discriminatory Taxes and Contributions.—The determination of what is a discriminatory tax is undoubtedly a difficult question in many cases. It seems plain, however, that contributions exacted from a limited number of firms and individuals are discriminatory in character, even if collected under the guise of being forced loans. In 1915, General Pelaez, commanding the Villa forces in Vera Cruz, demanded a forced loan of 50,000 pesos from the Penn Mex Fuel Company and gave the company seventy-two hours in which to comply. The Department of State telegraphed the Special Agent of the United States to request that the demand should be withdrawn and that interference with the company's affairs should cease.[1] In 1916, the local authorities in Vera Cruz sought to raise $500,000 for the purchase of cereals for the poorer classes by means of contributions. A threat was implied in the circular letter announcing the plan by the statement that the authorities would "be disposed to require, by other means, the aid of such persons who give signs of not preoccupying themselves for the public welfare."[2] The American firms and the sums which they were requested to contributed were: Arbuckle Brothers, $10,000; Pan-Mexican Coffee Company, $10,000; Pierce Oil Corporation, $5,000. The American consul was instructed to protest against this method of raising funds for the relief of the poor and to suggest that if such funds were necessary the authorities should resort to proper means of taxation as provided by law. In a large number of other cases contributions and forced loans requested from American citizens in Mexico were protested.[3]

A more difficult question as to discrimination was presented in 1915 by the military governor of Jalisco. This official sought to raise funds by contributions especially from foreigners and was dissuaded after vigorous protest. He then attempted to collect

[1] *For. Rel.*, 1915, pp. 1002–1003.
[2] *For. Rel.*, 1916, p. 778.
[3] See under the heading "Mexico: Forced Loans Imposed upon American Citizens," in *For. Rel.*, 1914, 1915, 1916, 1917.

a tax imposed particularly upon mercantile, industrial, and commercial establishments. Secretary Bryan protested against this tax on the ground that as the establishments of this character were largely owned by foreigners it seemed that the tax should be regarded as discriminatory against them.[1]

Confiscatory Taxation.—The Department of State has frequently entered protest against tax measures which impose a burden greater than it is considered the industry can bear, alleging that this amounts to confiscation of property. The tax decree of Carranza, dated Mar. 1, 1915, raised the taxes on mining property and decreed that payments must be made in gold instead of in the depreciated paper currency. The penalty for non-payment was loss of property. This meant a large absolute increase in the amount of taxes and many American mining men claimed that such levies could not be met from the proceeds of the industry in its then demoralized state. The State Department instructed its representative:

This great increase in tax, if unmodified, will inevitably result in confiscation of many properties, American owners of which are unable to work them because of disturbed conditions which also render it absolutely impossible for them to pay increased tax. Request immediate and material modification of this confiscatory decree.[2]

Protests against Taxes Directed against Large Mining Properties.—The purpose of the Mexican Revolution to split up large land holdings was applied to the breaking up of mining properties by the use of a progressive tax, the rate of which increased with the size of the mining property. In a decree of the Carranza government, dated May 1, 1916,[3] the following taxes were levied upon gold and silver mines:

A.	1 to 10 *pertenencias*,	$ 6 per year per *pertenencia*
B.	11 to 50 *pertenencias*,	$12 per year per *pertenencia*
C.	51 to 100 *pertenencias*,	$18 per year per *pertenencia*
D.	101 *pertenencias* or more,	$24 per year per *pertenencia*

In response to the efforts of the Department of State to obtain a more lenient tax rate the Mexican government responded that the rates were fair and that the application of a high tax to large

[1] *For. Rel.*, 1915, p. 998.

[2] *Ibid.*, 1915, p. 927. For complaint of mine owners see p. 931. For protest against the requirement of gold payment of export duties in 1914, see *For. Rel.*, 1914, pp. 743–744.

[3] See *For. Rel.*, 1916, p. 716.

holdings of mineral lands and of a low tax to small holdings was for the general benefit.[1]

The protest of the American government against the principle of such progressive taxation was set forth in an instruction of Jan. 25, 1917, which stated as follows:

Confiscatory operation of these taxes has been heretofore called to attention of *de facto* government with relation to cases of a number of American mining companies which have already been forced temporarily to surrender thousands of *pertenencias* on which large amounts of taxes had been paid and which were needed for future operations but could not be held because of exorbitant tax mentioned.

During the past two years the mining industry has protested continuously, both directly and through department, to General Carranza and Mr. Cabrera against confiscatory character of tax in question but neither the industry nor this government has ever questioned Mexico's right to impose taxes in accordance with laws properly emanating from Mexican Constitution. However, the government of the United States is protesting, and will continue to protest, most vigorously, against a system of taxation having for its avowed object, as stated by Señor Cabrera and the late Señor Amador, the absolute confiscation of the larger holdings of mining claims in Mexico, in which so many American citizens are interested.[2]

Several decrees drastically taxing the petroleum industry were viewed with suspicion by the Department of State as attempts at confiscation of oil under a retroactive application of the policy of nationalization set forth in Art. 27. A decree issued by Carranza, taking effect on May 1, 1917, the date on which the constitution went into force, placed a 10 per cent tax upon fuel oil and petroleum not intended for domestic consumption.[3] Secretary Lansing instructed the American ambassador to object to this tax as appearing "to contemplate the confiscation of American rights by retroactive legislation, impairing contractual obligations."[4]

[1] *Ibid.*, p. 719.

[2] *For. Rel.* 1917, pp. 1040–1041. For the controversy over a previous decree of March 1, 1915, embodying a progressive tax, see *For. Rel.*, 1915, pp. 900, 927, 936, 948, and 957.

[3] For text of the decree see *For. Rel.*, 1917, p. 1065.

[4] *Ibid.*, p. 1068. It seems from a survey of the diplomatic correspondence that no protest was made, however, as Ambassador Fletcher respectfully requested reconsideration of the instruction.

With regard to the question as to whether an export tax impairs the obligation of contract see controversy between the United States and Germany, *For. Rel.*, 1911, p. 204*ff.*

A subsequent decree of Feb. 19, 1918, issued by President Carranza placed a double tax upon the oil industry by taxing both the land and the production. Thus properties worked by the owners of the land were charged 5 pesos per hectare and also a royalty of 5 per cent of the product. In case landowners desired to work the property for oil they should make a statement setting forth certain data to the Ministry of Industry, Commerce, and Labor within three months. Oil properties not so registered were to be considered vacant and were liable to exploitation according to regulations to be issued.[1]

The diplomatic exchanges over this matter eventually became emphatic. The American ambassador presented the objections of his government on Apr. 2, 1918, in a comprehensive note, which pointed out that the decree seemed

. . . to indicate an intention to separate the ownership of the surface from that of the mineral deposits of the subsurface, and to allow the owners of the surface a mere preference in so far as concerns the right to work the subsoil deposits upon compliance with certain conditions which are specified. . . . The United States cannot acquiesce in any procedure ostensibly or nominally in the form of taxation or the exercise of eminent domain, but really resulting in confiscation of private property and arbitrary deprivation of vested rights.[2]

In an interview between Ambassador Fletcher and President Carranza, the American representative was informed that the decree was merely fiscal legislation and Mexico could not admit of any interference in the matter. The Mexican President continued "if this meant war or intervention he was prepared to confront this alternative, however regrettable."[3]

OTHER PROTESTS

Against Currency Regulations.—In at least one case the issue of paper currency by other governments has been the cause of diplomatic representations by the United States on the

[1] Text of decree in "Investigation of Mexican Affairs," Vol. II, p. 3155.

[2] *Ibid.*, p. 3157.

[3] *Ibid.*, p. 3160. Secretary Hughes protested against the raising of the tax on oil to 25 per cent in 1921 as confiscatory. As to the question of confiscation, the figures of the Mexican Minister of Industry and Commerce indicated that the net returns of American oil companies in Mexico were high despite the tax. See BEALS, CARLTON, "Mexico: An Interpretation," p. 241, B. Huebsch, New York, 1923.

ground that the depreciation of the currency diminishes, and therefore confiscates, outstanding obligations. In October, 1916, the Secretary of State raised objections to a decree of General Carranza which created an issue of currency and made it compulsory to accept the same at certain ratios for the payment of debts. The objection was made that the decree impaired the obligation of contract by applying its terms to all agreements without regard to the express stipulations of the parties. Secretary Lansing said:

As a practical matter, the decree will operate as a measure of confiscation of the vastly greater portion of indebtedness contracted prior to the coming into power of the *de facto* government of Mexico and still unpaid.

You will inform the appropriate authorities that because of the foregoing considerations, the government of the United States cannot be expected to recognize the right of the Mexican government to apply the terms of this decree to American citizens, and that it will so advise those of its citizens who may seek its advice.[1]

Due Process in the Annulling of Nicaraguan Concessions.—

The diplomatic activities of the United States in backward nations in which American capital has been invested have included efforts made from time to time to secure legislation which is in conformity with the interests of American capital and which introduces American ideas as to the processes of government. The means of pressure at the command of the United States to force through the suggested legislation are many and potent, as will be shown in the following chapter.

The granting of economic favors under the Zelaya administration in Nicaragua was looked upon with disfavor by citizens of the United States in that country because of the monopolistic nature of some of the concessions. Particular objection was raised by Americans in Bluefields to the concession of the Bluefields Steamship Company which was given an exclusive right to navigate the Escondido River.[2] Funds were accordingly

[1] *For. Rel.*, 1917, p. 1004. Compare, however, *Julliard* vs. *Greenman*, 110 U. S. 421. A protest against the issuance of treasury notes by the Haitian government in 1915 was based upon the grounds of violation of the terms of the contract with the National Bank of the Republic of Haiti, *For. Rel.*, 1915, p. 512.

[2] For complaints of American interests to the Department of State see *For. Rel.*, 1905, p. 695*ff*.

contributed by Americans and other foreigners for the purpose of overthrowing the Zelaya government.[1] After the revolution had proved to be successful, largely through the support of the United States, the American agent, T. C. Dawson, secured an agreement between the revolutionary chiefs which embodied a promise of the abolition of monopolies, contracts, and concessions granted under the previous governments and of the formation of a mixed claims commission to consider along with other claims, those arising from the abolition of the concessions. The composition and procedure of the commission was to be subject to agreement with the American agent after submission to the consideration of the Department of State.[2]

The original plan for the commission as conceived by the Nicaraguan government was that it should consist of a Nicaraguan and an American who, in case of dispute, should submit the case to the decision of a third member appointed by mutual accord. Secretary Knox secured the modification of this plan so that the commission should be composed of one Nicaraguan appointed by the Nicaraguan government, one American recommended by the United States but appointed by the Nicaraguan government, and an umpire appointed by the Department of State.[3] The American predominance in the commission was justified by the department as intended "to assure the justice and impartiality of the tribunal and to make it one to which foreign governments would be likely to look for the just consideration of the claims of their citizens."[4]

In his capacity of adviser as to the form and procedure of the commission, Secretary Knox opposed a clause in the Nicaraguan plan which provided that the method of cancellation of the contracts and concessions should be by presidential decree. As such executive action did not conform to the American conception of proper procedure the Secretary suggested an amendment which was accepted and which made the executive decrees reviewable by the commission. The Secretary explained his desire for this modification on the grounds that:

[1] MUNRO, DANA, "The Five Republics of Central America," pp. 97, 227, Oxford Univ. Press, New York, 1918.

[2] For the text of the agreement see *For. Rel.*, 1911, pp. 652–653.

[3] *Ibid.*, pp. 627–628.

[4] *Ibid.*, p. 640.

. . . . it is obvious that the plans recommended must adequately protect American interests by providing, among other things a legal procedure, recognized as appropriate here in analogous cases.[1]

SUMMARY OF THE DUE PROCESS DOCTRINE

The American doctrine of due process when forced diplomatically upon other countries has a double effect. In the first place, it brings about greater security for property as against political action. In the second place, the doctrine restricts the independence of action of the peoples to which it is applied by interfering with the function of the local government to regulate the affairs of the country and by displacing the concepts of the native law with the principles of the exotic Americanized common law. The extensive control over persons and property by the state in Latin countries and the large powers of the executive as compared with those of the courts have been the subject of attack. In the United States, the judicial department has been exalted to a position which it occupies nowhere else in the world, and to many Americans it seems only wise and just that it should be raised to a similar position in other governments. This feeling has frequently been reflected in diplomatic representations.

Objections to Procedural Law.—The due process doctrine has been invoked in protest against the methods of determining rights, particularly against executive decision without judicial review. Following are some of the matters to which procedural objections have been raised:

1. Executive determination without court review of:

(a) The forfeiture of mining claims for insufficient work.

(b) The question of public utility and compensation in cases of expropriation.[2]

(c) The amount of lands necessary for the accomplishment of the purposes of commercial corporations.[3]

(d) The expulsion of foreigners by executive decision.[4]

(e) The cancellation of concessions.

2. The restriction of the evidence as to the performance of positive exploitation acts on oil lands to require that the purpose

[1] *Ibid.*, p. 635.

[2] *For. Rel.*, 1917, p. 947; "Investigation of Mexican Affairs," Vol. II, pp. 3121, 3178. (Citations will be given in this summary only to those points which are not mentioned in the body of the chapter.)

[3] *For. Rel.*, 1917, pp. 947–948.

[4] *Ibid.*, p. 948.

of a contract of exploitation must be shown in the terms of the contract itself.

3. The provision of insufficient time for the payment of taxes with heavy penalties for non-payment.

Objections to Substantive Provisions of Laws and Decrees.— Following are some of the substantive provisions of laws and decrees against which objections have been raised:

1. The breaking-up of large mining properties by requiring the owner to work each five contiguous *pertenencias*.

2. The accomplishment of the same object by a progressive tax bearing more heavily on the larger properties.

3. The forfeiture of mines not continuously operated.

4. The retroactive impairment of title of petroleum land owners or lessors by requiring, in case of those who have performed positive exploitation acts, the acceptance of a fifty-year concession in exchange for former titles.

5. The impairment of title of those who have not performed positive acts by giving them only a preferential right to a concession in exchange for former titles.

6. The provision compelling foreign corporations owning 50 per cent or more of the stock of companies holding rural lands for agricultural purposes in Mexico to dispose of the same within ten years.

7. The exclusion of foreigners from acquiring concessions, or an interest in corporations owning land or concessions, in Mexico, unless they should agree not to invoke the protection of their governments.

8. The impairment of the obligation of contracts by compelling the payment of debts in depreciated currency.

9. The payment for expropriated lands by bonds on the basis of the value fixed by landholders for purposes of taxation.

10. The taking of land without adequate provision for compensation further than an unenforceable right to annual payments from the new occupant.

11. Taxation at a rate which is too high to permit of the profitable operation of the property.

12. Taxes or forced loans levied upon special persons or companies.

13. Heavy taxation of special industries which are largely in the hands of foreigners.

14. Taxation of petroleum lands, both upon the soil and the production, thus indicating to the Department of State an intention to nationalize petroleum through taxation.

The doctrine of "due process" in the diplomatic protection of property rights may be criticized on account of the unilateral character of its application, it generally being imposed by the action of a strong nation against one which is comparatively weak. It thus loses to a large extent its judicial character and becomes an instrument for advancing the cause of a party litigant. This defect of the doctrine could well be remedied by the provision of an international court representing the systems of civil as well as of common law in the western hemisphere, and endowing the court with jurisdiction to decide such matters as arise from the conflict of differing legal concepts. Only by submission of such cases to an impartial tribunal could the due process doctrine be rescued from the evils which are certain eventually to arise from the one-sided method of enforcement.[1]

[1] The suggestion of arbitration is made in the articles by Borchard and Bullington, previously cited.

CHAPTER VIII

ANTI-REVOLUTIONISM AND MANIPULATION

REVOLUTIONS BECOME A THREAT TO AMERICAN INVESTMENTS AND FINANCIAL CONTROL

Until the end of the nineteenth century, the United States maintained an attitude of neutrality with regard to the lightning-like upheavals which took place in the governments of the smaller Latin-American countries. Guided by the principles of international law and remembering the non-interference which had been so insistently demanded from other governments during the American Civil War, this country took the position that internal conflicts in other lands were not a matter of our concern. Nothing less sacred than the tradition of the American Revolution, reviewed with acclaim on each succeeding Independence Day, justified the use of violence on proper occasions in the overthrow of governments. Accordingly, the United States assumed a neutral status as between factions in foreign revolutions. Neutrality laws were applied, although the laxness of their enforcement was evidenced by the numerous armed expeditions which set forth from American soil to carry assistance to disturbers of Latin-American peace. The shipment of arms to the forces of both the beleaguered government and the insurrectionists was permitted. Recognition was duly extended to successful revolutionary factions after they were clearly and firmly established in power. In recent years, however, the time-honored policy of neutrality and non-intervention has been forced to give way before changing conditions and ideals. Today, excepting in rare instances, the United States frowns upon revolutions in Latin-American countries and is often willing to take a positive stand in support of the government against which the revolution is aimed. This new doctrine marks a striking reversal in the diplomacy of a state which owes its own origin to revolution.

Numerous explanations have been advanced for the change. The notion that the use of force is immoral, which seems to have

134

lain beneath President Wilson's policy against Huerta,[1] has a certain attraction for the idealistically inclined, but must be dismissed as of only minor importance in American diplomacy. Such a motive is connected with no national interest; and Americans, being a practically minded people, ordinarily do not borrow trouble by interfering in the affairs of others unless their own interests are involved. Undoubtedly, the desire to prevent European interference in Latin America was a strong reason for the origin of the doctrine of anti-revolutionism. European bondholders had held the public debt of several weaker countries in the region of Panama. European gunboats had cruised the waters of the Caribbean. And revolutions had always been an invitation to intervention by governments of creditor nations. But the possibility of European interference has greatly declined since the World War[2] and with its decline the opposition to revolutionary activities by the United States has increased. The strengthening of our policy has been coincident with the growth of American investments and institutions for financial control. The conclusion seems irresistible that whatever may have been the major cause for the origin of the American policy two decades ago, the principal reason is now economic.

The menace of revolutionary activities to American investments in weaker countries has been brought to the attention of the Department of State by innumerable protests on the part of business men who have felt their properties endangered in times of turmoil. American oil companies whose pipe lines have been cut and whose properties have been occupied, American railway companies whose locomotives and cars have been seized, mining men who have been forced to abandon their mines, wood-cutting firms whose river steamers have been taken—all of these and a great variety of other American concerns have deluged Wash-

[1] A good summary of this policy is in RIPPY, J. FRED, "The United States and Mexico," p. 333*ff*, Alfred A. Knopf, Inc., New York, 1926.

[2] The appearance of a British cruiser in Nicaraguan waters during the Revolution in 1927 caused a flurry of excitement in the United States and considerably strengthened the sentiment for intervention by creating an evidently groundless fear that the Monroe Doctrine was threatened. A British invasion of Central America at this date is so remote that it could not have been seriously considered by diplomats, whatever effect it may have had upon the public mind. For the comment of a shrewd scholar as to the remoteness of the European threat see Garner, James Wilford, "American Foreign Policies," p. 104, New York University Press, New York, 1928.

ington in times of disorder with requests for protection which the native government has been unable to afford against revolutionists.

It is true that revolutions may sometimes aid concession-seeking Americans. Sometimes, also, the overthrow of the existing government may appear to be beneficial to the majority of American interests, either because of the tyrannical character of the group in power or because of a legislative reform program which has aroused the ire of foreign property holders.[1] On the whole, however, revolutions are a menace to industry and commerce and are deplored by business men. The antagonism to violence has increased as the non-concessionary investment, representing bona fide capital, has come to predominate over that depending upon special contracts of exploitation. The shoe-string type of promoter, who without money sought to get rich by obtaining the grant of a monopoly and capitalizing its value at a large figure, often prospered through revolutions which brought favorable governments into power. The man who places money in productive enterprises and depends for a profit upon efficient operation can, however, see no advantage in civil warfare. The growing preponderance in American policy of the interest of the orthodox investor over that of the concessionaire was well set forth by Secretary Bryan who, in an instruction to the American Minister to Haiti in 1914, wrote as follows:

While we desire to encourage in every proper way American investments in Haiti, we believe that this can be better done by contributing to stability and order than by favoring special concessions to Americans.[2]

As the flow of American capital into unstable countries has continued, it has been inevitable that the preponderance of investment interests should become more pronounced and that there should develop at the same time a tendency on the part of

[1] An illustration of the antagonism of an American business representative toward a Latin-American government because of its legislative program was strikingly shown by the publication of a letter of Thomas F. Lee, Executive Director of the National Association for the Protection of American Rights in Mexico. Lee wrote in encouragement of certain Mexican revolutionists, promising "utmost help to the side of any capable, sincere and aggressive Mexican who desires to restore to his country the peace, prosperity, credit and honor it once claimed." Upon the publication of the letter Mr. Lee resigned his position. *The New York Times*, Jan. 20, 1922.

[2] *For. Rel.*, 1914, p. 370.

the United States to oppose domestic disturbances. The concept of a *pax Americana* for unstable countries in the Caribbean and Central America is today, for the most part, an investment policy.

The development of American financial control in weaker countries has given to the United States an incentive to oppose the overthrow of the established governments. This country, either officially or through private financiers, has acquired a right of supervision over custom houses and has in other ways gained the power of fiscal dictation in a number of unstable countries to the south. These institutions of control are more or less tied up with the existing government, and their success is threatened by civil war. They constitute another reason for the rendering of American aid in the suppression of revolutions.

Finally there have come into office, sometimes by American assistance, a number of presidents in Caribbean countries who are willing to conform to the economic policies of the United States, even as against popular opposition. Sudre Dartiguenave and Luis Borno of Haiti and Adolfo Diaz of Nicaragua are examples of the Latin American executive whose elevation to office has been due to a professed friendship for the aims of the great neighbor of the North. The United States particularly resents the conspiracies of native politicians to overthrow friendly governments of this kind. Courting the favor of Uncle Sam is often a surer method of retaining office than harking to the voice of the native electorate.

The United States, because of its economic and military power, has at its disposal a number of devices which it may use to prevent the success of revolutions. The power to refuse recognition, the ability to furnish the government with arms and to cut off the supply from the revolutionists, and the direct use of military forces are all effective weapons for the defeat of insurrectionists. These devices have not always been used for the purpose of preventing revolutions or for the protection of property, but have at times been employed to manipulate native governments. Reluctant officials have sometimes been compelled by these means to acquiesce in American demands for customs control or for other economic favors. Accordingly, as the methods of protection which this country has employed are noted and described in the following pages the use of the same methods for purposes of manipulation will also be commented upon. The deviation may be justified upon the grounds that the twisting of small governments to our purpose is an important part of the economic foreign policy of the United States.

RECOGNITION

The practice of refusing recognition to governments which come into power through revolution in countries in the Caribbean or in Central America is not in accordance with international law as its principles are recognized among nations of equal standing, and is a departure from the uniform early practice of the United States. In recognizing the Rivas government in Nicaragua in 1856, which had been set up the previous year by the American adventurer, William Walker, President Pierce stated that the policy of the United States had been to recognize *de facto* governments founded by violence in Europe and that:

> It is the more imperatively necessary to apply this rule to the Spanish-American republics, in consideration of the frequent and not seldom anomalous changes of organization or administration which they undergo, and the revolutionary nature of most of the changes.[1]

The growth of American investments and customs control has brought about a striking reversal of this doctrine.

No sooner had the United States secured an agreement for the control of the custom houses of the Dominican Republic than it adopted a program of supporting the government as against revolutionists, a program which shortly developed into a policy of non-recognition of governments established there through insurrection. In 1905, steps were taken by the United States to prevent arms from reaching revolutionists. In 1912, it was twice recommended to the Department of State that rebel forces should not be recognized by this country should they succeed in overturning the government by force.[2] Under Woodrow Wilson, clear and forceful expression was given to the policy. A group of Dominican revolutionists in 1913 were admonished that the United States could have no sympathy with those who sought to seize the power of government to advance their own personal interests or ambitions,[3] and that should they succeed the United States would refuse to recognize

[1] MOORE, JOHN BASSETT, "A Digest of International Law," (hereafter cited as *Moore's Digest*) Vol. I, p. 142, Govt. Printing Office, Washington, 1906.

[2] *For. Rel.*, 1912, p. 375.

[3] *For. Rel.*, 1913, p. 426.

them and would withhold from them the portion of the customs collections belonging to the Dominican government.[1] Under these instructions the American minister made such representations to the warring factions as to secure their acquiescence in the "American declaration that force of arms can never settle any question," and that "the last civil war of the country is over."[2] About five months after this solemn announcement of a régime of perpetual peace, the irrepressible opposition broke out in another revolution during which President Wilson proposed a plan of settlement and the erection of a new government. It was announced that as soon as the new government should be established the United States would insist that "revolutionary movements cease and that all subsequent changes in the government of the Republic be effected by the peaceful processes provided in the Dominican Constitution."[3] A similar representation was made in Haiti in the same year.[4]

When the Costa Rican revolutionary, General Tinoco, seized the reins of power in his country in 1917, Secretary Lansing made an emphatic summary of the Wilsonian policy as follows:

The government of the United States has viewed the recent overthrow of the established government in Costa Rica with the gravest concern and considers that illegal acts of this character tend to disturb the peace of Central America and to disrupt the unity of the American continent. In view of its policy in regard to the assumption of power through illegal methods, clearly enunciated by it on several occasions during the past four years, the government of the United States desires to set forth in an emphatic and distinct manner its present position in regard to the actual situation in Costa Rica which is that it will not give recognition or support to any government which may be established unless it is clearly proven that it is elected by legal and constitutional means.[5]

In 1926, General Emiliano Chamorro, who had come into the Presidency of Nicaragua as the result of a *coup d'état* was refused

[1] *Ibid.*, p. 427.

[2] *Ibid.*, p. 432.

[3] *For. Rel.*, 1914, p. 248.

[4] *Ibid.*, pp. 357–358. The much-discussed case of the refusal to recognize the Huerta government in Mexico in 1913 is an anomaly. Huerta had become President by nominally constitutional process (*For. Rel.*, 1913, p. 772) and the refusal to recognize him stimulated revolution. The attitude of President Wilson was idealistic and not, in the beginning, at least, connected with American economic interest. (For a discussion of the entrance of economic motives see above, p. 77.)

[5] *For. Rel.*, 1917, p. 306.

recognition by Secretary Kellogg, who stated that such recognition would not be in accord with the purpose of the Treaty of Peace and Amity between the five Central-American Republics of 1923, the object of which was to promote constitutional government by refusing recognition to factions coming into power by *coup d'état* or revolution. Secretary Kellogg stated that:

> The United States has adopted the principles of that treaty as its policy in the future recognition of Central-American governments as it feels that by so doing it can best show its friendly disposition towards and its desire to be helpful to the Republics of Central America.[1]

The United States informed the Sacasa leaders after the recognition of Diaz that no other faction would be recognized until after the election of 1928, even if it should be successful in seizing control of the country.

How a Government Worthy of Recognition May Be Established.—Having refused to recognize a revolutionary government in any instance, the Department of State is put to the task of finding a group of men who may be recognized and supported in order that the disturbances may cease and order may be resumed. The formula with which the United States has attempted to meet the situation on a number of occasions has been to secure an agreement between factional chiefs to suspend hostilities and to hold an election, all parties agreeing to abide by the result. The success with which the plan has been attended has varied. Where the successful revolutionary chief is strong he will naturally be unwilling to relinquish his power, particularly if it is stipulated that he is not to be a candidate in the forthcoming election. Thus, Huerta, in 1913, refused to agree to an election from which he was to be barred.[2] In 1914, a plan for an armistice and an election was successfully proposed in the Dominican Republic[3] and Jiménez, who was elected president, was subsequently recognized by the United States. A similar proposition was under consideration with regard to the Haitian situation in the same year, but the rapidity of Haitian political changes made it impractical to present the program to the

[1] Note set forth in Special Message of President Coolidge, printed in *Cong. Rec.*, Vol. 68, p. 1330.

[2] For the proposal of the Department of State in that instance see *For. Rel.*, 1913, p. 822.

[3] *For. Rel.*, 1914, pp. 247, 250.

various leaders.[1] Necessarily other means of deciding upon a government which justifies recognition must at times be used. The Carranzist faction was given recognition as the *de facto* government of Mexico following a conference between Secretary of State Lansing and the ambassadors from Argentina, Brazil, Chile, and the ministers from Bolivia, Uruguay, and Guatemala. The conference reported that the Carranzist party was the only one possessing the essentials for such recognition.[2]

Exceptions to the Policy of Non-recognition of Revolutionists.—In unusual circumstances when the general American interests are considered to be opposed by the government in power the United States has not been adverse to the recognition of a revolutionary government, and has even urged on the revolution. The outstanding illustration is, of course, the Panama Revolution of 1903, which was given such support by the United States as to insure its success. Recognition of the Panaman government followed immediately upon the heels of the outbreak. In this case, the desire of President Roosevelt to obtain the lease of a canal zone inspired the policy. Another illustration occurred in the Nicaraguan revolution of 1909–1910 in which the American business men in Bluefields and the Department of State opposed the Zelaya government, then in power. Secretary of State Knox withdrew recognition from the government of Zelaya and threw his support to the revolutionists. Shortly after the success of the uprising, recognition was extended to the new Estrada government upon the giving of certain assurances.[3] The fatal consequences to the Zelaya government of the withdrawal of American recognition were an object lesson to any Central-American executives who might desire to oppose the policies of the United States.

The recognition of Adolfo Diaz as the President of Nicaragua in 1926, following his election by the Nicaraguan Congress, occasioned an extended discussion in the American press and in Congress. The action was criticized as a departure from American policies on the ground that Diaz was really a party to the Chamorro revolution which had upset the Solorzano-Sacasa government, and that Dr. Sacasa, who had been Vice-president under the former régime, had a better constitutional claim to

[1] *For. Rel.*, 1914, p. 357.
[2] *For. Rel.*, 1915, p. 767.
[3] For a summary of the American policy see *For. Rel.*, 1911, 649*ff.*

the office. The Department of State may have been influenced in that case by a sense of loyalty to Diaz who as President in 1911 and thereafter had been faithful in his cooperation with the department.[1]

The announcement of the Department of State in October, 1927, that it would recognize the Nicaraguan Liberal leader, General Moncada, should he be chosen President in the 1928 election was another apparent exception to the principles of recognition that had been professed by Secretary Kellogg. The Central American Treaty of 1923, which Mr. Kellogg had acknowledged as his guide in the recognition of Central American governments, provides that recognition of a person elected President shall not be extended "if he should be the leader or one of the leaders of a *coup d'état* or revolution."[2] Moncada had been the leading general in the Liberal attack upon the Chamorro and Diaz governments. Nevertheless, the department interpreted the treaty as not to exclude the recognition of General Moncada because the revolution in which he had been a leader was unsuccessful. The distinction was probably introduced because of the personal desirability of Moncada, who held a leading place in the Liberal party and who was also friendly to the policies of the United States. The union in one person of American friendship and native popularity doubtless rendered desirable a departure from American policy.

Exchanging Recognition for Economic and Political Concessions.—The value of American recognition to the parties in power in the Caribbean and Central-American countries is so apparent that the United States has been on numerous occasions able to demand concessions in economic and political matters in return for recognition. The sale of American recognition for a price to factions that are willing to pay for it is not exactly in accord with the orthodox notions of international law but is, nevertheless, a potent means of dictating the

---

[1] For a criticism and defense of the department's policy in that case see the following references to the *Cong. Rec.*, Vol. 68: for President Coolidge's explanation of the legality of the Diaz government set forth in a special message to Congress, p. 1324*ff*; for Dr. Sacasa's case taken from *The New York Times* of Jan. 10, 1927, p. 1412*ff*; for an interesting debate over the terms of the Nicaraguan constitution between Senators Borah and Bingham, pp. 1558–1559.

[2] Art. II of the treaty. See Department of State, "Conference on Central American Affairs," p. 289, Gov't Printing Office, Washington, 1923.

policies of weaker governments without the necessity of the use of force.

In 1910, the United States secured certain pledges from the four principal revolutionary leaders in Nicaragua prior to the recognition of the Estrada government. On Sept. 10, 1910, Estrada gave promises of certain "reforms."[1] Desiring to have these incorporated in a more formal document which would bind the other revolutionary leaders the United States dispatched a special agent who secured a written agreement signed on Oct. 27, 1910, not only by Estrada but also by Adolfo Diaz, Luis Mena, and Emiliano Chamorro. This agreement included the following promises:

1. To adopt a constitution which would abolish the monopolies created by Zelaya, which had aroused the antagonism of American business men.

2. To create a mixed claims commission to pass on claims against the government, the form of which was to be in accordance with the agreement with the American agent after submission to the Department of State.

3. To punish the executioners of Cannon and Groce, the two American members of the revolutionary forces who had been executed by the Zelayists, and to grant an indemnity to their families.

4. To solicit the good offices of the United States in securing a loan to be guaranteed by a certain percentage of the customs receipts.

5. To bar the Zelayist element from the administration.[2]

Following this agreement and the induction of Estrada into office on Jan. 1, 1911, the United States extended recognition.

On several occasions the United States has negotiated with *de facto* governments in the Dominican Republic for the purpose of strengthening its control over the finances of that country. When Jiménez was elected President in 1914 the United States was tied by a promise to recognize the successful candidate. Nevertheless, the Department of State thought it wise to exact a promise from him to support stronger financial control by the United States prior to extending recognition, the specific aims being the acknowledgment of the position of the American Comptroller and the collection of internal revenues by the American customs receivership. The United States chargé was able to secure an evidently satisfactory promise in writing. Recognition was then extended and notice was given that revolutionary opposition would not be tolerated.[3] In 1916, when Dr. Henri-

[1] See *For. Rel.*,1910, p. 762.

[2] For the text of the agreement see *For. Rel.*, 1911, p. 652.

[3] *For. Rel.*, 1914, pp. 255–261.

quez was chosen President, Secretary Lansing instructed the American minister:

> Provisional government will not be recognized until it shows itself to be favorable to our interpretation of convention as to control, constabulary and other reforms and proves itself free from dominion of Arias.

Dr. Henriquez responded with a counter proposal which was not sufficient to satisfy the United States. Recognition was accordingly refused and military government was shortly afterward established.[1]

Similar bargains have been attempted in Haiti. In 1914, after the election of Davilmar Theodore as President by the Haitian National Assembly following a revolution, Secretary Bryan stipulated as necessary to complete recognition that satisfactory protocols should be signed which should contain an agreement to conclude a treaty granting to the United States control over the Haitian customhouses and providing for the settlement of disputes with the American railway and the National Bank of the Republic of Haiti in which Americans owned shares.[2] In 1915, it was made clear to President-elect Dartiguenave that the signing of a treaty giving control of the Haitian custom houses to the United States was a condition precedent to recognition, which was accordingly extended simultaneously with the signing of the treaty.[3]

The agreements of the American and Mexican commissioners in Mexico City in 1923 concerning the non-retroactivity of the clauses of the Mexican Constitution of 1917 regarding oil properties and land were in fact, if not in express stipulation, conditions precedent to recognition of the Obregon government by the United States. This was denied later by the Mexican Minister for Foreign Affairs, who, feeling the humiliation that the imposition of conditions upon his government by such methods would imply, contended that "the conferences of 1923 were not a condition for the recognition of the government of Mexico, and consequently can never be given that character."[4] The United States maintained emphatically that the opposite was correct. Secretary Kellogg, responding to the Mexican Minister for Foreign Affairs, alleged:

[1] *For. Rel.*, 1916, p. 235*ff.*
[2] *For. Rel.*, 1914, pp. 359, 364.
[3] *For. Rel.*, 1915, p. 490.
[4] "Rights of American Citizens in Certain Oil Lands in Mexico," p. 34.

I can only say to your excellency in this connection that my government continues to regard the proceedings of 1923 as a negotiation of the highest importance upon which two sovereign states may engage. Without the assurances received in the course of that negotiation recognition could not, and would not, have been extended.[1]

Thus it appears that the old doctrine of recognition has been radically changed by the United States. Before a new government in neighboring Latin-American states can secure recognition, it must ordinarily come into power by orderly processes. In some cases it must be prepared to meet American demands in political and economic matters before it can expect to be recognized.

ARMS CONTROL

Embargoes on Arms to Revolutionary Forces.—Until American investments in revolutionary countries began to suffer from political instability and until customs control and similar devices gave the United States a vested interest in the maintenance in power of friendly *de jure* governments, the policy of this country concerning the export of arms and munitions was one of complete freedom. Neither the principles of international law nor the neutrality statutes of the United States were construed as obliging the government to prevent shipments. Such a condition, however dear to the hearts of American rifle and cartridge manufacturers and concessionaire promoters of revolution, could not continue to exist following the growth of American economic interests in unstable countries. A few months after President Roosevelt had concluded an agreement with the Dominican government for the collection of the customs duties by an American receivership, a revolution being in existence against the Dominican government, the United States took steps to shut off materials of war from the revolutionists. There existed at the time a joint resolution of Congress which had been approved on Apr. 22, 1898, for the purpose of preventing American materials of war from coming into the hands of Spain. The resolution provided that the President might prohibit the exportation from any seaport of the United States of coal or other materials used for war, with such limitations and exceptions as might seem expedient.[2] The Dominican officials were

[1] "American Property Rights in Mexico," p. 10.
[2] 30 *Stat.* 739.

willing that an arms embargo should be applied with the understanding that the government could get arms in special cases when it so desired. Accordingly, on Oct. 14, 1905, President Roosevelt acting under the above-mentioned resolution issued a proclamation putting into effect such an embargo against Santo Domingo.[1]

The Arms Embargo against Mexico.—The revolution against Madero in Mexico brought the matter of arms control to the fore because of the danger in that country to American property which was then estimated to be worth about one billion dollars. The United States made strong demands upon the Mexican government to protect American investments from the disorders of the revolution but at the same time large quantities of arms and ammunition were going across the border to aid the revolutionists in their destructive activities. In 1912, the Mexican ambassador protested:

. . . while the Mexican government is concerning itself, as in duty bound, with the tranquility of the country and all its inhabitants, among whom are a number of citizens of the United States, and with looking after the inviolability of the property belonging to each one, those who rebel against its authority easily obtain from this country [the United States] all the elements necessary to inflict direct or indirect injury upon the residents of Mexican territory.[2]

Similarly Senator Root argued in the United States Senate:

The conditions are such that thousands of Americans in Mexico are now fleeing from their homes there and are abandoning their occupations, their mines, their manufactories, and their business because it is necessary to do so to prevent their lives from being destroyed by arms and munitions which are being sold and transported across the border from the United States.[3]

The joint resolution of Apr. 22, 1898 was insufficient to meet the emergency as it applied to seaports only. It was furthermore considered too broad inasmuch as it applied to coal and also might be proclaimed as against any country at any time. Accordingly, Congress amended the previous resolution by a joint resolution approved Mar. 14, 1912, which provided that when there existed in any American country conditions of

[1] *For. Rel.*, 1905, p. 399.
[2] *For. Rel.*, 1912, p. 744.
[3] *Cong. Rec.*, Vol. 48, p. 3258.

domestic violence which were promoted by the use of arms or munitions of war procured from the United States and that fact should be proclaimed by the President it should then be unlawful to export arms or munitions except under such limitations and exceptions as the President should provide.[1]   Under this resolution the United States proceeded to throw its munition resources upon the side of the established government as against revolutionary forces on numerous occasions by making exceptions in favor of exports to government forces while keeping the embargo intact as against the revolutionists.   Few revolutions in the neighboring countries of Latin America are hardy enough to succeed under such conditions.

The policy of arms control was applied in Mexico immediately upon the passage of the joint resolution of 1912 by a proclamation issued by President Taft on the date of the approval of the resolution.[2]   The President had at first intended to include in the proclamation a general exception permitting all shipments of arms and munitions intended for the Madero government, but upon the advice of the Department of State that such an exception might cause reprisals against Americans by the revolutionary leaders the general exception was omitted.[3]   After requests had been made by the Madero government, however, a policy was adopted of permitting shipments to government forces upon application through diplomatic channels in each specific case.[4] President Wilson, desiring to rid Mexico of the Huerta government, on Feb. 3, 1914, revoked the proclamation and permitted the unrestricted export of arms into Mexico.[5]   The reason for the revocation was that the Mexican question might be settled by "civil war carried to its bitter conclusion."[6]   An embargo proclamation was again issued on the recognition of the Carranza government as the *de facto* government of Mexico.   Permission was given, however, for the exportation of arms and munitions to the government forces excepting in the states of Sonora and Chihuahua and the Territory of Lower California, in which places the government was not yet in control.[7]   The embargo

[1] 37 *Stat.* 630. Text also printed in *For. Rel.*, 1912, p. 745.

[2] *For. Rel.*, 1912, p. 745.

[3] *For. Rel.*, 1913, p. 874.

[4] *Ibid.*, 1912, pp. 765–766.

[5] *For. Rel.*, 1914, p. 447.

[6] *Ibid.*, quoted from an instruction sent by Secretary Bryan.

[7] *For. Rel.*, 1915, pp. 772, 780, 781.

was made complete as against all factions when in 1916 the Pershing expedition into Mexico seemed threatened with attack,[1] but the government was again permitted to secure munitions when cordial relations were reestablished. The latter action was taken upon the advice of Ambassador Fletcher to whom leading Mexican generals had explained that there was dire need of ammunition on the part of the government. The ambassador recommended to the Department of State:

> It is to our interest that the government [Mexico] be given all proper support to enable it to pacify the country and restore normal economic conditions.[2]

A joint resolution of Jan. 31, 1922, supersedes the resolution of 1912. The new measure applies not only to American countries but also to any country in which the United States exercises extraterritorial jurisdiction. The resolution provides:

> That whenever the President finds that in any American country, or in any country in which the United States exercises extraterritorial jurisdiction, conditions of domestic violence exist, which are or may be promoted by the use of arms or munitions of war procured from the United States, and makes proclamation thereof, it shall be unlawful to export, except under such limitations and exceptions as the President prescribes, any arms or munitions of war from any place in the United States to such country until otherwise ordered by the President or by Congress.[3]

During the de la Huerta revolt in Mexico in 1923–1924, President Coolidge, acting under this resolution, imposed the embargo as against Mexico and permitted exceptions in favor of the Obregon government.[4]

Sales of Arms by the United States Government to Suppress Revolutions.—A striking feature of the anti-revolutionism of the United States has been the sale of arms by official action to certain governments that have been threatened by revolution.

[1] *For. Rel.*, 1916, pp. 789, 792.

[2] *For. Rel.*, 1917, p. 1082.

[3] U. S. Statutes at Large, Vol. 42, Part I, p. 361. The inclusion of countries in which the United States exercises extraterritorial jurisdiction was to make possible the restriction of the arms traffic in China. See the Agreement of the Diplomatic Body in Peking of May 5, 1919, *Treaties, etc. between the United States and Other Powers*, Vol. III, p. 3821.

[4] Proclamation printed in *The New York Times*, Jan. 8, 1924.

Such sales have been made to the Liberian government during the Kru revolt in 1916,[1] to the Cuban government when threatened with revolution in 1917,[2] to the Obregon government in Mexico during the de la Huerta revolution of 1924,[3] and to the Diaz government in Nicaragua during the Sacasa revolution in 1927.[4]

Manipulation through Arms Traffic Control.—Arms and munitions manufactured in the United States are superior in type and quality and cheaper in price than those which can be supplied in Latin-American countries. They can also be furnished in much greater quantities. Accordingly, when the United States diverts its exports of arms and munitions to one faction or another, the power which is thereby conferred is frequently sufficient to determine the issue of the conflict. Likewise, the removal of the preference and the placing of the factions on a basis of equality exerts an influence on the outcome, the total removal of an embargo being ordinarily favorable to revolution. When President Wilson in 1914 desired the overthrow of the Huerta government, and lifted the arms embargo, he greatly improved the chances of the Mexican revolutionists. A veiled threat of a similar action was made against the Calles government in 1927 by President Coolidge in the heat of the controversy with Mexico over the land and oil laws. On Mar. 28, 1927, the President terminated a convention of a year previous which had provided for the prevention of smuggling across the border and which required that each government should notify the other of shipments of merchandise.[5] The raising of the embargo on arms for the purpose of weakening the Calles government would have been of little effect so long as the United States was required to keep the Mexican government informed as to arms shipments. The termination of the anti-smuggling convention was considered to be in anticipation of the removal of the arms embargo and was regarded as a warning to Mexico.[6]

[1] *For. Rel.*, 1916, pp. 453–455.

[2] CHAPMAN, CHARLES E., "History of the Cuban Republic," p. 371, The Macmillan Company, New York, 1927.

[3] *Current History*, February, 1924, p. 853; *The New York Times*, Jan. 5, 1924.

[4] *State Department Press Release*, Mar. 23, 1927.

[5] Notice of termination announced in *State Department Press Release*, Mar. 22, 1927.

[6] *The New York Times*, Mar. 23, 1927.

Rarely has the United States gone so far in assisting a warring faction through arms control as in the aid extended to Adolfo Diaz in Nicaragua, in 1927. Exports of arms and ammunition from Mexico to the opposing Sacasa faction were strenuously protested by the Department of State. A supply of Sacasa arms and ammunition in a neutral zone was seized by American forces for the purpose of determining whether they had been shipped from the United States in violation of the President's arms embargo proclamation. When it was found that the supply had not come from the United States but from Mexico, some of the rifles and ammunition were "lost" in the river.[1] On Jan. 5, 1927, President Coolidge lifted the general embargo that had existed on the shipment of arms into Nicaragua in favor of the Diaz faction. This act was immediately followed by the shipment of arms by private exporters. Later, the United States government sold arms and ammunition to Diaz, the items being announced as 3,000 Krag rifles, 200 Browning machine guns with accessories, and 3,000,000 rounds of ammunition.[2]

ADVOCATING ANTI-REVOLUTIONISM AS A POLICY FOR CENTRAL AMERICAN AND CARIBBEAN REPUBLICS

The Central-American Treaties.—The United States has not only directed its own efforts against revolutions but has sought at various times to obtain the adherence of the republics of Central America and the Caribbean to a similar foreign policy. The Central American Peace Conference which met in Washington in 1907 was called by the United States for the purpose of taking steps to prevent wars and revolutions. In expressing to the delegates the desire of the United States to see the principles of liberty and order established in Central America, Secretary Root frankly stated that this condition would conform to the interests of the United States "from the most selfish point of view." He elaborated the statement by saying:

We in the United States should be most happy if the states of Central America might move with greater rapidity along the pathway of such prosperity, [as resulted from peace in the United States and Mexico] of such progress, to the end that we may share, through commerce and

[1] From the testimony of Stokely W. Morgan, Chief of the Division of Latin-American Affairs of the Department of State, before the Committee on Foreign Relations of the United States Senate, *The New York Times*, Mar. 10, 1927.

[2] *State Department Press Release*, Mar. 23, 1927.

friendly intercourse, in your new prosperity and aid you by our prosperity.[1]

Root was a keen-minded realist and was too frank to dismiss the subject with mere eulogies on peace. Not only did the five republics enter into the General Treaty of Peace and Amity but they signed an additional convention binding each other not to recognize any other government which should come into power as a consequence of a *coup d'état* or revolution so long as the freely elected representatives of the people had not constitutionally reorganized the country.[2] In 1923, another convention similarly drawn pledged the five republics not to recognize any government which might come into power in any of the five countries through a *coup d'état* or a revolution against a recognized government.[3]

On numerous occasions the United States has requested the republics in the Caribbean or Central America not to permit assistance to be given to revolutionary factions in other countries. A complaint was made in 1914 to the government of Haiti because of the smuggling of arms to Dominican revolutionists with the connivance of Haitian authorities. The protest was based upon the responsibility of the United States with regard to the Dominican customs. The following quotation will indicate the emphatic tone of Secretary Bryan's protest:

The government of the United States, in order that there may be no misconception of its attitude by the government of Haiti in this matter, desires to state that unless the Haitian authorities immediately desist from the shipment across the frontier of munitions of war for the use of Dominican revolutionists or from aiding and abetting these revolutionists or their agents in sending such shipments across the border, the government of the United States will be forced to consider what steps it will be necessary for it to take for the prevention of the further infringement upon the customs regulations above mentioned.[4]

Likewise representations have been made to the Dominican government to prevent the activities of Haitian revolutionaries within Dominican territory and also against the shipment of arms into Haiti.[5]

[1] *For. Rel.*, 1907, p. 688.
[2] *Ibid.*, p. 696.
[3] *Conference on Central American Affairs*, pp. 288–289.
[4] *For. Rel.*, 1914, p. 239.
[5] *For. Rel.*, 1915, pp. 470–471, 488.

In enforcing the embargo against the shipment of arms into Mexico in 1916, the United States sought the aid of Central-American countries. Secretary Lansing informed Salvador and Guatemala that, due to the interest of the United States in the restoration of law and order in Mexico, "the United States would consider it a very friendly act" if they would "prevent shipments of munitions of war to Mexico, pending the return of more nearly normal conditions in that country."[1]

During the Nicaraguan revolution of 1926–1927, the attempt to secure an agreement to a general arms embargo against Nicaragua became a matter of international importance. The Department of State took up the question of such an embargo with the governments of Costa Rica, Honduras, Salvador, and Guatemala, and those countries assured the department of their cooperation. An embargo was likewise requested of the Mexican government, which failed to agree to the suggestion and answered that as Mexico had no arms or munition factories the matter had little practical importance.[2] Subsequently, a heated controversy was publicly waged over the question whether the Mexican government had assisted in the export of arms into Nicaragua for the use of the Sacasa troops. Secretary Kellogg stated that "interference from outside sources" in Nicaraguan politics was viewed with concern in Washington, and gave out evidence that gun-running expeditions to Nicaragua had issued from Mexican ports.[3] Further evidence connecting these shipments with the Mexican government, although not very complete, created a furor of accusation and denial.

[1] *For. Rel.*, 1916, pp. 794–795.

[2] President Coolidge's message to Congress of Jan. 10, 1927, printed in the *Cong. Record*, Vol. 68, p. 1324.

[3] *The New York Times*, Nov. 18, 1926.

CHAPTER IX

THE PRACTICE OF ARMED PROTECTION

When diplomacy proves insufficient for the protection of American property abroad, the Navy Department is frequently called upon to furnish the required persuasive influences. The growth of the reliance upon force to safeguard American holdings in backward countries is a tendency of the last decade. The contention that American commerce and investments require an expanded navy has been put forth with increasing frequency and vigor during the last few years. Such an argument has an undoubted appeal when directed to many business men, and has proved to be effective in the halls of Congress. While large diplomatic movements and tendencies are ordinarily not reducible to measurement, the progress of the use of force in the widening regions of our economic influence can be traced roughly in the statistics of guns and tonnage that represent the growth of the American navy.

A summary of the demands made upon the Department of State during the revolutionary disturbances in Nicaragua in August, 1926, is set forth by the department in a recent publication.[1] A quotation from this pamphlet may serve to show vividly how investments in backward countries result in increased naval activity on the part of the United States.

On Aug. 19, 1926, the Otis Manufacturing Company telegraphed that further revolutionary disturbances in Nicaragua were reported, that an outbreak at Bluefields would be serious, and asked what steps were being taken by this government to protect property. The department replied on Aug. 21 that it was following developments closely and would take such appropriate action as possible to protect American interests which might appear to be in danger.

On Aug. 20 the Freiberg Mahogany Company telegraphed that interests in Nicaragua seemed to be in danger and said that sending

[1] Department of State, "A Brief History of the Relations between the United States and Nicaragua, 1909-1928," p. 65ff., Govt. Printing Office, Washington, 1928.

a warship to Bluefields would help. This was answered on Aug. 21 in the same words as the telegram from the Otis Manufacturing Company.

The Mengel Company also telegraphed on Aug. 20 and was answered in the same way.

On Aug. 20 Senator Ransdell telephoned to the department on behalf of the Otis Manufacturing Company. He said he understood that all proper steps would be taken by the department to protect American lives and interests, and he was assured that such was the case; the department was watching the matter closely. On Aug. 30 Senator Ransdell was informed by letter that warships had been ordered from Balboa, Canal Zone, to Bluefields and Corinto to protect American lives and property.

. . . .

The American Consul at Bluefields telegraphed on Aug. 31 as follows:

"Losses to Americans on the rivers will amount to two million dollars unless conflict stopped soon. If the five mahogany companies cannot get protection on all the rivers their losses will be one and one-half millions. Contending factions take their boats, recruit their men rendering them helpless, logs float out to sea. The two banana companies are also handicapped, their boats being taken and their laborers being recruited or frightened away."

NAVAL PATROLS

Patrols along the coasts of backward revolutionary countries are a regular feature of American naval activities, and protection is extended to American interests by the quieting effect of the presence of a warship or in more critical times by bombardment or the landing of bluejackets and marines. The three principal areas in which such patrols are maintained are in Chinese waters, in the Central American and Caribbean region, and in the eastern Mediterranean.

American war vessels have visited Chinese waters for the purpose of protecting American interests for over a century.[1] According to information issued in 1924 from the Department of the Navy, the vessels serving this purpose were organized into the Asiatic Fleet, the Yangtse Patrol, and the South China Patrol. The Asiatic Fleet consisted of an old armored cruiser, nineteen first-class destroyers, ten first-class submarines, a mine detachment of four vessels, an airplane squadron and its tender, and two large gunboats. While the principal base of the fleet

[1] For accounts of various naval visits, see PAULLIN, CHARLES OSCAR, "Diplomatic Negotiations of American Naval Officers," p. 167*ff.*, Johns Hopkins Press, Baltimore, 1912.

is in Manilla it sails to Chefoo, in North China, in May where it makes its summer base. On the way to and from Chefoo, calls are made at various Chinese ports. The South China Patrol consisted in 1924 of two river gunboats which patrolled the West River from Hongkong to some distance beyond Canton. The Yangtse Patrol consisted of several small river gunboats operating between Shanghai and Ichang, 1,000 miles up, and of two shallow-draft gunboats which were able to ascend 600 miles farther, through the great gorge of the Yangtse into the heart of China.[1] American commerce has increased on the Yangtse in recent years and the American Chamber of Commerce at Shanghai has as a consequence criticized the inadequacy of the naval protection, particularly on the upper river, and has demanded that more gunboats be sent.[2] As the conflict of the civil war of 1926–1927 began to approach Shanghai and to threaten the large investments at that place as well as at interior points on the river, the naval forces were greatly augmented.

The Caribbean and Central-American area, being frequently visited with revolution and being an important center of American investment and political interest, has been the recipient of more than ordinary attention by the United States navy. The Naval Intelligence Office said concerning this patrol in 1924:

The special service squadron in the Caribbean consists of five small second-class cruisers of little or no use in the line of battle. They are under the command of a rear admiral and are active in protecting our nationals and our tremendous fruit, sugar, and hemp trades, as well as oil and mining interests. The islands of the West Indies and the Central-American Republics are so often the scenes of revolutions, many of which lose their threatening aspect soon after the mere arrival of a cruiser flying our flag, though sometimes it is necessary to send a landing force ashore.[3]

Since the World War, the activity of American vessels in the eastern Mediterranean has greatly increased. Due to unsettled

[1] Office of Naval Intelligence, "The United States Navy as an Industrial Asset," pp. 4, 5, Govt. Printing Office, Washington, 1924.

[2] *Annual Report of the Navy Department*, 1923, p. 15.

[3] "The United States Navy as an Industrial Asset," p. 5. Additional vessels are sent into these waters in times of disorder such as in Haiti and Santo Domingo in 1915–1916 and in Nicaragua in 1912 and 1927. The table on page 158 shows the disposition of ten vessels in Nicaraguan waters in the latter year.

conditions in the countries in that region following the armistice, a number of destroyers were sent to Constantinople. From this point they cruised continually in the Black Sea, the Aegean, and the Mediterranean. The presence of the vessels, according to the naval account, did much to insure the safety of American life and property.[1]

Since the investment of large amounts of American capital in Liberia, the western coast of Africa has assumed a certain amount of importance to the United States and may be expected to claim its share of naval protection. During a Kru uprising in 1915, the U.S.S. *Chester* visited Liberian waters to assist in quelling the revolt.[2]

NEUTRAL ZONES

The Isthmus of Panama 1846-1903.—The declaration of neutral zones in disturbed areas in Caribbean and Central-American countries when American interests are threatened has now become a part of the protection policy of the United States. In Panama, this practice of establishing such a zone during revolutionary disturbances affecting the route of transportation across the isthmus has had a long history, being based on the American interpretation of the Treaty of 1846 with New Granada. Under that treaty the government of New Granada agreed to guarantee freedom of transit across the isthmus to citizens of the United States.[3] The discovery of gold in California and the building of the Panama Railway made the isthmus a center of American investment and commerce. The United States placed an interpretation upon the treaty which permitted the intervention of American naval and military forces for the purpose of maintaining freedom of transit during times of revolution. Intervention was frequently welcomed by Colombian officials as the general effect was to support the government against the revolutionists, although the United States at all times disclaimed any obligation to interfere as between the contending groups.[4] In 1903, during a revolution, the United States

[1] "The United States Navy as an Industrial Asset," p. 6.
[2] *For. Rel.*, 1915, p. 631.
[3] *Treaties Etc., between the United States and Other Powers*, Vol I, p. 312.
[4] For instances of intervention see *Moore's Digest*, Vol. III, p. 38*ff.* A clause in the treaty by which the United States guaranteed the neutrality of the isthmus was interpreted not to apply to domestic conflicts.

went much farther than it had gone on any previous occasion and prevented the landing of government troops on the isthmus. The nominal reason given for this action was the maintenance of the freedom of transit.

In Santo Domingo, in 1914, when President Bordas sought to drive insurgents from Puerto Plata by the use of artillery he was stopped by the Commander of the United States South Atlantic Squadron who opened fire upon him to prevent the bombardment of the city. When reproached for this interference in the conflict the Department of State informed the Dominican government that the bombardment contemplated by President Bordas was not permitted because of the damage which might have been done to foreigners and their property.[1]

Neutral Zones in Nicaragua.—The most generous uses of neutral zones during revolution has occurred in Nicaragua. In 1910, during the revolution against the Zelaya-Madriz government, while the government troops were preparing to take the city of Bluefields, the American naval commander at that place issued a proclamation to the effect that no armed conflict would be permitted in the city.[2] In 1912, when revolutionists were bombarding the city of Managua, the United States Minister to Nicaragua declared in the interests of humanity and for the protection of the lives and property of Americans, other foreigners, and non-combatants that the city should be considered as a place of safe refuge and that no further bombardment or other hostilities would be permitted.[3]

In the revolution of 1926–1927, greater use was made of the neutral zone than at any previous time. Requests were made by American companies for the establishment of such zones.[4] In February, 1927, it was announced that ten zones had been proclaimed. The warships and number of men used for maintaining the zones were as follows:[5]

[1] *For. Rel.*, 1914, pp. 240, 244.
[2] *For. Rel.*, 1910, p. 745.
[3] *For. Rel.*, 1912, p. 1041.
[4] Department of State, "A Brief History of the Relations between the United States and Nicaragua, 1909–1928," pp. 66-67.
[5] *The New York Times*, Feb. 22, 1927.

Location of zone	Warships	Number of men*
Puerto Cabezas........	Destroyer *Lawrence* Cruiser *Cleveland*	406
Prinzapulka...........	Destroyer *Coghlan*	106
Pearl Lagoon..........	Destroyer *Hatfield*	106
Bluefields.............	Cruiser *Denver*	343
Corinto...............	Cruiser *Galveston* Cruiser *Milwaukee* Cruiser *Raleigh*	1,329
Gulf of Fonseca........	Destroyer *Reuben*	106
Salinas Bay...........	Destroyer *Borde*	106
Managua and Loma....	....	541
Chinandega...........	....	373
Leon.................	....	470

* Sailors and marines. The figures are not clear as to whether they include officers in all cases.

On Apr. 18, Matagalpa was likewise declared a neutral zone, its neutrality being enforced by 325 marines. Granada then remained the only important city in Nicaragua which was not neutralized.

The military strength of Mexican factions being much greater than that of the contending forces in the Central-American and Caribbean countries, it has not seemed advisable to impose neutral zones in that country by force of arms. Attempts have been made during revolutionary disturbances to secure such zones in regions where American interests are particularly large through agreements between the opposing leaders. Thus, in 1914 and 1915, agreements were sought by the Department of State for the neutralization of the oil-producing region between Tampico and the Tuxpam River and at Ebana, west of Tampico, as well as of Mexico City and the railway between Mexico City and Vera Cruz.[1] In neither instance, however, could an agreement be obtained.

The International Settlement at Shanghai is the greatest center of foreign investment in China. Probably 30,000 foreigners, of whom nearly 4,000 are Americans, live there; and it is the port through which passes 40 per cent of China's foreign trade. For years the settlement has preserved its neutrality

[1] *For. Rel.*, 1914, p. 690*ff*; 1915, p. 676*ff*.

in the midst of China's civil wars.   The settlement police as
well as the military detachments of the several powers have
been prepared to defend this neutral status.   Sand-bag and
barbed wire defenses have at times been erected, and the domestic
disputes of China have been kept out.   A suggestion was made
by Secretary Kellogg in February, 1927, for an agreement
between the warring factions to preserve the neutrality of the
settlement.   The leaders refused their assent.   While not
strictly necessary the agreement was sought in order to prevent
any undesirable conflict over the question.[1]

Manipulation through Neutral Zones.—While the alleged
purpose for the establishment of neutral zones has been the
protection of American life and property, the opportunities for
manipulation have been so great that the assistance given to
favorite factions has frequently been of greater consequence than
the protection extended to citizens.   The neutral zone lends
itself to manipulation.   To declare a zone in the face of an
advancing army may not only amount to the creation of a safe
refuge for the troops within the zone which may be facing defeat
but may also have the effect of depriving the attacking force of
the advantage of occupying a strategic position or of securing
certain economic advantages, such as the control of customhouses
or railways.

Prior to the insurrection of 1903, the United States in the
exercise of its military power to keep the isthmus open for
transit of American citizens and property had intervened on
numerous occasions.   The general effect of the interventions
had been to assist Colombia in maintaining her sovereignty.
President Roosevelt alleged:

> Had it not been for the exercise by the United States of the police
> power in her [Colombia's] interest, her connection with the Isthmus
> would have been sundered long ago.[2]

The use of American forces in 1903 constituted a striking
reversal of this policy, for in that year the United States desired
the success of the revolutionists for reasons that are well known.
Accordingly, the Navy Department instructed the American
commanders:

[1] *State Department Press Release*, Feb. 5, 1927.
[2] Annual Message, Dec. 7, 1903, *For. Rel.*, 1903, XXXVIII; *Moore's
Digest*, Vol. III, p. 51.

Prevent landing of any armed force with hostile intent, either government or insurgent, either at Colon, Porto Bello, or other point.[1]

This instruction was designed to prevent Colombia from quelling the insurrection. President Roosevelt, disdaining diplomatic subterfuges, later stated: "I took the Canal Zone."[2]

The declarations of neutral zones in Nicaragua, previously described, have in each instance had the effect of assisting a group which has been favorable to American loans, customs control, and military intervention. When Commander Gilmore declared a neutral zone in Bluefields, in 1910, he virtually spread a protecting wing around the Estrada revolutionists who were about to be ejected from that city. Having protected them in their possession, the United States then took the position that Bluefields

. . . appears to remain as heretofore, under the *de facto* control of the Estrada faction. This government therefore admits the right of the Estrada faction to collect customs for Bluefields, and denies this right to the other faction.[3]

Not only were the government forces deprived of the military advantage which the occupation of Bluefields would certainly have given them but they were also deprived of the customs revenues which they would otherwise have received. The assistance thus rendered by the American naval officer was largely responsible for the success of the revolution, and the economic controls which were subsequently granted to the United States against the protests from members of the Nicaraguan public showed that the new government was not ungrateful.

One of the revolutionary leaders was Adolfo Diaz, who became Vice-president of the new government and shortly afterward President. Diaz was consistently friendly to the United States, and the United States in turn was anxious to keep him in power. When, in 1912, the revolutionists were menacing Managua, the declaration of a neutral zone compelled them to abandon the attack. In 1926-1927, the declaration of neutral zones was a most decided disadvantage to the Liberals. A neutral zone was declared in the revolutionary capital at Puerto Cabezas and the Liberals were given the choice of leaving the zone or delivering

[1] *For. Rel.*, 1903, p. 247.

[2] *Washington Post*, Mar. 24, 1911, quoted in NEARING, SCOTT, and FREEMAN, JOSEPH, "Dollar Diplomacy," p. 83, B. Huebsch and the Viking Press, New York, 1925.

[3] *For. Rel.*, 1910, p. 750.

up their arms.[1] All of the important ports and cities were neutralized, with the exception of Granada, thus insuring the control of the Diaz government over them. Diaz thus kept within his hands the customs service, the national railway, and the national bank, all three of which became collateral for an American loan for the purpose of suppressing the revolution.[2] The railway was likewise of importance to the Diaz government in the shipment of munitions.

LANDING PARTIES AND FORCES OF OCCUPATION

The direct employment of American troops is the most drastic method of protection and the most difficult to use with moderation. Criticism of the use of military forces has been widespread in the United States and the psychological effect abroad has been marked indeed. Violent animosities have been created among some of the people of Latin America against the United States. Hence, while the effectiveness of armed invasions cannot be questioned, the resulting state of mind of the rest of the world toward this country makes it imperative that this method be used with the utmost care, and that it shall be avoided except in extreme cases.

In Nicaragua.—An unusual combination of circumstances has given the United States government an interest in the suppression of revolution in Nicaragua. American mining and commercial companies have complained against the devastation committed by insurrectionists. American financiers have had an interest in Nicaraguan customs collections. The railway and the national bank have been pledged as security for a loan. Since 1910, for the greater part of the time, the administration of Nicaragua has been occupied by a faction which has been unusually compliant with the wishes of the Department of State. It has, therefore, suited the desires of this government to maintain the favorite Conservative faction in power. The further reason, sometimes given, that the treaty rights of the United States in a prospective Nicaraguan Canal make the maintenance of order a duty on the part of this country, has probably had more apparent than actual weight.

[1] *Current History*, Feb., 1927, pp. 735–736.

[2] Partiality for the Diaz government as against the revolutionists was admitted by the Chief of the Division of Latin American Affairs in discussing neutral zones before the Senate Committee on Foreign Relations, *The New York Times*, Mar. 10, 1927.

In 1912, shortly after the accession of Adolfo Diaz to the presidency, a revolution was begun by Luis Mena which threatened to overthrow the government. Not only did the above-mentioned reasons make interference by the United States desirable but an invitation for military intervention was issued by President Diaz as follows:

. . . my government desires that the government of the United States guarantee with its forces security for the property of American citizens in Nicaragua and that it extend its protection to all the inhabitants of the Republic.[1]

The United States hastened to send additional naval forces into Nicaraguan waters and eventually 2,600 men, 125 officers and 8 war vessels were used in the overthrow of the revolution. A stronghold of the revolutionists at Masaya was taken by assault. Mena surrendered and was deported to Panama.[2]

When most of the United States marines were withdrawn from Nicaragua, following the revolution of 1912, it was deemed wise to maintain a small force in the country as a stabilizing influence. The American minister in recommending the maintenance of such a force stated that "Withdrawal of all marines would be construed as the tacit consent of the United States to renew hostilities."[3] A force of 101 enlisted men and 4 officers of the Marine Corps was established as a Legation Guard on Jan. 9, 1913, and was maintained at approximately that strength until Aug. 3, 1925, when it was withdrawn. The effect of the maintenance of the guard was to prevent the overthrow of the established government for a period of over twelve years. On Oct. 25, less than three months after the withdrawal of the Legation Guard, General Emiliano Chamorro executed a *coup d'état* and seized the power of government.

Another important intervention took place in 1927. Adolfo Diaz, who desired to place his country under the protection of the United States, was again President. Complaints again came from American property owners in Nicaragua that they were endangered by the revolution. The intervention of the United States was first manifested by an arms control policy and the declaration of neutral zones, both of which favored the Diaz

---

[1] *For. Rel.*, 1912, p. 1032.

[2] For an account of the work of the marines see *Annual Report of the Navy Department*, 1912, p. 13; 1913, p. 38.

[3] *For. Rel.*, 1912, p. 1069.

government. More than 5,000 sailors and marines were sent into the country.[1] Later a more determined stand was taken. The President's personal representative, Col. H. L. Stimson, was sent to Nicaragua to arrange for a cessation of hostilities. He asked that the country should disarm and represented to the revolutionists that if they did not comply with his request their arms would be taken from them by the United States forces.[2] Thereupon most of the revolutionists capitulated.

The influence of American troops has been rather one sided in Nicaraguan politics. The Conservative party was maintained in power for a period from 1910 to 1925. No sooner had the Liberals secured a strong participation in the government after one of the fairest elections in the history of Nicaragua than the legation guard of the United States was withdrawn and the government was overthrown. Another Conservative government was established, and in 1927 the United States intervened with a large force of troops to defeat the Liberal revolution. Thus, the politics of Nicaragua have been manipulated in behalf of the Conservatives, which have been much more sympathetic to the aims of the United States than have their opponents. The Conservatives have given to interests of the United States the control of the customs, the bank, and the railway and have sold to the United States the right to build a canal through Nicaraguan territory.

Some of the Liberal forces refused to lay down their arms at Colonel Stimson's request, prominent among them being General Sandino. This recalcitrant Nicaraguan proceeded to occupy a mine belonging to an American at San Fernando in the northern part of the country. According to the American owner, the property which represented a $700,000 investment, was being ruined by the Nicaraguans. A request was made to the American minister for protection[3] and a detachment of marines, together with a unit of the native constabulary, was sent to recapture the mine. At Ocotal, on July 17, Sandino attacked the American position and was completely routed by a relief of airplanes which swooped down upon his troops with bombs and machine guns.[4]

---

[1] Cox, Isaac Joslin, "Nicaragua and the United States, 1909–1927." (World Peace Foundation *Pamphlets*, Vol. X, No. 7.)

[2] *State Department Press Release*, May 10, 1927; Cox, *op. cit.*, p. 800.

[3] *State Department Press Release*, July 1, 1927.

[4] *The New York Times*, July 18, 19, 1928.

His losses were estimated at about 300 killed and 100 wounded as against 1 killed and 2 wounded in the marine and constabulary forces. The hail of bombs and machine-gun bullets from the sky at Ocotal dealt a blow to insurrections in Central America. The engagement gave notice that the airplane has taken its place in the drive against revolutionism and that the hazards of disorders affecting American property have been tremendously increased. However, an energetic campaign of more than a year was necessary before the Sandino forces were dispersed.[1]

In Haiti.—Haitian domestic disorders reached a high point in the bloody excesses of 1915. "The Derelict of the Caribbean" had undergone a series of rapid changes in government in which the mortality rate among presidents had been remarkably high. The hazards of the executive office may be seen from the following list of presidents from 1908 to July, 1915 showing the manner of their exodus from office:

Simon, elected December, 1908; overthrown August, 1911.
Leconte, elected August, 1911; blown up in palace, January, 1912.
Auguste, elected August, 1912; poisoned May, 1913.
Oreste, elected May, 1913; overthrown January, 1914.
Zamor, elected February, 1914; overthrown October, 1914. (Killed in prison July 27, 1915.)
Theodore, elected November, 1914; overthrown February, 1915.
Sam, elected May, 1915; killed July, 1915.[2]

The killing of President Sam was a particularly gruesome orgy. A large number of political prisoners were shot in prison by an official of the Sam government on July 27. The President sought escape from the infuriated crowd by entering the French legation. The next morning the mob broke into the legation, seized the President, killed and dismembered him before the legation gates, and paraded hysterically with portions of his body held aloft on poles. The following day, July 29, United States sailors and marines were landed for the purpose of protecting American and foreign interests and for the preservation of order. Probably the chief reason for intervention was the fear that disorders in Haiti and financial difficulties would give

[1] For a detailed list of encounters with the revolutionary forces see Department of State, "A Brief History of the Relations between the United States and Nicaragua, 1909–1928," p. 71*ff.*

[2] "Inquiry into Occupation and Administration of Haiti and Santo Domingo," Vol. II, pp. 1777–1778.

European countries an excuse for customs control. The United States, accordingly, seized upon a moment when Europe was at war to take charge of the customhouses. The creation of a government which would look with greater favor upon American economic interests also loomed large among the reasons for intervention.

The American occupation took control of the customhouses and set to work to suppress disorders in the country. A force of marines[1] has been maintained in the country ever since, evidently waiting on the time when the Haitian *gendarmerie* shall have been sufficiently trained and disciplined to maintain order. A treaty, forced through shortly after the military occupation, gives the control of customs to the United States and is a strong additional reason for the discouragement of revolution in Haiti by the United States.

Manipulation of Haitian Government during Military Intervention.—The United States went far beyond the mere restoration of order in its military occupation of Haiti. In fact, it is doubtful if the history of American foreign policy reveals a more complete manipulation of a weaker government through the use of various methods of pressure to obtain financial controls and economic privileges in a nominally legal manner.

As has been intimated, the principal motive for intervention was the desire to take over Haitian customs control and thereby eliminate any excuse for intervention by European powers. The seizure of Haitian customhouses also suited American financial interests represented in the National Bank of the Republic of Haiti, which bank had sought to bring about cutoms control by the United States.[2]

---

[1] Stated in 1922 to have consisted on the average of about 60 officers and 1,500 enlisted men. By the end of 1927 the number of enlisted men had been reduced to 672.

[2] In explaining to the Department of State the action of the bank in 1914 in terminating a contract with Haiti to advance the ordinary monthly running expenses of the government the American Minister at Port au Prince said that this would precipitate a crisis in the affairs of Haiti and would make it impossible for the government to continue to operate. "It is just this condition that the bank desires," continued the minister, "for it is the belief of the bank that the government when confronted by such a crisis, would be forced to ask the assistance of the United States in adjusting its financial tangle and that American supervision of the customs would result." *For. Rel.*, 1914, p. 346. After intervention, bank officials successfully made representations to the Department of State for the purpose

A few weeks after the landing of American troops, all of the customhouses were taken over and administered by the forces of occupation. A treaty containing provisions for American customs control, an American financial adviser, and an American-officered constabulary was presented to Haiti for acceptance. The disinclination of the Haitians to accept these terms was strong, but was overcome by stronger methods of persuasion. The following manipulatory devices were used:

1. The signature of the treaty by the President was made a condition precedent to recognition by the United States.

2. The control of the customhouses by the United States left the Haitian government without revenues, and a period of official starvation ensued. For a time, the salaries of senators and deputies remained unpaid. When an allotment was made for the payment of the legislators it was understood that the matter of back salaries would wait until the chambers had agreed to the treaty.[1] Further promises were made that funds would be forthcoming to provide for every legitimate necessity of the Haitian government upon the ratification of the treaty.[2]

3. Banknotes to the amount of $100,000 which had been printed were to be withheld from the Haitian government until the signature of the convention.[3]

4. The United States promised that it would use its good offices to secure a loan for the Haitian government upon ratification of the treaty.[4]

5. The United States threatened that unless the treaty should be accepted either a military government would be set up until "honest" elections could be held or the control of the government would be permitted to pass to some other faction.[5]

Another instance of manipulation was seen in the installation and maintenance in power of a pliable president who, by various forms of pressure, was made subservient to the will of American

---

of securing the American occupation of all the Haitian customhouses and for a renewal of the deposits of the customs receipts with the bank according to its contract which had been abrogated by the Haitian Government. *For. Rel.*, 1915, p. 516.

[1] "Inquiry into Occupation and· Administration of Haiti and Santo Domingo," Vol. I, p. 637.

[2] *Ibid.*, p. 381; *For. Rel.*, 1915, p. 524.

[3] *For. Rel.*, 1915, p. 523.

[4] *Ibid.*, p. 447.

[5] *Ibid.*, p. 438.

officials. Just prior to the election of the President in August, 1915, Admiral Caperton, in charge of the American forces, was instructed by the Navy Department: "The United States prefers election of Dartiguenave."[1] The election, which was held in the presence of American marines, resulted in the choice of Sudre Dartiguenave. Concerning him General Cole said: "He was about the only politician in Haiti who was willing to accept office as President and father the American demands."[2] He would not have been chosen had he opposed American policies. He was not recognized until he had agreed to the signing of the desired treaty and he would have been ousted from power had he failed to act according to the wishes of the United States.[3] Dartiguenave continued in the presidency until he opposed the American occupation by a letter to President Harding, in 1921, requesting the withdrawal of the American marines upon the final organization of the *gendarmerie*. In 1922, he was succeeded by Louis Borno, who had become more satisfactory to the occupation officials.[4]

In the Dominican Republic.—The desire to maintain orderly government in the Dominican Republic has already been commented upon. In May, 1916, during a *coup d'état* in which Arias, the Minister of War, had seized control of the city of Santo Domingo, the United States landed troops for the protection of the American legation and consulate and of American life and property in general. President Jiménez was offered sufficient military aid to suppress the insurrection but he refused to accept it rather than face the disastrous consequences which he believed would follow the taking of the city of Santo Domingo by American troops. Being unable to oppose Arias successfully on

[1] "Inquiry into Occupation and Administration of Haiti and Santo Domingo," Vol. I, p. 315.

[2] *Ibid.*, Vol. II, p. 1784.

[3] See point 5, previous paragraph. See also the threat of Admiral Caperton to "proceed to the complete pacification of Haiti" if the treaty should fail, *For. Rel.*, 1915, p. 458; and see also the threat of General Cole to recommend the establishment of a military government if the President should fail to sign a decree dissolving the National Assembly in 1917. "Inquiry," Vol. I, p. 702.

[4] For a statement as to the use of bribery by Borno in the election in the Council of State see DOUGLAS, PAUL H., "The American Occupation of Haiti," *Political Science Quarterly*, Vol. XLII, p. 256. For another instance of manipulation see the amendment of the Haitian Constitution, above, p. 34.

account of the lack of ammunition, the President resigned. The United States then took action on its own account. An ultimatum was presented to Arias. He withdrew from the city which was thereupon occupied by American troops.

A new president, Dr. Henriquez, was then elected by the Dominican Congress, but the United States refused to recognize him unless he would agree to grant stricter financial control by the United States and to create an American-officered constabulary. When Henriquez refused these terms, the United States denied him recognition and also withheld from him the portion of the Dominican customs receipts which were due to the Dominican government. On Nov. 21, 1916, the Chief of the Division of Latin-American Affairs recommended to the Secretary of State that the Dominican Republic be placed under a military government. The reasons for this recommendation were that the coming elections would probably favor Arias, that Henriquez had not met the American demands, and that the withholding of the customs revenues from him had brought on an economic crisis for which the United States did not care to appear responsible. The plan was approved by Secretary Lansing and President Wilson and, on Nov. 29, the desired proclamation was issued by Captain Knapp who was in command of the United States cruiser force in Dominican waters. The reasons alleged in the proclamation were that the Dominican government had violated the Treaty of 1907 with the United States by increasing the public debt and that the United States desired to maintain domestic tranquility in the republic. [1]

Following the proclamation the American troops restored order to the country. Arms were taken from the populace, an uprising in Azua Province was suppressed, and some lawless bands were dispersed. The chief officials of the Dominican government refused, however, to cooperate with the military government and American officers were assigned to the cabinet posts. [2] The American occupation brought about order and economic improvement on the one hand and a restriction of civil liberties on the other. A plan for the gradual installation of a native Dominican government was agreed to in 1922 and the administration of affairs was placed in Dominican hands.

[1] For the above-described events see *For. Rel.*, 1916, pp. 220–249.

[2] See the reports of Captain Knapp, *For. Rel.*, 1917, pp. 709, 718.

On Sept. 17, 1924, the final detachment of American marines was withdrawn.

In Cuba.—The right of intervention by the United States provided for in the Platt Amendment was secured for the purpose of maintaining stable conditions in Cuba in order to eliminate any excuses which European governments might find to invade the country when their investments or other interests might be jeopardized. The third paragraph of the Platt Amendment provides as follows:

That the government of Cuba consents that the United States may exercise the right to intervene for the preservation of Cuban independence, the maintenance of a government adequate for the protection of life, property, and individual liberty, and for discharging the obligations with respect to Cuba imposed by the treaty of Paris on the United States, now to be assumed and undertaken by the government of Cuba.

The first interventions were for the purpose of suppressing disorders occasioned by dissatisfaction over elections. In recent years, the possibilities of European encroachment have dwindled, while the economic interests of the United States in Cuba have greatly increased. The value of property owned by Americans in the island has recently been estimated at about $1,150,000,000.[1] The significance of the American right of intervention is becoming predominantly economic in that it is an aid to the protection of the property of United States citizens.

The economic aspect of American intervention was indicated in 1917 during an insurrection which threatened the canefields and sugar mills in the eastern part of the island. Urgent appeals for relief were made to United States consular officers by Americans whose interests were threatened.[2] At the same time the imminence of the war with Germany made the sugar crop a matter of importance to the United States. Marines were sent into Cuba and a declaration was issued which warned the insurgents as follows:

The government of the United States, in emphasizing its condemnation of the reprehensible conduct of those in revolt against the Constitutional government in attempting to settle by force of arms disputes for which adequate legal remedies are provided, desires to point out that

---

[1] JENKS, "Our Cuban Colony," p. 299. See also the article "Cuba and the United States" by "O" in *Foreign Affairs*, January, 1928, p. 232, in which the holdings are placed at $1,500,000,000.

[2] See *For. Rel.*, 1917, p. 414*ff.*

until those in revolt recognize their obligations as citizens of Cuba, have laid aside their arms and returned to their allegiance to the Constitutional government, the United States cannot hold communication with any of them and will be forced to regard them as outside the law and beyond its consideration.[1]

A few months later, Secretary Lansing threatened to regard the insurgents as enemies of the United States if they did not at once cease their revolutionary activities;[2] and shortly thereafter the insurrection subsided.

AMERICAN-OFFICERED CONSTABULARIES

While the landing of American troops is the most effective method of suppressing revolution, nevertheless, there are grave objections to the use of such drastic measures. Not only is the occupation of territory by armed forces a grave shock to the sense of sovereignty of a people, even if such action is taken at the request of the established government, but there is also the unperformable task of the maintenance of discipline in a detachment of troops which is quartered among the people of a different race, color, and nationality. This task has baffled the military leaders of all conquering peoples, nor have the officers of the United States Navy or Marine Corps been able thus far to develop the spirit of obedience to such a point as to eliminate the problem. While offenses against native populations may be reduced to the minimum and frequently punished with adequate court martial sentences, there nevertheless remains the fact that crimes committed by the members of an army of occupation are certain to be considered as vastly more shocking to the populace than similar offenses committed by natives. To understand this, Americans need but to contrast the popular condemnation that arose over the "Boston massacre," with the complacency that follows the news of violence of a similar extent committed by a band of modern thugs.[3]

[1] *For. Rel.*, 1917, p. 388.

[2] *Ibid.*, p. 407.

[3] For evidence of offenses in Haiti and Santo Domingo see "Inquiry into Occupation and Administration of Haiti and Santo Domingo," pp. 425, 465–469, 474–480, 508, 579–591, 813*ff.*, 1536*ff.*, 1565*ff.*, 1786. KELSAY, CARL, "The American Intervention in Haiti and the Dominican Republic," *Annals of the American Academy of Political and Social Science*, Vol. C, pp. 142–144, 187–188. For offenses committed in Nicaragua see THOMAS, DAVID Y., "One Hundred Years of the Monroe Doctrine," pp. 298–299, The Macmillan Company, New York, 1923.

Because of these criticisms of armed occupation, it seems that a wise policy has been followed by the United States in seeking to build up native police forces or constabularies under American officers and to withdraw American troops. The constabularies, when sufficiently organized, will be able to maintain order and to protect American property and institutions for financial control. At the same time they will avoid much criticism that is levelled against a foreign occupation.

The Liberian Frontier Force.—Coincident with the undertaking of a principal part in a loan to Liberia and the control of Liberian customshouses the United States proposed a plan for rendering assistance in the organization and drilling of a Frontier Force. In pursuance of this plan, three former American army officers were appointed by the Liberian government, one to be a major and two to be captains. The work of reorganization was then undertaken under the supervision of the military attaché to the American legation in Monrovia. The Frontier Force was found to be in a demoralized condition. The President and Secretary of War of Liberia were ignorant of the number of men, officers, and guns. They did not know the location of the troops. The men had not been paid, the money for this purpose having been "jobbed" by Liberian officials. Into this hopeless array the American officers began at once the work of instilling some idea of military discipline. They also sought to procure better conditions with regard to pay, food, and clothing.[1]

The constabulary which consisted of the 3 American officers, 4 native lieutenants and 334 enlisted men soon became a dynamic force in Liberian affairs. The presence of the American officers seemed to impel respect among the natives. In one instance, when an American officer departed from an important post leaving the garrison under a native lieutenant, an uprising of the natives was staged. The revolt was timed to occur during the absence of the American commander but the accidental presence of another American officer, who had arrived to pay the troops, did much to save the situation.[2] During the Kru revolt in 1916, which threatened to interfere with customs collections at certain points, the Frontier Force engaged in a fierce battle with the revolting natives and defeated them with great slaughter. That section of the country then came for

---

[1] See report of American Military Attaché, *For. Rel.*, 1912, p. 665.

[2] *For. Rel.*, 1913, p. 683.

the first time in Liberian history under the actual control of the goverment. [1]

The Haitian Gendarmerie.—The Treaty of 1915 with Haiti, by which the United States obtained control of the Haitian customhouses, also provided in Art. X for a constabulary to be officered by Americans to be appointed by the President of Haiti upon nomination of the President of the United States. According to the treaty, the Americans are to be replaced when Haitians are found to be qualified to assume the duties of officers in the constabulary.   A board selected by the senior American officer determines the question of qualification.   At the close of 1927, the authorized strength of the constabulary, or Haitian *gendarmerie* as it is called, was reported to be 179 officers and 2,537 enlisted men. [2]

The *gendarmerie* has proved to be an effective force for the suppression of banditry.   The promotion of Haitians to occupy positions as officers has been slow, but, on the authority of Dr. Kelsey who made an investigation in 1921, "it has been hard to find Haitians whose standards approached those expected by the Americans." [3]   The following table of officers below field rank in 1917, 1922, and 1927 shows that the numbers of Haitian officers is increasing:

Year	U. S. Commissioned	Per cent	U. S. Non-commissioned	Per cent	Haitian	Per cent	Total
1917	9	10	80	85	5	5	94
1922	9	8	83	73	21	19	113
1927	15	10	83	54	55	35	153[1]

[1] *Sixth Annual Report of the American High Commissioner at Port au Prince, Haiti*, p. 25.

According to the *Annual Report of the Navy Department for 1924*,[4] the *gendarmerie* had by that time become "a well-trained, highly efficient organization."   A rifle team composed of native members captained and coached by American officers tied for

[1] *For. Rel.*, 1916, p. 456.

[2] *Sixth Annual Report of the American High Commissioner at Port au Prince, Haiti*, p. 23.   For an earlier personnel table see *For. Rel.*, 1916, p. 334.

[3] *Loc. cit.*, p. 139.

[4] *Pages 51–52.*

second place with the French team in the Olympic matches of that year, but lost by one point in the shoot-off, eventually standing third.

The Policia Nacional Dominicana.—In 1915, the United States insisted that the Dominican Republic should dissolve the inefficient and costly Dominican army, which was a tool for revolutionists, and that it should establish a constabulary which should be officered by Americans.[1] The reasons stated for this demand by the United States, aside from economy and maintenance of order, were that the new body would provide for the freedom of the customs from interference and for the full observance of the provisions of the convention with the United States. The Dominican government rejected the proposal as being "an abdication of the national sovereignty."[2] In 1916, when Dr. Henriquez was elected President, one of the conditions precedent to his recognition by the United States was that he should agree to the organization of the constabulary.[3] Again the demand was refused, although the President was willing to employ an American officer to supervise the reorganization of the army.[4]

After the United States had set up a military government in Santo Domingo, a force called the *Policia Nacional Dominicana* was organized under the auspices of the occupation officials. The new constabulary was divided into training-center forces, under American officers, and field forces, which were officered by Dominicans with the exception of the Intendant General who was an American. Recruits and cadets were attached to the training-center forces and upon completion of their training were assigned to the field forces.[5] During the occupation there was popular criticism of the *Policia* by members of the Dominican public.[6] Upon the withdrawal of the American occupation the Dominicans regained control of their constabulary. A new constitution, proclaimed in 1924, prohibits foreigners from belonging to it.[7]

[1] *For. Rel.*, 1915, pp. 298, 336–337.
[2] *Ibid.*, p. 338.
[3] *For. Rel.*, 1916, p. 235.
[4] *Ibid.*, p. 236.
[5] *Annual Report of the Navy Department*, 1923, p. 968.
[6] KELSAY, *loc. cit.*, p. 180.
[7] KNIGHT, MELVIN M., "The Americans in Santo Domingo," p. 125, Vanguard Press, New York, 1928.

The Nicaraguan Constabulary.—When it appeared that the United States was to withdraw its legation guard from Nicaragua, efforts were made to organize and train a native constabulary to take its place. In May, 1925, a bill was passed by the Nicaraguan Congress to provide for a constabulary of 400 officers and men. Major William B. Carter, former constabulary officer in the Philippines, was named chief instructor. The constabulary was, however, not able to prevent the *coup d'état* of October, 1925, when General Chamorro seized La Loma fortress in Managua. In 1927 and 1928, the native body cooperated with American marines in suppressing disorders, taking a part in the engagement at Ocotal and participating in numerous other skirmishes.

CHAPTER X

FINANCIAL SUPERVISION : CUSTOMS RECEIVERSHIPS

Loans from the financiers of the stronger industrial nations to the governments of the less developed tropical and subtropical countries, which have been increasingly numerous in the last few decades, have been frequently followed by the adoption of some kind of control over the fiscal affairs of the borrowing government. The demands of the financiers for prompt payment of interest and the regular accumulation of a sinking fund for the retirement of the debt have, in the absence of such control, been difficult for the governments of revolution-torn countries to comply with. Factions alternating in power have looted the treasury and internal disorders have frequently made necessary the diversion of all possible revenues to the military branch of government for the purpose of suppressing insurrections. The tendency in such countries has been to borrow money to meet emergencies until the load of the debt has become too heavy for the revenues of the country. Defaults and falling bond prices have ensued. Financiers have accordingly insisted upon the creation of controls to assure the application of a fixed portion of the revenues to the service of the debt. The purposes of the bankers are accomplished by pledging revenues, providing for their collection by the agents of the bankers or their government, and, in some cases, by limiting or supervising the loans and expenditures of the borrowing government.

Sometimes it has been found possible to obtain these ends by negotiation with bona fide governments which are willing to part with some of their important functions because of their desperate need of money. Controls in Salvador and Bolivia have been obtained in this way. In other cases, the debtor nation, staggering under a heavy load, is willing to submit to the financial guidance of one country in order to avoid the diplomatic nagging and possible intervention of other and more aggressive governments. Such was the situation in Santo Domingo and Liberia. Again the government seeking the control may manipulate a marionette executive into power and then make the desired arrangements. In Nicaragua a president of American creation granted financial control to the United States. Finally, military intervention may be necessary to procure the coveted right of administering the finances of some obdurate little republic. This method was found to be necessary in the case of Haiti.

In taking control over the finances of a weaker government the stronger power almost invariably acknowledges itself to be in much the same position as a trustee managing affairs for the principal benefit of the *cestui que trust.* Under fundamental rules of honesty, the controlling power should not permit the relationship to redound to the unmerited advantage of itself or its financiers at the expense of the debtor nation. Unfortunately, however, the high feeling of responsibility necessary to the fulfillment of such a trusteeship has not thus far been fully developed in the moral consciousness of any creditor nation. The sensibilities of debtor peoples have been outraged by force and brutality. Financiers have at times been enriched by a control which compels the payment of bonds at a price which renders a shockingly usurious return. The regulation of funds has frequently been used to force upon the debtor country political concessions to which the creditor nation is not entitled as a matter of right. No powerful nation in dealing with weaker countries seems to be able to resist the temptation to resolve doubtful questions in its own favor.

Despite flagrant abuses, however, financial control serves a useful purpose in restoring the public credit of bankrupt countries and in assisting to maintain stable government. Real encouragement is thus given to investment and economic development. There is unquestionably a need for a drift of capital from the industrialized countries into the backward areas, and it is doubtful if in the necessities of this great movement a large amount of financial control can be avoided. If fiscal domination is inevitable there is nevertheless a great opportunity for perfecting more equitable methods and for developing a stronger feeling of trusteeship in the statesmen of creditor nations.

THE EVOLUTION OF AMERICAN POLICY

During the debtor period of American history when large sums were being loaned to Latin-American countries by the bankers of Europe, the United States was exceedingly suspicious of any attempts by creditors to control the finances of borrowing nations in this hemisphere. The fear that political control would follow loans and investments was well supported by the facts of history. The French claims, which furnished a pretext for the invasion of Mexico in 1861, were partly based upon the default on bonds held by Frenchmen. It seems that the Mexican government had issued $15,000,000 worth of bonds for which it had received only $750,000. The bonds came into the hands of the French creditors of the original purchaser and the French government demanded that they be paid in full.[1] When the Mexican government suspended the payment of interest upon the foreign debt, France prepared to act. The consequent threat to the independence of Mexico is a familiar story. Great Britain and Spain, who acted jointly with France in the beginning of the intervention, were also moved partly by the suspension of interest payments. The blockade of Venezuelan ports and the seizure of Venezuelan gunboats in 1902 was due to the failure of Venezuela to make payments to the subjects of Germany, Great Britain, and Italy. The principal claims of Germany originated from defaults on government bonds held by Germans and on railway stock, the dividends of which had been guaranteed by the Venezuelan government.[2] In each of the two instances above mentioned the situation had held a threat of war for the United States. The American government was, accordingly, disposed whenever the intervention became a political threat to argue the case of the debtor nation against the designing creditor.

In sympathy with Latin-American opposition to armed invasion because of loans and investments, the American delegation at the Second Hague Conference advocated the adoption of what was known as the Porter Resolution, which was an adaptation of the Drago Doctrine. The resolution reads as follows:

The contracting Powers agree not to have recourse to armed force for the recovery of contract debts claimed from the government of one country by the government of another country as being due to its nationals.

This undertaking is, however, not applicable when the debtor state refuses or neglects to reply to an offer of arbitration, or, after accepting

[1] LATANÉ, JOHN HOLLADAY, "The United States and Latin America," p. 197, Doubleday, Page & Company, Garden City, N. Y. 1921.

[2] *Ibid.*, p. 250.

the offer, prevents any *compromis* from being agreed on, or, after the arbitration, fails to submit to the award.[1]

General Horace Porter, the American delegate with whose name the resolution was associated, made a notable speech in support of the measure before the First Commission of the Conference. The address deserves to rank among the best efforts of modern conference discussion. In the language of the commission's reporter the argument of General Porter was in part as follows:

The case is not infrequently that of an investor or speculator who withdraws his services and his money from his own country to risk a venture in another with the sole object of increasing his private fortune.

If he gains millions, his government does not share in the profits; but if he loses, he demands that it go even to the extent of war to secure sums claimed to be due and often grossly exaggerated.

The onerous rates exacted by a lender confirm the belief that he is assuming an extra-hazardous risk.

He not infrequently purchases in the market bonds of the debtor state at a low figure, and then makes his demands for payment at par.

In fact he is playing a game in which he expects to have recognized the principle of "Heads I win, tails you lose."

His foreign office, to which he appeals, has, generally speaking, no means at hand to make a thorough investigation of the subject, to procure and examine all the necessary documents, to inform itself as to the opposing evidence and form a correct judgment of the true merits of the case.

It has no jury to ascertain the facts, no competent and impartial court to guide it as to the law, no tribunal to pronounce upon the equity of the claim. In giving a decision the minister of foreign affairs must feel that he is violating a primary principle of the administration of justice in admitting that a case may be adjudged solely by one of the parties to the controversy.

If by so serious a means as that of armed force the amount of the claim be secured, the taxpayers of the coercing nations have to bear the expense of enriching an investor or speculator who has taken his chance of gain or loss in a foreign land, even if the cost of collection amounts to a hundred times the amount of his claim.

Perhaps there are no subjects which confront a foreign office that are more annoying and embarassing than the pecuniary claims of individual subjects or citizens against a foreign government, stated at their own valuation and pressed for payment even though this may entail the

[1] *The Proceedings of the Hague Peace Conferences, The Conference of* 1907, Vol. I, p. 616, Oxford Univ. Press, New York, 1920.

formidable question of an act of war. If it were made known that investors and speculators undertaking financial negotiations with a foreign government were expected to deal upon the principle of *caveat emptor*, or if it were understood at least that their home government would not proceed to a compulsory enforcement of their claims until such claims had been adjudicated and their true value ascertained by a competent court of arbitration, and that the debtor nation had then arbitrarily refused to abide by the award, foreign offices would be relieved of one of the most vexatious and perplexing of their duties.[1]

General Porter also stated that the exaggeration of the amounts claimed in such demands is "positively amazing" and that of thirteen large claims examined by mixed commissions during the preceding sixty years the greatest sum allowed in any case was only 80 per cent of the claim and the lowest was three-fourths of 1 per cent. He further described an instance of attempted collection of a claim by the Department of State in behalf of an American who had entered into a contract with a foreign government. The contractor claimed $90,000. After sixteen years of negotiations, during which a fleet of nineteen warships was sent and $2,500,000 in all was spent, the United States collected nothing.

Mere opposition to the financial imperialism of European governments had, even prior to the Porter resolution, been recognized by the United States as inadequate for the purpose of preventing their control over the backward countries of Latin America. There had developed a strong conviction that if the United States were to restrain European nations in the collection of their debts it must accept some responsibility for seeing that the obligations were paid. In 1861, when Great Britain, Spain, and France were contemplating the invasion of Mexico, Secretary Seward had under consideration a treaty with the Mexican government by which the United States was to assume the payment of the Mexican foreign indebtedness. Repayment to the United States was to be guaranteed by a specific lien upon all the public lands and mineral rights in Lower California, Chihuahua, Sonora, and Sinaloa. In case Mexico should fail to reimburse this country within six years, the pledged property was to become absolutely vested in the United States.[2] The matter was dropped, however, upon objection from the Senate.

[1] *The Proceedings of the Hague Peace Conferences*, Vol. II, p. 227.
[2] LATANÉ, *op. cit.*, p. 200.

In 1905, the situation in Santo Domingo seemed to be such as to create a danger of European intervention. Claims against that government were estimated at between $30,000,000 and $40,000,000, while the revenues of the republic were wholly inadequate to discharge such an obligation. As many of the creditors were European there was a real probability that they would be able to prevail upon their governments to seize some of the Dominican customhouses as security. This danger was increased by the fact that, in 1904, an American financial agent had taken over the customhouse at Puerto Plata under an agreement with the Dominican government to protect the interests of an American corporation, the San Domingo Improvement Company. Such a preference to an American creditor naturally suggested to European bondholders similar action by their governments.[1]

At this point President Roosevelt felt obliged to take steps to safeguard the Monroe Doctrine. On Feb. 4, 1905, a convention was signed giving to the United States the right to assume charge of all of the Dominican customhouses for the purpose of guaranteeing payments to the public creditors. When the Senate refused its assent to the convention, President Roosevelt carried out the arrangement under an executive agreement with the President of the Dominican Republic. In 1907, the arrangement was made more formal by the conclusion of a convention under which the President of the United States was given the power to appoint a General Receiver of Dominican Customs and other employes in his discretion. Provision was made for applying part of the customs receipts to the expenses of the receivership and the service of the debt. The remainder was to be turned over to the Dominican government. This arrangement is still in force.

To safeguard Central America against European encroachment, Secretary of State Knox made notable attempts to obtain customs control and refunding loans in Honduras, Nicaragua, and Guatemala in 1911, 1912, and 1913. Public opinion was not yet ready to back "dollar diplomacy" to this extent. The treaty with Honduras failed to obtain the consent of either the United States Senate or the Honduran Congress, the treaty with Nicaragua failed in the Senate, while the arrangement under

[1] STUART, GRAHAM H., "Latin America and the United States," pp. 220–221, The Century Company, New York, 1922.

negotiation between the Department of State and Guatemala was defeated by British opposition which appeared in the form of a warship along the Guatemalan coast. In Nicaragua, the bankers went ahead with a smaller loan than was contemplated by the proposed treaty, and by private arrangement they were able to obtain the right to select a Collector General of Customs, the same to be nominated by the bankers and approved by the Department of State. The arrangement was made in 1912.

Meanwhile the African Republic of Liberia, fearful of British financial and political domination, had asked for American assistance. In 1910, after a report by an American commission which had been sent to investigate Liberian conditions, the Department of State requested certain American bankers to participate in an international refunding loan. The loan agreement provided for an issuance of bonds up to $1,700,000.[1] The form of security proposed by the United States and accepted by Liberia and her creditors was the pledge of the customs receipts to be guaranteed by an international receivership consisting of an American Receiver General, designated by the President of the United States, and three Assistant Receivers of British, French, and German nationality, each designated by his own government.[2] The plan went into effect in 1912.

Some precedents for customs control were thus established by Mar. 4, 1913, when President Wilson took the oath of office. One of Wilson's first important pronouncements was to disavow the principle of revenue control in China. In refusing to request the American group to continue in the consortium plan for a reorganization loan to China in which the administration of certain taxes was pledged, the President said that the conditions of the loan seemed to touch very nearly the administrative integrity of China, and that he did not feel that his administration ought, even by implication, to be a party to those conditions.[3] But in the diplomacy of a great creditor nation and a rising world power such scruples could have no permanent place.

In the first half of 1914, the American government became concerned over the possibility of armed interventions by a

---

[1] The bonds actually issued amounted to $1,558,000.

[2] Text of the agreement is printed in BUELL, "The Native Problem in Africa," Vol. II, p. 865.

[3] *For. Rel.*, 1913, p. 170. The United States, however, had long been a party to a system of control of Chinese customs.

number of European powers in Haiti for the collection of interest upon the Haitian indebtedness to their nationals. France, Germany, and the United States were each desirous of obtaining control of the Haitian customhouses. When the United States proposed to take sole charge, both Germany and France raised objections. Those governments presented a plan for a tripartite control arrangement in which each country should be represented in the personnel of the collection service in proportion to the claims held by its nationals.[1] As only about 5 per cent of the claims were due to the citizens of the United States the proposition met with no favor in this country. After the outbreak of the European War and during a bloody uprising in Haiti, the United States grasped the opportunity to land troops. The seizure of customhouses speedily followed, and the Treaty of 1915 was concluded after what was probably the most striking application of pressure in the history of American treaty negotiations.[2] The agreement provided for customs control by the United States.

The Haitian treaty, coming in the administration of the most idealistic of presidents, was evidence of the passing of official objections to the control of revenues of weaker countries.[3] There remained one more task to be accomplished—the refunding of the indebtedness of the Caribbean and Central American countries in New York. This process is now well under way. Gradually British, French, and German capital has been retired from the public debts of those countries and American capital has become increasingly important. Financial control which was instigated to protect the investments of European bankers has remained and has been strengthened to protect the investments of Americans. The evolution of American attitude toward customs control from suspicion to cautious approach and finally to hearty and wholesale adoption has been the political concomitant of financial development. Today the United States has financial control over more backward countries than any other nation.[4]

[1] *The New York Times*, May 14, 1914.

[2] See above, p. 166.

[3] The objections to revenue control in China were withdrawn and a new consortium formed in President Wilson's second term.

[4] BUELL, RAYMOND LESLIE, "International Relations," p. 397, Henry Holt & Company, New York, 1925. See Chap. XVIII of that work for an excellent discussion of the general subject of financial control.

Financial control is the American adaptation of imperialism. Altogether such control appears to be a modern method which has great advantages over outright annexation. The troubles of local administration are largely avoided. The sensibilities of the controlled people are not outraged to the same extent as in occupation. A large amount of opportunity for native political experience and development is retained. And security for investment is largely achieved.

FORMS OF CUSTOMS RECEIVERSHIPS

The most important type of control from the standpoint both of the stabilization of finances and of political manipulation is the customs receivership. The revenues of the backward countries come largely from import and export duties. Because of the vital relationship between tariffs and the whole field of business, the control of the customs administration carries with it an important influence in the economic and political life of the country. Hence, the influence of the customs receivership has been profoundly felt even outside the fiscal system of the controlled state.

The Dominican Republic.—The first customs receivership to be placed under the authority of the United States was that in the Dominican Republic. A description of this receivership will serve to bring out the chief features of the form of control. Conventions between the United States and the Dominican Republic provide:

That the President of the United States shall appoint a General Receiver of Dominican customs, who, with such Assistant Receivers and other employees of the Receivership as shall be appointed by the President of the United States in his discretion, shall collect all the customs duties accruing at the several customs houses of the Dominican Republic until the payment or retirement of any and all bonds issued by the Dominican government in accordance with the plan and under the limitations as to terms and amounts hereinbefore recited.[1]

The General Receiver is responsible to the Bureau of Insular Affairs of the War Department. In the conduct of his office he is also guided by the policy of the Department of State as expressed through the American minister.

[1] Article I of the Convention of 1907, *Treaties, etc., between the United States and other Powers*, Vol. I, p. 419; also Art. I of the Convention of 1924, *Treaty Series*, No. 726.

There are three main purposes for which expenditures of the funds thus collected are to be made:

1. For the expenses of the receivership. Formerly 5 per cent of the customs collections were allotted for this purpose, but recently a fixed sum is set aside in the budget.

2. For the service of the indebtedness, including (a) interest payments, (b) amortization, and (c) the purchase and cancellation or retirement and cancellation of bonds as may be directed by the Dominican government.

3. The remainder is to be paid to the Dominican government.

In 1926, the cost of the receivership was $214,777.60, the amount accrued for the service of the indebtedness was $2,563,-953.54, and the amount paid to the Dominican government or disbursed in its behalf was $1,928,709.56.[1]

The number of employes in the Dominican Customs Receiver-ship on Dec. 31, 1926 was as follows:

Office of the General Receiver...........	25 (includes two Americans, the General Receiver and the auditor).
Special inspectors.....................	4 (includes two Americans).
Purchasing agent in New York.........	1 (an American).
Land ports, Haitian frontier............	3 (includes one American, the deputy receiver in charge).
Deputy receivers, entry ports...........	9 (no Americans included).

Adding the employes at the customhouses to the number, there were altogether 178 in the service of which 6 were Americans, 1 was a British subject, and 171 were Dominicans.[2]

Some controversy has taken place between the United States and the Dominican Republic over the terms of the treaty with reference to the appointment of officials under the General Receiver. By agreement, the President of the Dominican Republic has appointed the collectors and subordinate officials of the receivership. The power of the Dominican President to remove efficient employes for political reasons has, however, given rise to dispute.[3] The United States objected, in 1915, when the Dominican President sought to remove experienced deputy receivers against the protest of the General Receiver. At that time the Department of State sought to make the employes

---

[1] *Report of the Dominican Customs Receivership*, pp. 2–3, 1926.

[2] *Ibid.*, p. 96.

[3] *For. Rel.*, 1907, pp. 311–312; 1915, p. 299*ff*.

secure in their tenure by the adoption of civil service restrictions against political removals. The Dominican government, however, refused to agree.

Haiti.—In Haiti the General Receiver and "such aids and employees as may be necessary" are appointed by the President of Haiti upon nomination by the President of the United States. The duties of the receivership are to "collect, receive and apply" all customs duties.[1] The General Receiver now also holds the post of Financial Adviser.

Nicaragua.—The office of Collector General in Nicaragua was created in an agreement with the American bankers, Brown Brothers and J. and W. Seligman, for the purchase of $1,500,000 of gold treasury bills on Sept. 1, 1911. The Collector General is appointed by the Nicaraguan government upon the designation of the bankers and the approval of the Secretary of State.[2] A High Commission has been provided to settle disputes between the Collector General and the Nicaraguan government. It is likewise endowed with other important powers relative to the public debt and the budget. The High Commission is composed of one member who is appointed by the President of Nicaragua and one who is appointed by the Secretary of State of the United States. A third member with the power of arbitrator in case of dispute between the other two is also appointed by the Secretary of State.[3]

Liberia.—The 1912 international control over Liberian customs has been replaced by an agreement entered into in 1927 by the Finance Corporation of America, which was created for the purpose by the Firestone interests. Under the 1927 agreement, the Liberian customs, as well as other revenues, are collected under the "supervision" of the Financial Adviser who is designated by the President of the United States and appointed by the President of Liberia. He is removed by the President of Liberia upon request of the President of the United States. The Deputy Adviser and supervisors are nominated by the Financial

---

[1] Convention of 1915. For a dispute as to the extent of this function see *For. Rel.*, 1916, pp. 364–365.

[2] Text of the agreement is printed in Dunn, "American Foreign Investments," p. 340.

[3] Financial Plan of 1917, Art. I, Sec. 3 and Art. VII. The text of the plan is given in "Hearings on Foreign Loans," before the subcommittee of the Committee on Foreign Relations, United States Senate, p. 167, Govt. Printing Office, Washington, 1925.

Adviser, who must first report the names to the Secretary of State of the United States. They are then appointed and commissioned by the President of Liberia. They are subject to removal by the President of Liberia at the request of the Financial Adviser although under certain circumstances they can be removed without the Financial Adviser's consent.[1]

Salvador.—Participation in the appointment of customs collectors in Salvador by the Department of State is somewhat less direct, but there is, nevertheless, a definite connection between the collection arrangement and the department. In 1923, the government of Salvador provided for a refunding of its national debt by the issuance of approximately $18,500,000 of new bonds. The bonds were sold in the United States and were secured by an absolute first lien on 70 per cent of the customs revenues. The extension of the first lien to cover the whole of the customs revenues is provided for in case the 70 per cent should not prove to be sufficient. The collection of the customs duties is placed under the supervision of an agent of the New York bankers, this having been made possible by an exchange of notes with the Department of State. It is provided in case of disagreement between the agent of the bankers and the government of Salvador that the matter shall be referred to the Chief Justice of the United States Supreme Court through the Secretary of State. In case of default it is stipulated that a Collector of Customs is to be chosen and in such instance the Department of State agrees to assist the bankers in the selection of two nominees from which the government of Salvador shall appoint the Collector.[2]

Bolivia.—An arrangement which on its face is purely private was made for the supervision of the collection of Bolivian revenues by nominees of American bankers in 1922. The contract between the Equitable Trust Company of New York with regard to the $33,000,000 loan of that year[3] provided for a pledge of the import and export duties along with certain internal taxes. So long as any of the bonds remain outstanding the collection of all taxes, revenues, and income of the nation is

[1] The author has not been able to see a copy of this agreement and understands that it is unavailable. Dr. Raymond L. Buell who visited Liberia in 1926, has published the details in his work, "The Native Problem in Africa," Vol. II, p. 839*ff.*

[2] "Hearings on Foreign Loans," pp. 129–130.

[3] Only $29,000,000 was actually taken up.

placed under the supervision of a Permanent Fiscal Commission appointed by the President of Bolivia, two of the three commissioners being recommended by the bankers.[1] While the Department of State is not mentioned in the terms of the contract there is little doubt but that in line with its regular policies the support of the department will be given to the bankers in enforcing the agreement in case of dispute.

China.—The United States also has a share in the international customs control of China. The Maritime Customs Administration, which is mostly officered by foreigners, originated in an agreement made in 1854 between the Taotai of Shanghai and the British, French, and American consuls at that port. The agreement was necessary on account of the anarchy in the customs caused by the Taiping Rebellion. It provided that three foreigners should have charge of the customs at Shanghai. An Englishman, a Frenchman, and an American were chosen. Later the jurisdiction of the body spread to all of the maritime customs of China. By an agreement with Great Britain, China promised that so long as the British should lead in Chinese trade the Inspector General should be a British subject.[2] According to a description written in 1919 the service employed something over a thousand foreigners and about six thousand Chinese.[3] Despite the fact that the Maritime Customs Administration is an instrumentality of the Chinese government, few Chinese are admitted to the higher posts.[4]

The United States also considers that the surplus customs revenues are pledged as security for a number of American loans. In case of some of these obligations the Chinese government has promised that in times of default or failure of the specific security pledged the payments will be made from other sources. The Department of State has taken the position that

---

[1] See text of Art. V of loan agreement, "Hearings on Foreign Loans," p. 140; DUNN, "American Foreign Investments," p. 270; MARSH, MARGARET A., "The Bankers in Bolivia," p. 156, Vanguard Press, New York, 1928. Also see McQUEEN, CHARLES A., "Bolivian Public Finance," *Trade Promotion Series*, No. 6, Bureau of Foreign and Domestic Commerce.

[2] MacMURRAY, "Treaties and Agreements with and Concerning China," Vol. I, p. 105.

[3] KING, GERALD, in the *Far Eastern Review*, February, 1919, p. 67 *et seq.*, cited in WILLOUGHBY, "Foreign Rights and Interests in China," Vol. II, p. 772.

[4] WILLOUGHBY, *op. cit.*, Vol. II, p. 774.

this promise gives an automatic priority with regard to any surplus customs funds. On at least two occasions the department has objected when the Chinese government has sought to raise new loans by pledging the surplus customs receipts as security.[1]

RESULTS OF CUSTOMS CONTROL

Elimination of European Powers from the Caribbean Area.— The aim of the United States to prevent European powers from acquiring customs control in countries in the region of the Caribbean has been commented upon previously. This object has been achieved. Not only has American control assisted in maintaining regular payments of interest and principle upon bonds held by Europeans, but the European-owned bonds have been largely replaced by American-owned securities. The floating of the refunding issues has been made possible to a considerable extent by a feeling of security due to the United States customs control. The $16,000,000 issue of bonds for refunding in Haiti in 1922 is an illustration of the displacement of European capital.[2] With the weakening of European nations economically and politically by the World War, the growth in power of the United States, and the multiplication of American investments in the Caribbean and Central America, the actual danger of European encroachments is now reduced to a minimum if it has not entirely disappeared. In like manner customs control has helped to avoid the dangers of British and French intervention in Liberia.

Improvement of Credit.—American customs control has gone far to stabilize the finances of the controlled countries. The former uncertainties of revenue due to corruption and revolution have been largely eliminated and the regular application of a definite percentage of funds to the service of the public debt has done much to strengthen the credit of such controlled countries as the Dominican Republic, Haiti, Liberia, and Nicaragua.

The Dominican receivership has accomplished a great deal in reversing the previous tendency to increase the public debt. The amount of the debt has been decreased during a period of

[1] For one instance see WILLOUGHBY, *op. cit.*, Vol. II, p. 1008. For another see *The New York Times*, Aug. 26, 1926.

[2] Secretary Knox was the father of this policy although his attempts at general refunding in Nicaragua, Guatemala, and Honduras were unsuccessful. Customs control was an integral part of his plan.

substantial expenditures in public improvements. Interest payments have been regularly maintained. In 1905, the indebtedness of the republic was estimated at its nominal or face value to amount to over $40,000,000. Adjustments which involved a generous scaling down of these claims reduced the total to about $17,000,000 which was settled by cash payment. To accomplish this liquidation a bond issue of $20,000,000 was provided for in 1908. The margin between the $17,000,000 in claims and the amount of the bond issue was utilized in public improvements and the purchase of concessions. The 1908 bonds are now retired but additional issues have been necessary. At the end of 1926, the bonded indebtedness of Santo Domingo amounted to $15,000,000.[1] The value of the public improvements made during this period has been estimated to be considerably greater than the outstanding debt.[2]

In Nicaragua and Haiti there has been a vast improvement of public credit during the period of customs control. This improved credit may be measured by the rise in the price of government bonds. The Ethelburga interests of England paid 75 for the issue of 6 per cent Nicaraguan bonds in 1909.[3] American customs control was instrumental in making Nicaraguan bonds a safer investment. A bank credit of $1,000,000, bearing interest at 6 per cent, was obtained from American banks in 1927 at 99 cents on the dollar.[4] Just prior to American intervention in Haiti the credit of that country had been almost exhausted by a series of revolutions resulting in increased expenditures and a dissipation of government funds. A deficit of $1,281,288.15 for the fiscal year of 1912–1913 was partly covered by a 6⅔ per cent bond issue which, allowing for a fictitious rate of exchange permitted in the transaction, sold at 61. In the following year a deficit of $3,015,534.84 was partially covered by three 6⅔ per cent issues which sold at prices calculated to be 59, 56, and 47.[5] After seven years of

[1] *Report of the Dominican Customs Receivership*, 1926, p. 9.

[2] For a criticism of the high rates of interest charged in 1921, refuting somewhat the claims of sound credit, see the testimony of LEWIS S. GANNETT, "Hearings on Foreign Loans," p. 11.

[3] *For. Rel.*, 1913, p. 1043.

[4] Cox, *op. cit.*, p. 807.

[5] "Inquiry into Occupation and Administration of Haiti and Santo Domingo," Vol. II, pp. 1223–1224.

American customs control the 1922 6 per cent issue, amounting to $18,000,000, sold to the bankers at 92.1.

An improvement in credit is, however, not so easily arguable from a scrutiny of the price of bonds after fifteen years of customs control in Liberia. The 5 per cent bonds, issued under the 1912 agreement, of which $1,588,000 worth were sold, brought 93 to the Liberian government. The $2,500,000 7 per cent loan of 1927 brought 90. The lower price in 1927 was not due to customs control, of course, but to the desperate experiences of Liberia during the World War.[1] The bargaining power of the Firestone concession, which was expected to bring prosperity to Liberia, was instrumental in bringing about an acceptance of the terms of the 1927 loan.[2]

Control over Customs Rates.—The controversy which has continued for decades concerning foreign control of the tariff rates in China has well illustrated the power which such control gives over the economic life of the controlled country and the infringement of fiscal autonomy which results. A system of individual treaties between the powers and China has fixed the rates of duties which China is permitted to charge upon the imports of the treaty powers. The rates fixed in the treaties are specific but were in the beginning intended to correspond to a rate of 5 per cent on an ad valorem basis. As prices rose the specific duties became much less than 5 per cent. The rates were revised in 1902, 1918, and 1922 to correspond to an effective 5 per cent. The Chinese have objected vigorously to the control of their tariff rates. They feel that they have been deprived of needed governmental revenues and point out that the Chinese government is unable to use its tariff system for the protection of home industries. Accordingly, tariff autonomy is

---

[1] The price of the 1912 bonds had sunk to 55 in 1921.

[2] Whether the Department of State added its influence to persuade Liberia to accept the Firestone project and, therefore, the loan, which was a part of the plan, has been a matter of controversy. Dr. Buell, after consulting with citizens and officials in Liberia, arrived at the conclusion that such an influence was exerted. ("The Native Problem in Africa," Vol. II, p. 845.) This conviction was expressed at the Williamstown Institute of Politics in 1928, and was answered by a denial issued from the Department of State and also by a letter from President King of Liberia stating that the department exerted no influence with regard to the Firestone projects. (*The New York Times*, Aug. 30, 1928, Sept. 1, 1928; *State Department Press Release*, Aug. 31, 1928.)

demanded by Chinese nationalists as one of the attributes of sovereignty.[1]

Control over duties has been brought about in a number of the agreements for customs receiverships by provisions that the rates cannot be changed without the consent of the United States government or of the bankers during the life of the treaty or agreement.[2] Disputes over the matter of such changes have occurred from time to time. The United States has on several occasions refused to recognize as valid Haitian laws and decrees lowering the tariff rates without American consent.[3]

A controversy with the government of the Dominican Republic, in 1911 raised the question as to whether the levy of a new internal tax affecting imports was a violation of the terms of the treaty which provided that the import duties could not be modified except by previous agreement with the United States. A Dominican law of the previous year provided for the imposition of a stamp tax on foreign and domestic letters of exchange, on foreign lottery tickets which might be brought into the Republic, and on certain other articles of import. Another law provided for a municipal surtax to be levied by the commune of Santo Domingo upon articles of import. The United States protested that these were in substance and effect additional import duties for which the consent of the United States had not been obtained, while the Dominican government took the position that they were internal taxes and not affected by the treaty. The Department of State finally suspended protest but maintained its right to object as a matter of principle and to be consulted in the future on such matters.[4] In 1925 a law was passed, however, which placed an internal consumption tax on a large number of

---

[1] A notable treaty granting tariff autonomy to China and at the same time asserting the principle of most-favored-nation treatment was signed by the American Minister and the Nationalist Minister of Finance at Peking on July 25, 1928.

[2] Article III of the Convention of 1907 with the Dominican Republic; Art. IV of the Convention of 1924 with the Dominican Republic; Art. IX of the Treaty of 1915 with Haiti; Art. V, Sec. 4 of the agreement of 1911 between American bankers and Nicaragua; Art. I, Secs. 4, 5, and 6 of the Nicaraguan Financial Plan of 1917. For the provision in the 1927 Liberian agreement, see BUELL, "Native Problem in Africa," Vol. II, p. 842.

[3] "Inquiry into Occupation of Haiti and Santo Domingo," pp. 1406, 1432.

[4] See *For. Rel.*, 1911, p. 141, for this dispute. For an illustration of an agreement for changing import duties see pp. 139–140.

imported articles. The tax, according to the General Receiver, had the effect of reducing imports.[1]

The 1927 agreement with Liberia provides that the rates of revenues allocated to the service of the loan shall not be decreased without the approval of the Fiscal Agent, which is the National City Bank of New York.

Evidence that the control of customs rates may on occasion result in much damage to the controlled country was given by John A. McIlhenny, Financial Adviser to Haiti, before the Senate Committee in 1922. About 75 per cent of the Haitian customs revenues were at that time specifically pledged to the payment of certain debts while the Treaty of 1915 bound Haiti not to modify the duties without the previous consent of the United States. The export duties on coffee provided approximately 32 per cent of the customs duties. In normal times, most of the Haitian coffee had been sold in France, in which market it received special tariff concessions and from where it was distributed throughout Europe. The slump in the sales to France caused by the war made it desirable to find customers elsewhere, preferably in the United States. An export tax of 3 cents per pound, however, made it impossible for Haitian coffee to compete with Brazilian coffee in the American market. Haitian peasants, not being able to obtain a reasonable price, refused to bring their coffee into the towns. The inability to repeal the export tax made relief to the producers impossible.[2] The refunding loan of 1922, however, made possible the enactment of a more satisfactory tariff law through retiring the old debts to the payment of which specific tariff revenues had been pledged.

The Right of Intervention to Protect Customs Control.— Diplomatic intervention and the use of armed forces for the purpose of supporting and protecting the customs receivership constitute the ultimate guarantee of the rights of the bondholder. Specific provision is sometimes made in the control agreement for such protection. Article II of the Dominican Convention of 1907 provides that:

The government of the United States will give to the General Receiver and his assistants such protection as it may find to be requisite for the performance of their duties.

[1] *Report of the Dominican Customs Receivership*, 1926; p. 1; Knight, *op. cit.*, p. 126.

[2] "Inquiry into the Occupation and Administration of Haiti and Santo Domingo," Vol., II pp. 1234, 1235.

The provision is repeated verbatim in the Dominican Convention of 1924. A clause to the like effect is found in the Haitian Treaty of 1915. The agreement between Nicaragua and the American bankers of 1911 stipulates that the bankers have the right "to solicit the Department of State for protection against the violation of this agreement," while the financial plan of 1917 expressly provides for the submission of such disputes to the American controlled High Commission for settlement. The bankers of the 1923 loan to Salvador evidently believed with excellent reason that the provision for the reference of disputes concerning the loan contract to a federal judge carried with it the strong probability of American intervention to enforce any arbitral award. Their prospectus commented upon the subject as follows:

It is simply not thinkable that, after a federal judge has decided any question or dispute between the bondholders and the Salvador government, the United States government should not take the necessary steps to sustain such decision. There is a precedent in a dispute between Costa Rica and Panama, in which a warship was sent to carry out the verdict of the arbiters.[1]

Without specific clauses in the agreements, however, the growing policies of protecting American interests abroad make it more than probable that the department will not only support the receiverships in times of domestic trouble but will also be inclined to accept the advocacy of the bankers' case in controversies with the established government.

Political Control through Customs Supervision.—Customs supervision sometimes carries with it the ability to exert influence in the internal affairs of the controlled country through the power to withhold customs receipts from the government, or to increase the government allotment of funds in exchange for a consideration. The power of enlarging or withholding the governmental income has several times been used by the United States to compel the adoption of measures desired by this country.

During the desperate financial crisis of 1914–1915 in Santo Domingo, the Dominican government complained that the treaty allotment of funds was insufficient and asked the United States to increase the governmental portion during the period of the difficulty. Mr. Sullivan, the American minister, perceived

[1] "Hearings on Foreign Loans," p. 3.

the opportunity to obtain desired legislation from the Dominican government and telegraphed the following advice to the Department of State: "I believe that now is the time to demand reforms. Government never so reasonable."[1] The United States demanded and the Dominican government, for the time being, acquiesced in a plan for an American financial adviser and for the abolition of the practice of holding prisoners without trial or hearing. The use of such tactics was well adapted to the problem of dealing with the Dominican government according to Stewart Johnson, who became chargé upon the departure of Minister Sullivan. Mr. Johnson, in a series of recommendations to the Department, said:

> In my opinion only by trading concessions within our lawful power to grant or withhold can we hope successfully to impose upon the Dominican government measures for internal reform which as such we cannot in all cases clearly demand as of right.[2]

During the year 1916, the United States continued to negotiate with the Dominican government with regard to the powers of the Financial Adviser and also regarding the establishment of an American-officered constabulary. Finally, the American minister lost patience with the unwilling Dominican government and advised the General Receiver to suspend immediately all disbursements of Dominican funds "until a complete understanding is reached in regard to interpretation of certain articles of the Convention or until this government is amicable."[3] The loss of revenue caused consternation among Dominican officials but they refused to concede the American demands, and military intervention ensued.

The power which may be wielded through the restriction of funds was likewise illustrated in the negotiations leading up to the treaty of 1915 with Haiti. Following American military occupation in 1915, the United States forces took charge of the customhouses and funds were doled out to the Haitian government according to a limited schedule. The Haitian officials were told, however, that ample funds would be forthcoming so soon as the treaty should be ratified. This financial pressure and the promise of financial abundance undoubtedly had much

---

[1] *For. Rel.*, 1914, p. 196.

[2] *For. Rel.*, 1915, p. 320.

[3] *For. Rel.*, 1916, p. 252.

to do with securing favorable action by the Haitian President and Congress.

Control over customs has also in several instances been a decisive weapon in opposing revolutions. In 1913, Secretary Bryan informed the Dominican revolutionary leader, Jesús Céspedes and also Horacio Vásquez, who was suspected of revolutionary activities, that, if the revolution should succeed, the *de facto* government would not be recognized and the portion of the customs duties belonging to Santo Domingo would be withheld as long as an unrecognized *de facto* government should exist.[1] In the Nicaraguan Civil War of 1926–1927 the United States by the declaration of neutral zones protected the customs service which is under the American Collector General. By thus extending protection the stipulated revenues of the Nicaraguan government, which amounted to $80,000 per month for ordinary expenditures and $15,000 per month for extraordinary expenditures, were guaranteed to the recognized Diaz faction. The Sacasa forces were prohibited from collecting import duties on timber in places under their control although such duties were not included in the financial plan.[2]

Political power and the economic advantages to which it may give birth are sometimes the main reasons behind customs-supported loans, and are more important to the lenders than the profits which are to come from the loan itself. The importance of these subsurface advantages is well illustrated by the efforts of the Firestone interests to saddle a loan upon Liberia and thereby obtain sufficient control in the country to protect and advance their rubber-planting concessions. Mr. Firestone insisted that there should be a loan to Liberia as part of the general rubber concession plan, and his first proposal contained a clause for a control agreement which was so drastic that the Liberian government rejected it. The Liberian cabinet also took the position that any loan must come from interests wholly unconnected with Mr. Firestone. Then Firestone called into being the Finance Corporation of America which company eventually made the loan. Dr. Buell states concerning this company:

[1] *For. Rel.*, 1913, p. 427.

[2] Statement of Juan Sacasa, *The New York Times*, Jan. 10, 1927, reprinted in *Cong. Rec.*, Vol. 68, p. 1412.

While the Liberians may have believed that this is an independent organization, it is apparently an institution which Mr. Firestone established and financed for the purpose of making this loan.[1]

A second dispute arose over the permanence of the financial control. Firestone demanded a provision that no floating debt could be incurred and no loan obtained during the life of the bonds without the consent of the Financial Adviser. The bonds were to run for forty years. The intention was to prevent a refunding loan which would substitute French or British capital for American capital and likewise French or British financial supervisors for the American officials. It was feared that French or British rubber concessions might follow the displacement of Americans in Monrovia. Liberia, however, objected to being tied in this manner. The charges of the loan were heavy and more favorable rates could undoubtedly be obtained before the end of the forty-year period. After much negotiation and after Firestone had once threatened to call off the whole deal, a twenty-year compromise was reached. Thus it appears that to Mr. Firestone financial supervision in Liberia was obtained primarily for the purpose of controlling the Liberian government in matters not connected with the safety of the loan.[2]

[1] BUELL, "The Native Problem in Africa," Vol. II, p. 837.

[2] *Ibid.*, Vol. II, p. 837*ff.*

CHAPTER XI

FINANCIAL SUPERVISION : OTHER FORMS OF CONTROL

THE COLLECTION OF INTERNAL REVENUES

The establishment of a foreign-administered internal revenue service in a financially controlled country is in some ways a more serious matter than the setting up of a customs receivership. Customs collections are directly made upon foreign shippers and the indirect consequences upon the people, while highly important, are not so easily traceable. The foreign control of internal tax collections evokes greater popular resentment. Aside from the infringement of national sovereignty, proposals to surrender control of this function of government have sometimes offended native officials who have derived political benefit and financial gain from the ability to manipulate collections. On the other hand, the American government has not always been satisfied with customs control, but has found that the demands for increased allotments made upon it by the financially supervised government have made desirable control over internal revenues. The possibilities of violent fluctuations in foreign trade have made it precarious to rely entirely upon customs duties as security for loans. A well-developed system of internal taxation greatly supplements the customs revenues and acts as a stabilizer in times of need.[1] Furthermore, it is possible for a government whose customs are pledged to the payment of a foreign loan to place internal revenue duties on imported articles and thus sidestep the customs control. The Dominican government[2] and the government of Liberia[3] have both used this method.

In the Dominican Government.—For a year or so prior to the American intervention of 1916 in the Dominican Republic, the attention of the United States had been called to the deplorable condition of the internal revenue collection service. Revenue stamps had been given away or sold at a heavy discount. Min-

[1] "Inquiry into Occupation and Administration of Haiti and Santo Domingo," Vol. II, p. 1237.

[2] See above, p. 191.

[3] BUELL, "The Native Problem in Africa," Vol. II, pp. 808–809.

ister Russell reported that the internal taxes produced $450,000 per annum, whereas, by efficient and honest methods of collection, the sum could have been increased to at least $1,200,000.[1] A large annual deficit had occurred in Dominican finances. Consequently, requests had been made to the United States for advances of funds in addition to those provided by the treaty. These repeated supplications caused the Department of State to consider the possibility of obtaining control over internal revenue collections.

In 1914, when the Dominican government requested financial assistance from the United States in meeting back salaries, Secretary Bryan declared that the Department of State was willing to arrange the advance, provided the Dominican government would pledge and turn over the collection of alcohol and tobacco taxes to the Receivership.[2] The Dominican government countered with an offer to pledge the taxes without parting with the right of collection. Later in the year following the election of Jiménez the collection of these taxes by the receivership was made a condition precedent to his recognition.[3] Despite the fact that this condition was evidently accepted, the Dominican government continued to resist the transfer of the collection service. In June, 1916, however, after the refusal of another demand the Receivership proceeded to take charge of the collections over the protests of the Dominican officials.[4] After the American military government was established a number of reforms were made in the process of collection. Evaders of the taxes were penalized and the receipts began to increase at a rapid rate.[5] The income from the alcohol tax, which had averaged $210,000 annually in the years from 1909–1916, had soared upward to $809,270.21 by 1919. The entire internal revenue collections had increased from $450,000 in 1915 to $2,575,055 by 1923 and to $2,998,686 by 1924.[6] When the

---

[1] *For. Rel.*, 1915, p. 327.

[2] *For. Rel.*, 1914, p. 216.

[3] *Ibid.*, p. 256.

[4] *For. Rel.*, 1916, pp. 251–252.

[5] "Inquiry into Occupation and Administration of Haiti and Santo Domingo," Vol. II, pp. 994–995.

[6] For a good short summary of the Dominican financial situation see an article on Santo Domingo in the *Encyclopaedia Britannica*, 13th ed., Vol. 31, p. 464, written by Jacob H. Hollander, formerly Financial Adviser of the Dominican Republic.

military forces of the United States were withdrawn in 1924 the administration of the internal revenue service was turned back to the Dominican government.

In Haiti.—The United States found a similar condition in the internal revenue service in the Haitian Republic. In 1920–1921 the collections from this source amounted to but $360,000, whereas, according to the American Financial Adviser, an efficient administration of the system would have made possible the collection of $1,000,000.[1] American supervision of assessment and collection was proposed in 1921 but the Haitian authorities resisted the suggestion.[2] In 1924, however, the amenable Council of State approved a law creating an Internal Revenue Bureau which operates under the supervision and control of the American Receiver General of Customs. The director and other employes, according to this law, are appointed by the President of Haiti upon the nomination of the Haitian Minister of Finance and the Receiver General.[3] The first appointee to the directorship of the bureau was Dr. William E. Dunn, then serving as Acting Commercial Attaché of the United States Embassy at Lima. For the fiscal year 1925–1926 the internal revenue receipts under the new system reached the highest point in Haitian history, amounting to $831,034.06.[4] For 1926–1927 the collections were $830,657.59.[5]

In Nicaragua.—In 1917, the Department of State transmitted to the Nicaraguan government a plan providing that the collection of all revenues should be placed under the Collector General of Customs.[6] This proposal was not acceptable to Nicaragua. According to the financial plan adopted that year the Nicaraguan government retains the collection of all internal revenues. If, however, the aggregate of such revenues shall be less than $180,000 for any period of three months the collection will then be transferred to the Collector General. Such transfer has not thus far been necessary, but the possibility that the Nicaraguan

[1] "Inquiry into Occupation and Administration of Haiti and Santo Domingo," Vol. II, p. 1396.

[2] *Ibid.*

[3] *Current History*, August, 1924, p. 845.

[4] *Fifth Annual Report of the American High Commissioner at Port au Prince, Haiti*, p. 27, Govt. Printing Office, Washington, 1927.

[5] *Sixth Annual Report of the American High Commissioner at Port au Prince, Haiti, State Department Press Release*, Mar. 23, 1928, p. 32.

[6] *For. Rel.*, 1917, p. 1124.

government will lose this function probably acts as a stimulant to more effective collections.

In Bolivia and Liberia.—The Bolivian Loan Agreement of 1922 pledged a substantial list of internal revenues in addition to customs duties and provided that the collection of all taxes, revenues, and income of the nation should be made under the supervision of the Fiscal Commission. Similarly, the American Financial Adviser in Liberia has the power of supervision over the collection of all of the revenues of that Republic.[1]

CONTROL OVER INDEBTEDNESS AND EXPENDITURE

In practically all of the Caribbean and Central-American countries there has been present a strong temptation to incur obligations beyond the limits justified by sound finance. This tendency has invited European customs control in the past and, if unchecked, may conceivably threaten the success of customs receiverships and other supervisory policies of the United States. The guarantee of outstanding bond issues is uncertain when the debtor country has unlimited power to contract debts. Such lack of restraint also makes for instability of government. There is always the possibility that the revenues will become insufficient to maintain the service upon the debt and at the same time provide the government with sufficient money to meet its current obligations. When the revenues of a government become insufficient to pay salaries and bills for supplies, insurrection looms ahead. For these reasons, the United States has been inclined to restrict wherever possible the debt-creating power of the governments which are objects of its paternal interest. Such restrictions have not been confined to keeping down the figures of the "public debt," as the term is ordinarily understood, but have been expanded to limit obligations of other kinds.

Cuba.—Prevention of foreign financial control in Cuba, where the United States had long looked with suspicion upon the attempts of European powers to gain a foothold, led to the first provision for debt restriction. Article II of the Platt Amendment provides that the Cuban government

[1] A loan agreement negotiated between the United States and Liberia in 1920, but which failed to become effective, provided for a stronger system of control. The internal revenue collections were to be in the hands of the then existing receivership which was under the management of the American General Receiver.

. . . shall not assume or contract any public debt, to pay the interest upon which, and to make reasonable sinking fund provision for the ultimate discharge of which, the ordinary revenues of the island, after defraying the current expenses of government shall be inadequate.[1]

The United States has interpreted this clause as granting it the right to pass upon Cuban financial requirements and to give or withhold approval to external loans. The American interpretation was made clear in the loan transaction of 1922–1923. General Crowder, in No. 12 of his famous series of memoranda to the Cuban government,[2] set forth a number of conditions which he stated must be met by Cuba *"previous to the approval by the United States of a new external loan."*[3] The loan contract of 1923 used in its preamble the following language: "The government of the United States of America, being advised in the premises, has formally acquiesced in the creation of such public debt."[4]

Aside from the public debt of Cuba, the United States has taken a paternal interest in a number of concessions bestowed by the Cuban government and has entered objections at different times on the grounds that such concessions would result in an improvident strain on the treasury. In 1912, the Department of State raised an objection to the contract with the Cuban Ports Company, a British concern, stating that the obligation to pay to the company a specified portion of the ordinary revenues derived from the import tonnage tax regardless of whether or not such revenues were necessary to defray the expenses of the government, created a conflict with the terms of the above-quoted Art. II of the Platt Amendment. The contract was then revised to provide that if at any time the tonnage tax revenues were needed the Cuban government should have the right to terminate the contract upon the payment of compensation.[5] Later on the contract was terminated on other grounds but compensation was paid.

A concession to drain the Zapata Swamp was emphatically disapproved in 1912 as an "improvident and reckless waste of revenue and natural resources." The objection in this instance

---

[1] See Treaty of 1903, *Treaties etc. between the United States and Other Powers,* Vol. I, p. 362.

[2] Text given in DUNN, "American Foreign Investments," p. 287.

[3] My italics.

[4] DUNN., p. 290. See JENKS, *op. cit.,* p. 258*ff.*

[5] For the correspondence in this case see *For. Rel.,* 1917, p. 431*ff.*

was based upon Art. III of the Platt Amendment, which gives to the United States the right to intervene in Cuba under certain conditions. The American interpretative expansion of this article was stated as follows:

> Clearly this right of intervention . . . entitles this government to caution the Cuban government against adopting an improvident or otherwise objectionable fiscal policy on the ground that such policy might ultimately, either by itself or in connection with general conditions in Cuba, produce a situation there requiring the United States to intervene for any of the purposes recited in this article.

The President of Cuba took the position that Art. III of the Platt Amendment did not permit "meddling (*intromision*) in internal affairs," but nevertheless the United States successfully insisted upon its interpretation.[1]

In another instance, in 1912, the Department of State disapproved of a concession which it believed was sought by British capitalists to build the Caibarien-Nuevitas Railway. The reason for objection in this case was stated to be "that it is probably an improvident strain on the Cuban treasury."[2] The Cuban Secretary of State in reply informed the American minister:

> I cannot conceive that in the present legal status of the relations between Cuba and the United States any Cuban law, and much less any bill pending in our Senate or Chamber of Representatives, is at any stage pending the approval of the Department of State at Washington, or that it requires such approval to become effective.

[1] For the correspondence see *For. Rel.*, 1912, p. 309*ff*; 1913, p. 365*ff*. The objection to this concession appears to have been ill advised. At the outset the American minister explained that "The project of reclamation is merely a specious pretext for giving away incalculable millions in timber and charcoal woods." However, after American capital had appeared in the project and on investigation it was found that there was very little timber in the swamp the objections of the Department of State were speedily removed by some amendments. The belief of the American attorney for the concessionaires that an agreement existed with the Department of State by which the concession rights were to be transferred to an American company was said by Mr. Bryan to be an error as the department officials had no recollection of the agreement. The rights were nevertheless transferred to an American corporation, the Zapata Land Company, organized under the laws of New Jersey.

[2] The American minister had been instructed to emphasize in his representations to the President of Cuba the burden which the concession "would impose on the Cuban treasury in favor of capital which is neither American nor Cuban."

When it was known later that Colonel José Tarafa, of Cuba, was the principal party seeking the concession, that Martin Littleton and Roland R. Conklin of New York were associated with him, and that important British interests had been the real opponents to the proposed grant, the Department of State ceased to object.[1]

The Dominican Republic.—The Convention of 1907 with Santo Domingo provided in Art. III:

> Until the Dominican Republic has paid the whole amount of the bonds of the debt, its public debt shall not be increased except by previous agreement between the Dominican government and the United States.[2]

A great deal of controversy has taken place between the two governments regarding the scope of this agreement. The Dominican government has maintained that the term "public debts" applies only to the formally contracted debt of the country and not to obligations which pile up due to the inability to meet the ordinary current expenses of government.[3] The United States, on the other hand, has given a more liberal interpretation to the term public debts and has construed it as preventing an increase in floating indebtedness.

The increase in the current indebtedness of the Dominican government gave rise to apprehensions on the part of the United States, about 1910, when Dominican expenditures began to exceed the revenue alloted. In 1913, the United States approved a loan of $1,500,000 to fund the floating indebtedness,[4] but the sum turned out to be insufficient to take care of the outstanding accounts. Furthermore, the increase in indebtedness went forward at the rate of from $1,000 to $3,000 per day, and the current indebtedness was estimated at from $5,000,000 to $7,000,000.[5] In emergencies the Department of State requested

---

[1] JENKS, *op. cit.*, p. 111. The correspondence is given in *For. Rel.*, 1913, p. 381*ff*.

[2] The same provision is repeated in Art. III of the Convention of 1924.

[3] For the view of former President Henriquez see "Inquiry into Occupation and Administration of Haiti and Santo Domingo," Vol. I, p. 55.

[4] *For. Rel.*, 1913, p. 456*ff*.

[5] Practically all of the floating debt was settled by the Claims Commission in 1917, the total awards amounting to $4,292,343.52, "Inquiry into Occupation and Administration of Haiti and Santo Domingo," Vol. II, p. 979. For an excellent summary of the problem of the floating debt see *For. Rel.*, 1915, pp. 321–325.

that the receivership should assist the government by additional advances.   Assistance of this sort due to the revolutionary activities of 1914 was reported for four months to have been as follows:

For September, 1914........................	$114,194.17
For October, 1914..........................	97,267.98
For November, 1914 (estimated).............	58,147.19
For December, 1914 (estimated).............	75,000.00
	$344,609.34*

* *Ibid.*, p. 298.

The objections of the United States were directed not only at the growth in the amount of the floating debt but also at the irregular nature of the expenditures which made it impossible to live within the budget.   American officials reported a régime of graft which would have done credit to some of the politicians of the United States.   Honest creditors went unpaid while dishonest claims were allowed in wholesale amounts.   Politicians received salaries for offices which they held in name only.   In certain instances, the officeholders had not been within thirty miles of their alleged work.   The heads of some offices obtained the salaries of their employes and paid only a portion of the amount to the men, retaining the balance for themselves.   There were instances in which payrolls were pledged in advance to speculators for comparatively small amounts.   Payment for supplies which were never delivered was not infrequent and numerous accounts were found in which the sums due had been dishonestly increased.   Some officials had purchased office furniture and supplies at government expense and had sold them out the back door for their own gain.[1]   Such corruption brought about a feeling on the part of the United States that control over expenditures was necessary to prevent the growth of indebtedness.   Consequently, the creation of a financial advisership with power to disapprove of budget items and to pass upon the validity of each claim presented for payment became an objective of American diplomacy in the Dominican Republic.

From the first months of 1914 until military intervention in November of 1916, the proposal for an American financial advisership was almost continually an outstanding cause of

[1] "Inquiry into Occupation and Administration of Haiti and Santo Domingo," Vol. I, p. 98; Vol. II, pp. 974, 977.

controversy between the two governments. At times the Department of State requested this reform as a consideration in return for the advances of additional funds from the receivership and at other times demanded it as a matter of right under Art. III of the Convention of 1907 which prohibited the increase of public debt without previous agreement with the United States. In 1914, the United States procured an invitation from the Dominican government to send a financial expert with full powers of control over expenditures, and Charles M. Johnston assumed the position. His activities in slashing the budget soon created opposition among Dominican leaders and a commission was sent to Washington to ask President Wilson for a termination of the new office on the grounds that such control was contrary to the laws and constitution of the Republic. Following this request, the objectionable control was replaced by a devitalized advisership which was set up in the General Receiver's office and which was limited to the making of recommendations to the Dominican officials. The new office seemed not to satisfy the requirements of strict financial control. Demands were, accordingly, renewed for the reestablishment of the original office with its power of veto, but the Dominican government continued to resist the change up to the time of military intervention in 1916.[1] Following the intervention the officers of occupation assumed complete financial control in the Republic. Upon withdrawal in 1924, however, the supervision of the United States was reduced to the receivership of the customs duties and the attempts to control expenditures of the government through an advisership were abandoned.

Haiti.—The Treaty of 1915 with Haiti provided in Art. VIII:

The Republic of Haiti shall not increase its public debt except by previous agreement with the United States, and shall not contract any debt or assume any financial obligation unless the ordinary revenues of the Republic available for that purpose after defraying the expenses of the government, shall be adequate to pay the interest and provide a sinking fund for the final discharge of such debt.

The question of agreement with the United States as to the increase in the bonded debt is thus under control by treaty and the prevention of an increase in the floating debt without agreement has been made more certain by control over budget and

[1] For this controversy see *For. Rel.*, 1914, 1915, 1916.

expenditures through the establishment of an advisership which has become endowed with large powers.

The office of Financial Adviser was created in the Treaty of 1915 but the powers of the office under that instrument were not great, being confined to the devising of an accounting system, aiding in increasing the revenues, and making recommendations concerning improved methods of collecting and applying the revenues. The Haitian government agreed to "cooperate" with the Financial Adviser in his recommendations. There is in these stipulations no basis for a power of veto over either budget items or the payment of claims. In order to make this particularly clear the Haitian Chamber of Representatives in giving approval to the treaty added among its interpretative resolutions an explanation to the effect that the Financial Adviser was not to supersede the executive and legislative bodies in financial powers and that his functions were to enlighten and advise. The resolution alleged: "He is nothing but an official attached to the Ministry of Finance where he collaborates with his work and advice."[1] Secretary Lansing, however, explained that the United States was not bound by this interpretation.

Discontent with the conduct of Haitian finances soon moved the United States to expand the functions of the Financial Adviser. Payment of salaries to officials whose services were only nominal was objected to and protest was made against the discounting of salaries. Complaints were made against many budget items on the ground that they were needless and ill advised.[2]

In 1918, the American officials forced the Haitian government to agree to an increase in the powers of the Financial Adviser to cover approval of the budget and of expenditures. The method by which this concession was exacted from the Haitians was explained in an illuminating fashion before the Senate Committee in 1922 by Financial Adviser McIlhenny as follows: During October and November, 1918, a dispute had arisen between the Haitian officials and the Financial Adviser over the budget. The Haitian government proposed to increase its appropriations and to obtain the added revenues for that purpose from projected internal revenue taxes and from a loan. The Financial Adviser,

---

[1] *For. Rel.*, 1916, p. 324.

[2] "Inquiry into Occupation and Administration of Haiti and Santo Domingo," Vol. I, p. 409; Vol. II, p. 1395.

on the other hand, insisted that no increase should be made in the appropriations above the figures which he had set in the budget which he himself had framed. He further insisted that no payment should be made from the funds appropriated except upon warrants approved by himself. He absolutely refused to give permission for the proposed loan. The Haitian government answered that it did not recognize his right to control the framing of the budget or the payment of funds. For some weeks the question remained undecided. Finally the Haitian government was brought around to the American view by the vigorous application of financial thumbscrews. The commander of the American military forces instructed the national bank not to permit the Haitian government to withdraw its funds which were on deposit. Accordingly, the government found itself unable to pay any of its expenses. When placed in this desperate position the Haitian government acceded to the American demands and in a note of Dec. 3, 1918, addressed to the American minister, accepted the claims of the Financial Adviser to the control of expenditures. The Financial Adviser's budget was also adopted. The payment of Haitian expenses was then resumed.[1]

The procedure in the formulation of the Haitian budget which was adopted following this incident has been described as follows:

1. The secretaries in charge of the departments transmit their proposed schedules to the Financial Adviser.

2. After due study of these proposals the Financial Adviser meets the cabinet in full session to discuss them.

3. After an agreement is reached, the budget is approved by the Financial Adviser.

4. The budget is considered and approved by the American minister.

5. It is then enacted into law by the Haitian Council of State.[2]

The use of the powers of the Financial Adviser to press the Haitian government for concessions demanded by the United States seems to have been a rather unusual expansion of official duty. In an attempt to force through a new contract with the National Bank of the Republic of Haiti in 1920, the Financial

---

[1] For an account of the above episode see *Ibid.*, Vol. II, pp. 1435, 1436. For the text of the note of Dec. 3, 1918, see p. 1443.

[2] *Ibid.*, p. 1405.

Adviser under the orders of the American minister took action against the Haitian President, who had refused to sign. The salaries of the President, the department secretaries, the state councilors, and the palace interpreter were temporarily stopped, although they were later resumed upon the failure of the United States to obtain its demands.[1] It seems that a disputed clause in the contract permitting the Financial Adviser with the advice of the bank to regulate the amount of foreign money which could be imported and exported had aroused the ire of other financial interests in Haiti and that the United States was really espousing the cause of the National Bank in a contest with the Royal Bank of Canada.[2]

A great deal of criticism has been directed against the Financial Adviser by the Haitian people.[3] Mr. McIlhenny, the second incumbent of the office, went upon long visits to Washington to discuss matters connected with a loan. It was brought out by testimony before the Senate Committee that the greater part of his time had been spent in the United States.[4] During his absence from Haiti he conferred with the officials of the Department of State and testified that he looked to the Chief of the Division of Latin-American Affairs as his immediate superior. The spectacle of a non-resident financial dictator whose duty was to follow the orders of an official in a distant capital could hardly have inspired the Haitians with pride over the liberties of the republic. The fact that he drew a high salary while he was suspected of spending part of his time in dealing with his private affairs in the United States caused much adverse comment. In 1923, the position of Financial Adviser was consolidated with that of General Receiver of Customs and a more efficient operation of the two offices has resulted.[5]

Altogether, it seems that the financial advisership has reduced expenditures in Haiti by eliminating needless extravagance and expenditures due to sheer corruption. The credit rating of the

---

[1] *Ibid.*, Vol. I, pp. 795–802.

[2] DOUGLAS, PAUL H., "The American Occupation of Haiti," *Political Science Quarterly*, Vol. XLII, p. 388.

[3] KELSEY, CARL, "The American Intervention in Haiti and the Dominican Republic," *Annals of the American Academy of Political and Social Science*, Vol. C, p. 147; DOUGLAS, *loc. cit.*, pp. 374–375.

[4] "Inquiry into Occupation and Administration of Haiti and Santo Domingo," Vol. II, p. 1404.

[5] DOUGLAS, *loc. cit.*, p. 375.

country has thereby been greatly improved. On the other hand, the work of the adviser has been in direct conflict with the sovereign control of the Haitian government over its most vital function.

Liberia.—The original agreement with Liberia, which went into effect in 1912, did not specifically provide for a limitation upon loans. When, however, in 1915, the Liberian government borrowed $8,000 without consulting the Financial Adviser, the department protested that under the agreement it would be most natural to expect that he should have been consulted.[1] A number of reforms concerning loans and expenditures were incorporated in the 1917 demands upon the Liberian government which were accepted by that government. Among these were the following: no loans were to be made without the written consent of the Financial Adviser; the appropriations of the legislature were to be kept within the estimates submitted annually by the Secretary of the Treasury; the sanction of the Financial Adviser was to be necessary for expenditures outside of the budget; and while revenues continued to be insufficient to meet the budgetary appropriations, the Secretary of the Treasury and the Financial Adviser were to decide jointly what disbursements should be made currently within the budget.[2]

According to the terms of the 1927 agreement, the control over the expenditures of Liberia has been substantially revised. The Financial Adviser consults with the Liberian Secretary of the Treasury in the preparation of the budget. It is his duty to see that the projected appropriations shall not exceed the resources of the government and that all of the charges imposed in the loan agreement are provided for. If the Financial Adviser refuses to approve the budget as prepared by the Secretary of the Treasury, the provisions of the previous year's budget, so far as they pertain to the ordinary governmental operating expenses and the expenditures imposed by the agreement, shall take effect.

With regard to the expenditures to be made under the budget after it has been enacted into law, the financial interests concerned have profited from the experience with the pre-audit in Haiti. The officer who has control at this point is the Auditor. This official is appointed by agreement between the President of

[1] *For. Rel.*, 1915, p. 638.
[2] *For. Rel.*, 1917, p. 879.

Liberia and the Fiscal Agent of the loan, which is the National City Bank of New York. The powers of the Auditor are very great. All accounts against the Liberian government must, before payment, be presented to him. He then examines the appropriation to which the account is chargeable to ascertain that it is a proper charge and that the appropriation has not been exhausted. If the account proves to be legitimate and correct in amount, he approves the transfer to the government's disbursement funds of a sum sufficient to pay the amount due.[1]

Nicaragua.—In the Nicaraguan refunding negotiations conducted in 1917, the Department of State, acting on behalf of the bondholders, attempted to secure the appointment of a financial adviser. The suggestion evidently met with opposition in the Nicaraguan Congress, and the President of Nicaragua was forced to ask that it be stricken out of the proposals. He stated that he desired to supervise his own expenditures. A counter-suggestion was submitted through the Department of State, and a modified control of expenditures was adopted in the Financial Plan of 1917. The amount available for the Nicaraguan budget was limited to $80,000 per month for ordinary expenditures and $15,000 per month for unforeseen expenditures. If more than $95,000 was needed in any month the attention of the High Commission[2] was called to the situation. The commission was empowered to approve additional expenditures up to $26,666.66. Thus it was possible to allot $121,666.66 per month or $1,460,000 per year for budgetary purposes.[3] In 1920, a revision of the plan increased the allotment for ordinary and unforeseen expenditures from $95,000 to $105,000 per month which in addition to the $26,666.66 under the commission's control permitted an annual expenditure of $1,580,000. In 1926, another revision was deemed advisable because of the reduction in Nicaraguan obligations and the increased cost of government. The bankers and the Nicaraguan government accordingly agreed to a monthly limit of $115,000 upon ordinary and unforeseen expenditures in addition to the $26,666.66 which may be added by permission of the commission. Under the 1926 revision the monthly expenditures may now total $141,666.66 or $1,700,000 per year.[4]

[1] BUELL, "The Native Problem in Africa," Vol. II, p. 842.
[2] See above, p. 185.
[3] See the text of the plan, "Hearings on Foreign Loans," p. 172.
[4] Information concerning the 1920 and 1926 revisions has been supplied through the courtesy of former Commissioner Roscoe R. Hill.

The expenditures of Nicaragua have been somewhat reduced under this régime. They have, however, tended to press upon the upper limits of the amounts allowed and the High Commission has frequently thought proper to permit the government to draw upon the sums under its control. Following is a statement of the amounts expended under the budget over a series of years up to 1926:

Year	Budget Expenditures*
1910	$3,457,312.59
1913	3,000,000.00
1919	C$1,331,547.37
1920	1,528,077.71
1921	1,480,121.82
1922	1,503,225.83
1923	1,580,000.00
1924	1,580,000.00
1925	1,580,000.00
1926	1,580,000.00

* Cox, *op. cit.*, p. 858.

Considerable financial control over Nicaragua also resulted from the provisions of the Canal Treaty of 1914 under which the sum of $3,000,000 was to be paid by the United States for the canal rights. The treaty provided in Art. III that this sum was

. . . to be applied by Nicaragua upon its indebtedness or other public purposes for the advancement of the welfare of Nicaragua in a manner to be determined by the two High Contracting Parties, all such disbursements to be made by orders drawn by the Minister of Finance of the Republic of Nicaragua and approved by the Secretary of State of the United States or by such person as he may designate.

The practically bankrupt condition of Nicaraguan finances following the revolution of 1912 explains the willingness of the Nicaraguan government to agree to such terms.

The right of the United States to dictate how the treaty money should be expended and the urgent need of Nicaragua for funds gave to the Department of State a certain amount of power to bargain for financial concessions. In 1917, the Nicaraguan government desperately needed money for the payment of salaries to its officials and application was made for the release of some of the $3,000,000. The approval of the Department of State to the expenditure was, however, made contingent upon the ratification of the financial plan proposed by the bankers.[1]

[1] *For. Rel.*, 1917, p. 1746.

When this plan was finally agreed upon, payments of the treaty money began.[1] An American-controlled commission was, however, set up to supervise the expenditure of that part of the funds which actually reached the Nicaraguan government.[2]

Panama.—The United States has similarly exercised some control over the expenditure of moneys which it has paid to the Republic of Panama. The terms of the lease of the Canal Zone did not seem to anticipate this control. The Treaty of 1903 between the two countries sets forth the compensation for the lease as follows:

> As the price or compensation for the rights, powers, and privileges granted in this convention by the Republic of Panama to the United States, the government of the United States agrees to pay to the Republic of Panama the sum of ten million dollars ($10,000,000) in gold coin of the United States on exchange of the ratification of this convention and also an annual payment during the life of this convention of two hundred and fifty thousand dollars ($250,000) in like gold coin, beginning nine years after the date aforesaid.[3]

While there is here no suggestion that the United States was to retain any control over the money, the Department of State, nevertheless, has exercised a certain supervision over its disposition.

The Panaman authorities at one time sought to pledge the interest from $6,000,000 of the money, which was invested in bonds in New York, together with the annuity of $250,000 to raise funds for railway construction. The United States objected to such an incumbrance upon the moneys, taking the position that the purpose of the treaty payments was to create an income which would assure a permanent revenue for the maintenance

[1] A particularly exacting feature of this bargaining involved a federal statute to the effect that moneys shall not be paid out of the treasury to a debtor of the United States without first deducting the amount of such indebtedness. A protocol of 1909 between the United States and Nicaragua had provided that $550,000 should be paid to the United States by Nicaragua for the claimants under the Emery claim. When Nicaragua tried to have the interest remitted on this claim the United States took the position that the claim must be paid in full before any money could be paid to Nicaragua. This interpretation was seemingly liberal in the interests of the American claimants when it is considered that the money was due to the United States only as a collector for private parties and that the money to be paid out was really the money of Nicaragua.

[2] *Ibid.*, 1119. This body was the Commission on Public Credit which later evolved into the High Commission. See Cox, *op. cit.*, p. 732.

[3] *Treaties, etc. between the United States and Other Powers*, Vol. II, p. 1354.

of a stable government upon the isthmus. Therefore, the United States claimed the right to oversee the use of the money and felt bound to caution Panama against any discounting of the revenues.[1] The President of Panama protested that "He did not see what right the United States had to prevent Panama from using these funds which belonged to Panama and which she should be able to use as she pleased." Later on when Panama sought to borrow in New York for another railway venture, the Department of State gave permission to Panama to pledge the above-mentioned revenues providing certain conditions with regard to the loan and the location of the railway should be met.[2]

Bolivia.—The Bolivian loan agreement of May 31, 1922, provided that no external loan should be floated prior to Dec. 5, 1925, without the consent of the bankers. Regarding loans subsequent to that date, it provides that during the life of the bonds no external loan shall be contracted unless the taxes and revenues pledged for the service of the 1922 loan shall for a period of two years immediately preceding the new loan have produced annually one and one-half times the amount required for the service of the loan and during each of the two years the revenues of the Republic shall be sufficient to meet all of the ordinary expenses of government. The Permanent Fiscal Commission and the Minister of Finance have the power of deciding whether the conditions have been met.[3]

Poland.—An international loan was made to Poland in 1927 in which American bankers took the principal part. The amounts floated were as follows: $47,000,000 in New York, £2,000,000 in London, and $15,000,000 in France, Holland, Switzerland, Sweden, and Poland. The loan agreement provided for certain definite restrictions upon Polish fiscal freedom in order that stabilization might be achieved. Budgetary expenditures and loans are definitely limited. An American, Charles S. Dewey, has been appointed to supervise the carrying out of the provisions of the agreement.[4]

The various methods of American financial control are summarized in the following table:

[1] *For. Rel.*, 1912, pp. 1203–1204; 1913, pp. 1101–1103.
[2] *For. Rel.*, 1914, pp. 1032, 1035; 1917, pp. 1180–1181.
[3] Article 4, Sec. 7 of the loan contract.
[4] FISHER, H. H., "America and the New Poland," pp. 338–339, The Macmillan Company, New York, 1928.

CHART SHOWING PRINCIPAL FEATURES OF THE CONTROL OVER THE FINANCES OF BACKWARD COUNTRIES BY THE GOVERNMENT AND BANKERS OF THE UNITED STATES

Country controlled	Document which includes the control agreement	Relationship of American government or bankers to customs receivership or supervision	Control over customs rates	Collection of internal revenues	Control over indebtedness and expenditures
Bolivia...........	Contract of May 31, 1922 between the Republic of Bolivia and the Equitable Trust Company of New York	Permanent Fiscal Commission of three members appointed by the President of Bolivia, two recommended by bankers, supervises the collection of all taxes, revenues, and income	....	All revenues are collected under the supervision of the commission	No external loan may be contracted unless the taxes for the preceding two years have produced annually one and one-half times the amount required for the service of the loan and sufficient revenue to meet all the ordinary expenses of the Republic
Cuba............	Treaty of 1903 between the United States and Cuba incorporating the Platt amendment	....	....	....	Cuban government is forbidden to contract debts unless the ordinary revenues, after defraying current expenses of government, are sufficient to pay interest and to make reasonable sinking fund provisions. Under the intervention clause in the Platt Amendment, the United States has protested against allegedly improvident concessions on the ground that such improvidence might create conditions necessitating intervention

Dominican Republic..	Conventions of 1907 and 1924 between the United States and the Dominican Republic	The President of the United States appoints the General Receiver of Customs and assistant receivers	Import duties cannot be modified without previous agreement with the United States	Collection of internal revenues is now in the hands of the Dominican Republic	The Dominican public debt cannot be increased without previous agreement with the United States
Haiti............	Treaty of 1915 between the United States and Haiti and exchanges of notes	The President of Haiti appoints, upon nomination by the President of the United States, the General Receiver and such aids and employes as may be necessary	Customs duties cannot be modified in a manner to reduce the revenues therefrom without a previous agreement with the President of the United States	Internal revenue bureau is under the supervision of the General Receiver	The Haitian public debt cannot be increased without previous agreement with the United States. The Financial Adviser, who is also the General Receiver, approves the Haitian budget and the expenditures made under it
Liberia............	The contract of 1927 with the Finance Corporation of America and others	The Financial Adviser, who supervises the collection of customs, is designated by the President of the United States and appointed by the President of Liberia	The customs rates cannot be decreased without the approval of the Fiscal Agent, which is the National City Bank of New York	All revenues are collected under the supervision of the Financial Adviser	The Financial Adviser has power to see that the appropriations in the budget shall not exceed the resources of the government and that all of the expenditures included in the loan agreement are provided for in the budget. The Auditor has power to pass upon all accounts against the Liberian government before they are paid
Nicaragua..........	Agreement on gold treasury bills of 1911 between Nicaragua and American bankers and Financial Plan of 1917 approved by Nicaraguan Congress. Treaty of 1914 between Nicaragua and the United States	The Republic of Nicaragua names a Collector General of customs who is designated by the bankers and approved by the Department of State	Import and export duties cannot be altered without the previous approval of the High Commission. Exception is made for a 12½ per cent additional impost on import duties	Internal revenues are to be collected by Nicaragua unless the receipts for any three-months' period shall be less than $180,000, whereupon the Collector General shall collect them	Expenditures are limited to $115,000 per month for ordinary and extra-ordinary purposes. The High Commission may authorize additional expenditures up to $26,666.66 per month. The $3,000,000 allotted for the canal rights was expended under the approval of the Secretary of State of the United States

CHART SHOWING PRINCIPAL FEATURES OF THE CONTROL OVER THE FINANCES OF BACKWARD COUNTRIES BY THE GOVERNMENT AND BANKERS OF THE UNITED STATES (*Continued*)

Country controlled	Document which includes the control agreement	Relationship of American government or bankers to customs receivership or supervision	Control over customs rates	Collection of internal revenues	Control over indebtedness and expenditures
Panama...........	Treaty of 1903, as interpreted by the United States	....	....	....	The United States has exercised the power of advising as to the hypothecation of the $250,000 annuity paid for the Canal Zone lease and as to the revenues from a $6,000,000 fund invested in New York
Salvador..........	The contract of 1923 between the government of Salvador and American bankers	An agent of the bankers has supervision over customs collections. In case of disagreement between the bankers and the government of Salvador the matter is to be referred to the U. S. Supreme Court. In case of default a collector of customs is to be appointed by the government of Salvador from two nominees proposed by the bankers with the assistance of the Department of State			

THE COLLECTION OF THE INTERALLIED DEBTS: A PROBLEM IN INTERNATIONAL FINANCE AND POLITICS

Concerning the problem of the interallied indebtedness to the United States, Herbert Hoover has said: "The question is one of the most complex and difficult in character that the American people have ever confronted."[1] The United States has learned through disputes that have centered around the debts, as much as from any other matter, that it cannot enter a great world war, intertwine its economic affairs with those of allied governments, and then at the proclamation of peace retire to its former solitude. No question with which this government has to deal is more baffling to the average citizen, none more portentous, and to none are the principles of foreign policy learned by the American people in the days of isolation less applicable.

THE GENERAL CHARACTER OF THE LOANS

The Reasons for the Loans.—When the United States entered the World War, there were three considerations which prompted it to give large credits to the allied governments:

1. The allies were in dire need of munitions, supplies, food, and shipping. They had been actively fighting for nearly three years and their stocks were depleted almost to the point of exhaustion. The United States during that time had been building up a huge productive plant, which was capable of still greater expansion under the stress of actual participation in the war. The United States was the natural source from which the needs of the European allies were to be met. President Wilson in his War Message made this point clear. He said:

In carrying out the measures by which these things are to be accomplished we should keep constantly in mind the wisdom of interfering as little as possible in our preparation and the equipment of our own military forces with the duty—for it will be a very practical duty—of

[1] From an address delivered at Toledo, Ohio, Oct. 16, 1922.

supplying the nations already at war with Germany with the materials which they can obtain only from us or by our assistance. They are in the field and we should help them in every way to be effective.

The huge credits established for the allies were used almost entirely to purchase materials in the United States.

2. The credit of the allied governments was not good. Some of them were on the verge of bankruptcy. Senator Smoot estimated that if Great Britain, financially the strongest of the allies, should attempt to borrow at 3½ per cent, that government would realize only from 87 to 90 cents on the dollar.[1] The other allies would have been compelled to accept much less favorable terms than this. The United States, on the other hand, was able to sell 3½ per cent bonds to its own people at par.[2] Thus it may be seen that a great saving was to be made for the allies if they could obtain their credits through the United States government rather than by going to the private banking houses in New York.

3. Immediate military assistance could not at once be furnished by the United States. It was well understood that American troops could not appear on the European fronts in large numbers for at least a year after our entry into the war in April, 1917. Meanwhile, the best method of rendering effective service against the common enemy was by supplying credits and, through that method, materials to the allies whose armies were on the front.[3]

[1] *Cong. Rec.*, Vol. 55, p. 754.

[2] The rate on the First Liberty Loan was 3½ per cent. On the fifth or Victory loan it was 4¾ per cent.

[3] John Maynard Keynes, the brilliant English economist, who was temporarily attached to the British Treasury during the war, made the following comments concerning the value of American assistance:

"After the United States came into the war her financial assistance was lavish and unstinted, and without this assistance the allies could never have won the war, quite apart from the decisive influence of the arrival of the American troops."

. . . . . .

(Note 1) "The financial history of the six months from the end of the summer of 1916 up to the entry of the United States into the war in April, 1917, remains to be written. Very few persons, outside the half-dozen officials of the British Treasury who lived in daily contact with the immense anxieties and impossible financial requirements of those days, can fully realize what steadfastness and courage were needed, and how entirely hopeless the task would soon have become without the assistance of the

Opinions in 1917 Concerning Repayment.—It has frequently been stated in the discussions of the problem that the loans were a purely business transaction, but this is hardly an accurate statement. The security, the credit of the borrowers, the purposes for which the proceeds were to be applied, were all of such nature that as a business proposition the loans could not have been justified. They were political in character as, indeed, are practically all loans from one government to another. The nature of the loans is shown throughout the debates in Congress and the public discussions which attended the transaction. Everywhere it was emphasized that this was America's immediate contribution to the allied cause. It was understood that the loans were to be repaid, although that point was not emphasized. Some few, however, expressed doubts about repayment, while others felt that they should be considered as gifts.

Senator Kenyon was emphatic in expressing the hope that the loan to France would not be repaid.[1] Senator Cummins indulged in prophecy; and there were few public men in those unrealistic years who envisaged the future with the shrewdness and accuracy of the Senator from Iowa. His remarks are worth quoting at some length:

I am perfectly willing to give to any of the allied nations the money which they need to carry on our war, for it is now our war. I would give it to them just as freely as I would vote to equip an army or to maintain a navy of our own; but I shrink from the consequences that will, in all human probability, flow from the course which is suggested in this bill. I do not want the United States to become the bond creditor of Great Britain or of France or of Russia or of Italy; I do not want to enter the entangling alliance which the possession of these evidences of indebtedness will inevitably create. I should like to give to the allied nations $3,000,000,000, if they need the contribution, with never a thought of its repayment at any time or under any circumstances; I should like to give that or whatever sum may be thought needed as our donation to one phase of our own war; but I fear that in the years to come the fact that the United States has in its possession bonds of these great countries, which when they emerge from the war will all be bankrupt, will create an embarrassment from which the men of those times will find it difficult to

---

United States Treasury. The financial problems from April, 1917, onwards were of an entirely different order from those of the preceding months." "*The Economic Consequences of the Peace,*" p. 273, Harcourt, Brace and Howe, New York, 1920.

[1] *Cong. Rec.*, Vol. 55, p. 760.

escape. I think it will cost us more to take those bonds and to hold them against these governments than it would cost us to give the money, with a generous and patriotic spirit, to do something which for the time being, for the moment, we are unable to do with our own army and our own navy.[1]

On the other hand, there is little question that the majority of public men in this country and in France expected that the loans would be repaid, although there is evidence that many of them did not at that time have the slightest idea of the problems which would arise in repayment. The French ambassador at Washington, M. Jusserand, expressed a belief to Secretary McAdoo that the term for repayment should be fifteen years. The French Minister of Finance thought that the period should be extended to thirty years.[2]   In March 1919, when the question of the readjustment of debts had been raised by Italian delegates in the Financial Drafting Committee at the Peace Conference, the Treasury Department informed the French Deputy High Commissioner in Washington:

> You will appreciate also that the Treasury can not contemplate continuance of advances to any allied government which is lending its support to any plan which would create uncertainty as to its due repayment of advances made to it by the United States.[3]

When the Treasury Department had been assured that the French government had made no declaration in favor of the Italian suggestion, it continued to lend financial support to France.   After the date of this assurance, $690,000,000 in cash was advanced and credit was extended in lieu of payment for $407,000,000 worth of war supplies.   There was complete agreement upon repayment between the administrative officials of the two countries.

THE WORK OF REFUNDING

At the close of the war, the United States held against its allies certificates of indebtedness or demand notes bearing interest at 5 per cent.   It was desirable that these notes should be replaced by others at a lower rate of interest, providing for

[1] *Ibid.*, p. 757.

[2] *Annual Report of the Secretary of the Treasury*, 1926, p. 61.

[3] *Ibid.*, pp. 65–66.

definite dates of payment which would be within the capacity of the debtor nations. At the request of the administration, Congress passed an act creating the World War Foreign Debt Commission and authorized it to refund or convert the obligations due to the United States.[1] Certain restrictions were placed upon the power of the commission. The new rate of interest was in each case not to be less than 4½ per cent, the time of payment was not to be extended for more than twenty-five years, and it was provided that there should be no authority in the commission to cancel any part of the indebtedness except through the payment thereof. In placing these limits upon the terms which were to be offered, Congress had fixed standards which were impractical and the commission speedily found that it could not, even in the case of the most solvent of the debtor nations, adhere to the provisions of the act.

The first government to refund its obligations was that of Great Britain. In January, 1923, Stanley Baldwin, Chancellor of the Exchequer, and Montagu C. Norman, Governor of the Bank of England, on behalf of the British government, conferred with the World War Foreign Debt Commission in Washington and an agreement was eventually reached. Since that time twelve governments in all have made funding arrangements with the United States and two of the minor debtors, Liberia and Cuba, have paid their debts in full. The terms of the Congressional Act have been exceeded in all of the funding agreements but Congress has legalized each settlement as it has been made. In addition agreements have been signed with France and Greece that are as yet unratified.

The table on the two following pages presents the main facts concerning the debts and the terms on which they were funded. Some instructive comparisons of the debt agreements can be drawn from this set of figures. For purposes of estimating the relative values of the settlements, attention is particularly called to columns 5 and 10. It will be seen that Italy and Yugoslavia were leniently dealt with. The settlements negotiated with France and Belgium were moderate. That with Great Britain was comparatively firm. The obligations of almost all of the new states of Europe, Estonia, Finland, Hungary, Lativa, Lithuania, and Poland, which became indebted to the United States for surplus and relief supplies, were, in

[1] This act was signed on Feb. 9, 1922.

Country	1 — Sums due prior to funding: principal plus interest at the rates on the face of the obligation (5 and 6 per cent). In case of debts not funded, only the principal amount is given	2 — The amount of debt as funded. (The accrued interest was computed at reduced rates for purposes of funding.)	3 — Principal source of indebtedness (1) under Liberty bond acts; (2) surplus supplies sold on credit; (3) relief supplies furnished on credit	4 — Rate of interest on funded debt (Initial)	4 — Rate of interest on funded debt (Final)	5 — Average interest rates (approximate) On debt as funded	5 — Average interest rates (approximate) On original principal including back interest
Armenia	$11,959,917.49		(3)	Armenian government has ceased to exist			
Austria	24,055,708.92		(3)	Time for payment extended not to exceed twenty-five years			
Belgium	483,426,000.00	417,780,000.00	(1)	0.77–11	3½	1.790	1.840
Cuba	10,000,000.00			Final payment made in 1923			
Czechoslovakia	123,854,000.00	115,000,000.00	(1)	3	3½	3.327	3.433
Estonia	14,143,000.00	13,830,000.00	(1)	3	3½	3.306	3.404
Finland	9,190,000.00	9,000,000.00	(2)	3	3½	3.306	3.402
France	4,230,777,000.00	4,025,000,000.00	(3)	1	3½	1.640	1.955
Great Britain	4,715,310,000.00	4,600,000,000.00	(1)	3	3½	3.306	3.415
Greece[1]	19,659,836.00		(1)				
Hungary	1,984,000.00	1,939,000.00	(3)	3	3½	3.306	3.407
Italy	2,150,150,000.00	2,042,000,000.00	(1)	⅛	2	0.405	0.815
Latvia	5,893,000.00	5,775,000.00	(2 and 3)	3	3½	3.306	3.426
Liberia	35,610.46		(1)	Paid in full in 1927			
Lithuania	6,216,000.00	6,030,000.00	(2)	3	3½	3.306	3.420
Nicaragua[2]	166,604.14		(1)				
Poland	182,324,000.00	178,560,000.00	(2 and 3)	3	3½	3.306	3.408
Rumania	46,945,000.00	44,590,000.00	(1)	3	3½	3.321	3.358
Russia	192,601,297.37			Repudiated by the Soviet government			
Yugoslavia	66,164,000.00	62,850,000.00	(1 and 2)	⅛	3½	1.030	1.356

Country	6 Annual payments on funded debts		7 Term, years	8 Total amount to be paid	9 Present value on basis of 4¼ per cent	10 Percentage that present value at 4¼ per cent bears to amount of debt prior to funding
	Initial	Peak year				
Armenia.........						
Austria.........						
Belgium.........	$3,840,000	$12,868,000	62	$727,830,500.00	$225,000,000.00	46.5
Cuba...........						
Czechoslovakia..	3,000,000	5,886,475	62	312,811,433.88	91,964,000.00	74.3
Estonia.........	483,900	548,565	62	33,331,140.00	11,392,000.00	80.5
Finland.........	315,000	359,185	62	21,695,055.00	7,413,000.00	80.7
France.........	30,000,000	125,000,000	62	6,847,674,104.17	1,996,509,000.00	47.2
Great Britain...	161,000,000	187,250,000	62	11,105,965,000.00	3,788,470,000.00	80.3
Greece.........						
Hungary.........	67,770	78,885	62	4,693,240.00	1,596,000.00	80.4
Italy...........	5,000,000	80,988,000	62	2,407,677,500.00	528,192,000.00	24.6
Latvia.........	201,250	235,980	62	13,985,635.00	4,755,000.00	80.7
Liberia.........						
Lithuania.......	210,900	239,855	62	14,531,940.00	4,967,000.00	79.9
Nicaragua²......						
Poland.........	5,916,800	9,315,000	62	435,687,550.00	146,825,000.00	80.5
Rumania.........	200,000	2,248,020	62	122,506,260.05	35,172,000.00	74.9
Russia.........						
Yugoslavia......	200,000	2,490,605	62	95,177,635.00	20,030,000.00	30.3

The facts set forth in the above table were obtained mostly from the tables in the *Annual Report of the Secretary of the Treasury,* 1927, pp. 628, 630, and from the *Combined Annual Reports of the World War Foreign Debt Commission,* Washington, Govt. Printing Office, 1927, *passim.*

¹ According to an agreement of Jan. 18, 1928, the Greek debt, contracted under the Liberty bond acts, is to be funded as of Jan. 1, 1928. $18,125,000 is to be paid in sixty-two years on terms which have a present value at 4¼ per cent of $6,425,000 or about 32.7 per cent of the debt prior to funding. The United States agrees to loan $12,167,000 for refugee settlement work at 4 per cent for twenty years. This settles differences growing out of a loan agreement made during the war. Congress had not acted on the agreement at the end of 1928.

² This was the original amount of the Nicaraguan indebtedness. By 1927 it had been nearly retired, but in that year a new debt was incurred for military supplies. On Nov. 15, 1927, the total indebtedness was $299,127.99.

general, arranged on a basis approximating the British terms of settlement.

Capacity to Pay.—In making the agreement with Great Britain and in the subsequent refunding negotiations with other countries, the American commission has avowed the principle of the capacity of the debtor to pay. In each instance experts examined the financial and commercial data of the country under consideration. The Secretary of the Treasury, who was the chairman of the commission, has described how the American negotiators sought to reach adjustments which would not only permit the sums to be paid but which would also permit of economic development and financial stabilization in the debtor countries. "No settlement," he said, "which is oppressive and retards the recovery and development of the foreign debtor is to the best interests of the United States or of Europe."[1]   In explanation of the difference in treatment of the four principal debtors, Great Britain, France, Italy, and Belgium, Secretary Mellon has adduced the following statistics showing the percentages which the average annual payments bear to the budgets, foreign trade, and income of each:[2]

	Percentage of total budget expenditures	Percentage of total foreign trade	Percentage of national income	Average of the three foregoing indices
Great Britain...............	4.6	1.9	0.94	2.4
France.....................	7.33	2.64	1.47	3.81
Italy......................	5.17	2.87	0.97	3
Belgium....................	3.5	0.88	0.80	1.75

These figures tend to show the negotiation of settlements upon the basis of relative capacity to pay. They indicate that the British settlement is less burdensome when considered in connection with national capacity than the settlements with France and Italy. This is the more true when it is remembered that both France and Italy are obliged to make payments upon their debts to Great Britain. On the other hand, comparisons based upon average annual payments do not show the relative burden to be borne by the British. Because of the higher initial payments to be made by Great Britain, the obligations of that

[1] *Annual Report of the Secretary of the Treasury*, 1925, p. 53.
[2] *Combined Annual Reports*, p. 296.

country are more burdensome on the basis of present values than is indicated in the above table.

Some students of the question have doubted the success of the commission in its application of the principle of capacity to pay. A general feeling prevails among international economists that the heavy payments which must be made over a period of sixty-two years are clearly beyond capacity and will have to be revised. The great divergence in the various settlements, it is alleged, have been due partly to the different degrees of willingness of the debtors to settle. Professor F. W. Taussig denies that the principle of capacity to pay was applied in the British settlement.[1] Dr. James W. Angell questions the application of the principle in the following language:

It is hard to refrain from concluding that the so-called principle of "capacity to pay" was, within considerable limits, little more than a cloak for polite and perhaps half-conscious bargaining of a familiar order.[2]

The members of the Faculty of Political Science and Associated Schools of Columbia University united in a public statement to declare that the formula of capacity to pay was difficult, if not impossible, to apply to payments reaching over two or three generations. The statement reproached the funding commission for its allegedly haphazard methods as follows: "It is surely unjust to fix the burdens of future generations on the basis of guesswork."[3]

From this dispute two things seem to be clear. (1) The commission can justify, in a large measure at least, the difference in the settlements made with particular nations on the basis of "capacity to pay." (2) There is strong reason to believe that the settlements as a whole will in time work undesirable hardships in Europe and that in this sense they are beyond the capacity of the debtors.

If we are to view the settlements as strictly business transactions, as many Americans are wont to do, the figures lead to a first impression that the debt settlements are generous. It must be considered, however, that prices are now only two-thirds as high as war prices and that the medium with which the debts

[1] "The Interallied Debts," *International Conciliation*, No. 230, pp. 209–210.

[2] "The Interallied Debts and American Policy," *International Conciliation*, No. 230, p. 196.

[3] The statement is printed in the *Cong. Rec.*, Vol. 68, pp. 1317–1318.

are to be repaid will have a correspondingly higher value than that in which the original obligations were incurred. If the debtor nations were to repay the full amounts they would have to send to us 50 per cent more goods than they received.[1] Furthermore, the people of some of the debtor nations have not looked upon the debts as business obligations, but as transactions arising from the political and military necessities of a common war.

THE CANCELLATION ISSUE ARISES

The Russian Repudiation.—Following the entry of the United States into the war, loans totaling $192,601,297.37 were made to the Russian government. This was after the first Russian revolution. After the Bolshevist revolution of November, 1917, the debt was repudiated by the Soviet government. The decree of annulment was dated Jan. 21, 1918, and ran in part as follows:

1. All national loans concluded by the governments of Russian landowners and Russian bourgeoisie enumerated in specially published lists are annulled (annihilated) from Dec. 1, 1917. The December coupons of these loans are not subject to payment.

2. In the same manner are annulled all guarantees given by the said governments on loans for different undertakings and institutions.

3. Unconditionally and without exceptions, all foreign loans are annulled.[2]

In return the United States has for this and other reasons refused to recognize the Soviet government. The American position was made clear in President Coolidge's message to Congress of Dec. 9, 1923, in which he said:

Our government does not propose, however, to enter into relations with another régime which refuses to recognize the sanctity of international obligations.

One week later, the Soviet Commissary for Foreign Affairs addressed a note to the President of the United States informing him of its complete readiness to discuss the indebtedness. Secretary of State Hughes replied that there was no reason for negotia-

---

[1] Taussig, *loc. cit.*, p. 209.

[2] Text in Pasvolsky, Leo and Harold G. Moulton, "Russian Debts and Russian Reconstruction, p. 197, McGraw-Hill Book Company, Inc., New York, 1924.

tions. The Soviet authorities were at liberty to repeal their decree of repudiation, but until this was done and until Soviet propaganda in the United States should cease there remained nothing to discuss.[1] More recent dispatches indicate a willingness upon the part of the Russian authorities to admit the validity of the debt to the United States in return for recognition.[2]

Request of Allies for Cancellation.—Shortly after the armistice, suggestions for the cancellation of the interallied indebtedness were made by the allied governments. In a cablegram of Dec. 4, 1918, Secretary McAdoo was informed that the British government was suggesting the cancellation "of all loans made by one associated government to any other for the conduct of the war."[3] These suggestions continued to be made in one form or another, although the United States steadfastly refused to entertain the thought of cancellation. Indeed, early in 1922 when Congress passed the funding act, one of the provisions forbade the cancellation of any part of the indebtedness.

The government of Great Britain, which was indebted to the United States in a principal sum amounting to $4,074,818,-358.44, and which had credits against the insolvent allies amounting to almost $10,000,000,000 had embraced, from the first, the idea of general cancellation. Not only would Great Britain gain by foregoing her uncollectible claims against her debtors in exchange for relief from payment to the United States but the stimulus which cancellation was expected to give to the rapid economic recovery of Europe was considered vital to the reestablishment of sound business conditions in Great Britain. Furthermore, Great Britain was in an excellent moral position to urge cancellation from the fact that she was willing to give up a much larger paper claim against others than she was asking to be cancelled against herself. Accordingly, the British let it be known that they stood ready to absolve all interallied debts due to themselves in case they were relieved from payment; but in case the United States should insist in collection then Great Britain must secure sufficient sums from her debtors to meet the American demands.

---

[1] The notes in the case are printed in Pasvolsky and Moulton, *op. cit.*, pp. 241–243.

[2] For the embargo on loans to Russia, see above p. 93.

[3] Mountsier, Robert, "Our Eleven Billion Dollars," p. 23, Thomas Seltzer, New York, 1922.

The Balfour Notes.—In the famous Balfour notes addressed to the representatives of six debtor nations on Aug. 1, 1922, the following language was used:

> The policy favored by His Majesty is, as I have already observed, that of surrendering their share of German reparation, and writing off, through one great transaction, the whole body of interallied indebtedness. But, if this be found impossible of accomplishment, we wish it to be understood that we do not in any event desire to make a profit out of any less satisfactory arrangement. In no circumstances do we propose to ask more from our debtors than is necessary to pay to our creditors, and while we do not ask for more, all will admit that we can hardly be content with less.[1]

These notes undoubtedly constituted an invitation to the United States, and were, it cannot be denied, in line with the intelligent self-interest of Great Britain. From the standpoint of the United States, however, the Balfour notes helped to create an international situation of some significance. They clearly laid the foundation for European cooperation in opposition to the debt policies of the American government.

The French Answer.—In reply to the Balfour note the French Premier and Minister for Foreign affairs, Raymond Poincaré, outlined the policy of his government.[2] So far as the debts were concerned, he emphasized that they were contracted in the interest of a common cause and not for the individual gain of particular countries. "From the moral point of view," he said, "realization of this fact would justify the cancellation of these debts." However, when the reparation question should be settled, he promised, the French government would not be opposed to a general settlement. Reparations from Germany should, however, take precedence over all debt settlements. Poincaré said:

> The French government can in no case consider any settlement whatsoever of the debts she contracted during the war as long as the sums which she has advanced and which she will have to advance for reconstruction of her devastated regions have not been covered by Germany.

The growth of cancellation sentiment in France and the frank expressions of French opinion in certain quarters were answered by an embargo on French loans in the United States in 1925.[3]

[1] *International Conciliation*, No. 181, p. 535.

[2] *Ibid.*, p. 536*ff.*

[3] For a fuller description of this part of the dispute, see above, p. 89.

The French government then made efforts to fund its obligations and the Mellon-Berenger agreement was signed on Apr. 29, 1926. The French Parliament has, however, virtually repudiated the agreement by refusing to take action upon it. The sentiment of the French public against the plan was expressed by the venerable war premier, Georges Clemenceau, who in an open letter to President Coolidge published on Aug. 8, 1926, said:

Now it is an open secret that in this affair there are only imaginary dates of payment, which will lead up to a loan with solid security in the shape of our territorial possessions, as was the case for Turkey. Such a thing, Mr. President, I am bound to tell you we shall never accept.

The attitude of France remains today one of passive cancellation, and the embargo, although modified, still stands as to governmental loans.

MORAL AND QUASI-MORAL CONSIDERATIONS OF THE CANCELLATION PROBLEM

The arguments which have been given most weight on both sides of this rather bitter controversy are moral in character. This is one of the undesirable features of the matter as such contentions are too frequently exaggerated. They are unrealistic in that they have no clear connection with the future interests and welfare of the nations involved. They are in almost all cases wholly unconvincing to opponents. If the whole question could be removed from the so-called "moral" plane and settled with a sincere desire to attain the best future interests of all countries, the matter would lose much of its complexity. These contentions are, nevertheless, the most emphasized part of the discussion and should be enumerated.

The Sanctity of Contracts.—The initial American argument is based squarely on a fundamental principle of business ethics that an obligation entered into must be met. There was no talk of cancellation when the debts were incurred. After the credits have been advanced, the proceeds consumed, and the danger to the allied powers thus removed it is a breach of good faith to question the promise. In his message to Congress of Feb. 7, 1923, dealing with the settlement of the British debt, President Harding emphasized the demands of the United States as a creditor nation: "The call of the world today is for integrity of agreements, the sanctity of covenants, the validity of contracts." This contention because of its simplicity has an undoubted appeal to the average citizen. The debts were entered into, they must be paid; and that is all there is to it. The question is thus sheared of all mind-tiring subtleties.

On the other hand, it is not true that all international obligations that have been entered into should be fully observed. There is a well-accepted principle in international law that a change in conditions may sometimes operate to relieve a party from an obligation. When the changed conditions make it disastrous, almost self-destructive, for a nation to keep its word it has a duty to itself to seek to be relieved. Secretary Mellon acknowledged this right in the following words:

An insistence on a funding agreement in excess of the capacity of the nation to pay would justify it in refusing to make any settlement. None can do the impossible.[1]

The question is not then a moral one regarding the sanctity of a promise but an economic one concerning the condition of the debtor and the probable effect of the payments upon that condition. The World War Foreign Debt Commission and Congress have both acknowledged the advisability and justice of settlements on a basis other than that of strict performance. The one has signed and the other has approved agreements for adjustments the present values of which at $4\frac{1}{4}$ per cent vary from 80.7 to 24.6 per cent of the original debts. Further readjustments or complete cancellation could be based on similar principles should the advisability of such action become apparent.

Cancellation is Unfair to American Taxpayers.—The argument is advanced that it is not just that the taxpayers of the United States should be saddled with a debt which was incurred for the benefit of Europe. The American taxpayers must retire the bonds whether the debtor nations pay or not.

It is true that the bonds must be retired whether Europe pays or not; but to pay the debt due to American bondholders by taxation in the United States is a much simpler and easier transaction than to pay it from Europe. Payment of an internal debt may be likened to taking money from one pocket and placing it into another. There is a partial redistribution of wealth, which is taken from the taxpayers and given to the bondholders which parties are to a certain extent the same persons. The national wealth is not reduced in this way,

[1] *Combined Annual Reports of the World War Foreign Debt Commission*, p. 341.

excepting, of course, to the extent that the collection of taxes for the payment of bonds requires effort which might otherwise be expended in production. The chief problem of the payment of the debt internally is to get the money from the tax payers into the treasury. Payment of the debt by European nations requires two transactions: (1) getting the money into the treasury from the tax payers, a more difficult feat in Europe because of depleted resources; and (2) the still more difficult process of converting the money into form for transport to the United States. Without large private loans from the United States, this latter transaction would at present be impossible.

The Question of European Good Faith.—The allegation is made that European nations have not shown good faith in the matter of repayment. While protesting their incapacity to pay, they have not taxed themselves fully and have been proceeding with costly militaristic and imperialistic ventures. France, for example, has spent a great deal of money in the Ruhr, in Syria, and in Morocco on allegedly foolish campaigns. That government supports a huge standing army. Furthermore, she has loaned large sums to Central European governments for political purposes and at the same time has refused to tax the French people to the limit of their capacity. The per capita tax in France during the year 1923–1924 when cancellation sentiment was growing was $29.53 as against $45.27 in the United States.

Economists who have examined the French fiscal system, however, do not agree that France could secure materially greater sums by increased taxation. The French have a very much smaller income per capita than the people of the United States, which accounts for the fact that they have not raised as much in taxation per person. The French taxes amounted to about 20 per cent of their national income in 1924,[1] while the taxes in the United States were about 11.5 per cent of the American income. This is a much truer index of the relative fiscal burdens of the United States and France.[2]

As to the imperialism of European countries, it must be admitted that there has been a great present waste of wealth on this account combined doubtless with cruel and inconsiderate treatment of weaker peoples. Whether these efforts will result

[1] They are probably more than 22 per cent now.

[2] MOULTON, HAROLD G., "The French Situation," *Annals of the American Academy of Political and Social Science*, Vol. CXXVI, p. 2.

in a net future gain to the world is debatable.   Perhaps imperialism will prove unprofitable in the long run.   But can this thesis be maintained by a nation which is itself committed to imperialism and which attempts to justify it on the basis of future profits due to increased productivity in backward regions.   The conquest of backward countries has been such an integral part of the nationalistic systems of Europe that the people of those countries can never be expected to admit that others have the right to question them.   Europeans would be disposed to give a different turn to the argument.   They would doubtless point out that the United States is spending vast sums for its naval program and for the maintenance of warships and marines in Central America and the Far East.   They would ask: "Is it for these purposes that the European people are to be squeezed?"

The Debts as America's Contribution to the Allied Cause.— The main moral contention of the debtor countries has been that the debts were incurred in a common cause and should be taken as America's contribution to the war during the time after the United States entered the war and before American troops could bear an equal share in the fighting.   The debtor countries point to their enormous losses of men[1] and property which were much larger than those of the United States and claim that these far more than offset the loans.[2]

On the other hand, it is clear that losses prior to the date on which the United States entered the war do not concern this

---

[1] The losses of those killed and died in the military service of some of the allies were as follows:

	Total number killed and died	Proportion of dead to all troops in military forces of that country	Proportion of dead to all troops lost in war
Great Britain.....	908,371	10.08	10.73
France..........	1,357,800	16.07	16.11
Italy...........	650,000	11.57	7.68
United States.....	50,280	1.05	0.59

Taken from HARLOW, REX F., "A New Estimate of World War Casualties," *Current History Magazine*, June, 1925, p. 355.

[2] The validity of that part of the debts which was incurred for the sale of materials following the war is, however, not generally questioned.

question, for before that period the United States was a neutral country and in no sense involved in the struggle. The above-mentioned argument can have weight only for the relative efforts of the nations between the entry of the United States and the date on which American troops arrived on the front in sufficient numbers to bear their share of the fighting. The greater part of the casualties were suffered before the former date and much of the indebtedness was incurred after the latter date. Furthermore, it must be considered that the United States, in addition to the loans to the allies, was spending larger sums on its own preparations than were being spent by any of the allied governments.

It may also be questioned whether the duty of the United States to put forth effort in the war could have been said to have been equal to that of the European allies. The existence of the latter nations was menaced and they could not avoid exerting their entire strength. The national life of this country was not in jeopardy. The United States was more in the position of Japan, which country did not make the sacrifices in either money or men that were made by the United States, although Japan was in the war for a much longer period of time. No moral obloquy has attached to the Japanese on that account. This whole "moral" argument lacks reality for, if it were a controlling consideration, Japan, much more than the United States, would be the subject of European criticism. The distinction between the American position in the war and that of the European allies was clearly made by M. Poincaré in his note to Great Britain of Sept. 1, 1922, in which he said:

One cannot forget, nevertheless, that the United States entered the war without its existence being directly menaced and to defend with its honor the principles which form the basis of civilization. Whereas England, like France, had to safeguard not only her independence and the territory, but also lives and property and means of existence of her citizens.[1]

The United States Pictured as a War Profiteer.—The argument is often advanced that the United States got rich from the war and that, under the circumstances, it is not conscionable to collect more. The estimated national wealth of the United States in 1912 was $186,299,664,000. By 1922 this had soared to

[1] *International Conciliation,* No. 181, p. 540.

$320,803,862,000. The contention is urged by some European critics that it is hardly consistent for the United States to declare that it entered the war for certain high principles of justice and at the same time to insist so obstinately on increasing the already swollen profits which it derived from the conflict.

This argument must be examined critically. In the first place, the growth in the national wealth of the United States up until April, 1917, or during the days of American neutrality, cannot be held to affect this argument. The actual growth in wealth from April, 1917, until the close of the war was much less. The increase in values during the entire period was due largely to inflated currencies. Measured in "1913" dollars the wealth of the United States amounted to about $230,000,000,000 in 1923.[1] The per capita wealth in those terms showed an increase of only 1.4 per cent over that of 1914. Furthermore, at the close of the war the United States demonstrated its good faith by refusing to take any territory from Germany, although undoubtedly that refusal was based less on ethical than upon utilitarian grounds, it being considered to the best interests of the United States to refuse all overseas territorial acquisitions as well as mandates. On the other hand, the allies, especially France and Great Britain, received immense territories which were taken from the German and Turkish empires. They came out of the war greatly enhanced in point of size and are hardly in a position to point the finger of scorn at the United States because of incidental increases in wealth. The argument directed against the United States as a "profiteer" must be heavily discounted.

General Worthlessness of the "Moral" Arguments.—The moral arguments as a class illustrate primitive reasoning on international subjects. There are no definite standards by which these claims can be measured, and there is a tendency to exaggerate them on both sides. To attempt to settle an important world controversy by that method can only result in sending each set of contenders into its shell of self-righteousness from which it cannot be driven.

Successful statesmanship invariably approaches the world problem from the international point of view rather than from that of the single nation. From this standpoint, no settlement is justifiable which is not for the interests of the world at large.

[1] Fisk Harvey E., "The Inter-ally Debts," p. 305, Bankers Trust Company, New York, 1924.

No single nation can prosper permanently by an act that will lower general international standards of life. Before such a viewpoint can be taken by large populations, ethical standards must pass through a process something like the evolution from the individual to the social point of view in considering domestic problems.[1] It is submitted that such a change in view is necessary before the debt problem can be successfully solved.

ECONOMIC CONSIDERATIONS

The Transfer Problem.—When we come to consider the actual processes by which the debts may possibly be discharged, grave difficulties in the way of payment suggest themselves. The payment of an international debt has certain essential differences from the payment of debts between parties both of whom reside in the same country. If a farmer owes money to a banker in the city, he may bring his produce into town and sell it, and with the money thus obtained he may proceed to the bank and pay off the note. When a debtor desires to pay a creditor in another country, he must not only hold the value of the obligation in some form but must also transfer it to the other country. It is this process of transfer that constitutes the difficult problem in international payment. Situations are apt to arise in international exchange which will make large payments impossible without disastrous consequences for the debtor and creditor countries alike. The first and simplest method of international payment which occurs to the casual student of this problem is payment in cash. Payment in depreciated currencies would, of course, be unacceptable and gold would be required. It is not possible, however, to rely to any great extent upon gold for the payment of large sums. The total debt from the allies was estimated on Nov. 15, 1925 on the basis of the original sums to be $12,088,885,809.20 although the principal sums due have now been reduced by debt settlements. The total gold supply of the world, estimated in 1924, was $9,669,000,000 of which

[1] From the purely individual point of view, for example, there can be no justification for taxation for public education. The man with much property and no children has a perfect case against compulsory contribution for the education of the children of others so long as the premise of individualism is used as the starting point. When, however, the matter is looked at from the social point of view, it is seen that the state has excellent reasons for acquiring individual property by taxation for general welfare purposes.

$3,278,000,000 was in Europe.   If all of the gold in Europe could have been shipped to the United States, it would have been insufficient for the payment of the debts.   Of course the European governments, for currency reasons, could not part with any considerable portion of their reserves.   Moreover, the United States could not afford to accept any considerable supply of gold on account of the dangers of gold inflation.   Gold must then be discarded as a means of payment.

Payments might be made through the purchase in Europe of exchange or drafts payable in the United States.   These drafts might then be sent to America to liquidate the debt.   Thus, a French exporter may ship a consignment of gloves to New York and draw a draft on New York against the consignee for the purchase price.   This draft when accepted is equivalent to actual cash in the United States and may be obtained and utilized by the French government in payment of its American debts.   Payment by exchange has been declared to be the only practical method of paying large sums internationally.   There must, however, be a transfer of actual values in goods or a rendering of services which create sums due in the United States to Europeans before the drafts can be drawn.   There must also be a balance in favor of Europe before the drafts can be utilized for the payment of debts, *i. e.*, the amounts due for goods or services to Europe from the United States must be greater than the amounts due to the United States from Europe for goods and services.   From this arises the dictum that the debts can only be paid in balances of goods or services.   An analysis of some of the items in international payments will show the effect of building up balances in favor of Europe.

The Balance of Trade in Goods.—The so-called "favorable" balance of trade is the excess of exports of goods over imports. Europe might help to build up credits in the United States by securing a favorable balance of trade either directly with the United States or with a third country.   If the favorable balance of trade should be built up directly with the United States, European countries would need to send more goods to the United States than they would receive back from this country.   The kind of goods which Europe would be prepared to send would consist chiefly of manufactured articles.   *These cannot be sent here without a distinct modification of the present protective tariff,* which was erected for the main purpose of keeping such goods out of competition with the products of American factories. In case this change should come about, American factories would necessarily restrict their output and yield a considerable part of the American market to European products. This would be entirely opposed to present tendencies.[1]

The large export of American capital in recent years is largely indicative of the export of goods. The loans abroad have been the means by which credit has been extended. This tendency to send American capital abroad shows beyond doubt that at the present time it would be exactly contrary to the whole economic movement to attempt to pay the United States, except by granting further credit which is, of course, no payment at all.

Norman H. Davis, former Under Secretary of State, said concerning this:

> It does seem rather absurd, however, for us to be talking so much about what European governments can pay us when our bankers and investors are advancing to them, or investing in Europe, so much more than they are paying to us. Instead of taking their goods in payment, we have, during the last five years, actually sent to Europe about $9,000,000,000 or $10,000,000,000 through the purchase of foreign securities, or practically twice as much as the capital sum due our government as represented by the recent settlements.[2]

The interallied debts were contracted in abnormal times when the production of Europeans had largely been suspended; and they represented war supplies sent to those countries. To repay the debt in normal times will be difficult. It will require a reversal of the previous transactions and goods must come from Europe in huge amounts during a period, however, when the factories of the United States are producing at a great rate. It is this that makes repayment of the debts by trade balances a difficult proceeding.

Credits might be established in the United States through European exports of manufactured goods to third countries, which countries might send raw materials to the United States and thus adjust the payments by a triangular arrangement.

[1] PATTERSON, ERNEST MINOR, "The Effect of the Debt Situation upon Europe's Relations with the United States," *Annals of the American Academy of Political and Social Science*, Vol. CXXVI, p. 27.

[2] "The Problem Involved in the Settlement of International Obligations," *Annals of the American Academy of Political and Social Science*, Vol. CXXVI, p. 36.

That is, Europe might conquer the Chinese market for manufactured goods. China might send furs, oil, raw silk, and other materials to the United States. China would owe Europe, United States would owe China, and this would give Europe an indirect claim against the United States. Secretary of Commerce Hoover, in an address delivered at Toledo, Ohio, Oct. 16, 1922, suggested that the European debts might be paid by the triangular method and that the United States would thus import materials, such as rubber, coffee, sugar, woods, etc., which would not compete with American products.[1] In reply to Mr. Hoover, Prof. Edwin R. A. Seligman of Columbia University contended that such an arrangement would help to close the tropics to American products. He said:

> If the rubber and coffee are sent out by them to pay for more industrial products received from Europe, what will there be left with which to buy industrial products from the United States? It makes very little difference to us whether the wheels of industry are stopped here because of the plethora of exports of manufactured goods from Europe into the United States or because of the inability of the United States to send its wares to the tropics. In both cases there will be a falling off in the demand for our products.[2]

The Invisible Exchange.—A favorable balance for European countries might be made by building up credits in the United States through invisible items. This could be done (*a*) through the sums earned by European ships in carrying American goods; (*b*) through earnings of European banking houses and insurance companies in rendering services to Americans; (*c*) through remittances of Europeans who have emigrated to America and who send money home; (*d*) through the expenditures of American tourists in Europe; or (*e*) through interest due to European investors in American securities.[3]

Taking these items one by one, it will be seen that the tendency is against any credit balances to European nations through invisible exchange as a whole. (*a*) The policy of the United States at present tends toward the maintenance of a merchant marine and its operation, even at a loss. Before the war,

[1] *International Conciliation*, No. 181, p. 595.

[2] *Ibid.*, p. 612.

[3] For a discussion of invisible items see Bogart, Ernest L., "An Examination of the Reasons for Revision of the Debt Settlements," *The American Economic Review*, Vol. XVIII, No. 1, Supplement, p. 250.

European nations, particularly Great Britain, earned large sums annually for carrying American freight. During the last few years the sums due to the United States for carrying the freight of others have in a large way cancelled the sums due from the United States.[1] (*b*) American banking houses and insurance companies have been growing in strength, nor is it likely that this tendency will change. (*c*) The American immigration act has partially shut the doors against Europeans and has cut deeply into the remittances that might otherwise be sent home by European immigrants. (*d*) The expenditures of American tourtists in Europe are large and would be sufficient to provide sums for debt payments were they not far more than offset by other items. (*e*) The interest due to European investors in the United States has been greatly diminished by the fact that large quantities of American securities were repurchased following the opening of the war. The interest due to Americans investing in Europe is now greater than that due from America to Europeans. On the whole, there is little hope that the invisible items will give European nations sufficient income to result in an absolute surplus for the payment of the debts.[2]

The time must necessarily come when, with the continued export of American capital abroad in private investments, the growing interest returns will necessitate the payment of a balance from the rest of the world to the United States. The payments on private loans will be much larger than those proposed on the interallied indebtedness. To receive these payments, the United States will probably be compelled to modify its tariff policy to permit an "unfavorable" balance of trade. In this general readjustment it will undoubtedly be possible for the payments of debt installments to continue.

[1] The inconsistency in the policies of the United States was well illustrated in President Harding's message to Congress of Feb. 7, 1923, in which he urged the confirmation of the debt funding arrangement with Great Britain and also the passage of a ship-subsidy bill.

[2] Some analogies have been drawn from the payment of the French indemnity to Germany following the War of 1870. The effects of this payment were so depressing to German industry that Bismarck is reported to have remarked that the next time Germany defeated France he would insist upon paying an indemnity. For the methods of payment and economic effects see McKenna, the Rt. Hon. Reginald, "Reparations and International Debts," *International Conciliation*, **181,** p. 569; Moulton, Harold G. and Constantine E. McGuire, "Germany's Capacity to Pay," p. 220, McGraw-Hill Book Company, Inc., New York, 1923.

The debt payments represent a small figure as compared with the payments to be made on account of private loans and particularly as contrasted with the total payments made to the United States in the international exchange. During 1927, the United States received $205,981,429 in payments on the debts, about $738,000,000 because of private investments abroad, and approximately $9,000,000,000 for all items visible and invisible.[1] It has been suggested that the difficulties of repayment have been exaggerated by persons unfamiliar with the magnitude of international transactions. However, the maximum payments will be more than double the present payments. They will be collected to an increasing extent from nations other than Great Britain which in 1927 paid 78 per cent of the total. And they will be present as a disturbing and irritating element during whatever crisis may arise in the future over the ever increasing payments due to American private overseas investments.

At present, the payment of the installments as they fall due is made possible partially because large sums are being loaned abroad by Americans. The net result of the two transactions, so far as the debts are concerned, is to shift the ownership of the obligations gradually from the United States government to private American investors. The paying-back process will doubtless proceed so long as the loans continue. If the conditions of the money market should become such as to put an abrupt end for a time to foreign loans, however, many foreign issues would probably go into default because of the difficulty of arranging for the payment of principal and interest. Such defaults would create resentment in the United States, but the resultant economic troubles might disturb the complacency with which Americans in general view the high protective tariff.

The Effect of Cancellation upon Credit.—It is contended that the failure to observe international obligations would so shock the confidence of the financial world in the integrity of governments as to threaten the system of international credits. Herbert Hoover in his Toledo address of Oct. 18, 1922, said:

The repudiation of these loans would undermine the whole fabric of international good faith. 1 do not believe any public official, either of

[1] "The Balance of International Payments of the United States in 1927," Bureau of Foreign and Domestic Commerce, *Trade Information Bull.* 552, pp. 22, 30–31.

the United States or any other country, could or should approve their cancellation. Certainly *I* do not.

The United States has a great interest in this phase of the matter because of the large outstanding loans which the people of this country have abroad, and Europe has a similarly great interest on account of the need for rehabilitation and development.

There are, however, strong reasons for believing that revision of the interallied indebtedness by the United States would improve rather than injure international credit. Many well-informed economists feel that the debts cannot and will not be paid at anything like the present funded figures and that to hold blindly onto these obligations will in the course of time mean their necessary repudiation. If these transactions are not separated in principle from private business investments and dealt with on an entirely different basis, the whole system of credits will be affected when the ultimate and necessary default occurs. Intergovernmental debts for war purposes are not an integral part of the system of private loans for constructive purposes. They can very well be distinguished and dealt with upon different principles.

POLITICAL CONSIDERATIONS

The political effects of the insistence upon the payment of the war debts over a sixty-two-year period will probably not reach the height of their importance in this generation. They are matters of the future and their treatment must be conducted in the realms of prophecy and imagination. It is in these fields that "next step" statesmanship has so often been lamentably weak. Keynes, in his classic analysis of postwar settlements, "The Economic Consequences of the Peace," as early as 1919, made the following prophetic comment on the political possibilities of the debts:

A debtor nation does not love its creditor, and it is fruitless to expect feelings of goodwill from France, Italy, and Russia towards this country [Great Britain] or towards America, if their future development is stifled for many years to come by the annual tribute which they must pay us. There will be a great incentive to them to seek their friends in other directions, and any future rupture of peaceable relations will always carry with it the enormous advantage of escaping the payment of external debts. If, on the other hand, these great debts are forgiven, a stimulus will be given to the solidarity and true friendliness of the nations lately associated[1] . . .

A general bonfire is so great a necessity that unless we can make it an orderly and good-tempered affair in which no serious injustice is done to any one, it will, when it comes at last, grow into a conflagration that may destroy much else as well.[2]

Since the war there has been a general crystalizing of European feeling against the United States as the great commercial rival and financial dictator of Europe and as the general exponent of an allegedly severe capitalism—a particularly frightful bugaboo to the strong and increasing socialist factions on the continent. The business of playing the world creditor is one of the most delicate roles in international politics. A blundering policy which will cause the nations of Europe to forget their own animosities in their dislike for the new giant of industry and finance will, in the long run, undoubtedly be costly to this country as contrasted with whatever comparatively slight gain might be arguable from the collection of the war debts.

There are few responsible Americans who believe that the debts should be cancelled forthwith and without some consideration in return. It seems, however, that wise statesmanship would stand ready to participate in a general readjustment in which reparations, the debts, and any other economic disabilities would be subject to such revision as would appear calculated to advance the best interests of the world.

[1] Page 278.
[2] Page 280.

PART II
THE DIPLOMACY OF COMMERCE

CHAPTER XIII

HISTORICAL ASPECTS OF COMMERCIAL DIPLOMACY

The policies of the United States in support of foreign trade have been largely shaped in behalf of the two economic activities: shipping and manufacturing. At times, it is true, the producers of natural products have exerted an influence which has had its effects in Washington, but this impulse has not been consistent and perhaps at no time has it been dominant. In the early decades of American history, shipping was the chief care of our commercial diplomats, while in recent years the safeguarding of markets for manufactured goods has been of far more concern. In behalf of first one and then the other of these activities, the American government has since the Revolution been almost continually interested in the politics of foreign trade.

In order that the reader may see panoramically the influence of commerce in American politics the following aspects of the subject will be reviewed briefly:

   I. The shipping period:
      A. The struggles against the mercantilist system.
      B. The advocacy of neutral rights and the freedom of the seas.
      C. The drive against the markets of the Far East.
  II. The period of manufacturing.
      A. The demand for special favors.
      B. Pan-Americanism as an agency of trade promotion.
      C. The demand for equal treatment.

THE YOUNG NATION STRUGGLES AGAINST THE MERCANTILIST SYSTEM

Back in the pre-Revolution days the British mercantilist laws had tended to place an exasperating check on the commerce of the colonists. Parliament had stipulated that certain commodities could not be exported from the colonies except to Great Britain or her dominions, thus preventing colonial trade with foreign countries. Smuggling, carried on with the support of public opinion, went far to mitigate the rigors of the restrictions, but, nevertheless, the fetters on colonial trade continued to the time of the Revolution to be a cause for complaint against the mother country. The Declaration of Independence complained against the king " . . . for cutting off our trade with all parts of the world."

When the Revolutionary War had freed the colonies from Great Britain, the emancipated states found their commerce hampered by a long series of restrictions, which were a part of the well-accepted system of mercantilism. The new exclusions from the British possessions were particularly oppressive. As a part of the Empire the colonies had been admitted to other British markets and the intercolonial commerce had worn deep channels in American life. The trade was destroyed by the maritime warfare of the Revolution but attempts were made to reestablish it. The American commissioners who were sent to Paris to negotiate peace with Great Britain were instructed by Congress:

> . . . to endeavor to obtain for the citizens and the inhabitants of the United States a direct commerce to all parts of the British dominions and possessions, in like manner as all parts of the United States may be opened to a direct commerce of British subjects; or at least that such direct commerce be extended to all parts of the British dominions and possessions in Europe and the West Indies.[1]

The answer to this effort was the issuance by the British government of orders in council shutting out American vessels from the British West Indies and stipulating that only certain articles could be transported there from the United States.[2] It was said that the news of this order caused the price of American supplies to rise 300 per cent in the West Indies.[3] It is also reported that the exclusion of American commerce contributed to the starvation of 15,000 slaves in the islands during the next four years. The annual loss of trade to the United States is estimated to have been $3,500,000.[4]

The British order was a blow to postwar reconstruction, particularly in New England; for commerce and fishing were

[1] WHARTON, FRANCIS, "The Revolutionary Diplomatic Correspondence of the United States," Vol. VI, p. 188, Govt. Printing Office, Washington, 1889.

[2] *Ibid.*, p. 541.

[3] ADAMS, JAMES TRUSLOW, "New England in the Republic, 1776–1850," p. 118, Little, Brown, and Company, Boston, 1926.

[4] COMAN, KATHARINE, "Industrial History of the United States," p. 112, The Macmillan Company, New York, 1905.

vitally important to the future of the New England states. Prior to the Revolution, one-third of the commerce from Boston and New York had been with the West Indies.[1] The shipping fleets of those communities were in need of cargoes. "From Sandy Hook, however, to the stormy headlands of Maine," writes Ralph D. Paine, "it was a matter of life and death that ships should freely come and go with cargoes to exchange. All other resources were trifling in comparison."[2]

The American merchant marine staggered under the British broadside. Shipbuilding and fishing likewise suffered. The shipment of codfish to the West Indies had been an important part of the intercolonial commerce prior to the Revolution. The fishing fleets of New England, in 1764, had given employment to 6,002 men.[3] The inferior cod from their catches had been sent to feed the slaves in the British West Indies and had not only furnished a *quid pro quo* for West Indian products but had also produced a surplus of specie and bills of credit. This surplus enabled the colonists to make purchases in Europe, the balance of trade with which continent had been unfavorable to America. American fish was excluded from the West Indies under the orders in council above mentioned.

Merchants, shipowners, shipbuilders, and fishermen, embittered by the postwar commercial depression, complained against the British rule. In response the government of the Confederation exerted its influence to secure the removal of the barriers and to obtain entrance into other markets which were similarly closed.

Under the Articles of Confederation, the American government was impotent to wage an effective diplomatic battle for the removal of the restrictions. Singleness of action could not be secured among thirteen states each of which was master of its own commercial affairs. The need for centralized control of foreign policy was one of the reasons urged for the adoption of the Federal Constitution. When the Constitution went into effect in 1789 the problem of breaking down restrictions against trade was taken up with brighter prospects. The economic

[1] *Ibid.;* HERRICK, CHEESMAN A., "History of Commerce and Industry," p. 314, The Macmillan Company, New York, 1917.

[2] PAINE, RALPH D., "The Old Merchant Marine," p. 50, Yale Univ. Press, New Haven, 1921.

[3] WEEDEN, WILLIAM B., "Economic and Social History of New England, 1620–1789," Vol. II, p. 750, Houghton Mifflin Company, Boston, 1894.

influences making for the disintegration of the mercantilist systems also began to favor the success of the American plans.

The policy of the United States in opening the ports of other countries to American trade was backed by two methods of persuasion. In the first place, reciprocity was offered to foreign nations and the lure of the American market was held out in exchange for the right to enter the markets of others. In the second place, retaliation was employed and Congress enacted measures to shut American ports to the vessels of countries which did not admit the ships of the United States.[1]

An illustration of the policy of retaliation adopted for the purpose of forcing concessions is seen in the Act of Congress of Apr. 18, 1818, which prohibited the entry into American ports of British vessels coming from any British colony which was closed against American vessels. Pressure thus exerted upon British shipping interests was intended to secure from the British government a more respectful consideration of American claims. On July 25, 1825, the trade with the British colonies was thrown open to the vessels of all nations which should accept certain conditions. The United States, for the time under the Adams administration, failed to accept the conditions and a brief period of almost total non-intercourse ensued. Commercial pressure upon the government, however, finally brought results. Andrew Jackson had been in office but a few months when the policy of Adams was reversed and an agreement was reached with Great Britain which opened the ports of the United States to British vessels from the colonies and reciprocally the ports of the British colonies to American vessels. "The last remnants of the vicious system that was thus broken down," says Moore, "were removed in 1849."[2] While this was largely a diplomatic contest in behalf of American shipowners it was also, because of the close connection between national trade and shipping, a contest to remove restrictions which operated in practice against the export of American goods.

It has sometimes been emphasized that the keynote of this early commercial diplomacy was liberty. One eminent author

---

[1] See the message of President John Quincy Adams of Dec. 6, 1825, RICHARDSON, "Messages and Papers of the Presidents," Vol. XI, p. 300. See also MOORE, "Principles of American Diplomacy," Chap. V. A variety of special acts favoring American shipping were likewise passed which will be discussed in a later chapter.

[2] Op. cit., p. 171.

has attempted to show that the policy resulted from the doctrinaire devotion of the founders to the ideal of freedom, and that it sprang forth as a natural result of the philosophy of the Declaration of Independence. John Bassett Moore says:

The Declaration of American Independence, however, bore upon its face the marks of distinction, and presaged the development of a theory and a policy which must be worked out in opposition to the ideas that then dominated the civilized world. Of this theory and policy the keynote was freedom; freedom of the individual, in order that he might work out his destiny in his own way; freedom in government, in order that the human faculties might have free course; freedom in commerce, in order that the resources of the earth might be developed and rendered fruitful in the increase of human wealth, contentment, and happiness.[1]

While this statement attributes to our forefathers a philanthropy and idealism in their commercial policy which is more than human, it nevertheless accurately indicates the aim of liberty which was their purpose. But this purpose was based upon the immediate desire to provide trade for American ships and to sell such products as fish, lumber, and farm products rather than upon the humanitarian motive of developing the resources of the world for the increase of human contentment. The wealth, contentment, and happiness of British shipowners, for example, was of no concern to the United States.

THE UNITED STATES DEMANDS FREEDOM ON THE SEAS

The developing young maritime nation yearns for liberty. It was during the period when Holland was building her merchant marine that Grotius wrote "Mare Liberum." Without freedom, ships cannot sail the seas and the profits of the merchants and shipowners are cut off. There is likewise a depressing effect upon domestic industries which depend upon shipping and commerce. Some nations have been able to keep the seas open for their vessels by the maintenance of large navies. Others, without navies, have relied upon diplomacy. The United States, having seen the oceans closed against her ships in the early days of American history, joined with the advocates of freedom on the seas. This advocacy was not confined to negotiations for the removal of restrictions in times of peace. The contest for neutral rights during the European wars following

[1] *Op. cit.*, p. 2.

1793 was of the highest significance and is taken up in a subsequent chapter.

Defense of American Commerce in the Mediterranean.—The pre-Revolutionary commerce in the Mediterranean had been important to American merchants. American ships had sailed through the Straits of Gibraltar with one-sixth of our exports of wheat and flour and one-fourth of the dried and pickled fish. Under the protection afforded by British tribute, from 80 to 100 colonial ships had gone freely along the Mediterranean coasts. Twelve hundred American seamen were employed in the trade.[1] The Revolution saw a temporary cessation in this commerce, and when American ships again turned to the Mediterranean they found their routes infested with the corsairs of Morocco, Algeria, Tripoli, and Tunis. With the profits of counting houses in Salem, Boston, New York, and Philadelphia thus threatened and with the markets of the fisherman and farmer thus cut off, the government tried various methods of pacifying the warlike North Africans.

At first treaties were negotiated with the several Barbary states and tribute was paid. After an American vessel had been captured, a treaty was entered into with Morocco in 1787 at a cost of $10,000. The Dey of Algiers sent his fierce corsairs after American ships and thirteen were seized. The crews were kept in slavery, awaiting ransom. It cost the United States $800,000 to settle with the Dey, and a treaty was signed in 1795. The treaty stipulated that "the vessels of both nations shall pass each other without any impediment or molestation," but the United States was required to continue tribute by annual payments of twelve thousand Algerine sequins in maritime stores.[2] Treaties were signed with Tripoli in 1796 and with Tunis in 1797.

Becoming dissatisfied with the value of the tribute received from the United States, the Bashaw of Tripoli began war on this country in 1801. After a squadron had been sent into the Mediterranean and a number of encounters had taken place on land and sea, a treaty of peace was signed in 1805. After the War of 1812 had begun, the exacting and imperious Dey of Algiers, made bold by the temporary weakness of the United States in the Mediterranean, alleged that there was shortage in

[1] MOORE, *op. cit.*, p. 105.

[2] For the text see *Treaties, etc., between the United States and Other Powers*, Vol. I, p. 1.

his tribute and expelled all Americans from his domain. An American brig was taken. When the war with Great Britain was finished, the United States sent two squadrons to deal with the Dey, who was then brought to sign a treaty by which all rights to tribute were relinquished.[1] This marked the decline of the Barbary tribute system. Bombardments of Algiers in 1816 and 1824 by British fleets and the conquest of Algiers by France in 1830 were necessary, however, to the complete elimination of the Algerian seahawks from the Mediterranean.

THE UNITED STATES SEEKS TRADE PRIVILEGES IN THE FAR EAST

China.—American trading houses have been interested in commerce with the swarming millions of Asia since the beginning of our national existence. Some of the well-known early fortunes of New England were founded on the Canton trade, and stories are told of handsome profits from the early voyages. An American vessel of less than one hundred tons, which made a voyage to Canton with a cargo of furs, was reported to have secured a return of $60,000 on an investment of $9,000. Another venture yielded $150,000 on a capital of $40,000, and a third realized $284,000 on an investment of $50,000.[2]

An interesting account of the traffic is contained in William B. Weeden's "Economic and Social History of New England."[3]

For six months before a Canton ship left Salem, a small fleet of brigs and schooners were plying about and getting her with her cargo ready. They brought iron, hemp, and duck from Sweden and St. Petersburg; wine and lead from France, Spain, and Madeira; rum and sugar from the West Indies. Into these exchanges there went fish, flour, and provisions, iron and tobacco, from New York, Philadelphia, and Virginia. An important part of the outfit was in ginseng and specie. In the early voyages, neighboring merchants sent small ventures, paying from 20 to 33⅓ per cent of their value as freight. The first ships brought back tea largely, and the market was soon overstocked. Coffee then became a better return. This, with tea, muslins, silks, etc., was distributed to the Atlantic ports.

[1] Article II, "It is distinctly understood between the contracting parties, that no tribute, either as biennial presents, or under any other form or name whatever, shall ever be required by the Dey and Regency of Algiers from the United States of America, on any pretext whatever." *Treaties, etc., between the United States and Other Powers*, Vol. I, p. 7.

[2] FOSTER, JOHN W., "American Diplomacy in the Orient," p. 37, Houghton Mifflin Company, Boston, 1903.

[3] Vol. II, pp. 824–825.

The trade trickled through a Chinese wall of exclusion which the Imperial government had set up for the purpose of barring commerce from the West. All of the Chinese ports except Canton were closed against foreign trade. At that place vessels were admitted during certain months of the year when the winds were favorable. Foreigners were permitted during these months to come to Canton and maintain factories, *i. e.*, agencies for trade. Their business and personal affairs were, however, bound about with innumerable restrictions, which, to the occidental mind, seemed unnecessary and humiliating; and during the remainder of the year they were forced to retire to the Portuguese colony of Macao on the Pearl River below Canton. The fact that such trade as was permitted was exceedingly lucrative caused the traders to desire more, and they in turn stimulated their governments into action.

Great Britain was the first to challenge this system of restrictions with war; and in the Treaty of Nanking, signed in 1842 at the conclusion of military operations, the English secured the rights of trade and residence at Canton, Amoy, Foochow, Ningpo, and Shanghai. The tariff to be charged against British goods was fixed in a treaty of the following year at specific amounts equal to about 5 per cent ad valorem. Thus Great Britain secured herself against any substantial tariff restrictions on her exports to China.

When the news of the British treaty reached the United States, Congress was urged by the President in a special message to send a mission to China to negotiate a treaty of commerce. The Chinese had already promised that the American merchants would not come "to have merely a dry stick"[1] and it was considered that the time for securing a treaty was favorable. A bill was introduced in Congress to appropriate $40,000 to be placed at the disposal of the President to enable him to send a proper and imposing mission. This action was urged on by the merchants of the Atlantic seaports and was supported in Congress by John Quincy Adams, Chairman of the House Committee on Foreign Affairs, who well realized its importance to commercial interests. That some Congressmen were inclined to overemphasize the commercial importance of the treaty is indicated by the words of Isaac E. Holmes, a Representative from South Carolina.

[1] FOSTER, *op. cit.*, p. 75.

In the indirect language of the Congressional Globe, Mr. Holmes was reported as follows:

Mr. Holmes said he was one of those on the Committee of Foreign Relations who had voted to introduce this bill. In the present state of the commerce of the world, he regarded the present mission to China as more important than were all our other missions together. The trade of South America and Europe was fixed on an established basis. But, by the opening of intercourse with China, three hundred and twenty millions of people (hitherto shut out from the rest of the world) would be brought within the circle of commercial republics—for it was commerce that republicanized and civilized men . . .

The benefits of a commercial intercourse with China could not be too highly appreciated. No man now had it in his power to estimate how much of our surplus productions might be sold in that almost boundless country, and how much of our tobacco might be there chewed, in place of opium.[1]

The above extract from the debates of the time not only reveals the commercial importance attributed to the opening of the Orient but also indicates that the representative of the plantation as well as the spokesman of shipping had some faint notions as to the possibilities of a market in the Far East. If one can get the picture of millions of residents of China industriously chewing tobacco instead of opium and can visualize the corresponding prosperity of agriculture in the Southern states, which would certainly have followed, it becomes easy to understand the fervor with which Mr. Holmes supported the bill as well as the truth of the statement that "it was commerce that republicanized and civilized men."

Congress passed the bill and Caleb Cushing, a shrewd lawyer and diplomat, who had learned the needs of the American merchant marine in his home town, the busy shipping center of Newburyport, Mass., was appointed commissioner. Cushing went to China accompanied by an imposing suite and supported by a squadron of war vessels. In due course of time the Treaty of 1844 was concluded, providing for rights of trade and residence at the five ports mentioned in the British treaty and also for stipulations concerning the tariff which were similar to those secured by Great Britain.

[1] *Congressional Globe*, Twenty-seventh Congress, third session, Feb. 28, 1843, p. 325.

Since the time of the Treaty of 1844, the United States has had in mind two main policies concerning China. On the one hand, in company with European governments, this country has endeavored to break down Chinese barriers to trade. The number of open ports has now been increased to something over one hundred,[1] and in other ways commerce has been made less difficult. On the other hand, the United States has sought to keep China free from the restrictions by which other powers have sought to gain a preference in the Chinese trade. The fight against these preferences is the struggle for the "open door" and will be discussed at greater length in a succeeding chapter.

Japan.—Opening Japan to western trade was a task in which the United States bore the major role. During the seventeenth century the western trade with Japan, which had been highly profitable, was cut off abruptly. This was due largely to complaints made against foreign missions, but in the process of expulsion the European merchants were driven out along with the missionaries. From that time on until the middle of the nineteenth century Japan was almost entirely isolated from the rest of the world. The only intercourse with the West which remained came through the annual visit of two Dutch vessels to the Island of Deshima in the harbor of Nagasaki, where cargoes were unloaded and Japanese merchandise placed aboard. With the exception of the small Dutch commerce, western trade with Japan was stopped for more than 200 years.

The American appetite for Japanese trade had no doubt been whetted by tales of mysterious Nagasaki told by the shippers and sailors of the American ships *Franklin* and *Margaret*, for in 1799 the first and in 1801 the second of these vessels had been chartered by the Dutch to make the voyage. The supercargoes of both ships had written accounts of their strange experiences."[2] Later on the attempts of American traders to open commercial relations through the return of shipwrecked Japanese sailors were on two occasions repelled with decision. As the middle of the nineteenth century approached, it became apparent that Japanese commerce could not much longer be denied to the western world. The partial opening up of China had pointed in this direction. Con-

[1] WILLIAMS, E. T., "The Open Ports of China," *The Geographical Review*, Vol. IX, p. 306.

[2] PAINE, *op. cit.*, pp. 68–70.

templating the almost unlimited possibilities of trade which seemed to lie in the Far East, William H. Seward, as United States Senator from New York, remarked: "The Pacific Ocean, its shores, its islands, and the vast regions beyond, will become the chief theater of events in the world's great Hereafter."[1] The slim Yankee clipper with its enormous spread of sail had begun to cleave the waters of the Far East and had brought the Orient and Occident nearer in point of time. The *Rainbow*, launched in 1845, went out on her second voyage to China in ninety-two days and returned in eighty-eight, which was remarkable time in the sailing vessel period.[2]

American merchants who were feverishly seeking new trading areas brought pressure to bear upon their government, which was willing to act. Nor was the commercial and official sentiment content to follow the calm but tedious path of strictly pacific diplomacy. In 1852, Commodore Perry was dispatched with an imposing squadron to open treaty negotiations. While the Perry mission was yet in stage of preparation in the United States a member of the Senate, in opposing a resolution intended to secure information as to the object of the expedition, expressed what was probably a common feeling concerning the undertaking. He said:

Sir, you have to deal with barbarians as barbarians. These people, who are isolated from the world, not only socially but politically, are not expected to be regulated by the motives that govern the civilized portion of mankind. I think it a very laudable object to endeavor to extend our commercial intercourse so far as we can; and in doing so, I think the exhibition of our power there will command respect.[3]

With the arrival of the Perry mission, the Japanese were treated for the first time to the sight of steam vessels. The amazing spectacle presented by the squadron pouring forth its streams of black smoke and moving up the bay directly in the face of a head wind alarmed the people and threw the city of Yedo into a panic. John W. Foster, in his "American Diplomacy in the Orient," quotes a popular ballad which was sung among the Japanese at that time:

[1] Quoted in Foster, *op. cit.*, p. 135.

[2] Paine, *op. cit.*, p. 156.

[3] *The Congressional Globe*, April 1, 1852, Thirty-second Congress, first session, p. 942.

Through a black night of cloud and rain,
The Black Ship plies her way —
An alien thing of evil mein —
Across the waters gray.

And slowly floating onward go
These Black Ships, wave-tossed to and fro.[1]

This spectacular attempt at gunboat diplomacy was eminently successful. Commodore Perry brooked no interference with his ships but steamed past the forts and anchored well within the Bay of Yedo. In dealing with the Japanese he refused to permit evasion or to deal with subordinate officials, and was able to deliver the letter which he bore from the President into the hands of two Japanese princes of the highest rank. He then shortly withdrew his expedition with the promise that he would return the following year and take up the matter of a formal agreement. The treaty of the ensuing year, signed Mar. 31, 1854, provided for the opening of Nagasaki and two other ports for the landing of American ships and the purchase of supplies. In 1858, by a treaty of commerce and navigation, permission was granted to trade at six ports and a schedule of duties was fixed in the treaty. The United States had opened "the Land of the Rising Sun" to American trade. General intercourse between the Western world and Japan ensued.

INFANT INDUSTRY ENTERS THE FIELD OF COMMERCIAL DIPLOMACY

The clipper ship reached its zenith of influence about 1857 and in a few years it began to pass from the sea. With the decline of the American merchant marine, however, a motive force in American foreign relations, which in time was to be much more powerful than shipping, began feebly to stir. American manufacturing developed on a new scale in the decades following the Civil War, and by 1890 the industrialists were exerting on commercial policies an influence which gradually increased until it became dominant in the aftermath of the World War.

In the latter part of the nineteenth century American manufactured goods had difficulty in competing with the products of Europe. The control of the home market was insured by the

[1] Page 151.

raising of the protective tariff to great heights. There came a time, however, when production in certain lines began to outrun the domestic demand and manufacturers were looking around for foreign markets to conquer. Latin America in the late eighties appealed to the United States as a suitable field for the expansion of exports, but this field was preempted by Europeans against which the American manufacturers could not well compete. Special advantages were, accordingly, requested which would enable Americans to obtain a larger share of the trade. Such was the cry which infant industry uttered in the ears of the Department of State and the department sought for means of pacifying the lusty child.

James G. Blaine, Secretary of State in 1881, and again from 1889 to 1892, may be taken as typifying the commercial diplomat of that era. Blaine was a thoroughgoing protectionist and was also energetic in his attempts to extend American markets. He was an eloquent and forceful orator, although history has not recorded him as a careful or sophisticated diplomat. His attempts to increase American exports through the securing of special favors were, nevertheless, significant in the diplomacy of his time.

In dealing with Latin-American nations, Blaine placed much stress on the fact that practically all of the goods which the United States sent into those countries were charged substantial duties while the greater part of the exports from Latin America to the United States were admitted free. Blaine and his supporters considered this to be unfair treatment. "It was the application of the golden rule of commerce—the doctrine of fair trade—to insist that the countries whose products had so long been admitted free into our ports should admit our products free to theirs," wrote "A Supporter of the 'Pan-American' Idea."[1] This doctrine, emanating as it did from the mouths of high protectionists, must have seemed strange to European free traders who had been admitting American goods free while their own had been charged high duties in American ports. The art of sugar-coating a policy by attempting to explain it upon the basis of fair play and international morality was, however, not peculiar to James G. Blaine. The foible of rationalization is omnipresent in diplomacy. The plain reason for the difference in tariffs was, of course, that our imports from Latin America

[1] *The Review of Reviews* (American edition), June, 1892, p. 548.

were raw materials and foods, and consequently it was to our interest to admit them free. Latin-American countries taxed their imports from all countries alike and the purpose was revenue.

Among the commercial efforts of the United States during this period were the attempts to secure a customs union in the Pan-American Conference of 1889, and the use of the bargaining tariff for the purpose of obtaining advantages for American exports.

In the First International American Conference, held in Washington in 1889 to 1890, the United States brought forth a project for a customs union which should give all of the members of the conference substantial advantages in their trade with one another. This proposal was submitted in the Act of Congress calling for the conference and also in the invitation of the United States to the Latin-American nations. The reasons for the proposal were that it would give the United States preferences over European nations in Latin-American markets, and that it would not greatly affect our fiscal system as most of the Latin-American products were already admitted free to the United States. The project, however, met with fierce opposition.

Senator Roque Saenz Peña, delegate from the Argentine Republic, expressed forcefully the view of the Latin-American nations. Those countries could not afford to cut off their trade with Europe in order to gain freer intercourse with the United States. He said:

> The consumption of the nations of Latin America represented in this conference amounts to $560,000,000, but the United States share in those importations to the amount only of $52,000,000, not being 10 per cent of our purchases from Europe. The relation of these figures to the trade of the United States reveals the poverty of the exchanges with greater clearness. Out of their total export trade, amounting to $740,000,000, Latin America buys only $52,000,000; that is to say, 7 per cent of the total exports.[1]

The political effects of this combination were feared by Senor Peña whose apprehensions were expressed as follows:

> . . . it is easy to foresee the squirmings of Europe when she should feel the effects of a continental blockade, maintained, it is true, not by

---

[1] *International American Conference*, Vol. I, p. 113, Govt. Printing Office, Washington, 1890.

warships but by belligerent tariffs. It would not be countries bound together by political bonds that would enter into compacts inspired by a national sentiment. It would be the war of one continent against another, eighteen sovereignties allied to exclude from the life of commerce that same Europe which extends to us her hand, sends us her strong arms, and complements our economic existence, after having apportioned us her civilization and her culture, her sciences and her arts, industries and customs that have completed our sociologic evolutions.[1]

The proposal was overwhelmingly turned down by the conference.

Bargaining tariff laws, giving the President power to negotiate with other countries for a special lowering of tariff duties on American goods, were enacted in 1890 and 1897. The particular objective was the Latin-American market. The nature and effect of these acts will be taken up in a later chapter. For the present the matter may be dismissed with the comment that, except in a few instances, the general advantage accruing to the United States through its efforts to secure particular favors was not great. As the productive power of the United States increased, as the ability to compete in foreign markets was established, and as the menace of special arrangements as between countries in the Pan-European movement loomed on the horizon, the situation changed radically. The United States came to abandon and denounce the policy of favors in commerce and to demand, as of right, equal treatment for the exports of this country.[2]

Pan-Americanism as an Agency for Trade Promotion.—While the United States has ceased to demand or even to desire special tariff rates in Latin-American countries, the use of the Pan-

[1] *Ibid.*, p. 124. It is an interesting fact that thirty-nine years of commercial and industrial evolution have completely reversed the positions of the United States and Argentina. In the Sixth Pan-American Conference, held at Havana in 1928, the Argentine delegation favored and the American delegation opposed a clause in a treaty preamble which proposed the elimination of economic barriers as between American countries. Dr. Pueyrredon of Argentina argued that trade barriers are not compatible with the spirit of Pan Americanism while Charles Evans Hughes contended that the fixing of tariff duties is one of the attributes of sovereignty which cannot be relinquished by the individual states.

[2] In addition to arrangements made under the bargaining tariffs, the United States entered into three reciprocity treaties for the exchange of special favors. These treaties were not peculiar to the particular period around 1890 but were spread over half a century. The dates of the treaties were: with Canada, 1854; with Hawaii, 1875; with Cuba, 1902.

American movement to further our trade interests has not been neglected. It is a commonplace observation that in the councils of Pan-Americanism the United States has stood with some consistency for the removal of certain kinds of barriers to trade, other than tariffs; and that this desire for economic action has contrasted somewhat with the wish of many Latin-American countries for the adoption of political measures for the purpose of controlling the policies of the governments of the western hemisphere.

The following are some of the projects which have been urged in the various conferences between the American countries:

1. Patent, trademark, and copyright conventions which will permit an exporter to safeguard his property in all of the American countries with the least possible trouble and with the least possible expense.

2. Laws providing for the uniformity of customs regulations and classifications of merchandise.

3. Conventions which will eliminate local taxation of commercial travelers and which will permit them to secure entry for their samples without duty payments.

4. The development of the Pan-American Union as a clearing house of information on commercial and other subjects.

5. The development of transportation and communication.

While there is not sufficient space to detail all that has been accomplished with regard to the foregoing subjects, it may be helpful to discuss, as an illustration, a typical aim of American exporters in the Pan-American conferences, the protection of the trademark. In the United States, the *use* of a trademark is sufficient to vest ownership, while in Latin-American countries *legal registration* is necessary. Here is a confusion of law which might conceivably be disastrous to an American exporter of well-known goods. Unless the manufacturer should in some way register his mark in all of the countries to which the goods are to be shipped, it might transpire that another would secure the title to it by registration. The American exporter would then be unable to use his own trademark while he would be forced to submit to seeing someone else reap the fruits of his advertising and faithfulness in producing an article of quality over a long period of time.[1] It will be apparent that so far as the members of

[1] In 1927, an individual from a South American country visited the United States and called upon the manufacturers of radio apparatus. He then returned to his own country and registered in his own name some forty trade marks. Concerning this action James L. Brown, Chief of the Patent

the Pan-American Union are concerned, the United States is the only one which is particularly interested in the protection of trademarks. Countries which export raw materials and unmanufactured foodstuffs are not vitally concerned.

The aim of the United States has been to obtain agreement to a system by which one registration at an international office will provide for registration in all of the American republics. Such a plan was adopted in the form of a draft convention by the Fourth International American Conference, in 1910, but it did not receive a sufficient number of ratifications. In the Fifth Conference, in 1923, a less satisfactory plan was approved. The new convention provided for two Inter-American Bureaus or registration offices, one at Havana and the other at Rio de Janiero. Under this plan, when an American desires to protect his trademark in any of the countries adhering to the convention he registers it with the United States Commissioner of Patents. At the same time he pays a fee of $50 to cover the expenses of the Inter-American Bureau and also a sum equivalent to the registration fees required in the republics in which he desires registration. The matter is then referred to the Havana office where the details of the registration are taken care of. The convention, having been ratified by the United States, Brazil, Cuba, Paraguay, Haiti, and the Dominican Republic, went into effect on Sept. 30, 1926.[1]

"THE JOYOUS TRIUMPH OF MASS PRODUCTION" AND THE DEMAND FOR EQUAL TREATMENT

The great changes in American industrial life which became apparent at the time of the World War were aptly summarized by William S. Culbertson in his testimony before the Senate Committee on Foreign Relations in connection with the commercial treaty with Germany, of 1923:

---

and Trademark Section of the Department of Commerce, said: "Of course, protest was made to these applications for registration but such action was probably too late and now this individual may sell his rights to competitors of these American firms and may even confiscate the American goods should they arrive at a port in that country, bearing a trademark of which he is the registrant, and, accordingly, in the absence of fraud, the lawful owner." "Misappropriation of American Trademarks Abroad," *Commerce Reports*, June 4, 1928, p. 572.

[1] *Treaty Series* No. 751. See also KOSICKI, BERNARD A., "Trademark Protection in Latin America," Bureau of Foreign and Domestic Commerce, *Trade Information Bull.* 219, Apr. 4, 1924.

Beginning in 1914 a great economic change came over our national life. We suddenly realized that our commercial treaty structure was not adapted to the new conditions in which we found ourselves. The productive capacity of many of our industries expanded. The volume and the variety of American export trade increased. Many, many American products which had never found their way on to the shelves of any foreign country began to appear there during the period from 1914 down to 1920, and, as a matter of fact, down to the present time. We became interested in shipping. We changed, as it has been usually phrased, from a debtor to a creditor nation. Our whole attitude toward international commercial relations changed, as a matter of necessity, because of the expansion of our industrial and economic life.[1]

It is probable that if the United States had remained primarily an agricultural nation the problem of foreign markets would not be today such an important matter in our policies. It is true that in the earlier history of the country there was much bickering with other nations to secure freedom to send foods and raw materials into their territories or colonies. As time has passed, however, the exclusions against such commerce have disappeared. Modern nations with the industrial urge prefer rather to cultivate the importation of foods and raw materials and to reserve their barriers for the exclusion of manufactured goods. During the last few decades the character of goods comprising American foreign trade has changed, until manufactured products constitute the largest single class of exports, having usurped the premier place formerly held by raw materials. On the other hand, in imports the reverse has been true, and crude materials have displaced manufactured goods as the most important class. The table on page 263 in columns 3 and 5 sets forth this transposition.

From the "infant-industry" stage this country has now progressed to a position where it is able to compete with the world in many important lines of manufactured goods, and some fields are dominated almost completely by the American article. This ability to produce cheaply despite a high scale of wages is variously ascribed to (1) large-scale production, (2) an adequate supply of capital to maintain and improve plants and equipment according to the most progressive plans, (3) labor efficiency and industrial education, and (4) a rich supply of most of the basic

[1] "Hearings on Treaty of Commerce and Consular Rights with Germany," before the U. S. Senate Committee on Foreign Relations, p. 45, Washington Govt. Printing Office, 1924.

materials. The injury dealt to European industrial nations by the war has also given to the United States an important temporary advantage as a competitor.

THE RISE OF AN INDUSTRIAL NATION AS SHOWN BY THE STATISTICS OF ITS FOREIGN TRADE

	1	2	3	4	5	6
	Foodstuffs in crude condition and food animals, per cent	Foodstuffs partly or wholly manufactured, per cent	Crude materials for use in manufactures, per cent	Manufactures for further use in manufacturing, per cent	Manufactures ready for consumption per cent	Miscellaneous, per cent
Exports						
1821	4.79	19.51	60.46	9.42	5.66	0.16
1880	32.30	23.47	28.98	3.52	11.26	0.47
1910 to 1914	5.9	13.8	33.1	16.1	30.7	0.4
1926	7.1	10.7	26.8	13.9	41.5	
Imports						
1821	11.15	19.85	3.64	7.48	56.86	1.02
1880	15.01	17.69	19.74	16.59	29.43	1.54
1910 to 1914	12.0	11.5	34.4	18.2	23	0.9
1926	12.2	9.4	40.4	18.2	19.8	

The growth in the export of American manufactured goods since 1914 has been remarkable. Even allowing for the increase in prices, the 1926 exports are more than double those for the years preceding the World War.[1] The competitive power of the United States is particularly strong in certain lines of articles which are characteristic of recent industrial development and which seem to be well suited to the genius of American industry. A world leadership has been established in the quality and price of such products as machinery, automotive vehicles, and labor-saving devices.[2] In the manufacture of electrical equipment this country stands supreme. Generators, transformers, motors, switching equipment, radio apparatus, telephones, and wiring supplies have a large sale in other countries. In the field of agricultural machinery, American manufacturers have conquered the domestic market without the aid of a tariff and have sent abroad a large proportion of their production. American tractors,

[1] KLEIN, JULIUS, "Our Growing Trade in Manufactured Goods," *Commerce Reports*, Aug. 16, 1926, p. 398.

[2] *Ibid.*, p. 400.

harvesters, and other implements of power farming find a remunerative market in the great agricultural countries of Argentina, Canada, and Russia. Other articles which may be called American specialties are automobiles, motor cycles, bicycles, sewing machines, typewriters, adding machines, cash registers, and additional products of the later machine age.[1]

The supreme example of the all-conquering American product is the motion-picture film. Due to an abundance of capital, climatic advantages, and an unrivalled domestic market, the American producers and distributors have expanded their activities at home and abroad, until Hollywood has come to amuse, entertain, and possibly instruct the entire world. In 1926, it was estimated that the United States supplied upwards of 85 per cent of the pictures shown in the theaters of all foreign countries.[2] There has been a tendency for the percentage to decline with the growth of foreign producing industries but the United States still dominates the world market without a close rival in both short subjects and feature films. About 75 per cent of the short subjects shown in Norway, Sweden, Denmark, Germany, and the new Baltic states are American. In Great Britain, the Netherlands, Belgium, and Czechoslovakia the proportion is about 80 per cent, in France it is 95 per cent, and in practically all Latin-American and Far-Eastern countries it is from 90 to 95 per cent. The American feature film is supreme in the market of every country excepting Japan where Japanese features are in the majority. Even in Germany, which boasts the strongest producing industry outside of the United States, from 300 to 350 of the 450 feature films shown annually are imported from the United States.[3] Criticism of American films and a desire to develop the domestic product have led several countries to adopt protective policies. Legislation against foreign films has been passed in Great Britain, Germany, France, Austria, Hungary,

---

[1] See the compilation of articles entitled "Markets of the United States" in the *Annals of the American Academy of Political and Social Science*, Vol. CXXVII, No. 216.

[2] JOHNSTON, WILLIAM A., "The Motion Picture Industry," *ibid.*, p. 94.

[3] The above facts are from GOLDEN, N. D., "Short Subject Film Market of Europe," Bureau of Foreign and Domestic Commerce, *Trade Information Bull.* 522 and "Short Subject Film Market in Latin America, Canada, the Far East, Africa and the Near East," *Bull.* 544. See also NORTH, C. J., "Our Foreign Trade in Motion Pictures," *Annals of the American Academy of Political and Social Science*, Vol. CXXVIII, p. 100.

and Italy.[1] American exports are still continuing on a large scale, however, and about 30 per cent of the revenues of American distributors come from abroad.[2]

The growth of American productive power and the ability to compete in the foreign market for manufactured goods has brought about a profound change in the commercial policy of this country. Reciprocity, special favors, and a contracted interpretation of the most-favored-nation clause have been abandoned and equal opportunity in the markets of the world is demanded. Discriminations against American trade are now considered to be a potential barrier to success in the future, and the doctrine of equality has been selected as the most appropriate weapon for the battle against such trade obstacles.

[1] GOLDEN, N. D., "World Markets for American Motion Picture Films," *Commerce Reports*, Apr. 23, 1928, p. 202.

[2] *Ibid.*

CHAPTER XIV

BARGAINING TARIFF LAWS AND RECIPROCITY AGREEMENTS

THE IMPORTANCE OF MARKETS IN FOREIGN POLICY

In the foreign trade policies of most aspiring world powers, sales receive greater consideration than do purchases. This one-sided emphasis arises from the desire for a so-called favorable balance of trade, but it is greatly enhanced by the all-prevailing ambition for greatness in production. Western civilization is shot through with the industrial prejudice. The statesman dreams of huge factories pouring their streams of manufactured products into the channels of the world's commerce. Industries bring wealth and furnish employment to labor; and they are likewise a guarantee of military power. The importance of manufacturing is fully recognized in plans for the mobilization of resources in times of war. In disarmament conferences large industrial plants are taken into account as "invisible armaments." History is filled with illustrations of the conquest of undeveloped nations by those which are more advanced industrially. All of the bravery and cunning of the American Indian could not suffice to resist the advance of the European. The South, with its proud agricultural aristocracy and its splendid traditions of chivalry and horsemanship, was unable to repel the advance of the Northern "shopkeepers." Industry made Germany formidable and the lack of it made Russia impotent. The ambition for power, as well as the desire for wealth, has helped to spur governments onward in the paths of the "new mercantilism."

Industrializing nations tend to reserve their home and colonial markets for their own manufactures and seek to dispose of a growing share of their production in foreign countries. With competition and tariff barriers arising on all sides the problem of selling manufactured goods abroad is surrounded with increasing difficulties. The efforts of statesmen in every leading country are today directed to the opening of foreign markets and the prevention of discriminations against their national goods. There are, of course, times when the desire to import dominates

266

national policy for a period, as when the supply of a necessary raw material has been cut off or when a nation has become pressed for adequate food supplies. On the whole, however, among the materially advanced nations, exports have received greater emphasis than imports.

The following methods of assisting exports will be discussed in this and subsequent chapters:

1. Bargaining tariff laws.
2. Reciprocity treaties.
3. Most-favored-nation clauses.
4. Demands for the open door in the territories or spheres of other countries.
5. Closed doors in the colonial tariff system.

BARGAINING TARIFF LAWS

A bargaining tariff law, as enacted by Congress, is one with flexible schedules which gives to the President the power to change the rates on some or all imports from any country for the purpose of persuading or compelling that country to give more favorable treatment to its imports from the United States. Supported by such a law, the diplomatic officers of the United States may enter into long and complicated negotiations with foreign governments for the purpose of obtaining lower rates on American goods. John W. Foster, an experienced diplomat, was appointed executive agent to carry on the negotiations under the Tariff Act of 1890,[1] and John A. Kasson was appointed special commissioner for the negotiations under the Tariff Act of 1897.[2] At other times the work has been directed by the regular personnel of the Department of State.

Methods of Bargaining Provided in Tariff Laws.—The following methods of bargaining have been provided for in various tariff laws of the United States:

1. The penalty method by which the President has been authorized to raise the rates of duties as against the imports from another country in order to compel that country to treat American goods more favorably.

2. The concession method by which the President has been authorized to lower the rates of duties as against the imports

[1] See his "Diplomatic Memoirs," Vol. II, Chap. XXV, Houghton Mifflin Company, Boston, 1900.

[2] *For his experience see* OSBORNE, JOHN BALL, "The Work of the Reciprocity Commission," *The Forum,* Vol. 30, p. 394.

from another country in order to persuade that country to a better treatment of American goods.

As between the two methods, it would seem that the penalty method is more apt to arouse ill feeling by the appearance of coercion, and that the concession method is much more conciliatory. On the other hand, the concession method has the disadvantage of giving special treatment to a particular country. It thus violates the principle of equality, unless the concession is extended to all. If extended to all countries, the concession becomes equivalent to a general lowering of the tariff, a result which may not be in line with the national tariff policy. Furthermore, the concession method cannot be used with regard to goods which are on the free list.[1]

Objects of Tariff Bargaining.—The purposes of the United States in its tariff bargaining have been chiefly two:

1. To obtain special reductions on American goods in the tariff rates of other countries, the reductions being demanded on the grounds of reciprocity. For example, at one time when Brazil maintained a higher level of tariffs on American imports than the United States charged against Brazilian imports, the United States used the provisions of a bargaining tariff to demand a lowering of Brazilian duties on American goods and justified the demand on the grounds that reciprocal treatment is fair treatment. This was an earlier policy.

2. To secure equal treatment for American goods in the tariff rates of other countries. For example, when France has charged maximum tariffs against American goods and minimum tariffs against the goods of competing nations, the United States has on more than one occasion used the bargaining provisions of its tariff laws to demand that the discrimination be removed and has justified the demand on the grounds that equal treatment is fair treatment. This is the present policy.

Both the penalty and concession methods of bargaining have been used to obtain each of the objects above mentioned. As will be noticed, the two aims are directly opposed to one another. Before the World War the United States, being industrially weak, felt the necessity of special concessions and frequently sought them on the grounds of reciprocity. The great industrial development of the war period and the fear of foreign economic

---

[1] In addition to these methods of tariff bargaining there is, of course, the special reciprocity treaty, which will be treated later in the chapter.

combinations, however, have in recent years caused the United States to discard that policy and to demand equal treatment from all.

BARGAINING FOR CONCESSIONS

The Penalty Method as Used to Obtain Concessions. *The Tariff Act of* 1890.—The placing of bargaining tariff provisions in the McKinley Tariff Act of 1890 was largely due to the efforts of Secretary of State James G. Blaine. Secretary Blaine had for some time been desirous of securing concessions for American goods in the markets of Latin America for the purpose of developing American manufacturing interests. He also wished to correct an unfavorable balance of trade with those countries. He pointed out that in 1889 the trade of the United States with all American countries, excepting Canada, showed an excess of imports amounting to $142,000,000.[1] Computations showed that of the imports into the United States from the Latin-American republics, 87⅞ per cent were admitted free of duty while of the exports of the United States to those countries less than 10 per cent were duty free.[2] In the First Pan-American Conference of 1889–1890, the proposal of the American government for a customs union had been rejected with dispatch and instead the conference had resolved in favor of reciprocity agreements between single nations.

When, in 1890, following the conference, the House of Representatives passed a tariff bill which placed sugar on the free list, the Secretary of State was quite disturbed. This, in his opinion, was the free grant to Latin America of a valuable privilege which, if withheld, could be used as an offer to secure some corresponding concessions for American commerce. Blaine, accordingly, contended that duties on sugar and other leading imports from Latin America should be reestablished with a provision that they might be removed in the case of imports from countries which would agree to reduce their tariffs on imports from the United States. This, if enacted, would have provided for bargaining by offering concessions in exchange for concessions.[3]

[1] United States Tariff Commission, "Reciprocity and Commercial Treaties," p. 147, Govt. Printing Office, Washington, 1919.

[2] *International American Conference*, pp. 153–154.

[3] TYLER, ALICE FELT, "The Foreign Policy of James G. Blaine," p. 183*ff*., University of Minnesota Press, Minneapolis, 1927.

Congress, on the other hand, had made certain commitments concerning the reduction of duties and, accordingly, insisted that sugar and other articles be kept on the free list. A compromise was reached in which the penalty method of bargaining was inserted. Sugar, molasses, coffee, tea, and hides, constituting what was spoken of as the "tropical list," were to be free. The President was given the power, however, to suspend the free entry of these products whenever he should be satisfied that any of the countries exporting them to the United States was imposing duties and other exactions upon the agricultural or other products of the United States, which, in view of the free introduction of such sugar, molasses, coffee, tea, and hides into the United States, he should deem to be reciprocally unequal and unreasonable. A fixed schedule of rates was drawn up to be imposed by the President in case of such suspension. The act was not conceived in the spirit of giving concessions. Tea, coffee, and hides had been on the free list for twenty years and the removal of the duty from sugar was settled as a part of the domestic policy before the question of bargaining with other countries was introduced.[1] The act, then, provided a pure penalty method of obtaining concessions.

Under this act agreements for reduction of duties against American goods were concluded with ten countries as follows: Brazil; Dominican Republic; Spain for Cuba and Porto Rico; Salvador; German Empire; Great Britain for Barbados, Trinidad, Leeward Islands, Windward Islands, and British Guiana; Nicaragua; Honduras; Guatemala; and Austria-Hungary. Colombia, Venezuela, and Haiti failed to make concessions to the United States and the penalty duties provided for by the act were imposed upon the afore-mentioned classes of products coming from those countries.

The results of the concessions secured and penalties imposed under the act may be clearly traced in the statistics of American trade during the next four years. The exportation of American goods to the countries with which agreements were made was undoubtedly encouraged during a period when our exports as a whole showed a tendency to decline. Iron and steel products, which had been included in the concessions made by some of the countries, displayed very gratifying export increases to the

---

[1] Taussig, F. W., "Free Trade, the Tariff and Reciprocity," p. 121, The Macmillan Company, New York, 1920

countries which granted the reductions, although the exports of these commodities to other countries were practically stationary. The importation of the articles which were added to the free list increased, as might be expected.

The most marked effect of the operation of the act is shown in the results which followed the imposition of penalties upon the trade of Colombia, Venezuela, and Haiti for failure to give special rates to American goods. The importation into the United States of the affected articles from those countries showed in 1894 a 72.73 per cent decrease over the importation of the same articles for the three-year average from 1888 to 1890, inclusive. That the above-mentioned movements in commerce were due to the Act of 1890 and its administration is demonstrated by the fact that after the termination of this system by the Tariff Act of 1894 each of the effects which are above attributed to the workings of the bargaining tariff ceased to be observable. Thus, the exports to the countries with which we had had agreements began to decline. The imports of the commodities upon which duties were reimposed also declined. The imports from Colombia, Venezuela, and Haiti showed immediate and substantial increases when the penalty duties were removed.[1]

The Tariff Act of 1894 reimposed a duty upon raw sugar and increased that upon refined sugar. It furthermore repealed the provision giving power to the President to impose penalties. This brought to an abrupt end the arrangements with other governments by which the exports of the United States were to receive especially favorable treatment and led to numerous protests from those countries which had entered into the agreements. The Guatemalan minister, for example, pointed out that the reimposition of the duty on sugar meant financial ruin to his country as a great deal of capital had been invested in Guatemalan sugar production, relying on free access to the American market.[2] This experience with a bargaining tariff indicates a serious fault in Congressional control of foreign policy—that of uncertainty and liability to sudden reversals.

[1] An account of the passage of the act, the agreements reached under it, and the effects of the agreements and of the penalties is found in U. S. Tariff Comm., "Reciprocity and Commercial Treaties," p. 145*ff*. See also LAUGHLIN, J. LAWRENCE and H. PARKER WILLIS, "Reciprocity," Chaps VI and VII, Baker and Taylor, New York, 1903.

[2] "Reciprocity and Commercial Treaties," p. 162.

The Tariff Act of 1897.—In 1897, Congress passed the Dingley Tariff Act which contained provisions for tariff bargaining similar in character to those enacted in 1890. The list of duty-free articles was, however, quite different from the former "tropical list." Coffee, tea, tonka and vanilla beans were now included, while sugar, molasses, and hides were omitted. Excepting as concerned negotiations with the great coffee-producing country of Brazil, this was a much less formidable list. The President was authorized to impose duties upon the new list of products when imported from countries imposing duties or other exactions which, in view of the free entry of the above-mentioned articles into the United States, should seem reciprocally unequal and unjust. The bargaining power of this provision proved to be of little consequence on account of the unimportant nature of the products involved.

In one case, however, an exceedingly important agreement was effected. Persistent negotiations by the Department of States resulted, in 1904, in bringing Brazil to grant a considerable reduction on certain American products. More than 50 per cent of the Brazilian coffee crop was sold in the United States and the threat of a penalty tariff on this commodity evidently created genuine apprehension in Brazil. Accordingly, a reduction of 20 per cent was made in the Brazilian duties on American wheat flour and a number of manufactured articles. The agreement was opposed by the flour-milling interests of Brazil and by the Brazilian Congress. The President of Brazil, however, acted under an old law which permitted him to make reductions upon the products of any country which admitted coffee free. The reduction helped the exporters of American flour to resist partially the competition of Brazilian millers and Argentine exporters to Brazil. The exports of other preferred articles increased materially.[1] The agreement was abandoned in 1922 because of the new policy of equality adopted by the United States.[2]

The Policy of Securing Concessions by Threats of Penalties Repudiated by the United States in 1922.—In 1922, the tariff bill as it passed the House of Representatives provided penalty

[1] *Ibid.*, p. 285*ff.* For negotiations with Argentina over the matter see *For. Rel.*, 1911, p. 31.

[2] For the exchange of notes by which the United States and Brazil abandoned special dealing for unconditional most-favored-nation treatment see "Hearings on Treaty of Commerce and Consular Rights with Germany," p. 76.

duties which were similar in principle to those of 1890 and 1897. The penalties were to be imposed upon goods coming from any country which charged duties upon imports from the United States, which, as compared with the duties charged by the United States, were to be deemed reciprocally unequal and unjust. The clause was finally stricken from the act. Its rejection constitutes a definite repudiation by Congress of the use of penalties to obtain concessions. William Smith Culbertson, a leading authority in the field of commercial policy, makes the following comment concerning the wisdom and justice of providing penalty tariff rates for the purpose of wringing concessions from other countries, with particular reference to the proposal of 1922:

Probably no more objectionable method of tariff bargaining than this has ever been suggested. The aim of this method was not, at least primarily, to remove discriminations, but to batter down tariff rates, equally applicable to all countries, which American export interests might regard as being too high, but which the foreign country might think justified by its own fiscal and industrial needs. From the beginning of our history we have been very insistent upon our right to impose any duties which we thought our domestic needs required. Foreign nations have frequently objected to our high duties, but their claims have been denied. In view of this fact, it was inevitable that Congress should reject, as a *general* policy, a method designed to employ penalty duties for the purpose of forcing down the level of foreign tariffs.[1]

Remnants of This Policy in the American Tariff System.— American tariff acts still retain provisions for penalties to compel reciprocity in case of a few special articles. When these articles are admitted free into this country and another country imposes duties upon them when sent there from the United States, the President has power to impose a duty upon their importation here from that country. The penalty duty is to be equal to that charged in the other country. If a duty is already charged by the United States and the rate in the other country is higher, it is provided that the American duty shall be raised to an equal level. The efficacy of these provisions may be questioned upon the grounds that if the article is produced more cheaply in the other country than in the United States, we have no practical reason to complain about the imposition of a duty in the other

[1] "International Economic Policies," p. 115, D. Appleton & Company, New York, 1925.

country as a protection to a market which the United States could not invade at any event. If the cost of production is cheaper in the United States, a duty raised by this country would have no effect as it would be a needless protection to a market which the other country could not invade.[1]

A case which seems to be somewhat exceptional is found in the trade in lumber in the Pacific Northwest, covering the states of Oregon and Washington and the Canadian province of British Columbia. Here the costs of manufacturing lumber are about equal on the two sides of the boundary line, the Canadian producer having some advantage in the lower costs of logs and the American sawmill owners having an offsetting advantage in cheaper processes of milling. Canada levies a general import tax of 25 per cent ad valorem upon dressed lumber with jointed, tongued, or grooved edges. The American tariff law places lumber on the free list. This situation has not been satisfactory to American lumber manufacturers who have seen in it a distinct artificial advantage in favor of Canadian producers in that it opens the whole market of Canada and the United States to Canadians but restricts the Americans to the markets of the United States.[2] Accordingly, in the Tariff Act of 1922, the provision was inserted that whenever any country should place duties upon American lumber which was planed on one side and tongued and grooved, the President might enter into negotiations to try to remove the duty, and in case of failure he might proclaim equal duties upon similar lumber from such other country.

BARGAINING FOR EQUAL TREATMENT

The Concession Method: The Argol Agreements.—The United States occupied, in 1890, an industrial position somewhere between that of the manufacturing European countries on the one hand and the agricultural countries of Latin American on the other. In accordance with the general policy of industrial powers to seek free commercial relations with those countries whose industries are less developed than their own, the United States was desirous of securing lowered tariffs with Latin America. European countries, looking longingly at the American market,

[1] *Ibid.*, pp. 115–117.

[2] United States Tariff Commission, "Tariff Information Surveys on the Articles in Paragraphs 647 and 648 of the Tariff Act of 1913—Logs, Timber, Lumber, and Other Wood Products," (Rev. Ed.), Govt. Printing Office, Washington, 1922.

however, wished to see lower tariffs on their exports to this country. The United States had talked of fair trade and the golden rule to other countries on the American continent in 1890, but it had been little concerned about such considerations in its relations with Europe. In fact, this country was prepared to maintain and increase its high tariffs on manufactured goods for the purpose of protecting American industry against European products.

Resentment among the European nations caused them to consider measures of retaliation against the United States much in the same spirit as the United States had constructed the penalty provisions in connection with the "tropical list" in the Tariff Act of 1890. France, in 1892, had adopted a double-schedule tariff in which the maximum rates applied, with a few exceptions, to products from the United States. All other of the important western countries, excepting Portugal, were entitled to the rates of the minimum French schedule under the provisions of most-favored-nation treaties. The fetus of Pan-Europeanism was beginning to stir. Germany, Austria, Italy, Belgium, and Switzerland adopted the policy of granting concessions in their tariff rates which would become available to practically all of Europe through most-favored-nation treaties, but which would not apply to the United States. Furthermore, under the semblance of sanitary precautions, administrative discriminations were applied in some cases against American cattle and meat.[1]

The Dingley Tariff Act of 1897 gave to the President the authority to make certain specified reductions on a list of articles for the purpose of conciliating European countries. The list was as follows:

argols, or crude tartar, or wine lees, crude; brandies, or other spirits manufactured or distilled from grain or other materials; champagne and all other sparkling wines; still wines, and vermuth; paintings and statuary.

Under this provision a number of agreements were entered into, commonly referred to as the "argol agreements," which enabled the United States to secure the removal of some of the discriminations against American exports, and in a few instances to obtain special concessions.

[1] U. S. Tariff Comm., "Reciprocity and Commercial Treaties," p. 204.

The agreement concluded under this clause with France may be selected to illustrate the nature of the arrangements. France had already subjected American goods in most instances to the maximum rates of her tariff laws. In 1898, a proposal was under consideration in the Chamber of Deputies to double the rate on cotton-seed oil, a peculiarly American product which competed in the European market against vegetable oils from other countries. Such an action by the French Parliament would have been a severe blow to an important American industry. After negotiations between Mr. Kasson, the American commissioner, and representatives of the French government, the proposal to increase the duty on cotton-seed oil was dropped and a number of American products, such as canned meat, some wood products, and fruits, were given the advantage of the French mimimum tariffs. On its part, the United States applied the reduced duties to the French articles specified in the "argol list," excepting sparkling wines.[1]

Germany, Spain, Portugal, and Bulgaria consented likewise to place their minimum tariffs on certain American commodities. In general, it may be said that the effect of the law was in the direction of obtaining the removal of discriminations against American exports. Minor remissions or reductions of duties were also obtained from Italy, Great Britain, and The Netherlands.[2] The Tariff Act of 1909 provided for the termination of the concessions. The abrupt ending of the agreements was due largely to a reaction of the manufacturing interests against the principle of reciprocity. Believers in a high tariff feared that reciprocal concessions might lead to a further lowering of duties by the United States.

Securing Equal Treatment by Penalty Provisions.—American industry and trade has in the years following the war developed to a point at which the manufacturers are able to supply many important articles at a price which enables them not only to compete on a basis of equality with the manufacturers of other countries, but, if given an equal opportunity, to capture some of the best world markets. The former policy of the United States of seeking special concessions for entering the markets of the undeveloped countries of the American hemisphere has,

---

[1] U. S. Tariff Comm., "Reciprocity and Commercial Treaties," p. 205–206.

[2] *Ibid.*, p. 213; LAUGHLIN and WILLIS, *op. cit.*, Chap. IX; OSBORNE, *loc. cit.*

accordingly, given way to a policy of seeking equal treatment in all of the markets of the world. The aim is now to penetrate, also, the stronger countries which, because of the higher purchasing power of the people, offer a very promising territory. The stronger countries are, however, the very ones which have felt able upon occasion to maintain discriminatory tariff systems; and in some of them the American exporter finds his goods at a disadvantage as compared with the products of third countries. France, under its laws which provide for maximum and minimum rates, imposes in some cases the maximum schedules upon American goods, while the products of other countries enter at the minimum rates. Several other states of Europe have entered into treaties with their immediate neighbors granting especially favorable treatment in the matter of import duties.[1] These constitute a discrimination against the non-treaty countries, including the United States. American exporters have from time to time urged that measures be taken to remove these discriminations, which, if they should continue to grow, might greatly affect American sales in Europe.

The Tariff Act of 1909.—In 1909, Congress passed a two-schedule tariff in which the minimum rates were to be applied generally and the maximum rates were to be used against countries which discriminated against the goods of the United States. This law had no effect, as the minimum rates were applied to imports from all countries, although some of them maintained discriminations against American products.

Section 317 of the Tariff Act of 1922.—In Sec. 317 of the Tariff Act of 1922, a provision was incorporated at the suggestion of the Tariff Commission which gave the President the power to impose penalties upon the commerce of any country which should discriminate against the products of the United States. The President is by this act charged with the duty of attempting by negotiation to remove such discriminations as may exist against American goods. If the discriminating nation should refuse to end its unequal treatment, the President may place new or additional duties upon the importation of any or all of its products not to exceed 50 per cent ad valorem. If, then, the discrimination does not cease, the President may proclaim the

[1] McClure, Wallace, "A New American Commercial Policy as Evidenced by Section 317 of the Tariff Act of 1922," Columbia University Studies in History, Economics and Public Law, Vol. 114, No. 2, Chap. XI.

total prohibition of the importation of such goods from that country as he may deem the public interest may require. This clause is essentially different from the penalty clause in the Act of 1890 in that it seeks to secure equality of treatment, whereas the former provision was intended to bring about unequal treatment by gaining concessions in favor of the United States.[1]

Franco-American Tariff Dispute.—Differences arising with France over tariff matters in 1927 well illustrate the new American policy of equality and the use of the penalty clause in Sec. 317 in the attempt to compel equal treatment.[2]   In August, 1927, a reciprocity treaty between Germany and France was signed which not only provided for lowered rates upon certain articles on each side but also included a most-favored-nation clause which automatically extended to each the lowest tariffs granted by the other.   On Sept. 6, a new tariff was promulgated by France, in which the maximum duties were placed upon many manufactured products from the United States.   Under the new arrangement, American importers into France were compelled to pay about four times the rates paid by Germans on such classes of merchandise as electrical equipment, heavy machinery, light machinery and instruments, hardware and other metal products, chemicals, leather, textiles, earthenware, glassware, and specialty products.   In many of these articles there existed close competition as between American and German exporters.   The effect of this differential was to place the American dealers in a hopeless position and to deliver the French market to the Germans.

American business men immediately appealed to the embassy in Paris and to the Department of State in Washington for some diplomatic action which would bring relief and prevent the ruin of their market in France.   The Franco-German accord was seen by some Americans as a move toward the dreaded European economic union which held such disastrous possibilities for American trade in Europe.   Senator Borah, chairman of the Senate Committee on Foreign Relations, stated it was apparent that the European nations were entering an economic compact in order to "freeze out" the United States.[3]

---

[1] See McClure, *op. cit.*

[2] See Taussig, F. W., "The Tariff Controversy with France," *Foreign Affairs*, January, 1928, p. 177.

[3] *The New York Times*, Sept. 10, 1927.

The Department of State was not slow to respond to the appeals made to it and in its representations to France it set forth the doctrine of equality. A commercial treaty with an unconditional most-favored-nation clause was requested. Removal of the discriminations against American trade was demanded, and a threat of retaliation was made. An aide-memoire which the American chargé d'affaires was instructed to present to the French Foreign Office on Sept. 19, 1927, read in part as follows:

It is France alone, at the present time, which seriously discriminates against American products. Article 317 of the present American Tariff Law gives the executive the right to impose additional duties on goods coming from a country which discriminates in its tariff against the trade of the United States. The American government is very loath to increase its tariff on articles imported from France which is clearly at the present time practicing serious discrimination as contrasted with its treatment of similar goods imported from other nations which are competitors of the United States. It has so far refrained from doing so, since it believes that upon reconsideration the French government will realize the essential justice of the American principle already, as noted above, endorsed by representatives of the other nations of the world assembled in conference at Geneva, that it will hesitate to discriminate against a nation which has always maintained an intimate friendship with France, and will therefore see its way clear both to the negotiation of a treaty guaranteeing general most-favored-nation treatment and to suspending in the interim its manifest discrimination against American products.[1]

The French government took a position as against the United States which was similar to that which this country had taken as against Latin-American countries in the year 1890. France alleged that the high tariffs charged by the United States were unfair as contrasted with the much more favorable treatment which would be accorded American products in France under the French minimum rates. However, in order to restore harmony during the negotiation of a commercial treaty the French government on Nov. 21, 1927, restored the former favorable duties on American imports. This action has probably not settled but merely postponed the settlement of the difficulty arising from the fundamentally different positions and policies of the two countries.[2]

[1] *Department of State Press Release*, Oct. 3, 1927, p. 6.

[2] Withdrawal of American objections to borrowing by France in the United States for refunding and industrial purposes may have had something to do with the temporary settlement. See above, p. 91.

RECIPROCITY TREATIES

Reciprocity treaties belong to the period in American diplomacy of special bargaining. The three treaties which have been concluded have in each case been with a country with which the United States has had unusually close relationship because of geographical position. In the case of Hawaii and Cuba, at least, there have been strong political motives. The treaties with their dates are: the Treaty of 1854 with Great Britain concerning Canada, the Treaty of 1875 with Hawaii, and the Treaty of 1902 with Cuba.

Canada.—The desire for the Treaty of 1854 with Great Britain concerning Canada came largely from the Canadian side of the line. The British Corn Laws, which had existed until 1846, had given a tariff preference to Canadian grain, and had helped to entrench the Canadian farmer in the British market. Upon the repeal of the Corn Laws, the price of grain in England was lowered, Canadian grain lost its preferential position, and a slump in Canadian agriculture ensued. The best existing market was in the United States where a tariff of 20 per cent stood as a barrier. This the Canadians desired to remove. The exclusion of American fishermen from Canadian waters at the same time raised another vexing problem. The United States was willing to grant free access to its markets in exchange for fishing rights. The Treaty of 1854 not only settled the fishing dispute temporarily but provided for the reciprocal free admission of a long list of food stuffs and natural products.

The treaty stipulated that it could be abrogated after ten years upon the giving of a year's notice. At the end of the tenth year the United States gave such notice and at the end of the eleventh year the agreement was abrogated. There were several reasons. In the United States the treaty was regarded as giving to Canada much greater concessions than to the United States. The products which Canada wished to export to the United States were admitted duty free, while the products which the United States wished most to offer in exchange, that is manufactured goods, were not affected by the treaty. In addition, the need of increased revenues was very great in 1864 because of the heavy war expenditures. There was, furthermore, much bitter feeling over what was regarded as the hostile attitude of Great Britain and Canada during the Civil War, and the abrogation reflected the resentment of the United States.

For many years after the termination of the treaty, Canada continued to make advances for a return to reciprocity. Proposals were made to the United States in 1869, 1874, 1888, and 1889. In the twenty years following 1889, important changes took place in the two countries. In Canada, a strong national sentiment was developing and industrial groups were beginning to gain influence. In the United States, the manufacturing interests, which were becoming powerful, came to desire reciprocity with Canada to aid the export of their products. The newspapers supported the project because they wished to be assured of the free admission of wood pulp and paper.

In 1911, a plan for reciprocity was agreed upon between negotiators representing the two governments. Many natural products were to be free of duty, while rates corresponding approximately to the Canadian intermediate tariff were to be extended to certain classes of manufactured goods. A few minor manufactured products were to be on the free list in each country. The agreement would have had much more effect in stimulating the export of raw materials and foodstuffs from Canada into the United States than of manufactured goods from the United States into Canada. The arrangement was to be put into effect by concurrent legislation in the two countries. Congress passed the measure in July, 1911; but it met a different fate in Canada.

The Canadian Parliament was dissolved and the Liberal Premier, Sir Wilfrid Laurier, appealed to the country. The Conservative opposition attacked the policy of reciprocity with great vigor as a bartering away of Canadian political and economic independence. In appealing to Canadian nationalism they found plenty of material in the indiscreet utterances which had been made in the United States. Champ Clark, Speaker of the House of Representatives, had said:

I am for the bill because I hope to see the day when the American flag will float on every square foot of the British North American possessions clear to the North Pole.[1]

The result of the campaign was defeat for the grand old Liberal leader, and reciprocity between the two countries was removed from the realm of practical politics.[2]

[1] SKELTON, OSCAR DOUGLAS, "Life and Letters of Sir Wilfrid Laurier," Vol. II, p. 375, The Century Company, New York, 1922.

[2] An excellent account of the long reciprocity negotiations between the two countries is found in U. S. Tariff Comm., "Reciprocity and Commercial

Hawaii.—In commercial dealings with Hawaii prior to annexation, the United States was moved not so much by a desire to open up markets for American goods as by a wish to give Hawaiian sugar producers an overpowering interest in the American market. By placing Hawaii under the bonds of economic dependence, close political relations would be assured. Americans who had established sugar plantations in the islands were, of course, anxious for a reciprocity agreement. After two unsuccessful negotiations, a reciprocity treaty was concluded in 1875, which admitted free into the American market such articles as bananas, rice, sugar, syrups, and molasses. The duty was removed on a number of American exports to Hawaii, including agricultural implements, machinery, wool, cotton, woolen and cotton textiles, meat, breadstuffs, coal, iron, steel, and naval stores.

The treaty had a powerful effect upon the commercial relations between the two countries. The economic life of the islands was revolutionized. Whereas, in 1875, Hawaii had sent 17,909,-000 pounds of sugar to the United States, by 1885 this export had been increased to 169,653,000 pounds. By 1898 the amount had gone up to 499,777,000 pounds. The production of sugar in Hawaii, which had been 11,639 tons in 1875–1876, increased until it had reached 252,507 tons in 1898–1899. The remission of duties did not result in lowering the cost of sugar in the United States but rather in raising the price in Hawaii. The Hawaiian producer, rather than the American consumer, received the benefits. Accordingly, the treaty resulted in a rich bonus to the Hawaiian sugar planters, which bonus the United States was evidently willing to pay for the allegiance of the dominant commercial class in Hawaii. It was well understood that the continued prosperity of the sugar industry of the islands was dependent upon the continued goodwill of the United States.[1]

The exports from the United States to Hawaii, which increased from $947,260 in 1875 to $8,695,592 in 1898, were, after all, not

---

Treaties," which is a valuable piece of research in tariff diplomacy. The material concerning the two following treaties is likewise taken largely from the same source. LAUGHLIN and WILLIS, *op. cit.*, contain much material on the three treaties. For considerations bearing on the Canadian reciprocity problem of 1911 see also *Senate Docs.* Nos. 56 and 80, Sixty-second Congress, First Session.

[1] The treaty resulted in large increases in the real estate holdings of Americans in the islands, LAUGHLIN and WILLIS, *op. cit.*, pp. 74, 83–84.

a very important factor in American commerce, although the growth in amount shows the unmistakable effects of the treaty. The increase is, however, attributable to the economic prosperity of the islands as well as to the free admission of reciprocity articles.

The annexation of the islands occurred in 1898 and the reciprocity treaty was supplanted by the Organic Act of 1900. Since that time, Hawaii has been a part of the customs system of the United States and a régime of complete free trade has prevailed as between the two.

Cuba.—The only reciprocity treaty entered into by the United States which is still effective is the commercial convention with Cuba. The advantage to be derived from cementing the political relations between the two countries in the period following the Spanish-American War was more important from the standpoint of the United States than was the possible gain from the development of a market for manufactured goods. From the Cuban point of view, the proposed advantage in the sale of sugar in the United States was the all-important consideration. The list of those who testified at the Congressional hearings on the bill to make the convention effective indicates that its chief supporters were American importers of sugar, Americans with investments in Cuban sugar properties, and Cuban leaders. General Wood, the military governor of Cuba, likewise advocated reciprocity. In a letter to the Chairman of the Ways and Means Committee, General Wood declared that the island was in a critical economic condition and that it was the clear duty of the United States to help stabilize business conditions. He also held out the hope that the Cuban market might be captured by American exporters. Those who opposed reciprocity were the sugar producers of the United States, Hawaii, and Porto Rico, and the American tobacco interests.[1] The convention was negotiated in 1902, and in 1903 Congress passed the necessary legislation to put it into effect.

The provisions of the convention are as follows:

1. Goods on the free list at the time of the treaty are to be imported free as between the two countries during the life of the convention. In case the United States shall later place a duty on any goods which were free at the time the treaty became

---

[1] *House Doc.* 535, Fifty-seventh Congress, First Session; LAUGHLIN and WILLIS, *op. cit.*, p. 378.

effective, the duty shall not apply to such goods imported from Cuba.

2. Cuban exports to the United States of goods in the dutiable classes are admitted at a uniform reduction of 20 per cent in duty. Provision was made that during the life of the convention the rates of the 1897 tariff law on sugar should not be lowered for third countries. This is an exceptional instance in which a customs rate of the United States has been fixed by treaty. The provision was violated by the Tariff Act of 1913 which lowered the rate on sugar.

3. American exports to Cuba (excepting tobacco and tobacco manufactures, which must pay the regular duties) are admitted at reductions of 20, 25, 30, and 40 per cent. The main articles in each class are as follows:

(*a*) 20 per cent: all dutiable articles not in the other classes, including machinery, wood, meats, hides, skins, and leather.
(*b*) 25 per cent: salted, pickled, and preserved fish, and iron and steel products (excepting machinery and cutlery).
(*c*) 30 per cent: breadstuffs, cotton, cotton goods, boots, and shoes.
(*d*) 40 per cent: cattle (except for breeding), wool, and woolens.[1]

The convention has been of much assistance to Cuban exporters in making firm their hold upon the American market. The 20 per cent reduction in the American duty, amounting now to slightly less than four-tenths of a cent per pound for sugar of ninety-six degrees of polarization, has been of no small effect in diverting orders to Havana. Large investments of American capital[2] have likewise had a great influence in the rise of the Cuban sugar industry. Aside from the American dependencies, Cuba has become practically the only source of the sugar imports of the United States.[3] The table on page 285 shows the change which has come about since the treaty.

That the treaty has aided American sales to Cuba appears fairly certain. Not only have exports shown a substantial growth but the various categories of goods as classified in the treaty have increased roughly in accordance with the amount

[1] For the convention see *Treaties, etc., between the United States and Other Powers*, Vol. I, p. 354.
[2] See below, p. 395.
[3] Nevertheless, many Cubans believe that the convention should be revised and that the duty on Cuban sugar should be reduced, "Cuba and the United States," by "O," *Foreign Affairs*, Jan., 1928, p. 237.

of the duty reduction. Thus the 40 per cent class has shown the most increase, and so on.[1] Altogether, the treaty has been satisfactory to the United States. The concessions exchanged with Cuba constitute the one exception to the present American policy of equality, and reservations for the continuance of special treatment to Cuba are made in the most-favored-nation clauses in commercial treaties which the United States has been negotiating with various other countries.

SUGAR IMPORTS OF THE UNITED STATES

Year	From non-contiguous territories of the U. S., per cent	From Cuba, per cent	From other foreign countries, per cent
1902	23.27	25	51.73
1916	28.93	67.59	3.48
1926	28.03	71.14	0.83

Reciprocity Treaties Which Have Failed.—The strength of the past desire for reciprocity in the United States cannot be wholly measured by the three treaties just described. In addition to these at least thirteen treaties have been negotiated but have not become effective, the principal reason being the failure to receive the requisite two-thirds vote in the United States Senate. The countries with which these treaties have been negotiated, with the dates of signature, are as follows: the German Zollverein (1844); Mexico (two treaties, 1856 and 1883); Spain for Cuba and Porto Rico (1884); the Dominican Republic (1884); Great Britain for Newfoundland (1890); Great Britain for Barbados, British Guiana, Turks and Caicos Islands, Jamaica, and Bermuda (1899); Denmark for the Danish West Indies (1899); the Dominican Republic (1899); Nicaragua (1899); Ecuador (1899); the Argentine (1899); France (1899).[2]

From the dates of these treaties, it will be noticed that the heyday of the reciprocity enthusiasm was in the period from 1883 to 1899, during which time the executive department, at least, was attempting with a great deal of energy to develop a system of commercial treaties based upon exchanges of special tariff concessions. Congress, at times, seemed committed to

[1] U. S. Tariff Comm., "Reciprocity and Commercial Treaties," p. 343.
[2] *Ibid., passim.*

the same policy, but the strength of protection sentiment was such that the necessary two-thirds majority in the Senate was difficult to obtain. With allowance for this difficulty, reciprocity may be said to have been during this period the fully accepted policy of the government. As late as 1900 President McKinley stated in his annual message to Congress:

The policy of reciprocity so manifestly rests upon the principles of international equity, and has been so repeatedly approved by the people of the United States that there ought to be no hesitation in either branch of Congress in giving to it full effect.[1]

But the end of this policy was already in sight. In 1901, a convention called by the National Association of Manufacturers to consider the matter endorsed the principle of reciprocity only where it could be invoked without injury to any domestic interests.[2] This was construed as a repudiation of reciprocity. All of the treaties so laboriously negotiated in 1899 by Commissioner Kasson under the mandate of the Tariff Act of 1897 were then defeated in the Senate. There was a temporary return to the principle in the Treaty of 1902 with Cuba and in the Congressional approval of the agreement with Canada in 1911; but in recent years the policy of the United States has veered away from reciprocity and is now, excepting the treaty with Cuba, confessedly opposed to it.

[1] *For. Rel.*, 1900, xxvii, quoted in U. S. Tariff Comm., "Reciprocity and Commercial Treaties," p. 224. For the sentiment of business men prior to 1900 see House Report No. 2203, Fifty-fourth Congress, First Session, and HOXIE, R. F., "The American Colonial Policy and the Tariff," *Jour. of Political Econ.*, Vol. 11, p. 199.

[2] *Proceedings of the National Reciprocity Convention Held under the Auspices of the National Association of Manufacturers of the United States of America, Washington, D. C., Nov. 19 and 20, 1901*, p. 145.

CHAPTER XV

THE MOST-FAVORED-NATION CLAUSE

For purposes of commercial expansion the most-favored-nation clause, formerly the neglected step-child of American diplomacy, has in recent years been arrayed in new garments and brought forth to be introduced to the society of a somewhat reticent world. It has been shown that, with the revolution in the international economic status of the United States, the program of seeking special concessions for exports has given way to one of demanding equality of treatment from other nations. One agency for the obtaining of equal treatment abroad has been the penalty provision of Sec. 317 of the Tariff Act of 1922, which is to be used in retaliation for failure to give equality. The most-favored-nation clause has now been refashioned into an agency for securing the same result by more pacific means. The story of the radical change in the American attitude toward this clause may be somewhat tedious but it is necessary to an understanding of the evolution of the commercial policy of the United States.

GENERAL OUTLINE OF THE PROBLEM

The agreement of two nations to give to each other the same treatment that they extend to most-favored-nations has been called the "cornerstone of all modern commercial treaties."[1] Such a declaration, because of its important effect on subsequent agreements not contemplated at the time of making the original treaty, has been subjected to the most intense scrutiny. The interpretation of the clause, the determination of its effect upon other commercial treaty provisions, and the decision as to the particular form in which the promise shall be expressed have given rise to many difficulties.

For the purpose of analyzing the effect of the clause and its problems, it may be useful to represent the three countries in

[1] HORNBECK, STANLEY K., "The Most-favored-nation Clause," *Amer. Jour. of International Law*, Vol. III, p. 395.

the international triangle, which invariably forms around these disputes, as A, B, and X. Let us suppose that A and B conclude a treaty in which they agree to extend to each other most-favored-nation treatment. Later, to use an extreme case, A and X make a special reciprocity treaty in which each agrees to admit the goods of the other free of duty. Must A then admit the goods of B free because of the most-favored-nation provision? On this point a wide difference of opinion has existed. The commercial nations of Europe have ordinarily answered the question in the affirmative. On the other hand, powerful reasons of self-interest sometimes exist for refusing this interpretation. Let us conceive of A as a developing industrial state in the "infant industry" stage, maintaining a high protective tariff; of B as an industrial nation in the most advanced stage, selling its manufactured goods with great success in foreign markets; and of X as a tropical undeveloped country. It may be to the interests of A and X to interchange their products without restriction, but the citizens of A, particularly those interested in the promotion of home industries, would consider it as nothing less than a national catastrophe to admit the goods of B freely into competition with their own in their home market. It may well be supposed that the pressure in A for a restricted interpretation of the most-favored-nation treaty would be very great. The citizens of B, however, confident of their ability to conquer the markets of the world, would be found to take a broader view of this clause with its tariff-leveling tendencies. Thus national economic interests have injected strong prejudices into what has been frequently described in textbooks as a strictly legal question.

There have arisen two schools in the making and interpreting of most-favored-nation treaties. One believes in the "conditional" form and interpretation, which is that concessions given for a consideration from A to X are not extended under the most-favored-nation clause to B unless an equivalent has been received from B. The other school believes in the "unconditional" form and interpretation, which is that concessions given from A to X are thereupon extended freely under the most-favored-nation clause to B, whether they were given to X for a consideration or not. Following is an attempt to portray graphically the effect of the different forms and interpretations of these clauses:

ILLUSTRATIONS OF THE DIFFERENT FORMS AND INTERPRETATIONS OF THE
MOST-FAVORED-NATION CLAUSES

1. Showing the hypothetical treaty relations between A, B, and X.

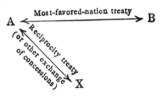

2. Showing the *conditional* clause or the *conditional interpretation* of the simple clause by which a concession given to X by A in return for an equivalent is denied to B. (The circles represent the tariff walls.)

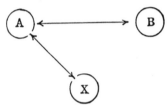

3. Showing the *conditional* clause or the *conditional interpretation* of the simple clause by which the concession given to X by A in return for an equivalent is extended by A to B in return for the same equivalent.

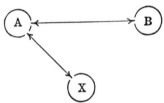

4. Showing the *unconditional* clause or *unconditional interpretation* of the simple clause by which a concession given to X by A for an equivalent is given immediately by A to B without the return of the equivalent.

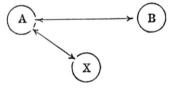

THE AMERICAN POSITION BEFORE 1923

Reasons for That Position.—Prior to 1923 the United States had clung to the conditional form and interpretation of the most-favored-nation clause with great consistency. Beginning with the Treaty of 1778 with France, which contained the first conditional most-favored-nation clause to find its way into commercial treaties, this government guarded jealously its favors and concessions. A number of reasons for this policy were to be found in the particular position occupied by the United States. In the beginning, the American government found itself hemmed in by a system of commercial restrictions. In order to secure better treatment, Congress passed retaliatory measures with the understanding that this government would be willing to withdraw its restrictions against any country that would reciprocate. To have extended such concessions gratuitously to all countries regardless of their treatment of American commerce would have destroyed the bargaining value of this policy, and the United States would have been left to face the restrictions of all countries save the one with which the concessions were originally exchanged.

The strong protective system that later developed added another powerful reason for the continuance of the conditional policy, *i.e.*, the guarding of the tariff wall. The United States became interested in securing single commercial agreements which would give to American exporters special advantages in certain other countries, particularly in the Western Hemisphere, and was willing to provide in return for a lowering of American duties to the particular nations involved. The whole protective system was, however, disposed against the extension of the lowered rates to other nations. These reasons go far to explain why the United States was for so long a period to be found on the side of conditional most-favored-nation treatment.

Almost every general form of the most-favored-nation clause used in the treaties between the United States and other countries has been the subject of dispute with regard to the conditional and unconditional interpretations. An examination of these disagreements shows that three main forms of the treaty clause have been involved in controversy.

The Conditional Interpretation of the Simple Most-favored-nation Clause.—The simple type of the clause merely states that most-favored-nation treatment shall be extended. Here the dispute has waged around the question of what is a "favor" or a "favored nation." The United States has insisted that a concession which it has given to a third country in exchange for value is not a favor but something bought and paid for by the third country. Accordingly, it need not be extended to a nation with which a simple most-favored-nation treaty exists. It is only necessary, according to this interpretation, to offer the other party to the treaty "as good a trade" as is offered to the most-favored-nation.[1] Outside of the United States this argument has sometimes been characterized as a play on words.

In 1803, when the United States made a treaty with France for the purchase of Louisiana, the following article was incorporated:

Article VIII: "In future and forever after the expiration of the twelve years, the ships of France shall be treated upon the footing of the most favored nations in the ports above mentioned [*i.e.*, Louisiana ports]."[2]

By an act of Congress passed in 1815 and by a treaty with Great Britain of the same year the United States removed the discriminating duties charged against vessels so far as British ships were concerned in return for a removal of discriminating duties against American ships by Great Britain. From that time on British ships were placed on an equal footing with American ships in the ports of the United States while the ships of other nations were still compelled to pay additional duties. The French minister at Washington protested in 1817, contending that this discrimination against French ships in Louisiana ports was a violation of Art. VIII of the Treaty of 1803. The Secretary of State, John Quincy Adams, contended that the treaty clause "does not say and can not be understood to mean, that France should enjoy as a free gift that which is conceded to other nations for a full equivalent." The French government denied that there was intended in the treaty to be any exceptions in the case of bargains and took the position that "a clause which is absolute and unconditional can not be subject to limitation or any modification whatsoever." Each nation continued for fourteen years to maintain its own interpretation without conceding the merits of the position of the other. France refused to make a settlement of the spoliation claims of citizens of the United States against that government until the question of the treatment of French ships in Louisiana should be disposed of. The matter was finally concluded by the Treaty of 1831 which not only made certain provisions for the adjustment of outstand-

[1] TAUSSIG, F. W., "The Tariff Controversy with France," *Foreign Affairs*, January, 1928, p. 179.

[2] *Treaties, etc. between the United States and Other Powers*, Vol. I, p. 510.

ing claims for indemnities but also provided for some reciprocal reductions in duties and included an agreement by France to abandon her protest under the Treaty of 1803. Such a settlement left the merits of the question undecided.[1]

Conditional Interpretation of Treaties Containing a "Covering" Clause.—A second and quite common type of treaty entered into by the United States has consisted of two clauses. One has dealt specifically with tariffs, and has promised that no higher duties shall be charged against the goods of the treaty power than are charged against the goods of other countries. A second clause has provided that if future concessions shall be made to third countries by either party to the treaty they shall also be given to the other party freely if the concessions have been freely given to the third country or upon payment of the same compensation if they have been given for a price. This second clause has been called the "covering" clause by some writers, on the assumption that it controls the first, and this has been the official position of the United States.

The Treaty of 1829 with Austria contained in Art. V this stipulation:

> No higher or other duties shall be imposed on the importation into the United States of any article the produce or manufacture of the dominions of Austria; and no higher or other duties shall be imposed on the importation into the dominions of Austria of any article the produce or manufacture of the United States, than are or shall be payable on the like article, being the produce or manufacture of any other foreign country.

In Art. IX appears the "covering" clause,

> If either party shall hereafter grant to any other nation any particular favor in navigation or commerce, it shall immediately become common to the other party, freely, where it is freely granted to such other nation, or on yielding the same compensation, when the grant is conditional.[2]

These provisions became the subject of dispute when in 1831 the United States entered into the treaty with France, above mentioned, by which it was provided that in return for a specified duty on United States long-staple cottons and the abandonment

---

[1] *Moore's Digest*, Vol. V, p. 257; U. S. Tariff Comm., "Reciprocity and Commercial Treaties," p. 405; HORNBECK, *loc. cit.*, p. 407.

[2] *Treaties, etc. between the United States and Other Powers*, Vol. I, pp. 31–32.

of certain claims under the Treaty of 1803 the United States should charge a specified lower rate of duty on French wines. The Austrian government then claimed that under Art. V, above quoted, the wines from Austria should be entitled to the same rates as those extended to the French. This was denied by the United States. The Secretary of State, Mr. Livingston, contended that Art. V should be read in connection with Art. IX, and that Austria was not entitled to the concession made to France unless it should give the same equivalent as the French.[1]

The courts of the United States likewise held to this interpretation when a similar situation was presented in the case of *Bartram* v. *Robertson*. The Treaty of 1826 with Denmark, renewed in 1857, had two articles quite similar to those in the Austrian treaty above cited. Article IV provided that no higher or other duties should be imposed on Danish imports into the United States than on similar articles from other countries, etc., while Art. I contained a "covering" clause requiring compensation where concessions were made to other countries for an equivalent. In 1875, the United States entered into a reciprocity treaty with the Hawaiian government by which sugar from the Hawaiian Islands was permitted to enter the United States free of duty. A firm which imported sugar from the Danish Island of St. Croix brought suit to recover the duties which had been paid following the taking effect of the Hawaiian Treaty. The plaintiff alleged that sugar from the Danish possessions should be allowed to enter the United States free, because of Art. IV of the Treaty of 1826. The Superme Court said concerning this claim:

> Our conclusion is, that the treaty with Denmark does not bind the United States to extend to that country, without compensation, privileges which they have conceded to the Hawaiian Islands in exchange for valuable concessions. On the contrary, the treaty provides that like compensation shall be given for such special favors.[2]

In these treaties the "covering" clause and the "no higher duties" clause seem to be squarely in conflict with one another. The fact that the two clauses have appeared over a long period of years together in treaties of the United States coupled with the fact that this country has always given them the conditional interpretation has established a precedent which has been suffi-

---

[1] *Moore's Digest*, Vol. V, p. 261; U. S. Tariff Comm., *op. cit.*, p. 407.

[2] *Bartram* v. *Robertson*, 122 U. S., 121.

cient warrant for the contention that the two clauses should be taken together and that the "covering" clause should control the most-favored-nation clause. Other governments with a traditional unconditional interpretation of most-favored-nation clauses have felt justified, however, in opposing the American view.[1]

A further interpretation, sometimes made by the diplomats of this country, that under certain circumstances, such as in the case of reciprocity treaties, the United States may refuse to permit most-favored-nations to render an equivalent seems hardly justifiable under the words of the treaty. In such cases the most-favored-nation is absolutely shut out from concessions granted to other countries. To call the excluded country in such cases a most-favored-nation seems to be a perversion of terms.[2]

A Contrary Interpretation Held as against Haiti.—Although the United States has consistently maintained the conditional interpretation in refusing to generalize concessions made by itself for a consideration, yet on one occasion, at least, it has been quite peremptory in denying this interpretation when taken by another country. The Treaty of 1864 with Haiti contained in Art. X the following agreement:

. . . no higher or other duties upon the tonnage or cargo of the vessels [of the contracting parties in the ports of each other] shall be levied or collected than shall be levied or collected of the vessels of the most-favored-nation.[3]

Article II contained a "covering" clause of the ordinary type. In 1901, the United States entered a protest against the action of Haiti in giving special lowered rates to French vessels. The Haitian government claimed that this was a reciprocity arrangement with France whereby in return for this concession France was to grant to the principal Haitian products the benefit of the French minimum tariffs. The Haitian government reminded the United States of the "covering" clause in Art. II, and contended that concessions given for a consideration did not need to be generalized. As has been shown, this was exactly

---

[1] For an analysis of the contentions of the United States and Germany over the two clauses see HORNBECK, *loc. cit.*, pp. 797–813.

[2] CULBERTSON, "International Economic Policies," p. 83; *Moore's Digest*, Vol. V, pp. 267, 283; U. S. Tariff Comm., *op. cit.*, p. 416*ff.*

[3] *Treaties, etc. between the United States and Other Powers*, Vol. I, p. 924.

the argument which the United States had advanced in a number of important controversies over the same point. David J. Hill, Acting Secretary of State, however, sent the following instruction to the American Minister in Port au Prince:

Referring to your No. 822, of Oct. 10, last, relative to the alleged right of the Haitian government to impose higher duties on United States vessels carrying French goods than on French vessels, I have to say that you may advise the government of Haiti that this government is of opinion that Art. X of the convention of 1864 between the United States and Haiti is quite independent of Art. XI [II] and creates absolute rights, which this government cannot fail to insist upon. Should, therefore, any higher charges be collected on American tonnage than that of any other country they will be reclaimed.[1]

Conditional Interpretation of the "No-higher-duties" Clause. The extremity of the view taken by the United States in the past is shown by the interpretation of a third type of provision which consists of the "no-higher-duties" clause without a "covering" conditional clause. From the natural meaning of the words in these treaties it would seem clear that the lowering of duties to one country would necessarily be followed by a lowering of duties to the treaty country. The Department of State has, however, maintained on several occasions the conditional interpretation.

In 1782, a treaty with The Netherlands was signed in which there appeared in Arts. II and III a mutual promise that the citizens of each country should pay no higher duties on imports into the other than those which the nations the most favored should be obliged to pay. There was no conditional covering clause. In 1787, the Dutch government protested against the fact that the state of Virginia exempted French brandies from certain duties if imported in French or American vessels while the brandies of The Netherlands were still subject to the charges. John Jay, Secretary of the Department of Foreign Affairs, was of the opinion that as the reduction on French brandies had been made gratuitously it should be extended to the subjects of The Netherlands. He was of the further opinion, however, that if the concession had been extended to France for certain values, it should not have been automatically extended to The Netherlands without the payment of the same compensation. Mr. Jay said that:

[1] *For. Rel.*, 1901, p. 278. See also HORNBECK, *loc. cit.*, p. 413.

. . . it would certainly be inconsistent with the most obvious principles of justice and fair construction, that because France purchases at a great price, a privilege of the United States, that therefore the Dutch shall immediately insist not on having the like privileges at the like price, but without any price at all.[1]

The Treaty of 1867 with the Dominican Republic contained in Art. IX the following provision:

No higher or other duty shall be imposed on the importation into the United States of any article the growth, produce, or manufacture of the Dominican Republic, or of her fisheries; and no higher or other duty shall be imposed on the importation into the Dominican Republic of any article the growth, produce, or manufacture of the United States, or their fisheries, than are or shall be payable on the like articles the growth, produce, or manufacture of any foreign country, or its fisheries.[2]

There was no "covering" clause. When the United States admitted Hawaiian sugar free under the Reciprocity Treaty of 1875, certain New York merchants importing sugar from Santo Domingo brought an action to recover the duties paid, claiming that, under the treaty, Dominican sugar should come in free on the same basis as Hawaiian sugar. The case was similar to that of *Bartram* v. *Robertson*, which tested the Danish treaty, except for the absence in this case of the "covering" compensation clause. The Supreme Court of the United States held that Dominican sugar could not be allowed the Hawaiian exemption.

. . . it [the treaty] is a pledge of the contracting parties that there shall be no discriminating legislation against the importation of articles which are the growth, produce, or manufacture of their respective countries, in favor of articles of like character, imported from any other country. It has no greater extent. It was never designed to prevent special concessions, upon sufficient considerations, touching the importation of specific articles into the country of the other. It would require the clearest language to justify a conclusion that our government intended to preclude itself from such engagements with other countries, which might in the future be of the highest importance to its interests.[3]

A dispute with Switzerland shows a slight variation from the one just described. The Treaty of 1850 with Switzerland

---

[1] U. S. Tariff Comm., *op. cit.*, p. 405.

[2] *Treaties, etc. between the United States and Other Powers*, Vol. I, p. 406.

[3] *Whitney* v. *Robertson*, 124 U. S. 193. Another reason given by the court for refusing the claim was that the Congressional act imposing the duty was subsequent to the Dominican treaty and therefore took precedence over it.

provided in Art. IX that neither party should impose higher duties upon products of the other than they would impose upon the produce of any other country. There was no conditional clause. Article X provided further that "each of the contracting parties hereby engages not to grant any favor in commerce to any nation, union of nations, state or society, which shall not immediately be enjoyed by the other party." When it is remembered that concessions given for a consideration have not been considered as "favors" by the American Department of State it will be seen that this article, from the viewpoint of the United States, adds nothing to the treaty.

The treaty was brought into question when in 1898 the Swiss minister at Washington presented a demand that Swiss imports be given as favorable treatment as those from France. It will be recalled that in 1898 the United States entered into an "argol" agreement with France whereby certain reductions were made in American duties on argols, brandies, still wines, paintings, and statuary in favor of the French products while France granted to the United States the minimum tariffs on certain American products.[1] The United States at first declined to accept the contention of the Swiss that the treaty entitled them to the reductions that were allowed on the French products and informed the Swiss minister that "a reciprocity treaty is a bargain and not a favor." After evidence had been brought forward to prove that it was the intention of the negotiators to provide for unconditional most-favored-nation treatment, however, the United States granted the Swiss claim. In this case the State Department maintained that its original position was correct so far as the construction of the words of the treaty was concerned, but admitted that "both justice and honor require that the common understanding of the high contracting parties at the time of the executing of the treaty should be carried into effect." In the following year, the United States gave a year's notice of the abrogation of the treaty in accordance with its provisions for termination. The reason for this action was that the existence of an unconditional most-favored-nation treaty embarrassed the government's attempts to secure reciprocal concessions with other governments.[2]

[1] See above, p. 276.
[2] *Moore's Digest*, Vol. V, p. 283; U. S. Tariff Comm., *op. cit.*, p. 428; HORNBECK, *loc. cit.*, p. 410.

The conditional interpretation of the "no higher duties" clause is in direct contradiction to the words of the treaty and seems to be indefensible. It can be explained only on the ground that sharp disputes involving national interests will frequently bring the disputants to read into the controverted words a meaning which is not there. There are many illustrations of this in diplomatic history, and, without a competent international tribunal, there is no satisfactory recourse.

Summary of the American Policy until 1923.—For almost a century and a half, the American government favored the conditional clause and the conditional interpretation of the simple clause. Beginning with the French treaty of 1778, which contained the first conditional most-favored-nation clause to find its way into commercial treaties, down to the year 1923, this government maintained with rare consistency the attitude that commercial concessions were not to be distributed with a generous hand to all nations. This was not due merely to the force of established tradition nor was it because of the influence of any American legal school. The reasons are to be found in the economic policies of the United States.

Summary of the Opposing View.—Conversely, as Great Britain and some other of the European nations developed the doctrine of free trade, they more strongly adhered to the unconditional clause with its tendency toward a universal lowering of duties. An indication of the British attitude in opposing the American policy may be seen in the following instruction given in 1885 by Earl Granville, Secretary of State for Foreign Affairs, to Mr. West, British Minister to the United States:

The interpretation of the most-favored-nation clause involved in the United States' proposals is, that concessions granted conditionally and for a consideration can not be claimed under it. From this interpretation Her Majesty's government entirely and emphatically dissent. The most-favored-nation clause has now become the most valuable part of the system of commercial treaties, and exists between nearly all the nations of the earth. It leads more than any other stipulation to simplicity of tariffs and to ever increased freedom of trade; while the system now proposed would lead countries to seek exclusive markets and would thus fetter instead of liberating trade. Its effect has been, with few exceptions, that any given article is taxed in each country at practically one rate only . . . But should the system contemplated by the United States be widely adopted, there will be a return to the old and exceedingly inconvenient system under which the same article in the same country would pay different duties varying according to its country of origin, the nationality of the importing ship, and, perhaps at some future time, varying also with the nationality of the importer himself.

.   .   .   .

Such a system would press most hardly on those countries which had already reformed their tariffs, and had no equivalent concessions to offer, and, therefore, Great Britain, which has reformed her tariff, is most deeply interested in resisting it.[1]

The Change in American Policy, 1923.—A great deal has already been said concerning the commercial changes which have come about in the United States during the period roughly coincident with the World War. In short, they may be summarized by the statement that this country has now become a seller of large quantities of manufactured goods in the markets of the world. The power to compete abroad in these lines has increased, and the danger from special discriminations has become more apparent. Fear of discrimination has given rise to such legislation as Sec. 317 of the Tariff Act of 1922, by which the President is armed to demand equality; and the unconditional most-favored-nation clause is another means by which it is sought to attain the same result.

The first official act showing the change to the unconditional type of most-favored-nation policy was the abrogation of the special arrangement which had been entered into with Brazil, in 1904. Under threat of placing a penalty tariff on Brazilian coffee, the United States had been able to compel Brazil to make some concessions in favor of American goods.[2] When, in 1922, Congress inserted a penalty provision in the tariff act for the purpose of penalizing just such special concessions as this when made between foreign countries, the inconsistency was apparent. The United States ceased to request the special concessions from Brazil, which it had been necessary to reenact each year, and after Jan. 1, 1923, they were done away with. The understanding was made formal on Oct. 18, 1923, by an exchange of notes between the Secretary of State and the Brazilian ambassador in Washington. The gist of the notes was that the two countries would give to each other unconditional

[1] *Moore's, Digest*, Vol. V, p. 270–271.
[2] See above, p. 272.

most-favored-nation treatment. The United States, however, made an exception of the special treatment which is accorded to American dependencies, Cuba, and the Panama Canal Zone.[1]

The treaty of Commerce and Consular Rights with Germany, which was signed on Dec. 8, 1923, was carefully drafted in Washington and was intended to serve as a model for subsequent commercial treaties. Article VII embodies the unconditional type of most-favored-nation clause. After the conventional "no higher duties" provision which declares that each power will impose no higher duties upon the products of the other than are imposed upon the products of any foreign country, the article has the following statement:

> Any advantage of whatsoever kind which either High Contracting Party may extend to any article, the growth, produce or manufacture of any other foreign country shall *simultaneously and unconditionally, without request and without compensation,* be extended to the like article the growth, produce, or manufacture of the other High Contracting Party.[2]

The words quoted in italics are deemed to make it sufficiently clear that unconditional most-favored-nation treatment is intended. On the side of the United States the special relations with Cuba, the dependencies,[3] and the Panama Canal Zone are excepted from the treaty.

The German treaty was the answer to threats of Pan-Europeanism in customs matters. An economic understanding of this character with the most important industrial nation on the European continent will safeguard the United States against any general system of discriminations so long as it remains in force. It is a wedge driven into the commercial heart of Europe. The significance of the treaty and the desirability of obtaining agreements of a like character with other European nations was clearly brought out by the tariff dispute with France in 1927. Germany and France had exchanged special concessions. Under the terms of the 1923 treaty the reductions which Germany had made on French imports were immediately extended to goods

[1] See the testimony of WILLIAM S. CULBERTSON before the Senate Committee, "Hearings on Treaty of Commerce and Consular Rights with Germany," pp. 75–77. The text of the notes is there set forth.

[2] *Treaty Series* No. 725. The italics are the author's.

[3] Colonies have traditionally been considered as outside of the operation of most-favored-nation clauses; HORNBECK, *loc. cit.,* p. 403.

from the United States. With France, however, the United States had no such treaty, and American goods were placed at a great disadvantage as compared with German goods.[1] Accordingly, the United States immediately submitted to France a proposal for a most-favored-nation treaty of the unconditional type. The negotiations have not yet been completed. If, however, such a treaty can be concluded, the fears of discrimination against American goods in France will be abated.

Since the signing of the German treaty, the Department of State has sought to conclude similar treaties and agreements with other countries. Considering the short time during which this policy has been followed, the number of nations with which agreements have been secured seems formidable. Treaties have been signed and ratified in the case of Hungary,[2] Estonia,[3] Honduras,[4] Salvador,[5] and Latvia.[5] Treaties signed with Norway and Austria have not yet been submitted to the Senate.[6] Besides the formal treaties above mentioned, unconditional most-favored-nation treatment has been provided in customs matters by exchanges of notes with Brazil,[7] Czechoslovakia,[8] the Dominican Republic,[9] Estonia,[10] Finland,[11] Greece,[12] Guatemala,[13] Haiti,[14] Latvia,[15] Lithuania,[16] Nicaragua,[17] Poland,[18] and Rumania.[19]

[1] See above, p. 278.
[2] *Treaty Series* No. 748.
[3] *Ibid.* No. 736.
[4] *Ibid.* No. 764.
[5] Ratifications not yet exchanged.
[6] In addition to these recent treaties an unconditional most-favored-nation treaty with Servia has been in existence since 1881.
[7] *Treaty Series* No. 672.
[8] *Ibid.* Nos. 673-A and 705.
[9] *Ibid.* No. 700.
[10] *Ibid.* No. 722.
[11] *Ibid.* No. 715.
[12] *Ibid.* No. 706.
[13] *Ibid.* No. 696.
[14] *Ibid.* No. 746.
[15] *Ibid.* No. 740.
[16] *Ibid.* No. 742.
[17] *Ibid.* No. 697.
[18] *Ibid.* No. 727.
[19] *Ibid.* No. 733. The author is indebted to Charles M. Barnes, Chief of the Treaty Division of the Department of State, for a statement enumerating the countries with which treaties and exchanges of notes have been concluded.

While much has been accomplished in obtaining treaties embodying the unconditional most-favored-nation principle, a survey of the list of agreements effected will show that, with the exception of Germany, the great trading nations of the world are not included. Canada, to the north, stands aloof. In South America, the leading commercial country, Argentina, has opposed the policy. In Europe, the leadership of the opposition has been taken by France. It is true that the 1927 Economic Conference at Geneva unanimously favored unconditional most-favored-nation treatment. When the United States reminded France of this endorsement, however, the French government responded that the Geneva Conference had also advocated the lowering of tariffs, and that the general adoption of the first proposal without the second would result in a disadvantage to the low-tariff countries. The French Foreign Office stated that in its negotiations with European countries for the reciprocal lowering of tariffs it had been noted that "most of the countries of Europe would consider it as not progress but as a step backwards in commercial policy" to grant unconditional most-favored-nation treatment to all countries alike without taking into consideration the protectionism of some and the liberalism of others. French officials claimed that the high tariff of the United States made it undesirable to extend unconditional most-favored-nation treatment to this country.[1] Thus it appears that in building a worldwide commercial treaty system incorporating unconditional most-favored-nation treatment the Department of State has encountered a formidable task.[2]

[1] The French Aide-Memoire of Sept. 30, 1927, *State Department Press Release*, Oct. 3, 1927.

[2] The American delegation to the World Economic Conference made a strong argument for equality of treatment in commercial matters and supported the recommendation for unconditional most-favored-nation treaties. See League of Nations, *Report and Proceedings of the World Economic Conference Held at Geneva May 4 to 23, 1927*, Vol. II, pp. 75, 88–90, Geneva, 1927.

CHAPTER XVI

THE OPEN DOOR AND THE CLOSED DOOR

THE GENERAL RELATION BETWEEN COLONIES AND MARKETS

The desire for markets has accounted for much of the zest shown in the competition for empires. The noble self-sacrifice displayed by the advanced industrial nations in their efforts to care for the spiritual and material interest of heathendom cannot be understood without knowledge of the fact that the "white man's burden" likewise includes the task of providing the natives with trinkets, clothes, and supplies at a substantial profit. It was the desire to dispose of surplus manufactures, according to Moon, that brought about "the imperialistic expansion of Europe in the last quarter of the nineteenth century."[1] To assert that the United States has taken lands for the drab purposes of trade would undoubtedly provoke a controversy which could result in no clear decision, due to the mixed character of the motives which have generally led to American expansion. But it cannot be gainsaid that the vision of greater markets was present in the minds of American political leaders at the time of the acquisition of our insular possessions, and that our colonial tariff policy has been formed to a large extent in response to influences which have pressed for a trade monopoly.

Does Trade Follow the Flag?—After all, what is the effect of the acquisition of colonies upon trade? English Liberalism in the middle period of the nineteenth century developed the conviction that the extension of political control does not necessarily result in an increase of national trade in the acquired territory. England was at that time supreme in industry and British manufactured goods could compete on their merits successfully without the artificial aid of tariffs or navigation laws. Culbertson says of this period:

The free-trade philosophy served as a convenient means of justifying the national aims of Great Britain during the period of her commercial and manufacturing supremacy. The movement was promoted by

[1] "Imperialism and World Politics," p. 28.

303

sincere idealists, unconscious of any nationalistic aim, and inspired only by humanitarian purposes. But it was underwritten by the business interests which, cramped in the home market, were in need of the export trade. Manufacturing had not developed in other countries sufficiently to offer them serious competition.[1]

Disdaining governmental assistance to commerce, the British Liberals rejected the doctrine that trade follows the flag and accepted rather the theory that economic tides run too strongly to be affected by political cross-currents. Colonies were no longer necessary to furnish markets for the produce of the home country. Sir F. Rogers, who had had long experience as Permanent Under-secretary of State for the Colonies, wrote in 1885:

I had always believed—and the belief has so confirmed and consolidated itself that I can hardly realize the possibility of anyone seriously thinking the contrary—that the destiny of our colonies is independence; and that in this point of view the function of the Colonial Office is to secure that our connection, while it lasts, shall be as profitable to both parties, and our separation, when it comes, as amicable as possible.[2]

In support of the contentions of the Liberals, numerous instances can be cited in which colonies have developed a greater trade with foreign countries than with the mother country. Canada, for example, has a much larger commerce with the United States than with Great Britain. The United States, a revolted colony, has been a better customer of England than any part of the British Empire. In these cases, economic factors have greatly outweighed the political. Alleyne Ireland in his work, "Tropical Colonization," published in 1899, went to some trouble to investigate the question from the statistical point of view. His conclusion was that despite political ties the British colonies and possessions were becoming commercially independent of the United Kingdom, and, in general, no evidence was discovered to the effect that trade follows the flag "in the sense that possession of a country produces any extraordinary development of trade between the dependency and the dominant country." He felt, however, that the possession of territory by the British resulted in safeguarding their trade to the extent that it prevented the acquisition of the territory by third countries and

[1] "International Economic Policies," p. 11.

[2] Quoted in VIALLATE, "Economic Imperialism," p. 7; see also MOON, *op. cit.*, p. 14*ff.*

the consequent diversion of trade from the United Kingdom by the erection of tariff walls.[1]

World opinion has, however, begun to question the efficacy of free trade in recent years and there has come a much stronger belief in the direct relation between territories and markets. The leading European countries began several decades before the World War to look anew for territories to furnish purchasers for their production.[2]

The colonial experience of the United States has been such as to induce a very different conclusion from that held by the Liberal school. The acquisition of colonial possessions by this country resulted in the undoubted establishment of commerce. Let us consider the case of the Philippine Islands as contrasted with that of Formosa. These two territories have some general similarities from the economic and geographic point of view. They are situated near the coasts of Asia about 300 miles apart. The first is a possession of the United States and the second, of Japan. Both the United States and Japan have sought to divert trade to themselves by means of tariffs. The result has been that the trade of the two, which would flow along similar lines if only economic forces were to be considered, has gone in opposite directions. In 1925, the United States had 66.4 per cent of the trade of the Philippine Islands and 2.3 per cent of the Formosan trade. Japan had 77 per cent of the trade of Formosa and 6.1 per cent of that of the Philippines. Colonial trade statistics show that similar situations exist in the commerce of many territorial possessions in this day of the mercantilistic renaissance.[3]

There are numerous reasons why the trade of a colony is diverted to the mother country:

1. *National Sympathy.*—Tastes and habits, which are extended from the mother country to the colony through the migration of citizens and through loyalty to the home tradition, can best be supplied by goods from the home country. Language and education are frequently matters of importance in influencing

[1] IRELAND, ALLEYNE, "Tropical Colonization," Chap. III, The Macmillan Company, New York, 1899.

[2] MOON, *op. cit.*, p. 526*ff.*, gives an excellent summary of considerations on both sides. See also VIALLATE, "Economic Imperialism," Chap. II.

[3] U. S. Tariff Commission, "Colonial Tariff Policies," Government Printing Office, Washington, 1922, contains many tables which support this statement.

trade. All of these factors are strongest in cases of "settlement colonies" where the population is to a large extent the result of migration from the home country, as in Alaska. In such territories as the Philippines, the presence of a few thousand Americans of business and official classes has had an undoubted influence on the sale of American goods.[1]

2. *Official Favoritism.*—In awarding concessions, colonial officials are inclined to favor their own nationals.[2] In case of loans, colonial officials will ordinarily approach their national financiers. The investors of the home country are often more willing to make colonial investments because of the belief that their properties will be protected, for in case of trouble they have readier access to the protecting government. For these reasons, the capital of the home country has an advantage in the development of the dependent territory, and investments draw goods in their wake, thus aiding commerce.

Aside from favoritism in official decisions, the governing class can sometimes influence the natives through their prestige, or by threats, to favor trade relations with the home country. Ireland states that the administrator of Mananjary, a district on the southeast coast of Madagascar, was reported to have threatened native traders with imprisonment if they bought goods from other than French firms, and he cites the following exhortation of the Governor-general of the island which was published in the *Official Gazette:*

You have been deceived several times by people who have told you that French merchandises are valueless goods and very dear. It was those people who are jealous who made this false statement to you, because, as everyone knows, the French goods are the best. Please look at the above picture. These are the French cottons bearing the following marks, "Liberté," "Tirailleur Malagache," "Cuirassier." The above-mentioned goods are not only of good quality, but are strong and cheap. All explanations can be read in this number of the *Vaovao.* When the people see you Malagasy, who have recently become French

---

[1] ROBINSON, A. G., "Commerce and Industry of Alaska, Hawaii, Porto Rico and the Philippine Islands," Bur. of For. and Dom. Comm., *Special Agents Series*, 67, p. 100.

[2] BUELL, "International Relations," p. 424. For illustration of favoritism shown in the awarding of oil concessions, see above, p. 60*ff.* The open-door policy in the Belgian Congo was largely nullified by administrative favoritism. Sometimes the law of the colony requires that concessions must be allotted to nationals.

people, buying these cottons, they will know that you are really faithful sons of France, and that you are true in your hearts to her.[1]

3. *Tariff Preferences.*—Most important of all influences are tariff systems which are designed to stimulate trade between the colony and the mother country. Such tariffs place obstacles in the way of trade between the colony and foreign countries while they leave commerce with the mother country free or subject to reduced duties. Tariffs which are intended to accomplish this object constitute the "closed door" in trade. They are in contrast with colonial tariff systems which apply equally as against foreign countries and the mother country and which constitute the "open door."

I. THE OPEN DOOR

The "open door" means the maintenance within colonial possessions of a tariff system which applies equally as against all nations. Tariffs and regulations for the obstruction of trade may be established, but they give no preferences in favor of the proprietary country. The term "open door" is sometimes used as a slogan by a government to prevent the establishment of the "closed door" in foreign territories in which it has commercial ambitions. It is in this latter sense that the doctrine has been most important in American policy.

The diplomatic branch of the United States government has adopted the open-door slogan on several notable occasions to protect the American exporter against the closing of doors abroad. In 1922, Charles Evans Hughes described the American policy as follows:

We are not seeking special privileges anywhere at the expense of others. We wish to protect the just and equal rights of Americans everywhere in the world. We wish to maintain equality of opportunity; as we call it, the *open door*.

He was speaking, however, only for the diplomatic branch. At the same time, the pressure of exporters and other influences upon those who have been engaged in framing colonial tariffs have brought about an opposite result in the American colonies. With two minor exceptions, the door in the dependencies of the United States has been tightly closed. Thus the United States has, like several other world powers, been enthusiastic for the

[1] *Op. cit.*, p. 121.

open door as a policy for others, while it has maintained the closed door for itself. This dualism is an evidence of the power of the business lobby. It has also been the cause of much misconception in the popular mind.

CLAIMS FOR THE OPEN DOOR IN OTHER THAN AMERICAN TERRITORIES—THE CONGO

The first instance in which the United States took steps to secure the open door to American trade was in the case of the Belgian Congo. In 1876, Leopold II, King of Belgium, founded the *Association Africaine Internationale*, which three years later became known as the *Association Internationale du Congo*, with claims over immense areas in the Congo Basin. The new association aroused the hostility of other powers interested in Africa because it infringed upon their claims to areas in the hinterland of their coastal possessions. In an attempt to conciliate this opposition, King Leopold adopted the policy of commercial equality. In 1884, the association explained to the United States, among the rest, that its intention was to extend equal treatment to the citizens of all nations. The United States then recognized the flag of the association as the flag of a friendly government. This act was declared by Secretary of State Frelinghuysen to be "in harmony with the traditional policy of the United States, which enjoins a proper regard for the commercial interests of their citizens."[1] During the same year the United States sent delegates to a conference of the principal commercial nations held in Berlin to discuss methods by which the Congo Basin might be kept open to the world's trade. The delegates were instructed that their part was to be merely deliberative. This cautious step into world politics was taken on account of the belief of the United States that the open-door policy was of sufficient importance to American trade to justify intermingling warily with the nations of Europe. The conference recognized the Congo Free State and resolved that freedom of trade should be guaranteed to all nations in that part of the Congo Basin under consideration. The convention was signed by the delegates of the United States. President Cleveland, who came into office shortly afterward, however, refrained from sending it to the Senate for concurrence, stating that "an engagement to share in the obligation of enforcing neutrality in the

[1] *Moore's Digest*, Vol. I, p. 117.

remote valley of the Congo would be an alliance whose responsibilities we are not in a position to assume."[1]

CHINA

The Threatened Break-up of the Chinese Empire, 1898.—The phrase "open door" is identified in the minds of most Americans with the policy of this country in China. American hopes of vast future markets in China seemed doomed to be blasted by the aggressions of European nations in the years following the Sino-Japanese War. In 1898, there occurred a series of onslaughts upon Chinese sovereignty which, for the time, threatened the dissolution of the empire, and with it the loss of such commercial equality as the United States had in the past enjoyed. Two kinds of territorial controls were obtained by the various powers from China. One was the lease of a port and the other was the sphere of interest over a larger area. The leases ran for terms of years, but to most intents and purposes they seemed tantamount to the transfer of absolute title. The spheres of interest gave predominance within certain areas to powers claiming the spheres.[2]

The promises and concessions which were extorted from China at this time and which seemed to threaten to destroy commercial freedom in that country may be briefly enumerated as follows:

March 15, 1897, a non-alienation pledge to France concerning Hainan.[3]
February 11, 1898, a non-alienation pledge to Great Britain concerning the Yangtse Valley.[4]
March 6, 1898, a lease to Germany of Kiaochow Bay in Shantung for ninety-nine years, together with railway and mining rights in the province.[5]
March 27, 1898, a lease to Russia of the Kwangtung Peninsula for twenty-five years, together with the right to construct a railway from Harbin to Port Arthur.[6]
April 10, 1898, a non-alienation pledge to France concerning the provinces bordering on Tongking.[7]

[1] *Moore's Digest*, Vol. I, p. 119.
[2] See above, p. 38.
[3] MACMURRAY, "Treaties and Agreements with and Concerning China," Vol. I, p. 98.
[4] *Ibid*, p. 104.
[5] *Ibid.*, p. 112.
[6] *Ibid*, p. 119.
[7] *Ibid*, p. 123.

April 26, 1898, a non-alienation pledge to Japan concerning Fukien Province.[1]

May 27, 1898, a lease to France of Kwangchow Wan for ninety-nine years.[2]

June 9, 1898, a lease to Great Britain of Kowloon for ninty-nine years.[3]

July 1, 1898, a lease to Great Britain of Weihaiwei for "so long a period as Port Arthur shall remain in the occupation of Russia."[4]

This succession of seizures was described by the Empress dowager as follows: "The various powers cast upon us looks of tiger-like voracity, hustling each other in their endeavors to be the first to seize upon our innermost territories."[5]   There was good reason for the opinion then held by many competent observers that the break-up of China was impending, and that the empire, which was old before Rome began, would speedily dissolve under the control of the more vigorous western nations.

During most of the period of the great scramble the United States was busily employed in the war with Spain.   The *Maine* was blown up in Havana Harbor on Feb. 15, 1898, four days after the British obtained their non-alienation agreement concerning the Yangtse Valley, and by the time the treaty of peace was signed on Dec. 10, 1898, the diplomatic forays had ceased.   The United States had acquired the Philippine Islands, however, and contemporary statements indicated that the possession of that territory so near to the coasts of Asia had awakened dreams of the establishment of a great commercial base at Manila from which the traders of this country might operate to secure their share of the Asiatic markets.   Yet at the same time the door to these markets seemed likely to be closed against American commerce.

The Origin of the Open-door Policy in China.—By the beginning of 1899, commercial leaders in the United States had developed a vague desire for the open door in China, without, however, having formulated any plans by which such a desirable condition could be guaranteed.   Lord Charles Beresford, who had been sent to China in 1898 by the Associated Chambers of Commerce of Great Britain for the purpose of an unofficial investigation into commercial possibilities in the light of the political situation, entered the United States in February 1899, on

[1] MacMurray, *op. cit.*, p. 126.

[2] *Ibid.*, p. 128.

[3] *Ibid.*, p. 130.

[4] *Ibid.*, p. 152.

[5] *For. Rel.*, 1900, p. 85.

his return voyage. Having been impressed by the strong desire for the open door among the trading classes of westerners in China and among the Japanese commercial leaders, he was pleased to find a similar feeling in the United States. In San Francisco, Buffalo, and New York he addressed commercial associations and listened to expressions of American opinion. Concerning the sentiment as he saw it, he said:

The principle of the "open door" is unanimously held to be the policy necessary for the increase of the United States' trade with China; but there the matter rests. I heard no sentiments expressed which conveyed to me any opinion on the part of any of the American Chambers of Commerce as to how the "open-door" principle was to be insured, although I did hear many opinions expressed that the time could not be far distant when the Chinese Empire would be added to the list of those countries which had fallen to pieces from internal decay.[1]

The United States was uniquely situated to promulgate the open-door policy. This country, largely due to the traditional sentiment against intervention in the affairs of other countries, had taken no territories, spheres, or leases in China. There was a strong sentiment among commercial groups in other countries for the open door, and there was reason to believe that Great Britain and Japan would sincerely and enthusiastically support the policy. Those countries, however, had made certain commitments which led toward the closed door, and they were not free to take the lead in the open-door movement.[2] Lord Beresford had called upon Secretary Hay during his journey through the United States and had presented arguments for the open door. W. W. Rockhill, formerly Secretary of the American Legation in Peking, was also in the United States during the summer of 1899 and pressed upon the Secretary of State the necessity of securing promises from the powers concerning the open door. At Hay's request Rockhill submitted on Aug. 28 a memorandum containing a statement of pledges to be obtained

[1] BERESFORD, LORD CHARLES, "The Break-up of China," pp. 442–443, Harper and Brothers, New York, 1899.

[2] With regard to Great Britain see HORNBECK, STANLEY, K., "Contemporary Politics in the Far East," p. 232, D. Appleton & Company, New York, 1916; BERESFORD, op. cit., pp. 454, 470; DENNETT, TYLER, "Americans in Eastern Asia," p. 641, The Macmillan Company, New York, 1922.

from the powers,[1] and on Sept. 6, Secretary Hay sent instructions to the American ambassadors to Great Britain, Germany, Russia, and on later dates to the diplomatic representatives in France, Italy, and Japan, requesting that they present the celebrated "Open-door Notes."

A quotation from the note to Germany will show the substance of these communications:

> Earnestly desirous to remove any cause of irritation and to insure at the same time to the commerce of all nations in China the undoubted benefits which should accrue from a formal recognition by the various powers claiming "spheres of interest" that they shall enjoy perfect equality of treatment for their commerce and navigation within such "spheres," the government of the United States would be pleased to see His German Majesty's government give formal assurances and lend its cooperation in securing like assurances from the other interested powers that each within its respective sphere of whatever influence—
>
> First. Will in no way interfere with any treaty port or any vested interest within any so-called "sphere of interest" or leased territory it may have in China.
>
> Second. That the Chinese treaty tariff of the time being shall apply to all merchandise landed or shipped to all such ports as are within said "sphere of interest" (unless they be "free ports"), no matter to what nationality it may belong, and that, duties so leviable shall be collected by the Chinese government.
>
> Third. That it will levy no higher harbor dues on vessels of another nationality frequenting any port in such "sphere" than shall be levied on vessels of its own nationality, and no higher railroad charges over lines built, controlled, or operated within its "sphere" on merchandise belonging to citizens or subjects of other nationalities transported through such "sphere" than shall be levied on similar merchandise belonging to its own nationals transported over equal distances.[2]

In brief, the powers were asked to pledge that within their leased territories or spheres of interest there would be no interference with treaty ports or vested interests and *that there would be no discrimination with regard to tariffs, harbor dues, or railway charges.*

In the course of time, favorable replies were received from the governments addressed. That they were not all enthusiastic

[1] HARRIS, NORMAN DWIGHT, "Europe and the East," p. 412, Houghton Mifflin Company, Boston, 1926; DENNIS, A. L. P., "The Origin of the 'Open Door,'" *Current History*, February, 1928, p. 651.

[2] *Treaties, etc. between the United States and Other Powers*, Vol. I, p. 246.

in their compliance may be seen from the following description by William Roscoe Thayer of the Russian attitude:

Russia would sign no paper, but her Foreign Minister, Count Mouravieff, gave an oral promise to do what France did. Later, he "flew into a passion" and insisted upon it that Russia would never bind herself in that way; that whatever she did she would do alone and without the concurrence of France. "Still," Hay adds, "he did say it, he did promise, and he did enter into just that engagement. It is possible that he did so thinking that France would not come in, and that other powers would not. If now they choose to take a stand in opposition to the entire civilized world, we shall then make up our minds what to do about it."[1]

Thayer's further statement that "not one of the governments concerned wished to agree to it," however, seems to go much beyond the evidence which he presents. There is good ground for supposing that Great Britain and Japan were anxious for the open door and that that fact was known in advance by the Secretary of State.

Supplementary to the policy outlined in the open-door notes, Secretary Hay later, following the Boxer troubles, sought to secure an agreement for the maintenance of the territorial integrity of China. On July 3, 1900, following the deliverance of the legations in Peking when the future of China seemed dubious in the face of threats by the infuriated powers, Hay sent another circular note to the allies. He declared that it was the policy of the United States to seek a solution which would bring about permanent peace and safety to China, which would preserve Chinese territorial and administrative integrity, and which would safeguard the principle of equal and impartial trade with all parts of the Chinese Empire. The preservation of Chinese territorial integrity was thus added to the open-door program. Here again it was the interest of the American exporter which prompted the policy. The United States was by treaty entitled to most-favored-nation treatment in China, which was a guarantee of equal treatment so long as the territory should remain under the control of the Chinese government. Should the empire be broken up, this equality of treatment would probably vanish.[2]

[1] "The Life and Letters of John Hay," Vol. II, p. 243, Houghton Mifflin Company, Boston, 1915.

[2] Other agreements entered into by the United States, which have recognized the open-door principle, are: The Root-Takahira Agreement of 1908, the Lansing-Ishii Agreement of 1917, and the Treaty Relating to Principles and Policies Concerning China, signed at the Washington Conference in 1922.

The Chinese policy of the United States is the result of the desire to aid the material interests of exporters and investors in a promising region which is scarcely likely to be an area of American political power. Other nations with great territorial possessions in Asia have regarded their vital interests as closely linked up with the Chinese situation, and they have shown the disposition to take determined action in that area. Because of the remoteness of China from the main interests of the United States, it has been considered unwise for this nation to extend its political and military system to that country. Accordingly, the doctrines of commercial and financial equality have been well calculated to preserve the opportunities of American citizens against the more aggressive methods of others. The character of the American policy has been well summarized by Tyler Dennett at the end of his work, "Americans in Eastern Asia," as follows:

In conclusion, we repeat that the tap-root of American policy in Asia is most-favored-nation treatment. An attitude of self-righteousness is neither becoming nor justified. American policy is not philanthropic; it is not, in its motive and history, benevolent; but it is beneficient, for the United States is so situated that American interests in Asia are best promoted by the growth of strong, prosperous, and enlightened Asiatic states. Indeed, it is difficult for an American to believe that the repression or weakening of any part of Asia is a benefit to any power. The United States is committed to its policy by geographical, economic, and political facts, and in the same measure is also bound to a policy of cooperation with all powers which sincerely profess a similar purpose.[1]

Protests against the Violation of the Open Door in Chinese Commerce.—The principal difficulties in the maintenance of equality for American trade have been encountered in South Manchuria, which after the Russo-Japanese War became a Japanese sphere. American commercial interests have complained against a, multitude of practices on the part of the Japanese, which, it is alleged, have embarrassed the trade of Americans in that section.

The fixing of rates on railways in South Manchuria by the Japanese has supplied one cause of controversy. In 1914, attention of the United States was called to the reductions in rates given to goods shipped into Manchuria from Japanese ports. The established route of trade for American goods entering Manchuria is through Shanghai, which is a center of

[1] Page 680.

distribution for American commodities. The discrimination in favor of shipments from Japan was, accordingly, such as to operate directly in favor of their own goods and against those of the United States. After an objection had been made on this point the Japanese issued an order permitting the same rates to goods shipped from Shanghai as from the Japanese ports, if they were carried in the ships of certain Japanese lines and consigned directly to points in Manchuria north of Mukden. This discriminated against American shipping. Furthermore, the American traders did not follow the practice of consigning their goods directly to points in Manchuria but transhipped them at the Port of Newchang. The American ambassador, accordingly, objected to these discriminations as inconsistent with the policy of the open door.[1]

Other methods of discrimination against the trade of foreigners in Manchuria have been alleged by American merchants and consular officials.[2] While many of these complaints have been concerned only with the preference of Japanese business men and bankers for merchants of their own nationality in such cases as treatment in banks, in hotels, and by shipping companies, and are not chargeable against the Japanese government, they nevertheless constitute a distinct handicap to foreigners within a Japanese sphere. Other complaints deal with the discriminatory acts of the Japanese administrative officials and are therefore violations of the spirit, if not the letter, of the open-door agreements. The following may be quoted from the annual report of the American Association of China for 1914:

American cotton formerly held a premier position in Manchuria. Under Russian occupation, every nation stood on an equal footing in Manchuria. The same duties and charges were assessed against all and facilities for distributing goods and doing business in general were satisfactory. Now it is all changed. Under Japanese administration, no chance to advance its own trade is overlooked and to competitors the means taken appear to be a departure from fair trading. In fact, they constitute a most serious violation of the open-door principle on which the diplomacy of the United States in China is based.[3]

[1] *For. Rel.*, 1915, p. 594*ff.*; 1916, p. 446*ff.*
[2] See MILLARD, THOMAS F., "Democracy and the Eastern Question," pp. 262–282, The Century Company, New York, 1919.
[3] *Ibid.*, p. 277.

The Twenty-one Demands and American Representations.—
At the outbreak of the European War many Japanese felt that
the time had come for them to take energetic action with regard
to their position in China. With the exception of the United
States, all of the great powers were busily engaged in the war.
One of the Japanese publicists avowed that "the opportunity of
a thousand years" had come.[1] A memorandum of the Black
Dragon Society of Japan, considered by Minister Reinsch as
authentic, expressed the views of an influential Japanese group:

> Now is the most opportune moment for Japan quickly to solve the
> Chinese question. Such an opportunity will not occur for hundreds of
> years to come. Not only is it Japan's divine duty to act now, but
> present conditions in China favour the execution of such a plan. We
> should by all means decide and act at once.[2]

On Jan. 18, 1915, Japan presented to China her famous
twenty-one demands, which became known during the following
month. On Mar. 13, Secretary Bryan addressed a note on the
question to the Japanese ambassador which reviewed the various
agreements between the powers for the open door in China.[3]
The fifth group of Japanese demands was specifically mentioned
by Mr. Bryan as a hindrance to trade in so far as it provided that:

> China shall purchase from Japan a fixed amount of munitions of war
> (say 50 per cent or more of what is needed by the Chinese government)
> or that there shall be established in China a Sino-Japanese jointly
> worked arsenal.

This clause was deleted from the final agreement between
Japan and China. Provisions for advisers on administrative,
financial, and military affairs were likewise stricken out following
the American objection that they were derogatory to the political
independence and administrative entity of the country. These
representations helped to preserve the integrity of China during
what was an exceedingly serious crisis.[4]

[1] WILLIAMS, "China Yesterday and Today," p. 502.

[2] *For. Rel.*, 1915, p. 134.

[3] *Ibid.*, p. 105*ff*.

[4] The discussion here has been primarily concerned with the open door for
commerce. This should be considered, however, in connection with the
open door for investments. See above, p. 38.

MOROCCO

The participation of the United States in the Algeciras Conference, which met to dispose of the Moroccan dispute between France and Germany, was evidently not based primarily on the economic interest of the United States in the open door, but rather on the desire of President Roosevelt to mediate between the two European powers. The proposal of a conference came from the Kaiser to the President, and the latter was instrumental in bringing about the meeting. Roosevelt wrote:

On Mar. 6, 1905, Sternburg came to me with a message from the Kaiser to ask me to join with the Kaiser in informing the Sultan of Morocco that he ought to reform his government, and that if he would do so we would stand behind him for the open door and would support him in any opposition he might make to any particular nation (that is to France) which sought to obtain exclusive control of Morocco.[1]

The President, however, felt that "We have other fish to fry and we have no real interest in Morocco."[2] And again: "Our interests in Morocco are not sufficiently great to make me feel justified in entangling our government in the matter."[3] In the interests of peace, however, Roosevelt agreed to give his assistance in arranging for the conference and the meeting was held in the early part of the following year in Algeciras. The result of the conference so far as the United States was concerned was the guarantee of "economic liberty without any discriminations." This guarantee was considered by Roosevelt to be of importance "at a time when we are everywhere seeking new markets and outlets for trade."[4]

THE OPEN DOOR IN AMERICAN DEPENDENCIES

American Samoa.—In 1899, the United States by treaty with Germany and Great Britain agreed upon a division of the

[1] BISHOP, JOSEPH BUCKLIN, "Theodore Roosevelt and His Time," Vol. I, p. 468, Charles Scribner's Sons, New York, 1920.

[2] *Ibid.*, p. 472.

[3] *Ibid.*, pp. 473–474.

[4] *Ibid.*, p. 503. The United States has continued its interest in the open door in Morocco. During the negotiations between Great Britain, France, and Spain, in 1923, over the reformation of the administration of Tangiers, the Department of State by identic notes reminded the governments concerned of the obligation under the Algeciras Convention to maintain the open door. Again, in 1928, when Great Britain, France, Spain, and Italy were about to confer, the department sent similar notes. *United States Daily,* Mar. 17, 1928, gives text of the 1928 notes.

Samoan Islands which had for ten years been under an unsatisfactory tripartite control. The United States secured the islands of Tutuila, Manua, and the other islands east of longitude 171° W. The advantage to the United States was in obtaining possession of the Island of Tutuila with its excellent harbor of Pago Pago, commonly said to be the best in the South Pacific. It was stipulated in the treaty that the United States, Great Britain, and Germany should be entitled to equal rights in commerce and shipping in the islands.[1] The United States was, accordingly, pledged to maintain the open door in American Samoa so far as the other two powers were concerned. The policy of the open door to the whole world has been maintained. The tariff on imports is established by regulations of the commandant and applies equally to the goods of all countries. The intrinsic value of the trade of this little insular possession is comparatively insignificant. The population of the American group of islands is estimated at 8,763. In 1926, the total imports were $148,163 of which $61,075 or 41.2 per cent came from the United States. The large importations for governmental use as compared with the total imports doubtless explains to some extent why the share of the United States in this trade is considerable.

The Canal Zone.—American rights in the Canal Zone were ceded by Panama in the Treaty of 1903, for $10,000,000 and an annual payment of $250,000, beginning nine years after the ratification of the treaty. The exact nature of the title under this arrangement has been the subject of some dispute, the United States claiming a cession of sovereignty and the government of Panama disputing this position. The merits of the controversy are not of sufficient concern here to necessitate a discussion of the treaty clauses involved. Reference must be made, however, to an interesting altercation over the policy of tariff collection within the zone which raised the question of the open door.

On June 4, 1904, or about seven months after the signature of the Canal Zone treaty between the United States and Panama, an order was issued by the War Department providing for the creation of two customs districts within the zone and for the collection of customs duties upon merchandise in the same way

[1] Article III, *Treaties, etc. between the United States and Other Powers*, Vol. II, p. 1596.

as American duties were charged upon foreign goods imported into the United States. Thus, articles from the United States would enter the zone free while those going from Panama into that area would have to bear the rather heavy rates of the Dingley tariff. In short, the status of tariff assimilation was established in the Canal Zone.[1]

The merchants of Panama had looked forward to a ready market for their goods in the Canal Zone, where the expenditure of a large amount of American money could be expected to create a situation of unprecedented prosperity. The erection of a tariff wall against them caused not a little dismay. Accordingly, the Chamber of Commerce in the city of Panama addressed a memorial to the President of Panama setting forth the grievances in part as follows:

> If customhouses be established in the zone, all merchandise and produce save those of the United States would be shut out, and the produce of this country, such as rice, corn, beans, rum, coffee, tobacco, cattle, etc., certainly a very small production, would be shut out from the very place where the people of Panama would expect to have a ready sale and receive some benefit thereby.
>
> Commerce, agriculture, and the cattle business would be strangled, and the government of Panama, which should derive its revenues from these sources, would suffer the same fate.
>
> Disaster would be general and all would be forced to emigrate. By Art. I of the treaty, the independence of the Republic of Panama is guaranteed by the United States. By the proposed establishments the Republic of Panama would be reduced to the worst kind of dependence and servitude that exists, that of starvation.[2]

The government of Panama heeded the request of its merchants and in its diplomatic intercourse with the United States pressed the point with some vigor. The question as to the full ownership of the zone was raised, and it was claimed by the representatives of Panama that, lacking complete sovereignty, the United States had no legal right to establish a tariff system. The United States maintained that its sovereignty over the

---

[1] For the text of the order see *For. Rel.*, 1904, p. 586. The order also contained a provision authorizing the Governor of the Canal Zone to enter upon negotiations with the President of the Republic of Panama respecting reciprocal trade relations. This provision was, at the time, unknown to the people of Panama.

[2] *Ibid.*, p. 585.

zone was complete; but as pacific relations in this vital strategic region were far more important than the commercial advantages to be secured through tariff assimilation, the point concerning customs was ultimately conceded to Panama.

The demands of Panama were satisfied by an order of the President of Dec. 3, 1904, revoking the previous order of the War Department, concerning the collection of duties, which had created customs ports within the zone. This made it necessary to ship most goods entering the zone through the ports of Panama or Colon. These ports were under the jurisdiction of Panama and the customs duties of Panama were collected. All of this was subject to the understanding that the tariff laws of Panama, which thereafter should apply, were to be modified in the direction of liberality. Materials for the construction, maintenance, and operation of the canal and supplies for employes of the United States and their families were to enter free, as had been guaranteed in the Treaty of 1903. Free trade was set up between the Republic of Panama and the Canal Zone. Accordingly, goods imported into the Canal Zone from the United States for persons other than employes of the canal, and commodities from other countries, excepting Panama, now pay the regular Panaman tariff. This has been properly classified as an open-door arrangement with the exception that goods and supplies for the employes of the canal are favored.[1]

There has been some complaint on the part of Panaman merchants that the War Department commissaries in the zone, which import their merchandise for government employes free and which have the additional advantage of reduced rates on the Panama Railroad, have been selling directly and indirectly to other than employes. It has been claimed that American and native employes have bought for their friends and that coupon books for commissary purchases have been transferred to non-employes. The commissaries have sold to ships passing through the canal. The Panaman delegation to the Third Pan-American Commercial Conference drew up a protest against these practices but was persuaded to refrain from presenting it.[2]

[1] For a good statement of the situation see U. S. Tariff Comm., "Colonial Tariff Policies," p. 625ff.

[2] *State Department Press Release*, May 14, 1927; *The New York Times*, Oct. 2, 1927.

II. THE CLOSED DOOR

There are two types of tariff systems which create a closed-door situation in dependencies: tariff assimilation and preferential tariffs. In the first, the colony is brought within the tariff system of the mother country and there is free trade as between them. When goods are shipped to the colony from third countries they pay the same tariffs as when shipped into the mother country. The colony is thus assimilated to the mother country in customs matters. The second or preferential type exists where a separate tariff system is created for the colony in which a preference is given to the mother country. This preference may amount to a reduction of duties or to completely free admission of products from the mother country. The United States has tariff assimilation for Porto Rico, Alaska, and Hawaii, while preferential tariffs exist in the Philippines, the Virgin Islands, and Guam. These are the American closed-door areas. Their combined population is about 13,500,000, as contrasted with about 37,000 in American Samoa and the Canal Zone. Thus it can be said that the United States maintains the closed door in her dependencies as compared with the open door at something like the ratio of 365:1.

PREFERENTIAL TARIFFS: THE PHILIPPINES

The Commercial Motive in the Acquisition of the Philippines.— Several reasons prompted the annexation of the Philippine Islands by the United States, and it is not the intention here to apportion the relative importance which should belong to each. There can be no doubt, however, that the desire for greater markets had its part in bringing about the acquisition and retention of the islands. At the time when Manila fell before the attack of the American Asiatic Squadron the powers of Europe were in the midst of their scramble for concessions in China, and the commercial element in the United States was being prepared to urge some kind of step which would assure to the United States a future participation in the Asiatic trade. As soon as American troops were established in the islands, a series of investigations was begun to ascertain their strategic, mineral, and commercial possibilities.[1] These investigations

[1] REYES, José S., "Legislative History of America's Economic Policy toward the Philippines," pp. 15–16 (Columbia Univ. Studies in History, Economics and Public Law, Vol. CVI, No. 2).

and the reports upon them antedated the decision of the administration in Washington to retain the Philippines.

Meanwhile those who were interested in the advancement of trade had shown some concern in the hitherto unfamiliar islands. Frank A. Vanderlip, who had served as financial editor of the *Chicago Tribune* and associate editor of the *Economist* and who, in 1897, had been appointed Assistant Secretary of the Treasury, in an article in the *Century* for August, 1898, expressed the opinion of the more alert among the commercial group. This article was written before the administration had made up its mind upon the Phillippine question. Mr. Vanderlip wrote:

It is as a base for commercial operations that the islands seem to possess the greatest importance. They occupy a favored location, not with reference to any one part of any particular country of the Orient, but to all parts. Together with the islands of the Japanese Empire, since the acquirement of Formosa, the Philippines are the pickets of the Pacific, standing guard at the entrance to trade with the millions of China, Korea, French Indo-China, the Malay Peninsula, and the Islands of Indonesia to the south.

John Barrett, who had been Minister to Siam, and who, during the war had acted as newspaper correspondent in the Philippines, contributed an article to the September issue of the *North American Review* in which he stressed the same motive.

We would have an unsurpassed point in the far East from which to extend our commerce and trade and gain our share in the immense distribution of material prizes that must follow the opening of China, operating from Manila as a base as does England from Hongkong.

During the period when such statements were being made, President McKinley was indecisive and open to the influence of opinion. Gradually the advantages of American ownership became apparent to him and in the making of this decision he was not unmindful of the interests of American trade. By the sixteenth of September, the decision to hold the Island of Luzon had been made. During a tour of the West in the following month, in a speech at Hastings, Iowa on Oct. 13, he indicated that this territorial expansion gave cause for commercial optimism:

We have pretty much everything in this country to make it happy. We have good money, we have ample revenues, we have unquestioned national credit, but what we want is new markets, and as trade follows the flag, it looks very much as if we were going to have new markets.[1]

A few weeks later he informed the Christian Endeavor Society of Boston that:

. . . the expansion of our country means the expansion of our system of education, of our principles of free government, of additional securities to life, liberty and the pursuit of happiness, as well as of our commerce and the distribution of the products of our industry and labor.[2]

During the discussion of the treaty in the Senate, the question of the Philippines was hotly contested. Commercial opportunities for American goods played a part in the debates and in the securing of a favorable vote. The argument was advanced by senators at the suggestion of William Jennings Bryan that the approval of the treaty with Spain would not commit this country upon the Philippine question but that the decision could be made later, after an appeal to the country. The treaty was approved and during the presidential campaign of 1900 the issue of imperialism proved to be more important than any other consideration. In the course of this contest, Senator Marcus A. Hanna, a man whose influence in the Republican party was very great and whose sympathy with commercial and financial groups was especially close during the campaign for reasons of party finance, remarked as follows:

If it is commercialism to want the possession of a strategic point giving the American people an opportunity to maintain a foothold in the markets of that great Eastern country, for God's sake let us have commercialism.[3]

Even in the strongholds of Democracy, the awakening manufacturing ambition and the desire to sell cotton goods in the Orient combined to counteract the influence of the great Democratic leader and anti-imperialist, William Jennings Bryan. The cotton producers were especially interested in the prospect of clothing the people of China with cotton goods instead of the more expensive silk, while the need of the Filipinos for a more adequate cotton covering was not to be denied. Senator McLaurin of South Carolina remarked before his constituents at Greenville on May 22, 1901:

[1] *Chicago Times-Herald*, Oct. 14, 1898; REYES, *op. cit.*, p. 21.

[2] REYES, *op. cit.*, p. 24.

[3] *Ibid.*, p. 38

The time has now come when we must have foreign trade, and not merely subsidiary to our industrial development at home, but as necessary to our continued prosperity. Our resources and population demand world-wide avenues of trade, and we cannot separate the commercial and political elements involved. What are we to do with our surplus products? This is the question engaging the attention of all the civilized nations of the earth. The only field unoccupied is the Orient. I believe that the time is near at hand when the cotton trade of the South will be with the Orient.[1]

And added Senator Pritchard of North Carolina:

When we consider the enormous undeveloped wealth of the South, it is a question of great importance as to whether or not the blight of Bryanism is to be permitted to arrest Southern progress.[2]

The desire for markets undoubtedly had some influence in the initial determination to keep the Philippines and in repelling the immediate counter-attacks against imperialism. Since that time, the question of independence has been periodically before the American people and throughout this conflict the American commercial interests in the Far East have constituted one of the most serious obstacles to granting the Filipinos their freedom. Col. Carmi A. Thompson, who was requested by President Coolidge to make a survey of the Philippine situation in 1926, reported as follows:

From the standpoint of American commercial interests in the Far East, it would be unwise to relinquish control of the Philippines at the present time. Our trade with the Orient has been expanding year by year and all indications point to an increased volume of business for the future. We need the Philippines as a commercial base, and the retention of the Philippines will otherwise be of great benefit to our eastern situation.[3]

The Open-door Ideal.—The Philippines were acquired during a period when grave apprehensions were felt that the markets of China were to be closed to the trade of the United States. During that time a marked feeling developed in this country that an open door to the trade of all nations was the only correct and morally defensible policy to be pursued by a strong nation which had acquired control over backward peoples.

[1] Quoted in the *Cong. Rec.*, Vol. 35, p. 2094.
[2] *Ibid.*
[3] *Sen. Doc.* 180, p. 3, Sixty-ninth Congress, Second Session

The belief in the moral and commercial advantages of the open door permeated the thinking business world. *The Commercial and Financial Chronicle*, a weekly newspaper representing the industrial interests of the United States, commented editorially on this question on Aug. 27, 1898 as follows:

Does anyone, for instance, seriously believe that because in our domestic fiscal legislation of other years we have carried the policy of protection to extremes, we will therefore now begin by shutting out goods of other foreign states from our newly acquired colonies? If so, he must imagine that America has shut its eyes to the diplomatic drama even now in progress on the Chinese coast; that it has forgotten the lesson taught by our own people to England in 1776, when England tried precisely this policy of trade discrimination. It is not our belief that the lessons of history have been wholly wasted on one of the most intelligent of modern nations.

President McKinley, whose Secretary of State, John Hay, was to go down in American history as the great open-door champion, firmly believed in the soundness of this policy, if the instructions to the Peace Commissioners above his signature are a true indication. In these instructions, dated Sept. 16, 1898 he declared:

Incidental to our tenure in the Philippine Islands is the commercial opportunity to which American statesmanship cannot be indifferent. It is just to use every legitimate means for the enlargement of American trade; but we seek no advantages in the Orient which are not common to all. Asking only the open door for ourselves, we are ready to accord the open door to others. The commercial opportunity which is naturally and inevitably associated with this new opening depends less on large territorial possessions than upon an adequate commercial basis and upon broad and equal privileges.

It is believed that in the practical application of these guiding principles the present interests of our country and the proper measure of its duty, its welfare in the future, and the consideration of its exemption from unknown perils will be found in full accord with the just, moral, and humane purpose which was invoked as our justification in accepting the war.[1]

During the discussions with the Spanish commissioners in Paris, the commissioners of the United States asserted that "it being the policy of the United States to maintain in the Philippine

[1] *For. Rel.*, 1898, pp. 907–908.

Islands an open door to the commerce of the world," they were prepared to grant to Spain for a term of years equal commercial privileges with the United States.[1]

Closing the Door.—In 1898, it was the sense of the American government that the open door was to be maintained in American territories to the same extent as it was to be requested in the territories of others. Such was without doubt the Golden Rule as applied to commerce. This idealistic policy lasted but a few brief months until American business interests became aware of the commercial possibilities in the Philippine Islands. And then a change began. By 1900, trade papers, chambers of commerce, manufacturers, and others interested in the export trade were helping to revise the Philippine tariff; and it was the declared intention of the Philippine administration to so shape the schedules as to give an advantage to American goods.[2] At that time there existed the treaty obligation by which the United States was bound to give equal treatment to Spanish goods and ships for a period of ten years. The letter of this treaty was not violated by the new tariffs, but the spirit of the treaty and the letter of the open-door declarations were both transgressed. Wines were so taxed as to give a preference to California products over those of Spain. E. R. Lilienthal, of the Crown Distilleries Company of San Francisco, wrote in gratitude to Colonel Edwards, Chief of the Division of Insular Affairs:

It is a matter of general recognition that our officials in their desire to prefer American interests have been hampered by the treaty of Spain, but all admit as the tariff is now framed a decided advantage has been gained and will be realized.[3]

Colonel Edwards himself described the result of the law as follows:

[1] *For. Rel.*, 1898, p. 950. Lord Beresford, in writing of his journey across the United States early in 1899, mentions a speech by one of the commissioners, Whitelaw Reid, in which Mr. Reid declared the open-door policy to be the best for American trade in the Philippines and China, and that the American government intended to commit itself to this policy in the Philippine Islands, "The Break-up of China," p. 437.

[2] See the statement by General Otis, "Correspondence Relating to Philippine Customs Tariff," *Sen. Doc.* 171, p. 18, Fifty-seventh Congress, First Session.

[3] *Ibid.*, pp. 260–261, quoted in Hoxie, R. F., "The American Colonial Policy and the Tariff," *Jour. Political Econ.*, Vol. 11, pp. 213–214.

While no different duty in favor of American goods is openly mentioned the articles were so described in the tariff as to allow an advantage of American goods.[1]

The law was promulgated by the Philippine Commission Sept. 17, 1901, and took effect Nov. 15, 1901.

In the tariff revision of 1905, consultation with American business men was again resorted to. The principle of legal equality in tariff rates was maintained and the actual preference to American goods was increased, thus satisfying the desire for a nominal observance of the treaty with Spain and at the same time giving the exporter some of the advantage for which he had been clamoring.[2]

The door which had been thus slowly swinging under pressure from American business men was closed with a bang as soon as the expiration of the Spanish treaty removed the obligation of equal treatment. In the Act of Congress of 1909, a Philippine tariff wall was maintained against the world at large, amounting to an average rate of about 20 per cent ad valorem,[3] while American goods were admitted into the islands free. Thus fell the principle of the open door. General Edwards, Chief of the Insular Bureau of the War Department, who had had previous experience in caring for the American exporter in the framing of Philippine tariff laws, had charge of drawing the schedules in this instance. In the performance of his task, he again consulted with the interested commercial groups in the United States. He described the process as follows:

Take the iron schedule, for instance, and it would be sent to the *Iron Age*, the jewelry schedule to the special jewelry magazine, the watch schedule to the watch magazine, and so forth, and invite recommendations and comment.[4]

He sought to favor American goods not only with suitable protective tariff rates but also by continued discrimination in descriptions and specifications. All special interests were recognized, according to General Edward's testimony, excepting those of which he had no knowledge.

The closing of the door in the Philippines did much to give the markets of the islands into the hands of American exporters.

[1] Hoxie, *loc. cit.*, p. 214.
[2] U. S. Tariff Comm., "Colonial Tariff Policies," pp. 595–596.
[3] *Ibid.*, p. 598.
[4] *Cong. Rec.*, Vol. 44, p. 2003.

In 1899, the Philippines bought from the United States but 7 per cent of their entire imports. By 1908, the percentage had increased to 17. Then came the Tariff Act of 1909. By 1913, the United States was supplying half of the Philippine imports.[1] In 1925, the imports from the United States were 57.9 per cent of the whole,[2] and in 1926 they were 60 per cent.[3] Iron and steel products from the United States increased from 8 per cent in 1899 to 76.16 per cent in 1925, while the percentages of cotton goods from this country increased from 0.51 to 52.29. The tariff on wheat flour so handicapped the Australian exporters as to prevent serious competition. The percentage of this commodity from the United States increased during the years above mentioned from 17.47 to 84.30. Likewise the tariff on rough lumber has given to the American exporters an almost complete monopoly of the Philippine market in competition with rivals in British Columbia.[4]

Guam.—A preferential arrangement exists in Guam, the tariff applying to the goods of foreign countries while those from the United States enter free. The tariff is put in force by the naval governor subject to the approval of the Department of the Navy.[5] In 1926, the imports from the United States constituted 58.4 per cent of all imports.

The Virgin Islands.—The Virgin Islands likewise have a tariff preference for American goods which enter free. The old Danish tariff applies to the goods of other nations. The imports from the United States dominate all others, being about 82.2 per cent in 1924. Prior to the purchase of the islands the Danish tariff applied to all nations alike.

ASSIMILATED TERRITORIES OF THE UNITED STATES

The greatest illustration of the efficacy of tariff assimilation in securing the trade of acquired possessions has been seen in the

[1] U. S. Tariff Commission, "Colonial Tariff Policies," p. 582.

[2] *Annual Report of the Insular Collector of Customs for the Fiscal Year Ended December 31, 1925*, Manila Bureau of Printing, p. 11, 1926. See also Buell, "International Relations," p. 425.

[3] U. S. Bureau of Foreign and Domestic Commerce, *Statistical Abstract of the United States*, 1926, p. 557.

[4] Smith, Franklin H., "Philippine Market for American Lumber," Bureau of Foreign and Domestic Commerce, *Special Agents Series*, 100, Government Printing Office, Washington, 1915.

[5] U. S. Tariff Commission, "Colonial Tariff Policies," p. 576. For a description of the tariff rates see *ibid.*, p. 618.

expansion of the continental territory of the original thirteen states westward to the Pacific. The added territories have been brought within the American tariff wall, and the result has been the opening of an enormous market to the producers and shippers of the original Atlantic strip. Similar results, although on a smaller scale, have been achieved by the inclusion of subsequently acquired territories in the tariff system of the United States.

Porto Rico.—The fixing of the tariff rates on goods passing between Porto Rico and the United States was a matter of bitter conflict in the early years of American occupation. The protected interests, such as the sugar producers in the United States, staunchly maintained that regular American tariffs should be charged against imports from Porto Rico. They took this position, not so much because of the fear of the competition from Porto Rico as from the apprehension that the policy, if once adopted, might be extended to the Philippines and to Cuba, if the latter should become a possession of the United States. On the other hand, the exporters, who desired the Porto Rican markets, the importers of products from Porto Rico, and the commercial leaders in the island combined to urge the abolition of tariffs.

In the first tariff arrangements under the military administration, American goods going into the islands were subject to the same duties as goods from other countries. In his message of Dec. 5, 1899, President McKinley advocated the abolition of all tariffs between the United States and Porto Rico, this position being taken largely because of the economic crisis in the island due to the cutting off of the old Spanish market for coffee. The problem was then put before Congress. After a bitter struggle between contending lobbies the Foraker Act was passed which applied the American tariff with some exceptions to imports into Porto Rico from foreign countries and provided that, until Mar. 1, 1902, the trade between Porto Rico and the United States should be subject to a tariff equal to 15 per cent of the regular American tariff plus the internal revenue taxes of the country of destination. Subsequent tariff enactments have eliminated all exceptions to the application of the regular American tariff in Porto Rico and have permitted the free passage of goods between the two excepting that the internal taxes of the country of destination must be paid. Thus the United States and Porto Rico repose within the same tariff wall, an example of tariff assimilation.[1] In 1926, 87 per cent of Porto Rican imports were from the United States.

Alaska.—Tariff assimilation has been applied to Alaska. The result is that a monopoly of the trade is in the hands of the United States, 98.3 per cent of the imports being of American origin in 1926. Canada, with the convenient ports of British Columbia, might be expected to compete substantially if the doors were open. Canadian goods, however, have been unable to invade the field to any marked extent. As the interior of Alaska is developed, the sales in that country will increase far beyond their present amounts and this will be of great commercial importance to the port of Seattle.

There does not exist and there is not likely to come any foreign competition for the trade of Alaska. In that respect the country [Alaska] is on the same basis as California and Oregon are. The competition is and will be almost exclusively domestic.[2]

Hawaii.—The tariff situation in Hawaii is the same as that in Alaska. This was not entirely an innovation at the time of annexation as the commercial relations between the two were very close. Under the Reciprocity Treaty of 1875 sugar and other important products entered the United States free while a substantial list of American products were admitted without duty into the islands. The system of tariff assimilation, which has existed since 1900, has increased the advantage of the United States because of the fact that the American tariff is higher than was that which had been in force under the Hawaiian government. Foreign sales in Hawaii are more important than in Alaska, due to the fact that many Japanese laborers in the islands buy rice from Japan, preferring it to the Hawaiian product. Hawaii is a port of call and the numerous trans-Pacific steamers that stop there have carried some of the trade from their own countries.[3] The imports from the United States were, nevertheless, 88.1 per cent of the total in 1926.

Expansionist Sentiment Now Non-existent.—Although colonies have proved to be useful in the extension of American trade, there seems to be no sentiment for further territorial

---

[1] U. S. Tariff Comm., "Colonial Tariff Policies," pp. 600–611. For the passage of the Foraker Act see also Hoxie, *loc. cit.*, pp. 203–205.

[2] Robinson, *op. cit.*, p. 30.

[3] *Ibid.*, p. 45.

expansion as an aid in the race for foreign markets.   Perhaps this is because colonial markets have not been important in American commerce, and such territories as the United States might acquire could scarcely provide a drop in the great bucket of American foreign trade.   At present, the expansionist ambitions of the United States are venting themselves in obtaining over certain countries a system of financial control backed by strong protection methods.   Such controls do not require annexation and do not affect trade through the manipulation of tariffs.

CHAPTER XVII

SHIPPING POLICIES

Brief Sketch of the History of the American Merchant Marine.
Before the Revolution, the colonists along the rugged New
England coast had already won for themselves a place upon the
sea. The comparatively lower cost of timber which favored
colonial shipbuilding and the initiative of a new people had
combined to insure for them success in ocean commerce. The
Revolutionary War played havoc with American merchant
vessels, but on the conclusion of peace the seaboard population
turned to the reconstruction of their shipping. Progress was
slow at first but great impetus was given to the movement by
the European wars following 1793. For over half a century
from that time the United States ranked as a leading maritime
power. American influence on the sea reached its climax in the
years from 1846 to 1860, when the graceful clipper became the
swiftest of cargo vessels. The Civil War marked the beginning
of a long, dull period in the shipping circles of this country.
During that conflict American ships aggregating about 1,000,000
tons were transferred to foreign registry, and many others were
destroyed. The energies of the nation were for the time turned
from commerce to war. Following the Civil War, the people
of the United States found an outlet for their energies in the
development of a vast internal empire and until 1914 they were
for the most part content to see their ocean-borne commerce
carried in foreign bottoms. The World War created an imperative need for ships. Congress provided for the erection of
shipyards. Steel and wooden vessels were turned out with
unprecedented speed and the United States government became
the owner of a huge merchant fleet. Since the war, severe
competition for the carriage of goods has reduced ocean
freight rates. Many of the vessels owned by the United
States government have been laid up and statistics of American
shipping employed in foreign trade show a marked decline in
tonnage.

The following table[1] will indicate the varying fortunes of the American merchant marine for more than a century and a quarter:

Year	American tonnage in foreign trade	Percentage of American water-borne foreign commerce carried in American vessels
1790	346,254	
1810	981,019	
1830	537,563	89.9
1860	2,379,396	66.5
1890	928,062	12.9
1910	782,517	8.7
1920	9,924,694	42.7
1927	7,309,146	34.1

THE IMPORTANCE OF SHIPPING TO THE NATION

The solicitude with which governments are disposed to regard the interests of shipowners is due to a number of causes which may be summarized as follows:

1. The importance of ships as a source of national income.

2. The greater aid which national shipping, as compared with foreign shipping, gives to national commerce.

3. The part played by shipping in plans of national defense and offense.

Shipping as a Source of National Income.—Shipping, profitably conducted on a large scale, has accounted for a considerable proportion of the wealth of maritime nations. Particularly has this been true in the case of small seaboard states whose marine activities have overshadowed the other industries of the people. The wealth of ancient Tyre came principally from its ships which distributed the wares of Egypt and Babylonia to the rest of the Mediterranean world. The prosperity of Venice in the Middle Ages sprang directly from the *entrepôt* trade carried on by her commercial fleets. The merchant marine of Great Britain, which carries the goods of all nations, is to no small degree responsible for the position of London in world finance. Many of the early American fortunes came from ships. The

[1] The figures are taken from the Bureau of Navigation's publication, "Merchant Marine Statistics 1927," pp. 22–23, 61–62.

argosies of such men as Elias Hasket Derby and Stephen Girard sailed the seven seas and brought profit to their owners by exchanging the widely differing products of the tropics for those of the temperate climates.

During periods of war and neutrality, shipping has been especially productive of income. The prosperity of American shippers during the period of the Napoleonic wars is well attested by the increase in tonnage in the foreign trade from 346,254 tons in 1790 to 981,019 tons in 1810. During the World War, enormous profits were made by American shipping. Freight rates soared to almost unbelievable heights and fabulous dividends were paid to stockholders in steamship companies. The American-Hawaiian Steamship Company paid 200 per cent in 1916 and 405 per cent in 1917. The Dollar Steamship Lines made profits of 322.9 per cent in 1916. The Luckenbach Steamship Company showed gains of 236.2 per cent in 1916 and 666.9 per cent in 1917.[1]

In the cold gray dawn of postwar reconstruction, American shipping has awakened to the realization that it is not organized on a basis to be productive of income. In this respect it has ceased for the present to be an advantage to the nation. Presidents Harding and Coolidge have deplored the deficits which have arisen from the operation of government-owned ships and have urged that the business be placed in the hands of private owners. On the other hand, private shipping interests, claiming inability to meet foreign competition, have sought subsidies and government aids in various forms. If the one factor of ship earnings were to be considered as all important, it would probably be better for the nation to permit its goods to be carried in foreign bottoms. At any rate, the shipping industry contributes but an infinitesimal part of the tremendous total of American national income, and its capacity for revenue is not sufficient to be seriously considered in the formation of the larger policies of the nation.

The Merchant Marine as an Aid to National Commerce.—The merchant marine, however, does not derive its chief importance from its direct contribution to national income but from its assistance to other enterprises. For that reason the governments of commercial peoples often lavish a care upon their ship-

[1] "Hearings on Treaty of Commerce and Consular Rights with Germany," p. 245.

ping interests which is far out of proportion to the capital involved or the number of people directly employed in the operation or building of ships.[1] In times of peace the great value of the ship consists in providing a method for transporting abroad the goods which it is desirable should be sold to foreign peoples and for bringing back the goods which it is desirable should be brought from abroad. If it can be shown that ships under the flag of a trading nation furnish better facilities for exports and imports than the ocean carriers under the flags of other countries, there is good reason why that nation should support a merchant marine even if it cannot produce a direct profit.

In the past, shipping under the national flag has furnished probably a more certain aid to national commerce than it does at present. Before the days of the packet ships, the merchant was also a shipowner. He assembled goods in his warehouses and exported them in his own vessels. In foreign markets they were disposed of and wares which were needed at home were obtained by exchange or purchase. There were no regularly scheduled lines of freighters which carried the goods of non-ship-owning exporters. Accordingly, the merchant with his fleets was the active force in foreign trade. If a country lacked ships, it depended upon the visits of the merchants of other countries. Sometimes these conducted commerce satisfactorily, but they could not be depended upon in times of war nor were their owners so well informed as to the nature of domestic industry and its export possibilities.

The extent to which trade depended upon the decisions of the shipowners was very great, but the shipmaster also played an important role. His part in the romance of early American commerce is well set forth in the following extract from Ralph D. Paine's interesting account of "The Old Merchant Marine:"

And so it happened that in the spicy warehouses that overlooked Salem Harbor there came to be stored hemp from Luzon, gum copal from Zanzibar, palm oil from Africa, coffee from Arabia, tallow from Madagascar, whale oil from the Antartic, hides and wool from the Rio de la Plata, nutmeg and cloves from Malaysia. Such merchandise had been

[1] The 450,000 men who operate the world's ships constitute but an insignificant number as compared with the millions engaged in agriculture and industry in single countries. SALTER, J. A., "Allied Shipping Control, An Experiment in International Administration," p. 7, The Clarendon Press, Oxford, 1921.

bought or bartered for by shipmasters who were much more than mere navigators. They had to be shrewd merchants on their own accounts, for the success or failure of a voyage was mostly in their hands. Carefully trained and highly intelligent men, they attained command in the early twenties and were able to retire, after a few years more afloat, to own ships and exchange the quarterdeck for the counting room, and the cabin for the solid mansion and lawn on Derby Street. Every opportunity, indeed, was offered them to advance their own fortunes. They sailed not for wages but for handsome commissions and privileges—in the Derby ships, five per cent of a cargo outward bound, two and a half per cent of the freightage home, five per cent profit on goods bought and sold between foreign ports, and five per cent of the cargo space for their own use.[1]

Today the situation is materially changed. Specialization has separated shipping from trade. Regular sailings of public carriers furnish reliable transportation for the goods of those who do not own ships. There has been something of a revival of the old merchant-owner combination in the fleets of huge commercial corporations, such as the United Fruit Company and the Standard Oil Company, but more often exporters or importers depend upon the service furnished by the shipping industry. The ports of a country may, with this system, be satisfactorily served by carriers under a foreign flag. The fact that about two-thirds of the ocean freight and three-fourths of the passengers to and from the United States are transported in the vessels of other countries indicates the part which foreign shipping has played in the great commercial development of the United States and the service which it has rendered to American industry.

There are, however, some good commercial reasons to be advanced for the development of a merchant marine under the national flag. From the standpoint of the United States, it is sometimes found that the liners of other nations do not always ply along the trade routes which are desirable for the American exporter. Perhaps such routes are not commercially successful. Perhaps the national habits of alien shipping or the policies of a subsidizing government have determined that the foreign-owned vessels shall primarily serve the commerce of the foreign country. Whatever the reason, there have been instances in which American exporters, desiring to ship their products to certain markets, have found no direct lines available. Prior to the World War

[1] PAINE, "The Old Merchant Marine," pp. 58–59.

the trade of the United States with South America and the
Orient was at a disadvantage as compared with British trade,
for the reason that the British exporters were better served by
direct shipping lines. In such a situation the natural attitude
of the American exporter and importer is to demand that action
be taken to develop a merchant marine under our own flag
which will furnish the desired facilities.[1] The effect of the
competition of United States ships in reducing ocean freight
rates, even below the level of profit, is likewise urged as a reason
for the maintenance of a merchant marine.

Shipping in War Time Emergencies.—It is in times of war that
the most acute need for shipping arises. The imperative demand
for ships during the World War will not soon be forgotten.
Following a temporary dullness at the opening of the war, there
ensued a period of activity in marine circles such as the world
had never before known. The cutting off of supplies from
belligerent countries necessitated longer hauls from more distant
ports. The loss of ships from submarine attack and the requisi-
tioning of ships by the governments for the transportation of
military supplies and troops combined to place an enormous load
upon the world's ocean carriers. Freight rates doubled, tripled,
and were finally multiplied by sixes and sevens. Ships which
were to be had at 2s.6d. per ton per month in 1914 were bringing
47s.6d. in 1917. In peace times British freight steamers had
usually sold for £6 to £7 per ton of dead weight freight-carrying
capacity, but in 1917 a sale was reported for as high as £60 per
ton.[2] J. Russell Smith, a leading authority, graphically describes
the effect of the war upon prices as follows:

The prices for old vessels are no less astonishing. In the summer of
1917, the French government paid £475,000 for a ship which ten years
ago sold to the Japanese for £32,000. By all the rules of good shipping
conduct this vessel in 1911 was ready for breaking up, yet this piece of
floating junk, which sold for $160,000 in middle age ten years before,
brought $1,800,000, so hard pressed were the Allies. These prices
arose from the enormous profits of the shipping business. Dutch
shipping companies paid 100 per cent dividends; Danish shipping shares
rose 100 points in a week, reached 1,000 on a par of 100, and made

[1] BARBER, A. B., "Foreign Trade and Our Merchant Marine," *Annals of
the American Academy of Political and Social Science*, Vol. CXXVII, p. 112.

[2] SMITH, J. RUSSEL, "Influence of the Great War upon Shipping,"
pp. 32–33, Oxford Univ. Press, New York, 1919.

profits in a year that were greater than the capital. It is no wonder that after America entered the war the cry of "ships, ships, and yet more ships" came continuously across the sea from the leaders in Europe.[1]

Nations began to bargain desperately for shipping facilities. Those countries which held valuable raw materials refused in some cases to permit their sale to other nations unless shipping could be alloted in return. Great Britain withheld coal and the United States withheld steel and food in the attempt to secure the use of ships. During the days of neutrality, American exporters paid the highest freight rates in history to British shipowners as a price for the lack of ships. Fortunate was the nation which, like Great Britain, possessed a large merchant marine. Under the terms of the British laws, registered ships could be requisitioned by the government and set to carrying freight for necessary purposes at reasonable rates.

The World War undoubtedly proved the inadequacy of peacetime shipping in great national emergencies. It has raised an important question: To what extent should unprofitable shipping be fostered to provide in advance for the uncertain contingencies of war? This question has frequently been raised in connection with the problem of the disposition of the government-owned fleet. It is also part and parcel of discussions on ship subsidy and national preparedness.

SHIPPING DIPLOMACY: THE FREEDOM OF THE SEAS

In the various diplomatic contests waged on behalf of the American merchant marine, none has been more dramatic than the defense of shipping interests during periods of neutrality. The doctrine of the "Freedom of the Seas" includes in a general way the various claims that have been made in behalf of our neutral shipping. The doctrine cannot be clearly defined but it arises largely from economic interest. It has been baptized in American blood, and because of its warlike associations it has become suffused with emotion in the popular mind.

The neutral nation desires that its freedom of action shall not be curtailed because of the wars of others. President Jefferson stated this position as follows:

. . . when two nations go to war, those who choose to live in peace retain their natural right to pursue their agriculture, manufactures, and

[1] SMITH, *op. cit.*, p. 33.

other ordinary vocations; to carry the produce of their industry, for exchange, to all nations, belligerent or neutral, as usual; to go and come freely, without injury or molestation; and, in short, that the war among others shall be, for them, as if it did not exist.[1]

Neutral ships are particularly in demand in times of war. They are not so liable to seizure as are the merchant ships of the belligerent countries, which are subject to capture on the high seas. Furthermore, the neutral countries are free to devote their efforts to commerce while the belligerents are mainly occupied in the more immediate tasks of fighting. Consequently, during war times the attractive offers made for the use of merchant vessels stimulate greatly the shipping activities of countries not engaged in the conflict. Neutral seaport cities hum with prosperity. The people who are engaged in shipping and in the other stimulated industries demand and receive diplomatic support for their activities.

The belligerent, on the other hand, feels fully justified in cutting off trade with his enemy. He cannot see why third countries have a "natural right" to step in and derive immense profits from wartime commerce. In so far as they assist his enemy they become, in fact if not in law, his opponents. Belligerents, accordingly, have always held their obligations to neutral commerce rather lightly. We have then on one side the interest of the neutral in an abnormal but remunerative commerce and on the other the war interest of the belligerent, whether self-preservation or conquest. It is difficult to see how a conflict of these interests can be avoided under a system of national independence and international disorganization.

The United States has, in general, been a strong defender of the interests of the neutral. American diplomatic officials have ardently advocated larger protection of neutral commerce in a multitude of negotiations. The same end has been sought at international conferences, called to codify the law of the sea. American scholars have frequently reflected the official view in their interpretations of international law. It is true that on rare occasions as a belligerent the United States has leaned in the opposite direction. In the Civil War and during American participation in the World War, the government was busy refuting many of the arguments which it had advanced in times

---

[1] *Moore's Digest*, Vol. VII, p. 677.

of neutrality. But, speaking generally, this country has been a fairly consistent advocate of the interests of the neutral.

There have been good reasons for this. Our periods of neutrality have been longer in time than our periods of belligerency. Our geographic position has been that of a neutral. Isolated in the Western Hemisphere, the United States has not been disposed to prepare after the European fashion for war as a normal and frequent occurrence. If there were a great power in South America with which hostilities were perennially probable, this country would doubtless lay its war plans to cut off European supplies from its southern rival. In such a situation the interests of the belligerent would dominate American thought and be emphasized in American policy. Under conditions as they have existed, however, the United States has been immune from danger in the New World, while the possibilities of entanglement with European powers have been remote. This country has, therefore, prepared intellectually and diplomatically to assist its own commerce during wars between other countries.

The Beginnings of the American Pro-neutral Doctrines.—In 1793, war broke out between France and Great Britain and for twenty-two years there was practically continuous strife in Europe. During almost all of the time the United States was a neutral nation and was engaged in attempts to maintain the rights of its shipping as against the decrees of belligerents. In the beginning, France opened the trade of her colonies to other nations and American ships swarmed into the West Indian waters. Great Britain by various devices enforced with some brutality sought to prevent this trade and scores of American vessels were seized and condemned. France, at the same time, issued orders designed to prevent the carrying of provisions to the British Isles. A horde of French privateers scoured the ocean to seize whatever offending vessels might come within their grasp. Later, more sweeping orders were issued. Great Britain declared a blockade of certain French ports which was much wider than she was able to make effective. She forbade neutral vessels to trade between ports under French control or to trade with any port which refused admission to British ships. Napoleon in the Berlin decree declared a blockade around the British Isles, and in the Milan decree he made subject to seizure all vessels which had submitted to search by British ships or which had touched at a British port. Thus the trans-

Atlantic commerce could be carried on only in violation of the decrees of one or the other of the belligerents and American ships in the European trade were in perpetual peril.

During this time, the government of the United States strove to uphold the rights of American shipping and was continually protesting to one or the other belligerent against the enforcement of the harsh decrees. The complaints which were presented through diplomatic channels were too many to enumerate but a few may be briefly summarized.

When the British, in attempting to prevent the use of American vessels in the trade between France and the French West Indies, invoked the Rule of 1756, which declared that trade not allowed to neutrals in times of peace could not be opened to them in times of war, the United States asserted that the rule was contrary to international law. The British supported the rule by the doctrine of "continuous voyage." According to this contention an American vessel transporting goods from a French colony to the United States, and then from the United States to France, was construed to have made a continuous voyage from the French colony to France. American officials protested against this doctrine. The capture of ships for the violation of a "paper" blockade was also a blow to neutral commerce. The United States contended that a blockade to be legal must be effective, and denounced the French and British blockades as ineffective and illegal. The inclusion of provisions as contraband of war by both French and British was declared to be contrary to the law of nations. Complaints were made against the seizure of ships by one belligerent for no other reason than that they had submitted to search by the other belligerent. The search of American vessels on the high seas for the purpose of impressment brought about heated exchanges with Great Britain, and was one of the causes of the War of 1812.

The United States likewise felt that the position of neutral shipping would be greatly improved by the adoption of the rule "free ships, free goods," *i.e.*, that enemy goods found upon neutral ships should not be subject to capture but should be protected by the neutral flag. The importance of the doctrine was doubtless overrated. President John Adams indulged in the following appraisal of its probable results if adopted:

The question, whether neutral ships shall protect enemy's property, is indeed important. It is of so much importance, that if the principle of *free ships, free goods* were once really established and honestly observed, it would put an end forever to all maritime war, and render all military navies useless. However desirable this may be to humanity, how much soever philosophy may approve it and Christianity desire it, I am clearly convinced it will never take place. The dominant power on the ocean will forever trample on it.[1]

While the United States realized that under the law as it then existed in the early nineteenth century enemy goods were subject to seizure, even when on neutral ships, this country, nevertheless, threw itself on the side of those who were seeking a change in the law.

The events of the Napoleonic wars placed their stamp upon American policy. A century later, the World War found the United States in a somewhat similar position. Europe was again at war and an enormous demand was created for American goods and American shipping. Great Britain, relatively more powerful upon the sea than ever, stood in the way of neutral commerce to the Central Powers. In its diplomatic contests with Great Britain, during the period of American neutrality, the Department of State was urged on more by the insistent demands of American copper, wheat, oil, and cotton interests than by the complaints of shipowners. Most of the exports from this country were carried in foreign ships. The percentages of such exports carried in American bottoms were for the neutral years, as follows: 1914, 9.7 per cent; 1915, 14.3 per cent; 1916, 16.3 per cent. Accordingly, the American argument was devoted to the defense of the rights of cargo owners more than shipowners.[2]

The first effect of the restrictions upon American trade was decidedly adverse. By extending the classifications of contraband goods, the British justified themselves in seizing almost any kind of cargo destined for their enemies. By the extension of the doctrines of blockade, continuous voyage, and ultimate destination, American commerce with neutral countries adjacent

---

[1] *Moore's Digest*, Vol. VII, p. 439. The principle was accepted in the Declaration of Paris in 1856. The United States refused to sign because of a failure to agree to the immunity of private property at sea, contraband excepted. The declaration was largely nullified during the World War by the extension of the doctrines of contraband and blockade.

[2] For illustrations of the requests for diplomatic assistance made upon the Department of State see *For. Rel. Supplement*, 1914, p. 270*ff*.

to Germany was greatly reduced. To these restrictions the United States filed protests which were largely unavailing. Eventually the regulations became endurable to American exporters who were able to find a market, mostly with the entente nations, for an unprecedented quantity of goods. The owners of American steamship companies were likewise immersed in prosperity.

The German government, by its unrestricted submarine policy, not only destroyed American lives but threatened to injure an immensely profitable export and shipping business. It is too soon to appraise the importance of the economic motive in the American entry into the war. Doubtless the historian of the future will give to the commercial and financial factors a far greater place than they held in the literature of the war period. The desire to maintain American commerce against the destructions of German submarines was, in any event, a factor in the rise of resentment against Germany.

The advocacy of neutral rights is still important in American diplomacy. Preparation to uphold such rights has played a part in the movement for a larger navy. The memory of the helpless position of the American commerce during the period of neutrality from 1914–1917 has helped to create a strong sentiment in naval and commercial circles for parity with Great Britain on the sea. Furthermore, the now questionable status of neutrality as among members of the League of Nations has made it probable that the American doctrines may be put to a severe test. When in some future European crisis the members of the League combine to punish an aggressor nation, the United States will be placed in a difficult but not unforsee-able position. Will this country then demand that traditional neutral rights be respected and, if so, will it be willing to back that demand with force? The probability that such a question will arise makes the problem of the defense of neutral commerce something more than a mere academic matter.

EXCHANGING GUARANTEES OF NATIONAL TREATMENT

Probably the most fundamental of peace-time shipping questions affecting international policy is whether national treatment should be given to the vessels of all nations in American ports. National treatment means the same treatment as is given to ships under the nation's flag.[1] It is to be distinguished from discriminatory treatment of foreign vessels. At various times Congress has been urged by shipping interests to levy higher charges against foreign ships than are levied against those under the American flag. It has been argued that such unequal treatment constitutes a form of subsidy in favor of the shipping of the United States which involves no charge upon the treasury. In international commerce, however, there are two ends to the voyage, one of which is in a foreign port. The foreign government may, and probably will, choose to answer discriminations with similar discriminations against American vessels. Reprisals might result in much harm to our merchant marine. Furthermore, exporters and importers naturally fear the possibilities of a shipping war in which they would be the innocent victims. Accordingly, the prevailing sentiment in the United States, as in other maritime countries, is for reciprocal national treatment of shipping in international trade.

The Early Application of Discriminations.—Discriminations have, however, played their part in American shipping history. Following the Revolution, a spirit of bitter competition existed as between the United States and Great Britain. American shipping men grew almost desperate in their attempts to rebuild the merchant marine. By 1789, the American tonnage was considerably below that of colonial days, a decline which was due to the ravages of the Revolution, the postwar depression, and the new barriers erected by the British Empire against American shipping. Great Britain, true to the spirit of her Navigation Laws and moved by an unfriendly feeling toward the emancipated colonies, closed the old trade routes to American ships until they were permitted to carry goods only in the direct trade with Great Britain. Even in this commerce American vessels were hampered by an oppressive system of duties. The West Indies and the British North American colonies were not open to ships from the United States. Thus the British restrictions and the navigation laws of other countries bore heavily upon the American shipping and ship building interests. A complaint from the shipwrights of Charleston to Congress is sometimes cited to illustrate the feelings of these groups. The communication attributes the depression in shipping to the

[1] An excellent discussion of national treatment is given in CULBERTSON, *op. cit.*, Chap. II.

"*ruinous restrictions* to which our vessels are subject in foreign ports."[1] Congress responded promptly to the demands of the shipping interests with a series of acts setting up discriminations against foreign ships in customs duties and tonnage dues.[2]

In the tariff act passed on July 4, 1789, shortly after the new Congress was organized, a provision was inserted providing that goods imported in American ships should pay 10 per cent less than the normal customs duties. In 1790, this discrimination was changed so that merchandise in American ships paid the normal charges and a duty of 10 per cent was added on all goods imported in foreign ships. In addition to the general discrimination in rates provided in the first tariff act, different duties were placed upon tea, according to the manner and vessel of importation. If imported directly in American ships from Europe, the duty was more than if imported from China in American ships, and if imported in foreign ships, the duty was higher still. The 1789 law also provided for discriminations in tonnage dues according to the following schedule:

	Cents per Ton
On American-owned vessels...........................	6
On vessels built in the United States but wholly or partly foreign owned....................................	30
On other vessels......................................	50

The Use of the Discriminations to Bring About Reciprocal National Treatment.—It is possible that the discriminations were originally imposed for the purpose of compelling the removal of the laws which kept American ships out of foreign ports, or they may have been intended by some to be a permanent advantage to American shipping in a world of seemingly perpetual navigation laws and regulations. Probably the policy resulted from mixed motives. Whatever may have been the original intention, after a few years the discriminatory laws came to be used principally as a basis for bargaining with other countries to secure in foreign ports the same treatment for American vessels as was accorded the ships of the countries in which the ports were located, *i. e.*, national treatment. In return, the

[1] SPEARS, JOHN R., "The Story of the American Merchant Marine," p. 102, The Macmillan Company, New York, 1910. Quoted from *American State Papers*, Vol. VII, p. 9.

[2] A complete account of the history of the discriminating duties is found in MAXWELL, LLOYD W., "Discriminating Duties and the American Merchant Marine," H. W. Wilson Company, New York, 1926.

United States held out the promise of national treatment in American ports. In 1815, Congress passed an act to abolish the discriminations in both customs duties and tonnage dues as against the direct trade with countries which should remove discriminating or countervailing duties against the United States.[1] It should be noticed that the statute was to affect only direct trade, that is, it applied to foreign ships coming from their own ports and carrying the produce of their own country. Indirect trade, such as the importation from England of the products of China or the carriage of French goods from France in British ships, was not to be freed from the discriminations. On July 3, 1815, four months after the law was passed, a convention was signed with Great Britain which is still in force. The convention provides, with regard to such charges as tonnage dues, for national treatment for British vessels in the ports of the United States and national treatment for American vessels in the British ports in Europe. It also provides for reciprocal national treatment with regard to the payment of customs duties in the direct trade between the United States and British territories in Europe whether such trade should be in British vessels or in vessels of the United States.[2]

The 1815 convention with Great Britain was the beginning of what was to develop into a complete commercial system of reciprocal national treatment for shipping in the trade between the United States and other countries. For a time, discriminations were kept up as to indirect trade and American vessels continued to be barred from the commerce with the British colonies in the West Indies and North America. Discriminations, accordingly, were maintained on the part of the United States and in 1818 American ports were completely closed as against British vessels coming from any British colony which was closed to American vessels. But subsequent legislation tended to mitigate the severity of the exclusions and in 1830 there was a reciprocal opening of American ports to British vessels coming from the British colonies and of the British ports to American vessels on terms of national treatment so far as direct trade was concerned. Here, indeed, was a reason for rejoicing along the Atlantic seaboard for American shippers had finally gotten into the coveted markets of the West Indies. Meanwhile Congress

[1] 3 Stat. 224.

[2] *Treaties, etc. between the United States and Other Powers*, Vol. I, p. 624.

had passed the Marine Reciprocity Act of 1828, which provided that the President might proclaim the removal of the discriminatory duties and tonnage dues as against the vessels of any country which should remove such discriminations as against American ships. The act was broader in its scope than that of 1815 and included indirect as well as direct trade. Following the enactment of this law, thirty or forty commercial conventions were concluded which provided for the reciprocal removal of discriminations against shipping. The President, in each instance, proclaimed the removal of discriminations against the shipping of the country with which the convention was concluded. "These conventions and proclamations, together with the law of 1828," says Culbertson, "are the legal basis of American shipping policy."[1] They have established national treatment so far as all ships engaged in our foreign trade are concerned.

The laws of the United States continue to provide for an additional 10 per cent duty to be collected upon goods imported in foreign vessels, with the proviso that the additional duty shall not be applied as against foreign ships that are entitled by treaty or statute to national treatment. The added tax of 50 cents per ton on foreign ships, in addition to the 2 or 6 cents now levied upon United States vessels, is still on the statute books, with the proviso that the larger tax shall not be levied if the President of the United States is satisfied that the nation of the vessel's origin has abolished all discriminating duties so far as they operate to the disadvantage of the United States. As treaties have been signed with almost all maritime nations the collections under the discriminatory provisions have been practically negligible since 1830.[2]

In the case of Soviet Russia, with which no commercial treaty exists, the discriminations are in full force and have prevented the use of Soviet ships in Russo-American commerce. Russian discriminatory charges against the ships of the United States, amounting to about twelve times the normal charges,[3] similarly prevent the entry of American vessels into Russian ports. The entire trade, amounting in 1926–1927 to $82,760,500,[4] is, accordingly, carried in foreign bottoms.

[1] *Op. cit.*, p. 439.

[2] MAXWELL, *op. cit.*, p. 143.

[3] Information furnished by the Soviet Union Information Bureau, Washington, D. C.

[4] *Soviet Union Review*, January, 1928, p. 13.

The Results of the Discrimination Policy.—The results of the discrimination policy inaugurated in 1789 have been a matter of sharp dispute. Spokesmen of the shipping interests and advocates of discriminatory duties have called attention to the great development of that part of our merchant marine which was engaged in foreign trade following the enactment of the laws. There was unmistakably such a development. The foreign trade shipping of the United States entering American ports in 1789 has been estimated at 300,000 tons.[1] The following table shows the tonnage increase during the next six years:[2]

Year	American tonnage in foreign trade entering home ports	Foreign tonnage entering American ports
1790	354,767	251,058
1791	363,662	240,740
1792	414,679	244,278
1793	447,754	164,676
1794	525,649	84,521
1795	550,277	62,549

Maxwell has pointed out that from 1790 to 1792, inclusive, the increase in American tonnage might be ascribed to the system of discriminating duties then in force, although there were other factors, such as the rise in confidence following the establishment of sound government. Doubtless the general economic reconstruction of the postwar period also partly explains the increase. During these three years, foreign shipping in American ports declined slightly. The next three years showed a great improvement in the position of the American ships as carriers for our foreign trade and a radical decline in the number of foreign ships which visited our ports. These tendencies were due to the war between Great Britain and France which began in 1793. The disasters of Europe brought wealth to the depressed shipowners of the United States. That the public men of those days did not consider the discriminatory policy to have been altogether wise is shown by the fact that after 1815 the discriminations were gradually withdrawn in return for the withdrawal of similar discriminations by other countries. The rise

[1] MAXWELL, *op. cit.*, p. 72.

[2] *Ibid.*, pp. 73–74.

of the American merchant marine to its zenith in the 'fifties came after the negotiation of commercial conventions had practically established national treatment of foreign ships in American ports.[1]

The Attempt to Revive Discriminations.—The World War brought violently to the attention of all nations which border on the sea the importance of shipping in times of war. The United States built up a great merchant marine suddenly, but grave doubts were soon entertained as to the ability to maintain it permanently. Accordingly, Congress, urged on by the maritime interests, sought soon after the war to give an artificial advantage to vessels under the American flag by a return to the system of discriminations. In Sec. 34 of the Merchant Marine Act of 1920, Congress expressed its disapproval of the commercial treaties which guarantee national treatment to foreign vessels and "authorized and directed" the President of the United States to give notice to all parties to such agreements that they would be brought to an end according to the provisions in the several treaties for termination after due notice.[2]

Congress was willing to scrap the commercial treaties without more ado, but the President, although authorized and directed to bring them to an end, refused to do so. The responsibility of the executive for the careful conduct of foreign relations tempered whatever enthusiasm he may have felt for the merchant marine, and he recoiled from the proposal to slash ruthlessly the whole commercial treaty structure. Presidents Wilson, Harding, and Coolidge have in turn declined to carry out the instructions of Congress.[3]

The negotiation of the Treaty of Friendship, Commerce, and Consular Rights with Germany, in 1923, caused a renewal of the argument upon the matter of discrimination. The treaty provided for national treatment of German shipping with regard

[1] MAXWELL, *op. cit.*, p. 92–93.

[2] A previous attempt to set up discriminations had occurred in 1913, but the law passed by Congress providing a 5 per cent discount in duties on goods imported in American ships had laid down the condition that it should not be interpreted to interfere with the various commercial treaties. The Supreme Court held the discount provision inoperative as contrary to the treaties. MAXWELL, *op. cit.*, p. 144.

[3] For the State Department memorandum of Sept. 6, 1920, setting forth the reasons for President Wilson's refusal, see "Hearings on Treaty of Commerce and Commercial Rights with Germany," p. 239.

to customs duties on imported goods and with regard to tonnage dues in exchange for similar treatment to be accorded to American shipping in Germany. The provisions are thus in line with the general American commercial policy. When the treaty came before the Senate, the friends of shipping made an attack upon the national treatment clauses and hearings were held before the Committee on Foreign Relations in which both sides of the question were presented. The result was that the Senate finally voted to approve the treaty. At the same time that body attached a reservation to the effect that the provisions for national treatment for German shipping should automatically lapse at the end of sixty days from the enactment by Congress of legislation inconsistent with such provisions. Congress has, however, enacted no such legislation and reciprocal national treatment seems to be firmly fixed as a part of the American policy.

Discriminations in Railroad Rates Provided for but Not Applied.—The Merchant Marine Act of 1920 provided that an additional discrimination might be permitted in the form of lowered inland railroad rates on goods imported or exported in American ships. Such a preference would no doubt prove to be of some importance to American shipping on account of the comparative long hauls to and from the American seaboard. A provision was inserted in the act, however, to the effect that the United States Shipping Board might certify to the Interstate Commerce Commission the inadequacy of American tonnage for the needs of American foreign commerce and that thereupon the Interstate Commerce Commission should suspend the operation of the clause. The insufficiency of American shipping for carrying the enormous trade of the United States, and the fear of railroad officials that discriminatory rates would redound to their disadvantage by diverting freight to Canadian ports have made it seem inadvisable to put this provision in effect. Accordingly, the Shipping Board, by certifying the lack of American shipping, has brought about the continuous suspension of the clause. This suspension has probably averted a shipping war which might have arisen on account of the resentment of foreign steamship companies against the discrimination.[1]

[1] ZIMMERMAN, ERICH W., "Ocean Shipping," p. 606*ff.*, Prentice-Hall, New York, 1921; CULBERTSON, *op. cit.*, p. 454*ff.*

THE COASTWISE TRADE MONOPOLY

Coastwise trade presents a different situation from foreign trade in that both ends of the voyage are in the one country. The creation of a monopoly without fear of foreign reprisal is, accordingly, possible. And so, while the policy of reciprocal national treatment seems to have been clearly established with regard to shipping in the foreign trade of the United States, this country has kept for its own flag a monopoly of the trade as between ports on the American coast. From the year 1789 this trade has been practically reserved for American vessels. The 1789 law placed an almost impossible tax upon foreign ships in this trade by providing that such vessels must pay a tonnage tax of 50 cents for each entry while American ships were charged a tax of 6 cents per ton payable but once a year. The Navigation Act of 1817 excluded foreign ships from the coastwise trade, and with the exception of the years 1917–1920, when the rule was relaxed because of the war emergency, the exclusion policy has remained in effect to this day. The monopoly of the coastwise trade is a great aid to American shipowners. The coastal and intercoastal trade involves an enormous movement of goods over routes some of which are much longer than the trans-Atlantic run. The American shipping engaged in the coastwise trade exceeds that in the foreign trade. The following table shows the tonnage which has been employed in the two services at various periods:

Year ended	Foreign trade, tons	Coasting trade, tons
Dec. 31, 1790	346,254	103,775
Sept. 30, 1840	762,838	1,176,694
June 30, 1860	2,379,396	2,644,867
June 30, 1890	928,062	3,409,435
June 30, 1910	782,517	6,668,966
June 30, 1921	11,077,398	7,163,136
June 30, 1927	7,309,146	9,432,869*

* Taken from Bureau of Navigation, "Merchant Marine Statistics, 1927," p. 22.

Shall the Coastwise Monopoly Be Extended to the Philippines?—There have been numerous demands on the part of shipping interests that the definition of coastwise commerce shall be extended to include goods carried between the United States and the insular possessions. Thus far only Porto Rico, the Hawaiian Islands, American Samoa, and a few unimportant small islands have been brought within the coastwise system, but there have been attempts to include the Philippines as well. In 1904, a law of Congress provided for applying the coastwise laws to the Philippines on July 1, 1906, but before the law became effective it had seemed unwise to shut out foreign shipping from this commerce and the law was not applied. Section 21 of the Merchant Marine Act of 1920 adopted explicitly the policy of reserving the trade between all of the insular possessions and the United States for American ships. The section provides in part:

That from and after Feb. 1, 1922, the coastwise laws of the United States shall extend to the island Territories and possessions of the United States not now covered thereby, and the board is directed prior to the expiration of such year to have established adequate steamship service at reasonable rates to accommodate the commerce and the passenger travel of said islands and to maintain and operate such service until it can be taken over and operated and maintained upon satisfactory terms by private capital and enterprise: *Provided*, that if adequate shipping service is not established by Feb. 1, 1922, the President shall extend the period herein allowed for the establishment of such service in the case of any island Territory or possession for such time as may be necessary for the establishment of adequate shipping facilities therefore . . . *provided further*, That the foregoing provisions of this section shall not take effect with reference to the Philippine Islands until the President of the United States, after a full investigation of the local needs and conditions, shall, by proclamation, declare that an adequate shipping service has been established as herein provided and fix a date for the going into effect of the same.[1]

Fear that the trade between the United States and the Philippines would suffer for lack of shipping has thus far made it undesirable to apply the law to those islands. In 1921 a survey showed that only 44.3 per cent of the merchandise exported from the United States to the Philippines was carried in American ships as contrasted with 49.8 per cent carried in British ships, while 52 per cent of the value of merchandise imported into the United States from the Philippines was carried in American ships as compared with 26.4 per cent in British ships. As

[1] Statutes at Large, 1919–1920, p. 997.

altogether only about half of the shipping service was under the American flag it seems as if the exclusion of foreign vessels would have been disastrous to the trade.[1]

The Canal Tolls Exemption to American Coastwise Trading Vessels.—A notable controversy with Great Britain arose in 1912 out of the desire of Congress to support the American merchant marine by extending favors to coastwise shipping. Under the Panama Canal Act of Aug. 24, 1912, it was provided that: "No tolls shall be levied upon vessels engaged in the coastwise trade of the United States." The British government had protested while the act was still under consideration that it was a violation of the Hay-Pauncefote Treaty of 1901 which states that:

The canal shall be free and open to the vessels of commerce and of war of all nations observing these Rules, on terms of entire equality, so that there shall be no discrimination against any such nation, or its citizens or subjects, in respect of the conditions or charges of traffic, or otherwise.

The exemption of American coastwise shipping from the payment of tolls was, according to the British government, a clear distinction in favor of American vessels and, therefore, a breach of the promise of equal treatment.

The United States took the ground that the promise of equal treatment meant equality as between nations other than the United States; that is, the clause was a promise of most-favored-nation treatment rather than national treatment. It was also alleged that as British ships could not participate in American coastwise trade the exemption of American ships in such trade was not a discrimination.[2] American shipping engaged in foreign trade would pay the same tolls as foreign vessels.

The British government answered that the promise in the treaty was a pledge of national treatment. The Hay-Pauncefote Treaty, it contended, was designed to supplant the Clayton-Bulwer Treaty, under which Great Britain had substantial rights with regard to the canal. The Hay-Pauncefote Treaty had given Great Britain a promise of national treatment as a consideration for the relinquishment of the prior rights. It was not reasonable to suppose that those rights would have been aban-

[1] Culbertson, *op. cit.*, pp. 463–465.

[2] See *For. Rel.*, 1912, p. 467; 1913, p. 540; and 1914, p. 317, for the correspondence and documents.

doned for the mere promise of most-favored-nation treatment to all countries. The exemption of American coastwise shipping, it was claimed, would injure British shipping in two ways. (1) A heavier burden would be placed upon foreign trade shipping going through the canal than would be necessary if the coastwise shipping bore its share of the costs of the canal.[1] (2) The exemption of coastwise shipping would make it possible for goods bound from abroad to an American port by way of the canal to escape the tolls by being landed at an American port and then being transported through the canal on an American coastwise vessel. This would deprive foreign vessels of a part of the voyage.

Sentiment in Great Britain was seemingly aroused against the United States for its alleged breach of the treaty. Ambassador Page wrote to the President:

And everywhere—in circles the most friendly to us, and the best informed—I receive commiseration because of the dishonorable attitude of our government about the Panama Canal tolls . . .

And this Canal tolls matter stands in the way of everything. It is in their minds all the time—the minds of all parties and all sections of opinion.[2]

Moved by the reports of Page and evidently desirous of making a bargain with Great Britain for the non-recognition of the Huerta government in Mexico, President Wilson came before Congress on Mar. 5, 1914, with a special message which he stated was upon a matter of great importance. The message was a request for the repeal of the tolls exemption. In language which stands as a classic rebuke to the use of sophistry for selfish gain in treaty interpretation, the President said:

Whatever may be our own differences of opinion concerning this much debated measure, its meaning is not debated outside the United States. Everywhere else the language of the treaty is given but one interpretation, and that interpretation precludes the exemption I am asking you to repeal. We consented to the treaty; its language we accepted, if we did not originate it; and we are too big, too powerful, too self-respecting a nation to interpret with a too strained or refined reading the words of our own promises just because we have power

---

[1] Secretary Knox pointed out, however, that the tolls as actually fixed did not include a heavier charge because of the exemption of coastwise shipping.

[2] HENDRICK, "Life and Letters of Walter Hines Page," Vol. I, p. 249.

enough to give us leave to read them as we please. The large thing to do is the only thing we can afford to do, a voluntary withdrawal from a position everywhere questioned and misunderstood. We ought to reverse our action without raising the question whether we were right or wrong, and so once more deserve our reputation for generosity and for the redemption of every obligation without quibble or hesitation.[1]

In response to this appeal, Congress passed an act repealing the exemption. The measure provided, however, that it was not to be construed as a waiver or relinquishment of the right of the United States to make the exemption in favor of coastwise shipping. Since that time several attempts have been made to reenact the exemption and American steamship companies have evidently not given up hope of attaining this end. In a recommendation made on May 9, 1925, the American Steamship Owners' Association, the Pacific American Steamship Association, and the Shipowners' Association of the Pacific advised: "that the Panama Canal Act be amended so as to provide that no tolls shall be levied upon vessels passing through the Canal engaged in the intercoastal trade of the United States."[2] The fear of reviving the controversy with Great Britain, as well as a belief in the injustice of such a course, has made it seem wise to reject this advice.

PURELY DOMESTIC POLICIES RELATING TO SHIPPING

There are a number of domestic policies for granting aid to shipping which are not international in their implications. Some of these which have been undertaken by the United States within recent years are as follows:

1. Government construction of ships.
2. Government operation of ships.
3. The sale of government ships to private owners at a low cost.
4. Loans to private builders and owners.
5. The granting of mail contracts to American ships.

The construction of ships by the United States government was carried on by the Emergency Fleet Corporation at a feverish pace following the entrance of the United States into the World War. By June 5, 1920, 2,160 vessels had been launched with a total dead weight tonnage of 12,219,461. Following the war,

[1] *For. Rel.*, 1914, p. 317.

[2] "Report on Matters Affecting the American Merchant Marine," *Sen. Doc.* 85, p. 127, Sixty-ninth Congress, First Session.

the construction of ships by the government was abandoned, the changed policy being set forth in the Merchant Marine Act of 1920. The ships continued to be operated by the government although in the 1920 act the policy of sales was set forth. Since that time, it has been the legislative and administrative intention to continue the operation of the ships until the service can be established on a firm basis, and then to sell them to private buyers who can guarantee to maintain the service. The sales have not proceeded as fast as has been hoped and it is difficult to predict at the present time whether the government is committed by the logic of events to indefinite operation. A revolving fund of $25,000,000, to be set aside from revenues from the sale and operation of government ships, was provided for in the 1920 act. The purpose of the fund was to make possible loans to private shipbuilders. The act also provided that wherever possible the United States mail-carrying contracts should be made with American shippers. A ship subsidy has been repeatedly requested by the private ship operators, but thus far Congress has refused to grant the request. As the above policies do not raise international issues, a detailed discussion of them is deemed to be outside the scope of this treatment.

CHAPTER XVIII

RAW MATERIALS: GENERAL CONSIDERATIONS

Foodstuffs, upon which human life depends, and raw materials which are the foodstuffs of the manufacturing industries, have since the dawn of history been counted among the stakes of diplomacy, colonization, and conquest. The Israelites were lured on through the desolate Sinai Peninsula by the prospect of "the land flowing with milk and honey." Captain John Smith placed the cod fisheries of the North Atlantic above the gold mines of the King of Spain, and the Canadian fisheries continued for over a century and a quarter after the American Revolution to be a cause for controversy between the United States and Great Britain. In the morning of civilization, the Island of Cyprus in the eastern Mediterranean was a prize successively struggled for by Phoenecian, Egyptian, and Greek because of the copper and iron so necessary in craftsmanship. Cyprian timber for the building of ships was likewise valuable in the eyes of the ancients. Timber was prized by Cromwell and his successors, who, as the English forests dwindled, sent their fleets to the Danish Sound to keep open the passage for supplies from the wooded lands along the Baltic.

As steel has come to occupy a foremost place in modern construction, the interest of statesmanship in coal and the steel-making minerals has correspondingly increased. In the Republic of Austria stands a massive red mountain of iron, the Erzberg, the value of which was recognized by the Romans. Feudal princes contended for it. Today it is described as a "political magnet" exercising its powers of attraction upon the Fascist leaders of ironless Italy. The coal mines of the Saar have furnished a cause for Franco-German jealousy since the war. The richer veins of the Ruhr also provided fuel for European hate as the armies of France moved into that area in 1923; but the coal of the Ruhr may yet be the cause of a close economic cooperation between France and Germany as the industrialists of the two countries press upon their governments the modern necessities created by world competition. Asia, responding to the industrial urge, has discovered that it has some international raw-material problems. Japan, like Italy, lacks the basic materials of industry. These exist in China. At the spot where the Han River flows into the Yangtse are located the beginnings of a great iron-and steel-producing system. Japanese troops were for years quartered in this prospective Pittsburgh and the twenty-one demands of 1915 included an ultimatum regarding guarantees for Japanese interests in the Han-Yeh-Ping Company.

The automobile, too, has had its influence upon international relations. Oil has been the innocent cause of a score of disputes as gigantic combinations of producers and distributors have ransacked the world for petroleum supplies. The balloon tire has brought about smoothness and ease in motor transportation, but not in world politics. The arguments of Britons and Americans over the restrictions on the export of crude rubber from British possessions served for a brief time to disturb the tranquility of Anglo-American friendship. And the squirmings of little Liberia under the hand of a great American rubber manufacturer remind us that the self-determination of small nationalities is sometimes a secondary matter to security in raw material supplies.

Wherever the earth has been found capable of producing wealth there has been a potential cause for rivalries among ambitious peoples. The important place of the humble rocks, soils, and fuels in international conflicts has sometimes been hidden by the resort to exalted phraseology concerning abstract rights and ethics. An instance taken from recent history may help to emphasize the obscured importance of the raw-material motive in international affairs. The best iron ore in Europe lies in the Lorraine deposits. This fact accounts, in part, for the conflicting ambitions of Germany and France concerning that territory. The Germans were well aware of the mineral value of this section when they included it in their demands of 1871.[1] The industrial value of their conquest became apparent as millions of tons of iron ore were produced each year to become steel in the smelters and furnaces of the Ruhr. The part which Lorraine played in the industrial rise of Germany may be indicated by the fact that in 1913, 21,135,000 tons of iron ore, or

[1] HAZEN, CHARLES DOWNER, "Alsace-Lorraine under German Rule," p. 86, Henry Holt & Company, New York, 1917.

more than three-quarters of the entire German output, came from this section.[1] Meanwhile, the French mourned openly for their fellow Frenchmen who were under German rule, and more secretly for their lost industrial assets.

The return of Lorraine caused the French blast furnaces to blaze anew. The revision of the ore output of the two countries and the shifting in their relative positions in steel production may be illustrated by the following figures in millions of metric tons:[2]

	Iron ore		Steel	
	1913	1925	1913	1925
Germany......................	28.6	5.5 (estimated)	17.6	12.5
France........................	21.9	35.7	4.6	9.0

When the close connection between steel output and national power is considered, it will be seen why the ore of Lorraine should have been an important element in the *revanche* complex.

Much of the rivalry over raw materials is due to the fact that both minerals and agricultural products are unevenly distributed over the world's surface. Coffee and rubber do not grow in the colder climates and mineral deposits are so widely scattered that there is no country which has a complete supply within its own boundaries. Each country must depend upon others for some of the most vital industrial ingredients. The fact that nearly one-third of the world's mineral tonnage moves across international boundaries[3] indicates that the problem of mineral supply is one of much more than purely domestic concern.

The Industrial Importance of Raw Materials.—The need of manufacturing nations for raw materials and foodstuffs has assumed new importance today because, as has been observed, the leading western nations are seized with industrial ambitions. Such aspirations not only raise the question of markets in which to sell goods but also make necessary the materials from which the manufactured products are to be made. They likewise

[1] Hazen, *op. cit.*, p. 86.

[2] Figures gathered from Tower, Walter S., "The New Steel Cartel," *Foreign Affairs*, January, 1927, pp. 252, 254.

[3] Leith, C. K., "The Political Control of Mineral Resources," *Foreign Affairs*, July, 1925, p. 545.

create the problem of a food supply for the laboring population. In recent years, the consumption of the materials of industry has moved at a faster pace than ever before.

The world has used more of its mineral resources in the last twenty years than in all preceding time, and there is nothing to indicate any slackening of the acceleration which has occurred during this period.[1]

There is, therefore, some concern among manufacturers as to the future of their supplies, and a consequently greater attempt by governments to insure freedom of access to the sources of these

WORLD PRODUCTION AND APPARENT UNITED STATES CONSUMPTION OF
PRINCIPAL COMMODITIES
(Figures are approximate only)

Commodity	World production	United States apparent consumption	Per cent	Source
Coal, 1925............	Millions, short tons, 1,500	582[1]	38.8	Commerce Yearbook, 1926, Vol. I, Table 30, p. 285
Pig iron, 1925........	Thousands, long tons, 75,598	36,701	48.5	Commerce Yearbook, 1926, Vol. I, p. 367; Vol. II, p. 626
Copper, 1926.........	Thousands, short tons, 1,632	904	55.4	Yearbook Amer. Bureau Metal Statistics, 1927, p. 37
Rubber, crude, 1925...	Thousands, long tons, 515	386	75.0	Commerce Yearbook, 1926, Vol. I, Table 5, p. 454
Coffee, 1925..........	Thousands, pounds, 2,864,026[2]	1,258,488[3]	44.0	Commerce Yearbook, 1926, Vol. II, p. 611
Petroleum, crude, 1925	Thousands, barrels, 1,067,566	801,025[4]	75.0	Commerce Yearbook, 1926, Vol. I, pp. 298, 309
Tin, 1925.............	Long tons, 146,100	76,646[5]	52.4	"Tin in 1926," by J. W. Furness, Bureau of Mines, pp. 29, 31
Silk, raw, 1925........	Thousands, pounds, 88,050	63,764[6]	72.4	Commerce Yearbook, 1926, Vol. II, pp. 513–621
Nitrate soda, 1925.....	Thousands, metric tons, 2,524[7]	1,174[8]	46.5	Commerce Yearbook, 1926, Vol. II, pp. 129, 132

[1] United States production.
[2] World exports.
[3] Imports into United States minus exports from United States.
[4] Indicated consumption.
[5] Imports for consumption.
[6] Imports of raw silk.
[7] Chilean production of nitrate soda.
[8] Chilean exports to United States.

[1] LEITH, *loc. cit.*, p. 541.

materials, if perchance, they lie outside the territories of the manufacturing state. The plight of the unhappy British cotton-mill owner, cut off from his supply of raw cotton during the American Civil War, illustrates the possible position of the manufacturer who depends upon a single foreign source for his materials.

The problem of maintaining adequate industrial supplies has a special meaning to the United States which consumes more of such materials than any other country. The development of large-scale production, now established on a wider basis than has ever before been possible, has made of American industry a gigantic and voracious machine that demands in enormous quantities the products of every zone. The table on page 360, furnished by the courtesy of the Treasury Department, shows the scale of consumption of certain principal raw materials in this country.

The Military Importance of Raw Materials.—War colleges and general staffs are no less interested in sources and supplies of materials than are the boards of directors of industrial corporations. The military aspect of the question is likewise, at times, a matter of general public concern, for the prospect of a nation being deprived of the materials which are essential for national defense is one which, with or without reason, may be made to arouse the powerful national emotions of fear, ambition, or cupidity.

The demands made by the armies and navies in the World War created the necessity of supplies on a scale never before dreamed of, and gave to the question of raw materials a new meaning in international relations. Colonel William P. Wooten said, before the Williamstown Institute of Politics, in 1923:

Coal and iron are the bases of modern industry. They are also the bases of modern war. About one ton of steel is required for the ordinance and transport components included in the initial equipment of a modern soldier. The annual national consumption of steel for military purposes by the Western European belligerents in the World War was from two to two and a half tons for each soldier in the field. Steel, of course, means coal and iron. Hence the inherent ability of a nation to sustain a prolonged war may almost be gauged by its coal and iron production.[1]

[1] In CULBERTSON, WILLIAM S., "Raw Materials and Foodstuffs in the Commercial Policies of Nations," Annals of the American Academy of Political and Social Science, Vol. CXII, pp. 269–270. The paper by Colonel Wooten is entitled "Raw Materials and Foodstuffs in the War Plans and Operations of the Army."

Accordingly, national plans for defense or offense must be carefully drawn with regard to securing adequate sources of coal and iron. This particular problem has been of much more importance to other nations than to the United States. The German General Staff had planned in advance of the World War the seizure of coal mines in France, Belgium, and Poland, and of the iron basins of France which were adjacent to German Lorraine. The execution of these plans followed immediately on the outbreak of war.[1] France was, accordingly, placed in an extremely disadvantageous position as to the manufacture of the essential equipment for her soldiers and was forced to rely heavily upon her ally, Great Britain, whose resources were already overtaxed.

Because of the motorization of equipment, the conversion of shipping for the use of oil as a fuel, and the invention of new military devices, such as the tank and the airplane, it was found that during the last war oil had taken a new place of importance in military operations.[2] A mental picture of modern war conditions will indicate the basis for this anxiety. Along the front lines tanks are moving to the attack, while overhead airplanes are sweeping through the sky, both propelled by oil. Powerful tractors are bringing the heavy artillery into position. From the rear, troops, munitions, and supplies are being brought forward in trucks, passing enroute the motor-driven ambulances, which are carrying the wounded out to the hospitals. Farther back, the ocean lanes are being kept open by battleships, cruisers, and destroyers, while transports and supply ships move freely from the overseas base of supplies, all of them carrying a smaller bulk of fuels and able to get up greater speed in less time due to the oil-burning engine, now considered to be the most effective mode of ocean propulsion. The World War was said to have been in its last stages a contest between the automobile driver of the allies and the locomotive engineer of the Central European governments. In this contest the chauffeur had certain undoubted advantages.

Other materials which are necessary for military operations are too numerous to indicate in detail, and two or three further

[1] Spurr, J. E., "Political and Commercial Geology," p. 39, The McGraw-Hill Book Company, Inc., New York, 1920; Smith, George Otis, "The Strategy of Minerals," p. 127*ff.*, D. Appleton & Company, New York, 1919.

[2] See above, p. 57.

illustrations will suffice. Cartridges require copper and zinc, which are the components of brass. Cotton, wool, and rubber are necessary in army supplies and are frequently difficult to obtain. Finally, food supplies for both military and civilian populations are ordinarily a cause of anxiety for every belligerent government and the problem is a particularly difficult one to solve if control of the seas is not complete.

The Position of the United States with Regard to Raw Materials and Foodstuffs.—A brief resumé of the physical resources of the United States with relation to their adequacy to fill domestic needs is necessary in order to determine how important the question of supply is likely to become. Such a survey will also throw much light on the position which the United States may occupy in the world, both from the industrial and military standpoints. For this purpose a classification involving the following main categories will be employed:

I. Energy resources:
    A. Coal
    B. Oil
    C. Waterpower

II. Industrial materials:
    A. Minerals:
        1. Those of which the domestic supply is adequate, such as iron, copper, lead.
        2. Those of which the domestic supply is considerable but inadequate for domestic needs, such as bauxite, tungsten, gold.
        3. Those of which the domestic supply is inconsiderable, and regarding which the United States is almost, if not completely, dependent upon external sources, such as tin, nickel, manganese.
    B. Non-mineral industrial materials:
        1. Those of which domestic supply is adequate, such as cotton, cottonseed oil, lumber (excepting tropical hard woods).
        2. Those of which the domestic supply is considerable but inadequate for domestic needs, such as wool, pulp wood, hides, and skins.
        3. Those of which the domestic supply is inconsiderable, and regarding which the United States is almost, if not wholly, dependent upon external sources, such as silk, rubber, jute.

III. Foodstuffs:
    A. Those of which the domestic supply is adequate, such as wheat, corn, butter.

B. Those of which the domestic supply is considerable but inadequate for domestic needs, such as sugar, fish, figs, and dates.

C. Those of which the domestic supply is inconsiderable, and regarding which the United States is almost, if not wholly, dependent upon external sources, such as coffee, bananas, tropical nuts.

1. **Energy Resources.**—The United States may derive great hope for her industrial future in the magnificent supplies of energy resources within her boundaries. The following table illustrates the supremacy in this field:

ENERGY RESOURCES*

(Figures are in millions of horsepower-years)

	Coal	Petroleum	Waterpower
United States.................	500,000	400	37
China.......................	200,000	60	20
Germany.....................	48,000	2	2½
Canada......................	40,000	40	22½
Great Britain................	27,000	(?)	1
Australasia..................	19,000	(?)	4
Russia......................	17,000	280	16
Poland and Czechoslovakia.....	14,000	45	1
India.......................	11,000	70	27

* CULBERTSON, WILLIAM S., "Raw Materials," p. 7.

Coal, besides furnishing a fuel for steam and electrical power, is one of the two basic ingredients of the steel industry. Oil is an important fuel in motor, aerial, and ocean transportation and is also used extensively on railways. The fact that the United States has approximately five times as many motor vehicles as the rest of the world testifies as to the place of this fuel in American life. The prediction, frequently repeated on good authority, that the American fields will be depleted in twenty years, indicates that an acute oil problem is looming ahead which must be solved either through security in foreign supplies or the discovery of a substitute fuel. The rapid development of electrical power within the last few years has placed a new emphasis upon the potential water power stored in the lakes and streams of the United States. Here are the sleeping giants that will help to turn the wheels of industry in the future, and they are an undoubted element of strength in the American industrial system.

II. Industrial Materials. Minerals.—The United States is more richly endowed with industrial minerals than any other country. A study by Joseph B. Umpleby for the year preceding the war showed that the United States held first place in the production of thirteen out of the thirty most important minerals, was second in four, and had a production equal to 5 per cent or more of the world's supply in four others. Mr. Umpleby found by multiplying the production of these commodities by the average United States price for the year that the United States contributed over 36 per cent of the entire value as compared with less than 15 per cent for Germany, 10.5 per cent for the United Kingdom, while no other country produced in excess of 5 per cent.[1]

The iron ore deposits of the United States come first in importance in the mineral class.[2] The industrial civilization is built upon steel, a product of iron. Iron and its products stand first among the metals, the production of pig iron being from 94 to 96 per cent of the entire metal output. The iron deposits of this country exceed those of Lorraine, which have been the rich mineral prize of Europe. The United States ranks first in actual reserves and when potential reserves are considered there is no close second.[3] Outside of the United States other rich iron supplies are found in Newfoundland, Cuba, and Brazil, which are all conveniently located with reference to this country. With unrivaled coal and iron deposits the United States is self-sufficient so far as the two major elements in steel making are concerned. Among other important industrial minerals found in this country are copper, lead, zinc, silver, and phosphate. These minerals involve no political problem of supply to this country but their significance in estimating the place of the United States in the general scheme of international relations is none the less very great.

Although well supplied with most of the important minerals, it must not be supposed that the United States is self-sufficient in the metal industries. Many of the minor but essential

[1] Smith, *op. cit.*, p. 289.

[2] Coal might be classified here but it has been placed among the energy resources.

[3] Tower, *loc. cit.*, pp. 250–253.

ingredients of steel are not produced here in sufficient quantities to supply the large American demand. Manganese is an illustration of an indispensable mineral for which the steel industry of America is dependent almost entirely on foreign sources. "In modern steel making manganese is as necessary as iron itself; one eminent metallurgist has said that steel is not steel unless it contains manganese."[1] The amount that goes into steel is comparatively small but the improvement in the quality of the product which it brings about through the removal of oxygen, and to some extent sulphur, is very great. If used in larger quantities, manganese serves as an alloy and produces a tougher quality of steel. There is but little manganese ore in the United States. Russia, India, Brazil, and perhaps Africa are the great potential sources. Due to this necessity, American capitalists have negotiated with the Soviet government for concessions in the Russian Caucasus where there are extensive deposits. If this field develops, the importations to the United States from Russia should become considerable. At present, an import tariff is maintained on manganese for the purpose of stimulating home production. Such a policy, however, seems to be a futile and unwise attempt to develop production at home. Unlike the products of the farm, minerals, when once consumed, are irreplaceable. It would appear then that the effort to stimulate local production is not only likely to fail for the most part but also in so far as it succeeds it is in contradiction to good conservation policy.

There are other minerals for which the American manufacturers are destined to depend upon foreign countries. Nickel, which is used for toughening steel, is imported mostly from Canada. Chromium, another of the "medicines" of steel, comes mainly from Rhodesia, New Caledonia, and India. Tin ore, which is so indispensable to the canned-fruit and vegetable industries, is produced mostly in the Malay Archipelago and Bolivia. These illustrations will be adequate to emphasize the point that the United States is not sufficient unto itself and that despite great wealth in minerals an open commerce in such products is necessary to the continuation of American industry at its present speed.

Non-mineral Industrial Materials.—The broad and productive fields and forests of the United States furnish a substantial part

[1] Smith, *op. cit.*, p. 185.

of the non-mineral supplies of American industry. The fact that this country lies in the temperate zone and the further fact that land has risen in value with the growth in population make necessary a dependence on foreign supplies in many particulars. There are important industrial materials which are tropical products and cannot be produced here. There are other commodities which, although they can be grown in this country, may be obtained with less expense from the more sparsely settled portions of the earth where on account of cheap lands the cost of production is lower.

Some important materials are produced in ample quantities to supply domestic need. Lumber and cotton are examples. The remaining forests of the South and West produce approximately the quantity of lumber consumed in this country, the imports being about offset by exports. Neither exports nor imports of lumber are large as compared with domestic production and consumption. Timber differs from other products of the soil in that it is difficult to reproduce and for reasons of conservation it is on the tariff free list. Cotton is the outstanding example of an industrial material supplied to the world by the United States. The American crop regularly amounts to more than one-half of the world's production and more than one-half of this crop is exported. Foreign countries have a vital interest in the American supply, and, should the United States attempt with vigor to restrict export or production in the interest of price stabilization, the policy would undoubtedly have an important effect upon the industries of Europe and might lead to international complications. In one important case, that of the American Civil War, the failure of the cotton supply led to a very cool attitude on the part of some groups in Europe toward the United States. Great Britain has, in recent years, made considerable progress in the project of developing independent supplies within her own territories. This movement, however, cannot in the near future affect the supreme position of American cotton in the world market.

In another class of materials, domestic production and import combine to furnish the American supply. Wool is sheared in large quantities from American sheep, but the demands of American industry make necessary the importation of equally large amounts from Argentina, Australia, China, and the United Kingdom. The American production is stimulated by a tariff of 31 cents per pound upon improved wool. The problem in this case, and the principle applies elsewhere, is whether artificial stimulus should be given to sheep raising in order to maintain a certain security of supply at home, or whether free importation should be permitted and the energies and land now utilized in this effort be turned, in part, to the production of some other commodities more suited to the economic situation in the United States. Pulp wood is another commodity in which the supply comes from both domestic production and importation. The immense demands of the press for newsprint paper have made the domestic production of pulp wood inadequate and more than half of the supply is imported. Canada is the chief source of supply. The Canadian provinces have placed an embargo upon the export of pulp wood from crown lands and threats have been made at various times to extend this embargo to include all pulp wood. These threats have been met with protests from American pulp and paper interests.

There are, finally, numerous important products of the soil which are consumed in large quantities by American industries but which are not produced in this country. Such commodities furnish some very interesting and vexing problems of supply, and in several instances during the last few years questions concerning them have attracted nationwide attention. Egyptian long-staple cotton, camphor, rubber, sisal, jute, and silk are illustrations of this class of products. Rubber, to take the best-known example, is extracted from tropical trees which thrive best near the equator. The United States, which consumes about three-quarters of the world's production, must rely entirely upon foreign sources for its supply. The large tire manufacturing industry of the United States, employing about one hundred thousand workmen and selling its products to millions of consumers in this country and abroad, imports annually over 450,000 tons of crude rubber, mostly from British possessions. Any tendency to restrict international trade in such commodities will, we may be sure, bring about strong protests from such influential interests.

III. **Foodstuffs.**—The United States must look forward to a time when it will face a food problem. In the decade prior to the World War, the acreage devoted to the production of export foodstuffs showed a marked tendency to decrease. This diminution of the American export crops led James J. Hill, the Empire

Builder, to conclude that the United States was headed toward an agricultural deficit.[1] The decade of the war brought about a change in agricultural tendencies. The decrease in the production of livestock reduced the consumption of grains and freed them for export; while the production and export of agricultural products were stimulated by the war which made an unprecedented demand upon this country. The exportation of foodstuffs increased considerably. This, says Dr. L. C. Gray, economist of the Department of Agriculture, "is a temporary digression from the long-time trend toward increasing scarcity of land in relation to population."[2] Dr. Gray further predicts that in a comparatively short time the United States, pressed by the necessities of food, will be forced to make a choice similar to that of Great Britain at the time of the repeal of the Corn Laws, as to whether industry will be favored by free importation of foodstuffs or whether agriculture will be sustained and stimulated through protection.

At present the United States has a large exportable surplus of the most important grains that go into the American food budget. Wheat and corn are the foremost products in this class. As to these there is no problem, excepting such as may arise in the attitude of consuming nations toward any attempt to restrict the supply artificially.

Of foodstuffs that are both raised and imported in considerable amounts by the United States, sugar is probably the most important example. F. Schneider, Financial Editor of the New York *Sun*, has described the role of sugar in world politics as follows:

Since its first appearance, sugar has exercised an important effect on the development of world commerce. It has influenced the course of discovery; it has created great political issues. Conversely, the commodity itself has reacted often to the pressure of political events; its industrial history has been altered by the policies of sovereigns, ministries, and parliaments. It has influenced politics and been a prey to politics.[3]

[1] See GRAY, L. C., "Relation of Population Growth and Land Supply to the Future Foreign Trade Policy of the United States," in CULBERTSON, "Raw Materials," p. 191

[2] *Ibid.*, p. 198.

[3] "Sugar," *Foreign Affairs*, January, 1926, p. 311; see also LAUGHLIN and WILLIS, "Reciprocity," Chap. V.

As sugar has been deemed of great importance by European nations, so has it played a major part in American policies concerning foodstuffs. A large area in the United States is adapted to the growing of cane and beet sugar, but at the same time the warm islands of the Caribbean and the Pacific have distinct advantages in cheaper production. In order to maintain the domestic output, a protective tariff has been ordinarily maintained upon sugar, although temporarily under the McKinley Act of 1890 the tariff was eliminated and a bounty substituted. Reciprocity treaties with the sugar-producing countries of Hawaii and Cuba were entered into in 1875 and 1902, respectively, and a number of executive agreements for lower foreign tariffs upon American goods were based upon the allowance of free entry of sugar into the United States under the Tariff Act of 1890. In the case of the treaty with Hawaii, the free entry of sugar from that country served as a great stimulant to sugar planting and revolutionized the economic life of the islands, creating at the same time powerful interests which were favorable to annexation to the United States.[1]

There are several important articles of food for which Americans must depend entirely upon importation. Foods and beverages from the tropical and subtropical countries, although they cannot be grown here, have by long-developed habit become a regular part of the bill of fare. Coffee, about two-thirds of which is produced in Brazil, has an inalienable place upon the American menu. Bananas, pineapples, cocoanuts, cocoa, and tea, likewise exotic, have similarly established themselves. Foods and beverages of this kind are not essential to the existence of life in the United States and a complete stoppage of imports would have little more effect than the more or less painful disruption of habits. Nevertheless, this cannot be said to be unimportant in the economy of a nation which is willing to pay large sums in the aggregate to continue the purchase of such commodities. With the exception of coffee, however, considerable percentages of all of these products are grown in more than one country and, accordingly, there is no possibility of a monopoly or severe restriction in imports in times of peace or in war time, providing the sea lanes remain open.

---

[1] See above, p. 282.

METHODS OF SECURING MATERIALS AND FOODSTUFFS

Tariff Policies.—Export tariffs on goods from continental United States are unconstitutional and, therefore, this powerful weapon for maintaining a supply of raw materials at home is impossible to apply, except to exports from the possessions. Discussion of this phase of tariff making will be reserved until the subject of the attempts to remove restrictions imposed by other countries is taken up. Several considerations concerning the levy of import duties should be considered:

1. Import duties on manufactured goods tend to develop industry and thus give domestic raw materials a home market. Protection on manufactured articles also indirectly encourages the importation of raw materials from countries that might otherwise fabricate them for the American market.

2. Raw materials which cannot be produced in the United States should be placed on the free list in order to facilitate their importation. Thus rubber, which is produced in the tropics, and nickel ore, which is mined mostly in Canada, are free of duty. Also materials produced in abundance for export, such as cotton, may well be free, although tariff policy is here unimportant as there will be practically no imports.

3. Where a material can be produced in the United States but the supply is not equal to the domestic demand, the determination as to whether a duty should be charged depends upon several factors. If the article is an agricultural product and the output can be increased by the raising of prices, the problem is simply whether it is worth paying the higher price in order to have a domestic supply. In the case of wool and sugar, Congress has taken the view that domestic production should be encouraged, and has imposed a duty. Hides and skins, on the other hand, are admitted free. If the article is not reproducible, as in the case of minerals, and we may also include timber which is difficult to replace, conservation of domestic supplies demands that there be no protective duty. Under free trade, the United States can draw upon the supplies of other countries and preserve its own forests and mines for an emergency. Thus forest products are admitted free. Domestic producers, however, demand that duties be imposed in order to stimulate home production. Frequently special groups are able to bring such strength to bear upon Congress that in the general tariff log rolling they are

able to secure protection in opposition to what seems to be the better policy of conservation. An example is the case of manganese. Before the war the United States produced less than 1 per cent of the manganese used in this country. Under a protective system the meager American deposits will be exploited. Sound policy dictates that every encouragement should be given to the importation of manganese. Nevertheless, Congress has heeded the demands of the domestic producers and has placed upon it a duty of 1 cent per pound.[1]

The commercial treaty or reciprocity agreement, in so far as it brings about a greater importation of raw materials, is a special application of the principle of tariff reduction or free trade to the particular country with which the treaty or agreement is made. Thus in the Hawaiian Treaty of 1875 certain products, among them sugar, were admitted from Hawaii free into the United States. The Cuban Treaty of 1902 provided for a reduction of 20 per cent upon goods coming from Cuba. This localized our sugar imports until practically all of them from foreign territory are Cuban. The effect here is possibly that we have created a sugar supply nearer to our own doors, which is therefore more likely to be certain and accessible. The argol agreements, in which the United States offered tariff reductions in exchange for similar concessions, are other illustrations of the principle of securing materials by a lowering of tariff duties.

Territories and Raw Materials.—The need of imperial expansion to obtain needed raw materials has recently been emphasized by the demands of Germany for the restoration of her lost colonies. Dr. Schact, President of the Reichsbank, expressed a conviction prevalent among German industrialists when he said: "The fight for raw materials plays the most important part in world politics, an even greater rôle than before the war."[2] Here a question may be raised as a companion to the riddle "Does trade follow the flag?" Do colonial materials flow into the mother country?

Many instances may be cited in which the raw materials of a colony are sold, not to the mother country, but to foreign lands.

---

[1] SPURR, JOSIAH EDWARD, "Steel-making Minerals," *Foreign Affairs*, July, 1926, pp. 605–606. Other illustrations of protected minerals are given on pp. 607, 611.

[2] Quoted by JACOB VINER in "National Monopolies of Raw Material," *Foreign Affairs*, July, 1926, p. 585.

Three-fourths of the cotton of French Indo-China goes to Japan and China. All of the cobalt and two-thirds of the nickel of the French possession of New Caledonia go to Belgium. The crude rubber from the plantations in British territory comes mostly to the United States.[1] If this were the case universally, the acquisition of territory for the purpose of securing raw materials would be a futile endeavor. The experience of the United States with its dependencies has, however, been somewhat different from that indicated above. The percentages of the exports (mostly foodstuffs and raw materials) of the principal American possessions that come to the United States are: from the Philippines, 73 per cent; from Porto Rico, 92 per cent; from Hawaii, 98 per cent; and from Alaska, 99 per cent.[2]

The question of minerals and agricultural products has played some part in the annexation and retention of the Philippine Islands. As soon as American forces were in the Philippines, in 1898, a number of investigations were ordered to determine the mineral possibilities of the islands. These reports were known to the President prior to his decision to retain the archipelago and may possibly have had some bearing on that decision. The mineral deposits of the Philippines have been the subject of subsequent investigation, and some resources of importance have been disclosed. The islands have a supply of iron ore, which thus far has not proven influential in American policy further than to cause some apprehension as to their fate should they become independent. Japan has very little iron ore and might wish to acquire convenient iron deposits in the Philippines. More important than the mineral resources of the islands are the actual and potential products of the soil.

The Filipino leaders have clearly seen that the development by Americans of a large and important source of raw materials, such as rubber, in the islands will make independence impossible. Colonel Carmi A. Thompson, in advising against Philippine independence in the near future, stressed the point that the Philippines are certain to become a source of supply for tropical products which cannot be produced in the United States. He stated:

[1] MOON, THOMAS PARKER, "Raw Materials and Imperialism," in "International Problems and Relations" (*Proceedings of the Academy of Political Science, July,* 1926), p. 185.

[2] *Statistical Abstract of the United States,* 1926, pp. 555–557.

After the introduction of capital, the island should carry on a large export business of commodities which the United States cannot produce in sufficient quantities for our requirements, or at all. And while the Philippine market should not be limited to the United States, we will be the natural outlet for a large proportion of their products.

Besides the principal items now raised, such as rice, tobacco, sugar, copra, and hemp, the Philippines, within a comparatively short time, should be able to supply the United States with a large part of its requirements of rubber, coffee, camphor, pineapples, lumbang, hardwood lumber, and many other tropical commodities."[1]

With regard to three of these commodities, rubber, camphor, and coffee, the United States has been confronted with governmental controls of its supplies by other countries and, accordingly, would consider it advantageous to secure its materials from sources within its own territories.

The possibility of rubber planting in the more southern of the islands has attracted attention in the last few years. There are reported to be at least 1,500,000, acres of land suitable for rubber growing in Mindanao and adjacent islands, but the Philippine land laws restrict the purchaser or leasor to 2,530 acres, or, by a possible interpretation, 5,060 acres. The lack of an adequate labor supply would also be a handicap to the establishment of the industry on a large scale, unless the Philippine Legislature or the Congress of the United States would permit the immigration of Chinese coolies. The establishment of this industry would undoubtedly mean that the chances for independence would be less, not only on account of the American capital invested but because the users of rubber in the United States would certainly exert an influence in favor of retention.[2]

Investments in Raw-material Production Abroad.—Much American capital has found its way during the last few years into the production abroad of the materials which are necessary in the conduct of American industries at home. A considerable part of the tin ore, which made possible the operation of American smelters during the years 1915–1923, was mined in Bolivia

[1] "Conditions in the Philippines Islands," *Sen. Doc.*, 180, Sixty-ninth Congress, Second Session, pp. 7–8.

[2] WHITEFORD, HARRY N., "Rubber and the Philippines," *Foreign Affairs*, July, 1926, p. 677; *Committee on Interstate and Foreign Commerce, House of Representatives*, "Hearings on Rubber, Coffee, Etc.," pp. 108–119, 237, 243, Govt. Printing Office, Washington, 1926.

by American capitalists. American companies are becoming increasingly important in the ownership of nitrate properties in Chile. Steel-making minerals which are not produced in the United States have attracted American capital. There are important investments in the manganese fields of the Georgian Soviet Republic. The Vanadium Corporation of America owns the largest vanadium deposits in the world situated in the Peruvian Andes. Recently, the production of rubber has attracted the interest of American capitalists. American companies have placed much money in the plantations of the Dutch East Indies, the extensive Firestone project in Liberia is planned to cover a million acres with an investment of $100,000-000, while Henry Ford has secured important concessions in Brazil.[1]

The need of raw materials is sometimes emphasized as a reason for the giving of strong protection to American investments abroad. Such protection, when extended in good faith, represents the efforts of a manufacturing nation to safeguard the supplies of its industrial materials.

[1] For a general article on this question, see EARLE, EDWARD MEAD, "International Financial Control of Raw Materials," in "International Problems and Relations," (*Proceedings of the Academy of Political Science, July,* 1926) p. 188.

CHAPTER XIX

RAW MATERIALS: THE CONTEST AGAINST RESTRICTIONS

Should Commerce in Raw Materials be Free as a Matter of Principle?—The view has been vigorously set forth in recent years that restrictions upon the export of raw materials are wrong in their nature, and that they are far more objectionable from the standpoint of international ethics than are restrictions on the importation of commodities. This position has been taken at different times by the spokesmen of such countries as Italy, which is peculiarly dependent upon others for the raw materials of its industries. Certain leaders in the United States have expressed a similar conviction. In fact, nothing more clearly stamps the United States as a nation under industrial influence than the vigorous objections to the controls of natural products which have been voiced in recent years in this country. Powerful manufacturing interests have given shape to American policy, although at times the injury to other kinds of consumers has likewise been the reason for complaint. The chief advocate of the right of American industry to obtain its raw materials without restraint has been Secretary of Commerce Hoover. The following statement is representative of his sentiment on this subject:

The world has often enough seen attempts to set up private monopolies, but it is not until recent years that we have seen governments revive a long-forgotten relic of medievalism and of war-time expediency by deliberately erecting official controls of trade in raw materials of which their nationals produce a major portion of the world's supply, and through these controls arbitrarily fixing prices to all of the hundreds of millions of other people in the world. It is this intrusion of governments into trading operations on a vast scale that raises a host of new dangers—the inevitable aftermath of any such efforts by political agencies to interfere with the normal processes of supply and demand.[1]

There is, however, no reason to distinguish in principle between restrictions on the export of commodities and restrictions on

[1] "Hearings on Crude Rubber, Coffee, Etc.," p. 2.

imports, or to say that either should give rise to diplomatic complaint, except as judged by the effects in the particular case. If an import or export restriction is not destructive of existing industrial systems already built up in other countries, it cannot be said to be a menace to friendly relations. Thus, the protective tariff of the United States, which was imposed early in our history, has not, as a general rule, caused any diminution in production abroad. The importation of goods from foreign countries has, generally speaking, increased substantially despite the tariff, the increase being due to the enlarged purchasing power of the United States. Instances may be found here and elsewhere in which particular tariffs have been imposed suddenly and have affected an established trade. A shock of this kind to the existing economic system of foreign countries is certain to arouse ill feeling. It is well known that during the period of the Articles of Confederation some bitterness was occasioned by prohibitive import duties which were placed in New York upon garden products from New Jersey and firewood from Connecticut. The affairs of many citizens of New Jersey and Connecticut were disarranged and retaliatory action was resorted to in both of the aggrieved states.

An export restriction, if not severe, or if imposed in the infancy of a trade in raw materials so that the consuming industries become gradually accustomed to the handicap, should give rise to no political protest, whatever may be the criticisms of the economist. If, on the other hand, an enterprise comes to depend upon the ability to purchase a particular material and then suddenly the supply is stopped by the action of a foreign country, which has a monopoly of the commodity in question, the result is apt to be a heavy loss to the dependent industry. Capital may be destroyed, workmen may be thrown out of employment, and bitter feeling is sure to result. The vested interest must be taken into consideration in international relations, for the destruction of such an interest sets loose psychological forces which have their political reactions.

Beyond this there is a more fundamental question. Is it not better to maintain complete freedom to buy and sell according to economic needs? The answer to this question depends upon whether one is more interested in an effective world economic order or in the self-sufficiency of particular nations. The United States has decided against freedom of selling in the American market[1] and can hardly expect that its demand for freedom to purchase in the world market should receive any great consideration as a matter of principle.

Foreign governmental restrictions upon raw materials which are used in the United States have been the occasion of much public discussion and probably much diplomatic representation by the United States within the last few years. Secretary Hoover has enumerated nine governmentally controlled combinations in raw materials for which the United States spent $1,031,555,097 in the fiscal year ending June 30, 1926.[2] In addition, there are some twenty or thirty other commodities for which the United States is dependent upon external sources and which might be controlled in a similar way by the action of one government or by the agreement between two governments. The possibility of reducing the manufacturers of the United States to a condition of dependence upon a world-wide system of monopolies and restrictions has appeared to Secretary Hoover to be a matter of vital concern, and the task of preventing the further development of such a system is in his opinion a major problem in American economic foreign policies.[3]

There are two main purposes which have caused governments to restrict the export of raw materials, (1) protection to home industry and (2) price fixing or stabilization.

PROTECTIVE RESTRICTIONS ON THE EXPORT OF RAW MATERIALS

A country which has a virtual monopoly in the production of an industrial raw material frequently finds that other countries are purchasing that material and building up important industries through its manufacture. The producing country, should it be ambitious to develop industries of its own, may consider it advantageous to check the export of the raw material until it has gone through one or more stages of manufacture. The

---

[1] JACOB VINER remarks concerning the American tariff in this connection that it is "the most severe and the most important interference with the law of supply and demand which the world has ever known." *Foreign Affairs*, July, 1926, p. 598.

[2] The nine materials thus controlled are long-staple cotton, camphor, coffee, iodine, nitrates, potash, mercury, rubber, and sisal.

[3] Secretary Hoover's speech, delivered at Erie, Pa., *The New York Times*, Nov. 1, 1925; *Current History*, December, 1926. See also *Annual Report of the Secretary of Commerce for the Fiscal Year Ended June* 30, 1926, pp. 35–41.

advantages to domestic capital and labor and the increase in national power which are presumed to arise through the stimulation of industry have been mentioned previously. The possibility that the prevention of exportation will operate to encourage the development of supplies elsewhere, in case the material is reproducible, or that it will stimulate scientists in their efforts to develop a substitute, makes a policy of restriction oftentimes of questionable value. There are, nevertheless, a number of instances in which protective export restrictions are used today. Two main methods are employed to accomplish this object; namely, taxation and embargo.

Protective Taxation.—The simple export tax for the purpose of assisting home industries was frequently used during the days of mercantilism. Thus, the English taxed wool, which they produced in large amounts, in order to assist the fabrication of that material at home. The protective export tax has been revived by some countries in recent years, as in the case of the Indian duty on hides and skins, the Swiss tax on cattle, as well as hides and skins, and the Swedish and Norwegian taxes on wood and timber.[1]

The preferential export tax is used to retain raw materials within a colonial system. This tax is levied against exports to outside countries but is remitted in part or wholly when the material is to be manufactured somewhere within the empire. In 1903, the Federated Malay States were supplying 60 per cent of the world's tin ore. During that year, a tin smelter was built by the International Tin Company at Bayonne, N. J., and the company made inquiries for the purpose of securing ore in the Federated Malay States. Fearing that this new competition would prove disastrous to the smelters at Singapore, the British imposed a preferential export tax upon tin ore from the Federated Malay States. The tax, which was in addition to the already existing export taxes, amounted at that time to about $11.50 per *pikul* (133⅓ pounds) and was imposed on all exports excepting such as the British Resident might guarantee would be smelted in the colony of the Straits Settlements, where the Singapore smelters are located. In 1904, the exemption from the duty was extended to include exports to the United King-

[1] Fisk, George Mygatt, and Paul Skeels Pierce, "International Commercial Policies," pp. 59–64, The Macmillan Company, New York, 1923; Viner, *loc. cit.*, p. 585.

dom, and in 1916, those to Australia. The tax effectively prevented the American smelter from obtaining tin ore from the Federated Malay States.[1] Later, the investment of American capital in the tin mines of Bolivia provided, for a time at least, an answer to the British export taxes. Between 1915 and 1923, Bolivian tin ore was exported in large quantities to smelters in the United States. By 1923, the American smelters were found to be unsuccessful, due to high costs, and were closed. Bolivian tin ore is now smelted in England.[2]

Two other preferential export taxes which were imposed upon raw materials produced in the British Empire have been repealed. Palm kernels exported from West Africa were crushed before the war for the most part in Hamburg. Crushers were also operated in Hull. At the beginning of the war, several crushing plants were erected in the United States. The kernels are valued chiefly for their oil which is used in the manufacture of soap. In 1919, a preferential tax of about £2 per ton was placed upon kernels shipped out of the British possessions in West Africa. The tax had the effect of diverting the kernel trade to Great Britain, but has now been removed.[3] A former tax on hides and skins exported from India likewise attracted some attention in the United States. During the World War, India prohibited the general commercial tanning of skins in order to free her industries for war purposes. This stimulated the tanning industry in the United States. To reestablish her industry, India, in 1919, placed a tax of 15 per cent upon the export of untanned hides and skins with a rebate of two-thirds of the tax if the tanning was to be performed in the British Empire. The effect of the tax was to damage American tanning interests. The United States attempted to meet this and other discriminations by an import duty of 20 per cent on tanned leather while untanned hides were left on the free list. The Indian preferential tax has since been repealed.[4]

[1] U. S. Tariff Commission, "Colonial Tariff Policies," pp. 337–340. In 1916 an export tax was placed upon tin ore exported from Nigeria, excepting such as should be smelted in the United Kingdom or in a British possession.

[2] MARSH, "The Bankers in Bolivia," p. 37.

[3] U. S. Tariff Commission, "Colonial Tariff Policies," p. 340; CULBERTSON, "Raw Materials," p. 49.

[4] U. S. Tariff Commission, "Colonial Tariff Policies," pp. 344*ff.*; see also JAMES, GORTON, "British Preferential Export Taxes," *The American Economic Review*, Vol. XIV, p. 56. For a good general treatment of this and

The United States had at one time a preferential export tax upon materials shipped from the Philippine Islands. Under the Philippine Tariff Act of 1902, goods which were dutiable in the United States paid an export tax equal to the American duty only, while goods which were on the American free list were subject to no export duties when shipped into this country. Manila hemp, which was on the American free list, was subject to a general export tax in the islands of 75 cents per 100 kilos. This gave to the American manufacturer an advantage in the purchase of hemp equal to the amount of the duty. The advantage was all the more certain because Manila hemp was a natural monopoly of the Philippines and could not be purchased elsewhere in any considerable quantities.

An example of a production tax, with a rebate if the material is to be fabricated at home, is seen in the British Columbia tax upon timber.[1]

Embargoes. *Pulp Wood.*—Pulp wood is important in the paper industry, as it is the raw material from which newsprint and several other grades of paper are manufactured. The fact that the newspapers are dependent upon a supply of newsprint paper gives to the domestic manufacturers of this grade an effective voice, possibly out of proportion to their importance. The great supply of pulp wood upon which American paper consumers must depend is located in Canada. In 1926, the United States produced and consumed well over one-half of the paper of the world. The paper consumption of that year has been estimated to have required 12,341,000 cords of pulp wood. 5,479,000 cords were from domestic sources; 4,973,000 were imported from Canada in the form of pulp wood, pulp, and paper products; and 1,889,000 cords were imported from other sources. The growing dependence of the United States upon other countries, particularly Canada, for pulp and paper is shown in the following table, which gives the source of the pulp wood for the paper consumed in and exported from the United States, over a number of years:

---

other phases of the raw material problem see DONALDSON, JOHN, "International Economic Relations," pp. 427–590, Longmans, Green and Co., New York, 1928. Professor Donaldson's excellent work came to hand after this volume had gone to press.

[1] See below, p. 384.

Year	Domestic, per cent	Canada, per cent	Other sources, per cent
1899	78.0	20.2	1.8
1904	72.9	22.5	4.6
1909	70.2	22.4	7.4
1914	60.0	26.8	13.2
1919	59.9	36.9	3.2
1921	54.3	34.5	11.2
1923	45.8	38.2	16.0
1925	45.7	38.6	15.7
1926	44.4	40.3	15.3*

* Department of Commerce, *Commerce Year Book*, 1926, Vol. I, p. 547.

The question as to whether the manufacture of pulp wood into paper will take place in Canada or the United States has had much interest for politicians and industrialists on both sides of the border. Canada would undoubtedly prefer that the manufacture should take place on that side of the line where it would give employment to Canadian labor. An abundance of timber and waterpower gives Canada certain natural advantages in such manufacture. American pulp and paper companies are interested in preventing such a development. The removal of the American duty on newsprint, in 1911, resulted in the building of mills for the production of that type of paper in Canada. Since 1911, the export of newsprint from Canada to the United States has consistently increased and Canadian production now exceeds that of the United States. A tariff has been retained by the United States on higher grades of paper.

Canadian efforts to develop the manufacture of paper have in recent years centered around an embargo on pulp wood. A number of provinces have placed embargoes upon the export of all pulp wood cut from Crown lands. Such action has been taken in Ontario, Quebec, New Brunswick, and British Columbia, which are the important pulp wood provinces. The embargo is of importance as 92 per cent of the Canadian lands which contain the pulp woods belong to the Crown, although a great deal of active cutting is done in the 8 per cent of lands which are in private hands. The effect of the embargo is to retain the pulp wood until it has gone through one stage of manufacture, that is, until it has been made into wood pulp. Practically all of the provinces permit the export of pulp.

Ontario has gone farther. In making license contracts with companies for the cutting of wood on Crown lands the minister of Lands and Forests has laid down the requirement that the wood must be manufactured into paper before exportation. This is a good illustration of the attempt to build up domestic manufactures by a protective embargo. The companies which have been manufacturing pulp for the American market will, under the contracts, either sell their product to Canadian mills or manufacture it into paper on the Canadian side. It has been estimated that the inclusion of this clause in the contracts will greatly increase the investment and the wage bill in the Ontario pulp and paper mills.[1]

In 1922, as a result of the resentment in Canada over the Fordney-McCumber Tariff Law, which was presumed to have injured Canadian agriculture, the Canadian Parliament authorized the government to impose an embargo upon all pulp wood, thus cutting off the supply from private as well as from Crown lands. The exportation of such wood runs somewhat above 1,000,000 cords per year. This embargo has not as yet been imposed but attempts to force the government to apply it have created an issue in Canadian politics from time to time. The possibility of an embargo is held as a threat against the United States. Canadian paper interests have hoped to use this threat for the purpose of securing the removal of the American tariff from all kinds of paper. Even without a complete embargo, it is apparent that in the course of time the Canadian paper mills will absorb practically the entire Canadian output of pulp wood.

In contesting these restrictions the United States has at times provided retaliatory duties which may be levied upon paper or wood pulp. The provisions at first, in 1897, were very broad and permitted duties on wood pulp and paper. Gradually, because of pressure from American consumers, the scope of the proposed retaliations has been narrowed until, since 1922, they include only book paper. These attempts by Congress have not been successful in removing Canadian restrictions.

Timber.—Protective embargoes and taxes have been employed by various Canadian provinces for the purpose of developing the lumber industry. Embargoes have been used to prevent the

---

[1] *The New York Times,* Feb. 2, 1926. The Ontario Minister of Lands and Forests was kind enough to confirm the statement as to his policy in a letter to the author, of May 9, 1928.

export of timber cut from Crown lands in the provinces of Ontario, Quebec, and New Brunswick until the logs have been manufactured into lumber. The same thing is done in British Columbia and, in addition, the export of logs cut from private lands is prevented by a heavy tax. The magnificent forest, probably the greatest in the world, which lies in the Pacific Northwest, is being cut into lumber by mills on both sides of the international boundary. The American mills have more efficient and cheaper milling processes. If there were no restrictions on trade, they would be able to secure some of their timber supply from British Columbia where the price is lower. It is this export of logs to the American mills that the provincial government seeks to prevent. The embargo upon timber cut from Crown lands is supplemented by a heavy tax of $2 per thousand feet upon all cut timber, with a provision of a rebate of the tax, over and above 1 cent per thousand feet, when the logs are manufactured or used in the province.[1] This restriction has caused some sentiment in the Pacific Northwestern states in favor of import duties on Canadian lumber. The demands of lumber consumers, however, have been considered by Congress and lumber is retained upon the free list.[2]

GOVERNMENTAL RESTRICTIONS FOR THE PURPOSE OF PRICE FIXING AND STABILIZATION

Governmentally controlled monopolies in the production or marketing of raw materials have created much discussion during the last few years in the United States. These monopolies have been due largely to postwar fluctuation of prices and to efforts to bring about stability. The United States was more than once engaged in controversy with other governments concerning monopolies prior to the World War, but the growth of industries depending on materials produced abroad has now aroused in this country a more pronounced opposition to governmental control than formerly existed. The effective and vigorous representations by rubber manufacturers in the last few years have, for example, done something to create public opinion and to determine official policy in the matter.

The principal reason for the establishment of raw material monopolies by governmental action is to be found in the desire

[1] CULBERTSON, "Raw Materials," p. 39.
[2] *Cf.* above, p. 274.

to aid the producing industry. Raw materials in many cases are furnished by a large number of small producers. Unrestricted competition between these producers is apt to result disastrously to them for two reasons. (1) The small producer is at a great disadvantage in price bargaining with the large purchasing corporation. (2) Due to the fact that the amount of production depends upon weather considerations and upon the area which is planted more than it does upon the needs of the market, the uncontrolled output of a large number of producers is apt in any given year to bear only an approximate relation to the demand. Years of surplus and deficit alternate and cause price fluctuations. Coffee and rubber planters as well as cotton and wheat growers have gone through years of overproduction with the consequent depression of prices to a point where the industry has ceased to be profitable.

Such considerations, although not confined to agriculture, have ordinarily brought about a demand in farming communities for cooperation. Where the raw material is produced largely for export, as in the case of rubber, coffee, and cotton, the demand for some system of cooperation is intensified. In such a situation the interests of the entire country as well as those of the particular industry are deemed to be affected and governments sometimes step in to compel a unified policy either in producing or marketing. Conflicts of interest between producing and consuming nations are then likely to arise and an international problem is created.

The various types of governmental controls that have been adopted by producing nations are:

1. Government ownership of all or part of the production system.

2. Governmentally supported combinations of producers.

3. Governmentally supported marketing monopolies.

4. Restrictions on production or export.

5. Financial operations for purposes of price stabilization, or price raising.

Government-owned Monopolies. *Camphor.*—Formosa is the source of the greater part of the world's supply of camphor. Since 1899, Japan has had a complete monopoly over the refining process. The government licenses the production of crude camphor and buys the product. By its monopoly the Japanese government is able to control production, prices, and distribution. The power to fix prices is, however, limited by the possibility of substituting synthetic camphor manufactured from turpentine whenever the price rises high enough to justify. In 1917, the price of camphor went up to the high point of $4 per pound. The manufacture of synthetic camphor in the United States was then undertaken. As the price dropped to somewhere below $1 per pound the synthetic camphor industry closed down.[1]

The British monopoly of phosphates in the Island of Nauru furnishes another illustration of a government-owned monopoly. In 1919, the governments of Great Britain, Australia, and New Zealand purchased the phosphate works in the island, which is now a Class C Mandate of the British Empire, for the sum of £3,500,000. The British Phosphate Commission has direct charge of the working of the concession. The phosphates are sold at cost price to the three governments and, until their requirements are met, no sales are made to others. Sales to other purchasers are made at the market price. This monopoly is of some importance due to the fact that the Island of Nauru is said to have the largest reserve of high-grade phosphate in the world. The United States is not affected, however, as this country has a sufficient supply of phosphates for its own purposes.[2]

Monopolies of Producers. *Potash.*—In some kinds of mining, where production is conducted on a relatively large scale and is limited to a comparatively few areas, it has been feasible to promote monopolies among the mine operators, the combination thus being formed in the first stages of the producing process.

Influential groups in the United States have for some years been affected by a monopoly of potash producers in Europe. The importance of the European combination to this country can be best realized by considering the dependence of American agriculture upon potash. The American people consume $50,000,000 worth of food per day or about $18,250,000,000 worth per year. By far the greater part of the consumption is of domestic produce. The immense drain upon the land which is caused by the production of this food has created a major economic problem in the necessity for replenishment of wornout soils. The three factors in commercial fertilizers are phosphoric

[1] CULBERTSON, "Raw Materials," p. 69; "Hearings on Crude Rubber, Coffee, Etc.," p. 32.
[2] CULBERTSON, "Raw Materials," p. 70.

acid, nitrogen, and potash. Phosphoric acid may be secured in abundance from the phosphate deposits in the western states. Nitrogen is procured from Chilean nitrates, although it may be obtained from the air. For the third factor—potash—the United States is forced to rely upon Germany and France to the extent of about 200,000 tons per year, whereas the domestic production has been in the neighborhood of 20,000 tons.[1] "Potash is a necessity. Neither the Chemical industry nor agriculture can flourish without it."[2]

The Potash War of 1909–1911.—The powerful *Kali-Syndikat* organized among the potash producers of Germany in the years prior to the war, possessed a monopolistic control of the production and distribution of potash salts. The Prussian government owned three of the German mines and was instrumental in the organization of the syndicate, which was supported and approved by the Imperial government. In 1909, there arose a heated controversy between the United States and Germany over the interests of the American purchasers and the German producers of potash, which illustrates the nature of a state-supported monopoly as well as the strength of national interests in an important raw material controversy.[3]

The *Kali-Syndikat* was composed of all the potash miners of Germany. It marketed the product, controlled the price, and allotted the division of trade among its members. Such a control permitted the raising of prices several dollars per ton above the costs to the producers. On June 30, 1909, at midnight, a restriction which forbade sales excepting through the organization, expired. Between 1 and 2 a.m. the president of the syndicate issued a mandate to the members to convene at nine o'clock that morning to consider a renewal of the regulations. In the brief interval between midnight and the issuance of this call, certain American buyers, who were eagerly awaiting their opportunity, entered into huge contracts, mainly with the Aschersleben and

[1] For an excellent account of the potash problem see HOAR, H. M., "Potash," Bureau Foreign and Domestic Commerce, *Trade Promotion Series*, No. 33, pp. 83, 87, Washington, Govt. Printing Office, 1926. The domestic production for 1924 was 22,896 short tons of pure potash (K_2O) while the importation amounted to 200,365 short tons.

[2] SPURR, JOSIAH EDWARD and FELIX EDGAR WORMSER, "The Marketing of Metals and Minerals," p. 486, McGraw-Hill Book Company, Inc., New York, 1925. The chapter on Potash is by Charles H. MacDowell.

[3] *For. Rel.*, 1911, pp. 198–243, contains an account of this contest.

the Sollstedt mines. The latter of these mines was purchased that night by American capitalists. The contracts aggregated more than $20,000,000, and called for deliveries over a period of seven years from Jan. 1, 1910. The new prices were about 45 per cent below those previously maintained by the syndicate.

When the members of the syndicate convened at 9 a.m. and received reports of these transactions, they felt that the life of the potash trade was threatened. For a time they were utterly demoralized, but after a period of negotiation a "Fighting Syndicate" was formed which did not include the Aschersleben and Sollstedt mines. The American purchasers offered to give up a substantial part of the advantage which they had gained under their midnight contracts for the sake of peace. This offer was rejected and the aroused German mine owners threatened retaliatory action which would be backed by the German government unless the contracts should be entirely nullified. The Americans refused this and continued to make bargains with the Aschersleben and Sollstedt mines at the low price of their former contracts. About 90 per cent of the American potash trade for the next few years aggregating about $35,000,000 was contracted for. A grim struggle ensued between the German mine interests and the American purchasers.

Various measures were shortly brought before the Bundesrat for consideration for the purpose of so controlling potash production and sales as to make the fulfilment of the American contracts impossible. This legislation was watched anxiously by the United States government, and on Jan. 8, 1910, a telegraphic instruction was sent to the ambassador at Berlin which read in part as follows:

Repudiation by German potash interests is contrary to the sense of business integrity, and the department cannot conceive that governmental sanction of such action as represented by potash interests will be given, since to do so might be construed as evincing an unfriendly intent and operating to perpetrate an international injustice.[1]

On May 10, 1910, a law was passed which provided for the fixing of the quotas of sale for the various potash mines with the further provision that in case any mine owner should exceed the amount fixed he should pay a duty on the excess sold. This duty was so high as to make such excess sales unprofitable. The

[1] *For. Rel.*, p. 201.

quota system prevented the two mines under American contract from supplying the amounts contracted for except by the payment of the stipulated duties. The law was vigorously protested by the Department of State prior to its enactment. Six days before its passage the American ambassador was given instructions, which were presented in a note of May 5, as follows:

. . . the American government cannot but regard the enactment of such a bill as indicating such an unfriendly if not indeed hostile attitude toward this branch of American commerce and industry as may give rise to grave apprehensions.[1]

The German government pointed out that the law did not violate the American contracts, for those contracts included a provision for the payment of any government charge that might be imposed. It was further contended that this restriction was somewhat analogous to the passing of a protective tariff by the United States which

. . . infringes upon contracts previously concluded by imposing the higher rates of the new tariff. Although contracts concluded by German nationals are often seriously impaired thereby, the Imperial government has never made representations in such cases, much less called such procedure an unfriendly act, as was done in the American note of May 5, or gone so far as to threaten rupture of previously friendly commercial relations.[2]

Furthermore the Bundesrat had been authorized to reduce the duties upon previous contracts so that the price would not be higher than the old syndicate prices. The Americans

. . . would receive potash salts at the same prices as they paid before July 1, 1909, and they would only lose the purely speculative profit they endeavored to obtain by taking advantage of the unfortunate condition of the German potash market.[3]

The negotiations were continued in a spirited manner and intimations of tariff reprisals were made by the Secretary of State. Finally, a conference was held in Hamburg in October, 1911, in which the American potash purchasers met with the German mine owners and settled their outstanding differences. The American "midnight contracts" were given up and new contracts were made with the syndicate at substantially the

[1] *For, Rel.*, 1911, p. 204.
[2] *Ibid.*, p. 209.
[3] *Ibid.*

prices that had prevailed until June 30, 1909. The two independent mines were compelled to reenter the syndicate. On the other hand, American purchasers received a refund of 60 per cent of the tax which had been paid upon the potash purchased under their contracts since the passage of the control measure of May, 1910. Most of this refund was, however, paid out again in settlement of the claims of the two mines against the American purchasers for the relinquishment of the contracts. Thus, the contemplated profits of Yankee enterprise were abandoned in the face of Bismarckian statecraft and the old monopoly was reestablished.

Since the war, the French government has been in possession of the Alsatian mines, with the exception of a single group. These mines were taken over by France from the former owners following the war. Threatened with severe competition with one another, the German syndicate and the French government have come to an agreement by which sales territory has been assigned to each group and an understanding has been reached as to the maintenance of price levels. This is one of the monopolies which Secretary Hoover has publicly deplored. The United States has refused to acquiesce in loans made by American bankers to the German syndicate. In 1925, the syndicate planned to obtain a loan of $50,000,000 of which $25,000,000, was to have been floated in the United States. The announcement of a policy by the State Department to oppose such loans made it necessary to abandon the hope of American aid. A loan of approximately $40,000,000 was offered in Europe where it was quickly oversubscribed.[1]

The German-French potash combination has likewise come under the fire of the United States Department of Justice which has brought suit against it in the United States District Court for the Southern District of New York. The United States government alleges that the German syndicate and the *Societe Commerciale des Potasses d'Alsace*, a French government controlled corporation which is the sales agent of the French government mines, have constituted a combination in restraint of trade and have thus violated the Sherman Anti-trust Act, as well as a clause in the Tariff Act of 1894 which is aimed at foreign importing monopolies. Exceptions to the suit were filed in which it was alleged that the suit is, in effect, an action

[1] See above, pp. 95, 97.

against the sovereign government of France. The lower court has not as yet[1] rendered a decision.

Nitrates.—Nitrogen, as has been pointed out, is one of the principal components of commercial fertilizer. It is important from the standpoint of national defense, being employed in the manufacture of explosives. It is also used in a number of important industries. About 60 per cent of the amount of nitrate consumed in the United States goes into agriculture and the remainder into the manufacturing of dyes, artificial leather, explosives, or the making of metals. The great source of nitrate upon which this country must at present depend is Chile.

Production of sodium nitrate in Chile is almost entirely controlled by the Chilean Nitrate Producers' Association. Only two companies, both of them American owned, are outside the association, which was organized during the distressing slump in the price of nitrate following the World War. The national welfare of Chile is seriously affected by the price of this commodity. One-half of the governmental revenues are derived from a nitrate export tax. General business depends upon the prosperity of the producing companies and at the end of the war there were about 60,000 Chilean laborers employed in the nitrate fields. The government supported the organization of the association of 1919 and four of the eighteen directors are appointed by the President of Chile. The organization is a governmentally supported combination of producers.

The powers of the association are very great. It allots production quotas to the members and fixes the price of the product. The price-fixing decision of the Board of Directors in May or June of each year is productive of a fight between two factions. The companies which have rich fields and efficient methods of production favor low prices, while the less efficient companies and those with wornout fields want high prices. The government directors usually side with the low-price faction. British capitalists own extensive nitrate fields in Chile and are influential in the association. The British influence has been reported to be on the side of high prices.[2]

The recovery of nitrogen from the air offers the greatest hope of a substitute for Chilean nitrate. German scientists have

---

[1] 1928.

[2] "Hearings on Crude Rubber, Coffee, Etc.," p. 30; CURTIS, HARRY A., "Our Nitrogen Problem," in CULBERTSON, "Raw Materials," p. 173.

made some substantial strides in the development of this process, and have made their country independent of Chilean supplies. The fixation of nitrogen is still in the experimental stage in the United States, and further development of it awaits Congressional action upon the government power and nitrate plants at Muscle Shoals. The construction of a power project and nitrate plants at Muscle Shoals was begun during the war because of the need of nitric acid for explosives. The nitrate plants were completed during the summer of 1919 but have not been operated. Congress has debated the policy of governmental operation as against a lease to a private company, but thus far no definite action on the matter has been taken. The operation of the nitrate plants would provide a certain proportion of the nitrates necessary for American agriculture and would doubtless stimulate the further development of the industry in the United States.

Iodine.—Iodine, a by-product of nitrate production, is also controlled by a combination of producers in Chile. Chile produces about 65 per cent of the world's output of iodine and American imports are entirely from that country. The *Combination de Yodo*, consisting of the Chilean iodine producers, assigns production quotas and controls prices and exports. This combination is "nominally voluntary but favored by the government to such an extent that it is generally believed that any iodine producer who should attempt to remain outside of it would suffer in some direct and many indirect ways."[1]

Marketing Monopolies. *Sisal.*—Sisal is the fiber from which binder twine is ordinarily manufactured. Yucatan farmers produce 75 per cent of the world supply and most of their production is exported to the United States. The creation of a monopoly for sales purposes has been resorted to on more than one occasion.

In 1915, the Congress of the State of Yucatan granted power to the Governor to create a purchasing commission with the power to borrow money in order to acquire the sisal crop. The *Comisión Reguladora del Mercado de Henequén* was formed, commonly known as the *Reguladora*, with the exclusive right to purchase sisal from the producers. The *Reguladora* then demanded 23 cents per pound from foreign purchasers. The

[1] Statement of C. C. Concannon in "Hearings on Crude Rubber, Coffee, Etc.," p. 31.

Food Administration of the United States sought to obtain supplies at 11 or 12 cents. A compromise was reached at 19¼ cents which was considered exorbitant inasmuch as the prewar price had been around 5½ or 6 cents per pound. A campaign for conservation of binder twine was, accordingly, inaugurated in the United States. Substitutes were officially suggested and were used as far as possible. Consumption was reduced, and in 1920, there was a surplus of 540,000 bales of sisal on hand. Prices broke and fell to 2½ cents. The *Reguladora* was bankrupted.

In 1922, a new governmental agency, the *Comisión Export-adora de Yucatan*, was created, which was likewise financed in the United States. This commission was given a sales monopoly by the imposition of an export duty upon all sisal excepting that which should be exported by the commission. Under this control method the price of sisal advanced from 3½ or 4 cents per pound to 6½ or 7 cents. The operations of this agency have not created the same dissatisfaction in the United States as did the manipulations of the *Reguladora*.[1] A suit brought against the Sisal Sales Corporation, an agent of the commission, by the Department of Justice has been dropped following certain changes in the practice of the corporation.

Laws Restricting Production and Export.—In order to prevent an oversupply of a raw material from being thrown upon the world market, various devices have sometimes been adopted to restrict production and export. Governmental and producers' monopolies normally exercise this control. The Japanese camphor monopoly, the Spanish quicksilver monopoly, and the producers' combinations in potash, nitrates, and iodine have kept a tight rein upon both production and export.

Where such monopolies do not exist, governments have sometimes passed laws or made regulations which limit the production or export of the commodities of the disassociated producers. The acreage of coffee planting has been restricted in São Paulo and a close supervision on exports has also been maintained by the requirement that all coffee must pass through the government-owned warehouses. The government of Yucatan has likewise limited the acreage of the sisal farmers. The Egyptian government, because of large crops and the fear of

[1] CROSSETTE, LOUIS, "Sisal," Bureau of Foreign and Domestic Commerce, *Trade Information Bull.* 200, p. 7.

glutting the market, has on two occasions, in 1915 and 1921, restricted the production of long-staple cotton.

Sugar.—Notable attempts at the restriction of both production and export have been made in the Cuban sugar industry. Like many other agricultural commodities, sugar experienced violent price fluctuations in the period following the World War. Due to a shortage, the price began to rise rapidly in the early part of 1920 and by May 19, Cuban sugar had reached a pinnacle price of 22½ cents in New York. From that point it began a disastrous decline and by Dec. 13, 1920, it had reached 3¾ cents. Cuba was swept from the revelry of the "dance of the millions" into the doldrums of a moratorium, all within a few weeks. The sugar market recovered, but a return of low prices a few years later stirred the government to action. In the spring of 1926 it ordered the sugar mills to limit their output to 90 per cent of their estimated production and the order was enforced by a prohibitive tax upon the excess above this percentage. Subsequently, extraordinary powers were given to the President who was authorized to fix quotas for every province and mill. The 1926–1927 crop was arbitrarily limited to 4,500,000 tons and that of 1927–1928 to 4,000,000 tons.

In addition to the limitation of production, the Cuban government has embarked upon an export limitation program, which is the more remarkable in that it looks toward the bringing of all sugar exporting nations into a great international combination. In 1927, a National Sugar Defense Commission was created to advise the President with regard to his powers. Of the 4,000,000 tons of the 1927–1928 crop, 3,200,000 were allotted for export to the United States; 150,000 tons were to be consumed in Cuba and the rest was to be marketed in Europe and elsewhere by the commission.[1]

Seeking to obtain the cooperation of other nations in the stabilization plan, Colonel José Tarafa, the head of the Cuban commission, visited Europe in November, 1927. An agreement was signed in Paris on Nov. 15, 1927, between Colonel Tarafa and representatives of producers in Germany, Poland, and Czechoslovakia. An international committee was created to consist of two members from each signatory country. The function of the committee will be to seek a rational apportionment

---

[1] JENKS, "Our Cuban Colony," pp. 276–277.

of sugar exports as among the various countries in order that useless competition may be avoided. A provision has been made for the addition of other countries to the agreement.[1]

The United States is evidently not disposed to criticise the sugar control. Such an attitude may seem strange in view of the fact that this country imports more than 3,000,000 long tons of Cuban sugar per year, which is over one-half of the American consumption. The acquiescence of this country in the control of sugar as contrasted with its opposition to coffee, rubber, and sisal monopolies, is understandable, however, when it is realized that powerful American interests are in sympathy with the movement to stabilize the price of sugar. Unlike coffee, rubber, and sisal, Cuban sugar is largely owned by American capitalists. In 1926–1927, 62½ per cent of the Cuban output was manufactured in American-owned mills and 8 per cent in American-Cuban mills. The American-controlled companies have 84 active mills and more than 4,000 miles of railway. They own or lease 6,274,000 acres of land in Cuba or 22 per cent of the area of the island. The value of American property in the Cuban sugar industry is in the neighborhood of $600,000,000.[2] The announcement of the signing of the Paris agreement was greeted in New York by a rise in the shares of some of the largest of the interested American companies. The sugar producers in the United States, Hawaii, and the Philippines are likewise favorable to sugar stabilization. Accordingly, it will be easy to see why the official wrath vented against the controls of other products is not displayed against the sugar stabilization system.

Rubber.—A sliding scale restriction of the export of rubber from British Malaya and Ceylon has been accomplished by making the exportable percentage vary directly with the price. Enforcement of the restriction has been brought about by a prohibitive export tax which has been levied whenever the export for any plantation has exceeded the percentage permitted. The rubber restrictions have probably attracted more public attention than any of the other raw-material controls, the unusual interest being largely due to the energetic protests of American manufactures and the support given to those protests by the United States government.

[1] *The New York Times,* Nov. 16, 1927.
[2] JENKS, *op. cit.,* pp. 284–287.

The development of plantation rubber in the British and Dutch eastern possessions is a fascinating story of a transformation in tropical agriculture brought about by science and investment. Crude rubber is produced by the coagulation of the juice of the rubber tree which grows best in areas lying within about 10 degrees of the equator. Until the visit of Sir Henry Wickham to Brazil, in 1876, rubber had been secured only from trees which grew in the wild state. Sir Henry developed the idea that rubber trees could be grown under cultivation. He was permitted to take seeds to England on the pretense that they were botanical specimens. In London, he experimented with the culture of young trees, and plantations were subsequently started in Ceylon, Malaya, and the Dutch East Indies. In 1910, the price of crude rubber soared to $3 per pound and capital in large quantities was poured into the business of rubber growing. Since that time the production from the plantations has expanded rapidly and it now greatly exceeds the output of wild rubber. The following table will indicate something of the phenomenal rise of the new industry:

	Plantation rubber, tons	Wild rubber, tons	Total world production, tons
1910	7,269	73,477	80,746
1920	304,671	36,464	341,135
1930 (est'd)	621,000	20,000	641,000*

* "Hearings on Crude Rubber, Coffee, Etc.," pp. 8, 17, 18.

Price fluctuation has played a part in the brief but adventurous history of plantation rubber. The fact that the trees do not bear for about seven years after planting makes impossible a close correlation of supply and demand. Investments that are attracted by high prices cannot have an immediate effect upon output. Prices may remain at a high level for some years after additional capital has gone into the plantations, thus inviting further investment. Far-sighted investors may take account of these facts, but, nevertheless, the industry has developed by jerks. Furthermore, the war and the peace played their part in causing price oscillation. During the war the demand for rubber raised the New York price to as high as 90 cents per pound, and the average for the war years was 67.2 cents. With the armistice came a slackening in demand. Dealers found themselves with large stocks on hand and the average yearly price sank to the unprofitable level of 16.3 cents in 1921 and 17.5 cents in 1922. The British producers then demanded legislation which would permit a fair return on the investment and which would tend to prevent these violent changes in prices.

The Stevenson Plan was the regulatory device adopted. This plan was placed in effect by colonial legislation, under the direction of a committee, appointed by the British colonial secretary, of which committee Sir James Stevenson was chairman. The measure provided for a sliding scale prohibition on the export of rubber, which was to be increasingly severe in times of low prices while the restrictions were to be abated as the price went up. The restrictions were enforced through a prohibitive export tariff, to apply not only on excess exports but also on all exports for the month by the party exceeding the quota. Standard production was defined as the 1920 output of each plantation. For the first three months under the plan, only 60 per cent of standard production could be exported. If the price of rubber should remain at more than 30 cents for three consecutive months, an extra 5 per cent could be exported in the following quarter. If the price should remain at more than 36 cents, an increase of 10 per cent was to be granted. On the other hand, if the price should drop to less than 24 cents per pound during any quarter, the percentage to be released would be decreased by 5.

The rise of the price of rubber during the third year of the operation of the plan led to consternation on the part of the American rubber buyers and to diplomatic protests to the British government. In the early part of May, 1925, the price started to go up. The month opened with a New York quotation of 45 cents per pound, which reached 69½ cents by the first of June. By July 20, the price had risen to $1.21 per pound in what was virtually a runaway market. During this skyrocket ascension the Rubber Association of America in a lengthy memorandum complained to the State Department concerning the effect of this restriction upon industries in the United States. The complaint reads:

It is the view of the special committee appointed for this purpose by the Rubber Association of America that if the British government could be made to understand fully what the present situation is in the American rubber manufacturing industry and how the future of that industry is threatened by a continuation of the present operation of the scheme, it would see the desirability and necessity of relaxing its restrictive provisions.[1]

Just what representations were made through the diplomatic service is not yet a matter of record, but according to W. O. Rutherford, Vice-president of the B. F. Goodrich Company, of Akron, who was in close touch with Ambassador Houghton in London:

> We made our presentation and our ambassador in Great Britain, Mr. Houghton, carried on the work. I am here to say that he has done and is doing a very splendid piece of work.[2]

Herbert Hoover, Secretary of Commerce, took the contest into the open by speeches and letters which were given prominence in the press. In an address delivered at Erie, Pennsylvania on Oct. 31, 1925, Hoover expressed the following opinion as to the danger to international good feeling in such controls:

> But the moment that a government, directly or indirectly, fosters or establishes these combinations, then that government has taken the responsibility for the prices. Whether these prices be reasonable or high, the populations of the consuming countries direct their attention upon the selling government and the matter becomes one of national emotion among all consumers. These peoples at once appeal to their government for action that it should use its great powers for their protection. Every day for the past year our government departments have had to deal with exactly this thing. And at once we have higgling of merchants, lifted to the plane of international relations, with all of its spawn of criticism and hate . . . The world will never go to war over the price of anything. But these actions can set up great malignant currents of international ill will.[3]

A number of defenders of the British point of view chose to answer this and similar criticisms.[4] They insisted that the effect of the Stevenson Plan upon the rise in the value of rubber had been greatly overestimated and that the chief cause of higher prices was the increased demand for rubber by the tire manufacturers in the United States, which demand had grown

[1] "Hearings on Crude Rubber, Coffee, Etc," p. 65.

[2] *Ibid.*, p, 99.

[3] *The New York Times*, Nov. 1, 1925. See also *Current History*, January, 1926, pp. 310–311.

[4] See particularly a statement by Sir Robert Horne in *The New York Times*, Jan. 3, 1926.

quite large since the advent of balloon tires.   It was urged that
the Stevenson Plan, by stabilizing the price, had rendered a great
service to the rubber industry.   It was pointed out that there
was no discrimination in this plan against purchasers in the
United States, for British rubber importers were hit by the
same restrictions.   British spokesmen further argued that there
was no reason to complain, for the American protective tariff
was a much greater restriction upon British trade than the
Stevenson Plan could possibly be upon the trade of the United
States.

The result of the international debate was, for a time, indecisive.   Due to the high prices of rubber, the restrictions under
the Stevenson Plan were gradually modified until early in 1926
the export of 100 per cent of standard production was permitted.
It should be remembered that this was not the entire current
production, but an amount equal to that for 1920.   In due time
the price of rubber returned to normal levels.   In October,
1926, the British colonial office announced a new set of restrictions,[1] under which the amount to be exported at the then
prevailing prices would be reduced to 80 per cent of standard
production.   In the course of time, however, the British government, probably responding to the sentiment of the rubber
industry, made an inquiry into the operation of the plan.   The
findings were adverse to its continuance and on Apr. 4, 1928,
Prime Minister Baldwin announced in the House of Commons
that the rubber export restrictions would be terminated on Nov.
1.[2]   The rise in the production of the Dutch plantations as
contrasted with the slower increase of the restricted British
plantations was largely responsible for the dissatisfaction with
the Stevenson Plan.

Financial Operations to Support Prices.—There have been
instances in which governments have made or sponsored heavy
purchases of a commodity in the market in order to check falling
prices.   During a rapid decline in the price of silk in 1921, the
Japanese government loaned large sums of money to a Japanese
corporation in order that it might buy stocks of silk and thus

[1] *The New York Times*, Oct. 25, 1926.

[2] *Parliamentary Debates*, House of Commons, Vol. 215, p. 1946.   On June
7, 1928, it was stated in the House of Commons that a new plan of restriction had been confidentially submitted to the Secretary of State for the
Colonies.   It is hinted that this scheme would include Dutch and British
rubber interests.   *Ibid.*, Vol. 218, p. 343.

steady the price. The interest of the Japanese people in the silk industry is necessarily large as Japan produces 75 per cent of the world's silk. This interest accounts for the government's willingness to intervene. The valorization of 1921 was not considered oppressive by American manufacturers who had on hand large supplies of silk which had been purchased at high prices. They were naturally anxious that the price should not decline too abruptly.[1]

Coffee.—One of the most important contests in which the United States has participated concerning a controlled commodity has been that with Brazil over the valorization of coffee. The consumption of coffee in the United States amounts to well over 1,200,000,000 pounds per year and, accordingly, a rise in the price of 1 cent per pound for the period of a year increases the American bill by more than $12,0C0,000. In 1926, the United States imported 1,493,316,000 pounds, of which 1,013,-344,000 came from Brazil.[2]   On more than one occasion the price stabilization efforts of Brazilian governmental agencies have been the cause of protests by the United States.

The attempt by the government of São Paulo, the largest coffee-producing state in Brazil, to stabilize prices in 1906 gave rise to the first misunderstanding between the two countries on this matter. The coffee planters were heavily in debt and European financiers took steps to foreclose their mortgages on the plantations. The government of São Paulo then decided to take drastic action to save the industry. A plan was devised for buying up the surplus coffee upon the world market and holding the acquired stocks for higher prices. Foreign financial assistance for this purpose was sought. At first the bankers of Europe refused to give their aid. Finally the help of Herman Sielcken, who represented the National City Bank of New York, was secured, and other bankers, some of them European, were later brought into the project. Total loans to the extent of $90,000,000 were obtained.

The Coffee Valorization Committee of the state of São Paulo was formed and, beginning in 1906, purchases of coffee were made in the various commercial centers of the world through the agency of private banking and coffee firms. One of the

[1] "Hearings on Crude Rubber, Coffee, Etc.," p. 29.

[2] Department of Commerce, "Commerce Year Book," 1926, Vol. I, p. 136; Vol. II, p. 611.

firms thus employed was Crossman and Sielcken, of New York. Altogether the committee purchased almost 9,000,000 bags of coffee. This huge stock was to be sold gradually according to a fixed schedule so that the price would not be unduly depressed. In September, 1911, it was alleged that the committee still held between 5,100,000 and 6,000,000 bags.

In 1911, an investigation was called for by G. W. Norris of Nebraska, then a member of the House of Representatives. Congressman Norris claimed that the activities of the valorization committee had artificially enhanced the price of coffee, that this increase was costing the people of the United States about $35,000,000 per year, and that such part of the committee's work as was carried on in the United States was in violation of the Sherman Anti-trust Act. An investigation by the Department of Justice followed and an action was instituted in May, 1912, against Sielcken and other agents of the committee in the Federal Court of the Southern District of New York on the grounds that a conspiracy in restraint of trade existed.

The Brazilian ambassador complained to the State Department against these proceedings and asked that the suit be dropped. He claimed the action was directed at a sovereign state contrary to the rules of international law. The American ambassador in Brazil reported that feeling throughout Brazil was exceedingly sensitive on the matter and that the continuation of the suit would embarass American enterprises which supplied materials to the Brazilian government as well as others that were negotiating with the government concerning the construction of a military port. He later commented on a conversation with the Brazilian Minister for Foreign Affairs as follows:

> The Foreign Minister fears that it may be difficult to prevent public opinion in Brazil from erroneously inferring that the government of the United States is unfriendly to Brazil. He believes that the people of Brazil will draw this inference from the fact of the revival of this delicate subject upon which Brazil is peculiarly sensitive and which would automatically disappear within a short time. The Embassy is firmly of the belief that it would be most advantageous to our position in Brazil to postpone further legal action until after the adjournment of the Brazilian Congress on December 31, since American commerce and industry is likely to derive considerable advantage from pending legislation which should be closed by that date.[1]

[1] *For. Rel.*, 1913, p. 59.

After some negotiations, it was agreed that the Attorney General should drop the suit on condition that the committee should sell the entire stock of valorized coffee in New York, which was said to amount at that time to 932,000 bags. This was done in the course of a few months and the suit was dismissed.

Valorization was resorted to in 1917–1918 and again in 1921–1922. In each case the financial operations were very large. In 1917–1918, about $75,000,000 was raised through an issue of paper currency, and in 1921–1922 a loan of $45,000,000 was negotiated. In both instances a rise in price was caused by the government purchases and later a fall in price followed the sale of the government-owned stocks.[1]

The valorization operations just described involved the purchases of coffee in the various coffee-trading centers of the world. Other devices have been adopted by which production and the quantity to be exported are fixed by law. Eleven large government warehouses have been erected in the interior of São Paulo in which the coffee is to be stored under government control. This restrictive arrangement came in for some caustic criticism in the United States when, in 1924, the price of coffee began to rise, some grades of coffee increasing as much as 15 cents per pound. In 1925, the state of São Paulo attempted to obtain financial assistance for the purpose of protecting the price of coffee. American bankers were approached but at the instance of the federal government they declined to participate in the plan.[2]

Summary of Methods Used to Combat Monopolies.—The United States has made use of numerous weapons in its fight against the control of raw materials by foreign monopolies. The following is a resumé of some of the methods used:

1. Diplomatic representation. The correspondence of the State Department with Germany which was conducted with a great deal of feeling concerning the potash monopoly has been mentioned. During the last few years additional correspondence has evidently been carried on with various governments regarding similar subjects, although this has not as yet been made public. During the hearings before the House Committee on Interstate and Foreign Commerce there were hints of diplomatic

---

[1] "Hearings on Crude Rubber, Coffee, Etc.," p. 24.

[2] See above, p. 94.

activity, but if the correspondence was placed before the committee it was read in secret session.

2. The United States has declared that loans by Americans to foreign monopolies of raw materials will not be acquiesced in by the State Department. American capital has been used in the past in the price-raising activities of the Yucatan *Comisión Reguladora del Mercado de Henequén* and of the Coffee Valorization Committee of the state of São Paulo. In each instance the efforts of the American capitalists concerned have been the subject of much criticism due to the increased cost to the American public. The present official antagonism to loans of this character is expressed by Secretary Hoover as follows:

We have considered it vital that the support to these controls should not be given by nor become entrenched among American investors. We have asked our banking houses in their own interest not to arouse against themselves that criticism of the American consuming public that would inevitably follow if they were to engage in the financing of these monopolies, and thus become parties to mulcting of the American consumer. I am glad to say that our bankers have cooperated in such a policy.[1]

The State Department has advised against loans to the German potash syndicate and to the state of São Paulo for the valorization of coffee. The government policy has not failed to arouse some discontent among investment bankers who see the business of financing these enterprises transferred to London and continental centers.

3. Government encouragement of economy in the consumption of controlled materials has probably had some effect in combating the foreign controls. The official propaganda to bring about economy in the use of binder twine was said to have helped to lower the cost of sisal and the Department of Commerce has stated that its efforts in cooperation with the tire manufacturers for conservation in the use of rubber have had great effect in reducing the price.[2]

4. The government has rendered assistance in the efforts to build up a supply of the controlled materials in American territory. In 1923, Congress appropriated $500,000 for a survey by the Department of Commerce of the possibilities of growing

[1] "Hearings on Crude Rubber, Coffee, Etc.," p. 4.

[2] *Annual Report of the Secretary of Commerce for the Fiscal Year Ended June 30, 1926*, p. 39.

rubber in new areas. This survey was carried out by the crude-rubber section of the rubber division of the department. The Department of Agriculture has from time to time made experiments in the types of substitutes for controlled commodities which can be grown in American soil. The search for potash has been encouraged by the government. The Department of Agriculture has sought to develop the growth of sisal and according to Secretary Hoover:

> The Department of Commerce has facilitated the interest of Americans in the planting of coffee in Colombia and Haiti and Central America.[1]

The prospect of securing a supply of nitrates which will make this country somewhat independent of the Chilean monopoly has created some sentiment for operation of the Muscle Shoals nitrate plants.

5. Through the Bureau of Standards, a number of research investigations have been carried on for the express purpose of developing substitutes for controlled materials. The bureau has sought to develop synthetic rubber, and to improve the methods of reclaiming used rubber. That these efforts have been attended with some success may be judged from the following estimate by a bureau official:

> The bureau has cooperated with the manufacturers in the past with the result that the life mileage of tires has more than doubled, without increasing the amount of crude rubber used per tire.[2]

The United States is today waging a fight for freedom in the commerce of raw materials, and its work in this regard may be compared superficially with the efforts of the British Liberals to extend the doctrines of free trade in the second half of the last century. Economic forces are, however, more important factors in the success or failure of government monopolies than are the attitudes of state departments and foreign offices. The probability that the consumers of controlled raw materials will develop their supplies elsewhere or that substitutes will be resorted to and thus deprive the controlling state of its monopoly and its markets will doubtless have more effect in relaxing a restrictive policy than will the complaints of the governments

---

[1] "Hearings on Crude Rubber, Coffee, Etc.," p. 298.

[2] See *Ibid.*, p. 337, for the "Program of Fundamental Research Work Relating to Rubber," a memorandum of bureau experts.

of consuming nations. The raw material controversies, never-theless, have their place in the study of international political rivalries. They are capable under modern publicity methods of developing heated sentiments in consuming communities. They constitute one of the problems which an industrializing nation, such as the United States, may expect to encounter in the future.

CHAPTER XX

CONCLUSION: THE ECONOMIC DIPLOMACY OF THE FUTURE

The improvement of national economic conditions by political means is an effort worthy of the highest statesmanship. It is salutary and wise to direct policies toward making better the material circumstances of life. We might almost say that here is a standard by which all doctrines and slogans should be measured. The chief question is whether the standard can be correctly applied in view of the influences which are brought to bear to compel the adoption of unwise and shortsighted measures under the pretense that they will promote the national economic welfare. As a counteractant against sudden and special influences a few general principles which will serve as a foundation for sound policy should be kept in mind.

In developing a truly economic policy it is imperative to consider the effect upon the nation as a whole. This is a day of powerful lobbies. Because of superior organization, effective publicity methods, and a shrewd sense of self-interest, an active minority may often affect public policy much more than the uninformed and less-vitally interested majority. The over-emphasis given to the desires of a comparative few sets up strong temptations to commit political errors. There can be no general economic gain in sending forth a fleet of warships each time a few investors or concessionaires feel that they have been wronged, although the profit to the individuals specially concerned may be very great. The vigorous appeals of particular groups should be appraised with a definite realization of the tendency to overstatement of advocates under the psychological influences of partisanship and self-interest. The public official, like the artilleryman, must make proper corrections for the direction and velocity of the wind.

A far-sighted view of economic consequences is essential. To the "practical" man the present is vastly more important than the future. This year's dividends outweigh the profits of fifty

406

years hence. The future generations, which may suffer from the improvidence of the present, are not here to present their case. They cannot compete in the influencing of public or official opinion with accomplished and highly paid press agents who are with us in the flesh. Every nation is thus forced by the mechanics of its thinking to discount its own future. When the question of permitting the slave trade was considered in the eighteenth century, no thought was given to the unborn Americans of the twentieth century. The immediate profits to Yankee skippers and to southern plantation owners were, however, highly effective arguments. The *Real Politik* of the German Empire brought returns to bankers and traders. These gains and much more were destroyed during the World War and the Germans of the next generation were left to brood bitterly over the near-sightedness of their fathers. Political influences set up by present policies may have an enormous economic meaning for the future. The insulted sensibilities of a weak but rising nation may not affect the profits of this generation, but they may destroy those of the next. Theorists are sometimes able to calculate the importance of such factors. The balanced idealist has a better approach to political economy than the business man, not because of any understanding of the technique of trade or banking, but because, uninfluenced by present profits, he has his eyes more clearly fixed on the future.

A world outlook and intelligent cooperation in world affairs are necessary to satisfactory participation in future world business. Understanding and sympathy must be characteristic of the successful trading or creditor nation. Knowledge of foreign markets and fiscal systems is of value, but much more than this is required. Political trends abroad will have their reactions upon the dollar. As the connection between governments and business becomes closer throughout the world, an acquaintance with the national aspirations of other peoples must be cultivated. The United States government is developing groups of officials trained in world affairs. But an intelligent corps of diplomatic, commercial, and financial experts is not sufficient. Education of large scholarly groups among members of the general public is likewise necessary to give strength and balance to national opinion. Colleges must continue to contribute to this end. Organizations for the spread of knowledge with regard to international affairs must be developed. Already a half dozen such associations of major caliber have taken their place in American intellectual life, each conducting its researches, publishing its periodicals, and creating its scholars. The prestige which has become attached to such societies is one of the hopeful signs indicating the gradual passing away of the psychic fogs of isolation and suspicion among influential members of the American public.

The amicable settlement of the disputes which are certain to arise is one of the essential conditions of confidence in business. International economic relations are continually raising problems which are difficult of adjustment through diplomacy. Defaults in bond payments, breaches of concession contracts, questions of the confiscation of property through social legislation, damages to property in times of domestic violence, misunderstandings over commercial treaties—all of these are types of vexatious controversies which this country will encounter in increasing numbers. At present, the United States has fallen behind in the movement for the friendly adjustment of disputes. The failure to join the World Court, which amounts to a refusal to become associated with the most practical and hopeful institution of its kind, has marked this country as clearly backward in the development of machinery for the friendly settlement of international difficulties. The lack of a strong psychological attitude in favor of judicial settlement was evidenced by the failure to support the Central American Court of Justice when a decision was rendered contrary to the interests of the United States. The protest against an adverse decision by the American member of the board of arbitration which sat upon the Norwegian shipping claims was taken to indicate the lack of strong confidence in arbitration tribunals in this country. A great world creditor and trading nation which is slow to arbitrate will undoubtedly find its pathway strewn with difficulties. As the American public becomes more internationally minded, however, the disposition to settle controversies by court process will inevitably be strengthened.

The entrance into legislative conferences for the purpose of settling world problems will likewise be an aspect of the maturing economic policy of the United States. At present, this government is remaining cautiously in the rear of the movement. Since 1918, a great advance has taken place in the use of such gatherings to bring about international legislation.[1] The literature of the League of Nations reveals a surprising number of legislative conferences held under its auspices. The evolution of the attitude of the United States toward the efforts of the League is worthy of note.[2] At first this country refused to answer the communications of the League. From that position, the government has advanced to one of unofficial observation. More recently, official delegates have been sent to a few conferences. If the United States has changed from an attitude of total aloofness to one of cautious participation within less than a decade, it may be argued that closer and more confident cooperation can be brought about in the future, whether with the League of Nations or other representative international agencies. Such a development would seem to be a necessary and natural accompaniment of the growth of American commerce and finance.

The economic diplomacy of the United States is in its infancy. The giant industrial and commercial forces that have recently been unleashed have yet to find their full manifestation in governmental policies. The agencies which are to compel their translation into politics are, however, energetically at work. The American business man has reached a place in the sun. The banking, trading, and manufacturing classes, which in other periods of history have been despised and repressed, have now risen to a position comparable to that held by the mandarins of Manchu China, the landed aristocracy of the feudal period, the clergy of Puritan New England, or the military caste of imperial Germany. The business groups are the most intelligently class conscious elements in American society. From Boston to Los Angeles and from Seattle to Miami, chambers of commerce, luncheon clubs, boards of directors in their meetings assembled, and trade journals give thought to the service which government can render in the promotion of industry, commerce, and finance. Wealth and talent are at their command. They are inspired by an irrepressible enthusiasm and a dogmatic self-righteousness. Can anyone doubt but that as the decades of the twentieth century pass by, their influence in the molding

[1] See Hudson, Manley O., "The Development of International Law Since the War," *Am. Jour. International Law*, Vol. 22, p. 341.

[2] Bassett, John Spencer, "The League of Nations a Chapter in World Politics," Chap. XV, Longmans, Green and Company, New York, 1928.

of policies will continue to be powerfully exerted? This is inevitable. It is right that in a system of representative government their voice should be heard. But such influences should be given weight only in so far as they are in line with the dictates of wise statesmanship, taking into consideration the interests of the whole nation, today and tomorrow.

PRINCIPAL SOURCES

Academy of Political Science, "International Problems and Relations," *Proceedings*, July, 1926.

ADAMS, RANDOLPH GREENFIELD, "A History of the Foreign Policy of the United States," The Macmillan Company, New York, 1924.

American Journal of International Law.

Annals of the American Academy of Political and Social Science.

BERESFORD, LORD CHARLES, "The Break-up of China," Harper & Brothers, New York, 1899.

BORCHARD, EDWIN M., "The Diplomatic Protection of Citizens Abroad," Banks Law Publishing Co., New York, 1915.

BUELL, RAYMOND LESLIE, "International Relations," Henry Holt & Company, New York, 1925.

——, "The Native Problem in Africa" (2 vols.), The Macmillan Company, New York, 1928.

Cox, ISAAC JOSLIN, "Nicaragua and the United States, 1909–1927," World Peace Foundation *Pamphlets*, Vol. X, No. 7.

CULBERTSON, WILLIAM SMITH, "International Economic Policies," D. Appleton & Company, New York, 1925.

——, "Raw Materials and Foodstuffs in the Commercial Policies of Nations," *Annals of the American Academy of Political and Social Science*, Vol. CXII.

Current History Magazine.

DAVENPORT, E. H. and SIDNEY RUSSEL COOKE, "The Oil Trusts and Anglo-American Relations," The Macmillan Company, New York, 1924.

DENNETT, TYLER, "Americans in Eastern Asia: A Critical Study of the United States with Reference to China, Japan, Korea in the Nineteenth Century," The Macmillan Company, New York, 1922.

DENNY, LUDWELL, "We Fight for Oil," Alfred A. Knopf, Inc., New York, 1928.

DUNN, ROBERT W., "American Foreign Investments," B. Huebsch and the Viking Press, New York, 1926.

FISCHER, LOUIS, "Oil Imperialism," International Publishers, New York, 1926.

FISH, CARL RUSSELL, "American Diplomacy," 3rd ed., Henry Holt & Company, New York, 1922.

FISK, GEORGE MYGATT and PAUL SKEELS PIERCE, "International Commercial Policies," The Macmillan Company, New York, 1923.

Foreign Affairs.

FOSTER, JOHN W., "American Diplomacy in the Orient," Houghton Mifflin Company, Boston, 1903.

————, "A Century of American Diplomacy," Houghton Mifflin Company, Boston, 1900.

GARNER, JAMES WILFORD, "American Foreign Policies," New York University Press, New York, 1928.

HACKETT, CHARLES WILSON, "The Mexican Revolution and the United States, 1910–1926," World Peace Foundation *Pamphlets*, Vol. IX, No. 5.

HARRIS, NORMAN DWIGHT, "Europe and the East," Houghton Mifflin Company, Boston, 1926.

HOBSON, C. K., "The Export of Capital," Constable and Company, Ltd., London, 1914.

HORNBECK, STANLEY K., "Contemporary Politics in the Far East," D. Appleton & Company, New York, 1916.

HURLEY, EDWARD N., "The New Merchant Marine," The Century Company, New York, 1920.

International Conciliation, particularly Nos. 181 and 230, dealing with the interallied debts, and No. 166 treating of the diplomatic situation concerning oil.

ISE, JOHN, "The United States Oil Policy," Yale University Press, New Haven, 1926.

JENKS, LELAND HAMILTON, "Our Cuban Colony," Vanguard Press, New York, 1928.

JONES, CHESTER LLOYD, "Caribbean Interests of the United States," D. Appleton & Company, New York, 1916.

Journal of Political Economy.

KNIGHT, MELVIN M., "The Americans in Santo Domingo," Vanguard Press, New York, 1928.

LATANÉ, JOHN H., "A History of American Foreign Policy," Doubleday, Page & Company, Garden City, 1927.

————, "The United States and Latin America," Doubleday, Page & Company, Garden City, 1920.

LAUGHLIN, J. LAWRENCE and H. PARKER WILLIS, "Reciprocity," Baker & Taylor, New York, 1903.

MACMURRAY, JOHN V. A., "Treaties and Agreements With and Concerning China," (2 vols.) Oxford Univ. Press, New York, 1921.

MARSH, MARGARET, "The Bankers in Bolivia," Vanguard Press, New York, 1928.

MAXWELL, LLOYD W., "Discriminating Duties and the American Merchant Marine," H. W. Wilson Company, New York, 1926.

MCCLURE, WALLACE, "A New American Commercial Policy as Evidenced by Section 317 of the Tariff Act of 1922," Columbia University Studies in History, Economics and Public Law, Vol. 114, No. 2.

MILLARD, THOMAS F., "Democracy and the Eastern Question," The Century Company, New York, 1919.

MOON, PARKER THOMAS, "Imperialism and World Politics," The Macmillan Company, New York, 1926.

————, "Syllabus on International Relations," The Macmillan Company, New York, 1925.

MOORE, JOHN BASSETT, "A Digest of International Law," (8 vols.) Govt. Printing Office, Washington, 1906. (cited *Moore's Digest.*)

———, "Principles of American Diplomacy," Harper and Brothers, New York, 1918.

MOWRER, PAUL S., "Our Foreign Affairs: A Study in National Interest and the New Diplomacy," E. P. Dutton & Company, New York, 1924.

MUNRO, DANA G., "The Five Republics of Central America," Oxford University Press, New York, 1918.

NEARING, SCOTT and JOSEPH FREEMAN, "Dollar Diplomacy: A Study in American Imperialism," B. Huebsch and the Viking Press, New York, 1925.

NOYES, ALEXANDER D., "The War Period of American Finance, 1908–1925," G. P. Putnam's Sons, New York, 1926.

OVERLACH, T. W., "Foreign Financial Control in China," The Macmillan Company, New York, 1919.

PAINE, RALPH D., "The Old Merchant Marine," Yale University Press, New Haven, 1921.

Political Science Quarterly.

REYES, JOSÉ S., "Legislative History of America's Economic Policy towards the Philippines," Columbia University Studies in History, Economics and Public Law, Vol. CVI, No. 2.

RIPPY, J. FRED, "The United States and Mexico," Alfred A. Knopf, Inc., New York, 1926.

SALTER, J. A., "Allied Shipping Control: An Experiment in International Administration," The Clarendon Press, Oxford, 1921.

SMITH, G. O., "The Strategy of Minerals," D. Appleton & Company, New York, 1919.

SMITH, J. RUSSELL, "Influence of the Great War upon Shipping," Oxford University Press, New York, 1919.

SPEARS, JOHN R., "The Story of the American Merchant Marine," The Macmillan Company, New York, 1910.

SPURR, J. E., "Political and Commercial Geography," The McGraw-Hill Book Company, Inc., New York, 1920.

STUART, GRAHAM, "Latin America and the United States," The Century Company, New York, 1922.

TAUSSIG, F. W., "Free Trade, the Tariff and Reciprocity," The Macmillan Company, New York, 1920.

THOMAS, DAVID, Y., "One Hundred Years of the Monroe Doctrine," The Macmillan Company, New York, 1923.

DE LA TRAMERYE, PIERRE L'ESPAGNOL, "The World Struggle for Oil," Alfred A. Knopf, Inc., New York, 1924.

United States Government Publications, Washington, Govt. Printing Office:

U. S. Dept. of Commerce, *Annual Report.*

———, *Commerce Reports* (issued weekly).

———, *Commerce Year Book* (issued annually).

———, *Merchant Marine Statistics* (issued annually).

———, *Special Agents Series* (issued by number).

———, *Statistical Abstract of the United States* (issued annually).

————, *Trade Information Bulletins* (issued by number).

————, *Trade Promotion Series* (issued by number).

U. S. Congress, *Congressional Record* (cited *Cong. Rec.*).

U. S. Dept. of the Navy, *Annual Report.*

————, Office of Naval Intelligence, "The United States Navy as an Industrial Asset," 1924.

U. S. Dept. of State, "A Brief History of the Relations between the United States and Nicaragua, 1909–1928," 1928.

————, "American Property Rights in Mexico," 1926.

————, "Annual Report of the American High Commissioner at Port au Prince, Haiti."

————, "Conference on Central American Affairs, Washington, Dec. 4, 1922 to Feb. 7, 1923," 1923.

————, "Papers Relating to the Foreign Relations of the United States," (issued for the years 1870 to 1917. Cited *For. Rel.*).

————, *Press Releases.*

————, *Proceedings of the United States-Mexican Commission Convened in Mexico City, May 14, 1923, 1925.*

————, *Treaties, Conventions, International Acts, Protocols and Agreements between the United States of America and Other Powers* (3 vols. Vols. I and II cover the years from 1776 to 1909 and were published under the editorship of Williams M. Malloy in 1910. Volume III covers the period from 1910 to 1923 and was published in 1923. Cited as *Treaties, etc., between the United States and Other Powers*).

————, *Treaty Series* (Published currently).

U. S. Dept. of the Treasury, *Annual Report.*

U. S. Dept. of War, *Report of the Dominican Customs Receivership* (by fiscal periods).

U. S. Federal Oil Conservation Board, *Report to the President of the United States,* Part I, 1926.

U. S. Federal Trade Commission, *Report on Foreign Ownership in the Petroleum Industry,* 1923.

U. S. House of Representatives, Committee on Foreign Affairs, "Hearings on the Foreign Service of the United States," 1924.

————, Committee on Interstate and Foreign Commerce, "Hearings on Crude Rubber, Coffee, etc.," 1926.

U. S. Senate, *Doc. No.* 285, Sixty-sixth Congress, Second Session, "Investigation of Mexican Affairs" (2 vols.).

————, *Doc. No.* 11, Sixty-seventh Congress, First Session, "Restrictions on American Petroleum Prospectors in Certain Foreign Countries."

————, *Doc. No.* 39, Sixty-seventh Congress, First Session, "Oil Prospecting in Foreign Countries."

————, *Doc. No.* 64, Sixty-eighth Congress, First Session, "Diplomatic Correspondence with Colombia in Connection with the Treaty of 1914, and Certain Oil Concessions."

————, *Doc. No.* 97, Sixty-eighth Congress, First Session, "Oil Concessions in Foreign Countries."

————, *Doc. No.* 166, Sixty-eighth Congress, Second Session, "Isle of Pines."

————, *Doc. No.* 96, Sixty-ninth Congress, First Session, "Rights of American Citizens in Certain Oil Lands in Mexico."

————, *Doc. No.* 180, Sixty-ninth Congress, Second Session, "Conditions in the Philippine Islands."

————, *Doc. No.* 210, Sixty-ninth Congress, Second Session, "Oil Concessions in Mexico."

————, Committee on Foreign Relations, "Hearings on Treaty of Commerce and Consular Rights with Germany, 1924."

————, Subcommittee, "Hearings on Foreign Loans," Vol. I, 1925.

————, Select Committee on Haiti and Santo Domingo, "Inquiry into Occupation and Administration of Haiti and Santo Domingo," 1922.

U. S. Tariff Commission, "Colonial Tariff Policies," 1922.

————, "Reciprocity and Commercial Treaties," 1919.

U. S. World War Foreign Debt Commission, *Combined Annual Reports,* 1927.

VIALLATE, ACHILLE, "Economic Imperialism and International Relations during the Last Fifty Years," The Macmillan Company, New York, 1923.

WILLIAMS, EDWARD THOMAS, "China Yesterday and Today," Thomas Y. Crowell Company, New York, 1923.

WILLOUGHBY, WESTEL W., "Foreign Rights and Interests in China," (Rev. Ed., 2 vols.) The Johns Hopkins Press, Baltimore, 1927.

ZIMMERMAN, ERICH W., "Ocean Shipping," Prentice-Hall, Inc., New York, 1921.

INDEX

A

I

L

M

R

Date